To.

R.C. Sunrma
By: Julie Sunrma
25 DEC 13

ANCIENT GREECE

ANCIENT
GREECE

EVERYDAY LIFE
IN THE BIRTHPLACE
OF WESTERN CIVILIZATION

ROBERT GARLAND

STERLING
New York

To my son Richard, to my daughter Ling Ling.

STERLING
New York

An Imprint of Sterling Publishing
387 Park Avenue South
New York, NY 10016

Please see page 365 for image credits.

This edition published by arrangement ABC-CLIO 130 Cremona Drive Suite C,
Santa Barbara, CA 93117-5505, USA.

ISBN 978-1-4549-0908-8

Distributed in Canada by Sterling Publishing
c/o Canadian Manda Group, 165 Dufferin Street
Toronto, Ontario, Canada M6K 3H6
Distributed in the United Kingdom by GMC Distribution Services
Castle Place, 166 High Street, Lewes, East Sussex, England BN7 1XU
Distributed in Australia by Capricorn Link (Australia) Pty. Ltd.
P.O. Box 704, Windsor, NSW 2756, Australia

For information about custom editions, special sales, and premium and corporate purchases,
please contact Sterling Special Sales at 800-805-5489 or specialsales@sterlingpublishing.com.

Manufactured in China

2 4 6 8 10 9 7 5 3 1

www.sterlingpublishing.com

Title Page: A SYMPOSIUM SCENE *shows a reclining youth holding a musical instrument in one hand while a young female dances. Tondo from Attic red-figure cup, ca. 440–480* B.C.E.

Frontispiece: GRAECIA VETUS. *Robert de Vaugondy, 1752. A map of Greece featuring the ancient regions of Macedonia, Thessaly, Epirus, Achaia, and Peloponnese.*

CONTENTS

PREFACE

In 1908, the British Museum mounted its first exhibit on Greek and Roman life. Although that exhibit—intended to illustrate daily life through everyday objects that were commonly used in the home—has changed repeatedly over the years, the essential formula has remained constant, testifying to the high level of interest in the subject among the general, museum-going public. The pioneering work on the present topic, however, was undertaken by German historian W. A. Becker, whose *Charicles or Illustrations of the Private Life of the Ancient Greeks* was first translated into English in 1845. Still in print, it offers a narrative account of the life of a young aristocrat named Charicles. Though *Charicles* has undoubtedly stood the test of time and is supported by a daunting body of literary evidence, one must get to the evidence by wading through the translator's exsufflicate late Romantic purple prose, of which this description of a young woman is an example: "A rich profusion of light hair descended on her neck in luxuriant ringlets, while the finely-penciled arch of the eyebrows was of a jetty black: in the delicate whiteness of her cheeks rose a soft tinge to natural vermilion." More important, *Charicles* avoids all the brutish nastiness of life in ancient Greece, which provides a necessary insight into the living conditions of any preindustrialized population.

The daily life of ancient Greece was one where parents routinely buried children, where famine and disease made common cause, where life expectancy was little more than half of what it is today, where there was no antidote to physical pain, where terror and anxiety stalked the mental horizons of even the most enlightened, and where, despite all the forces that sought to repress it, culture remained politically vital. It was a routine that has much to tell us about the plight of millions today. Not the least of the benefits of studying the Greeks from this angle is that it helps us put the glittering accomplishments of their civilization into their proper, somewhat somber and sobering context. We know both them and ourselves better as a result.

Hamilton, New York
June 2008

AUTHOR'S NOTE

All translations of Greek text included in this book have been made by the author. Bibliographic references that are provided refer to any standard edition of Greek texts, not to specific copyrighted translations. Students can refer to any English translation of the works cited. Translations of inscriptions that appear in Greek epigraphical works are also included, but no sources are provided for these because they can be consulted easily only by those who read Greek. In other instances, the author has noted "in fragment from a lost work" because the fragments in question appear only in scholarly Greek anthologies. Finally, the author has used standard Greek notation for those Greek authors who wrote only one work: that is, only the section of the work is noted, and no title is given. Greek names are transliterated in their Greek, rather than Latinized, form (e.g., Herodotos, not Herodotus), except in cases where this might create unnecessary confusion (e.g., Aeschylus, not Aiskhylos).

Finally, I would like to thank Roger Just and Pavlos Sfyroeras for teaching me so much about Greekness, ancient and modern. I am most grateful to Annette Goldmacher, for help with the index.

ANCIENT GREECE TIMELINE

B.C.E.

The conventional divisions:

ca. 1600–ca. 1100	The Mycenaean Period
ca. 1100–ca. 900	The Dark Age
ca. 900–ca. 725	The Geometric Period
ca. 725–ca. 625	The Orientalizing Period
ca. 650–480	The Archaic Period
480–323	The Classical Period
323–31	The Hellenistic Period
ca. 1600	Mycenaeans come into contact with Minoan civilization based on Crete
ca. 1650–1500	Shaft graves built at Mycenae
ca. 1200?	The Trojan War
ca. 1025–950	Period during the Dark Age that provides the least amount of archaeological data
ca. 1100	Collapse of Mycenaean civilization
ca. 800	Earliest evidence of writing in Greece
776	Traditional date for the first celebration of the Olympic Games
ca. 735–715	First Messenian War
ca. 730	Colonization movement begins
ca. 725	Homer composes *The Iliad*
ca. 700	Homer composes *The Odyssey*; hoplite armor is invented
669	The Spartans are defeated by the Argives at Hysiai
ca. 660	Sparta crushes the Messenian Revolt

INTRODUCTION

There are serious limitations to any book that calls itself *Everyday Life in the Birthplace of Western Civilization*. To begin with, it is impossible to confine our description of daily life to a single chronological period. The evidence is far too fragmented and disjointed. Similarly, we cannot assume that the picture that we build up incorporates more than a small part of the geographical whole that we identify as the Greek world. There are vast areas about which we know very little because the people who inhabited them, though essentially Greek, have left few traces of their way of life in either the literary or archaeological record. To speak of the daily life of "the Greeks," to borrow a phrase of Paul Cartledge (*The Greeks,* 37) "must therefore be construed often, or perhaps usually, as in some sense just a manner of speaking."

In the Classical era, we know most about Athens and its surrounding countryside, and it is Athens that I shall be concentrating upon in this book. This is due not only to the fact that Athens' population has bequeathed to us a wealth of archaeological data in the form of household objects, remains of buildings, depictions on vases, inscriptions on stone and other materials, and so forth, but also because Athens was an extremely literate society whose literature contains plentiful allusions to daily life. However, I also draw heavily on the Homeric poems, especially *The Odyssey*, because this provides us with arguably the most detailed picture of daily life in ancient Greece of any period. After Athens, we probably know most about Sparta in the Classical age. This is not because Sparta possessed any of the attributes that I have just ascribed to Arhens—Sparta was in many ways the exact antithesis of Athens—but because historians and philosophers were fascinated by Spartan society and wrote a great deal about it. We know relatively little about other major centers, such as Corinth, Thebes, and Megara, on the Greek mainland. And when we move outside the world of the city-states or *poleis,* as these communities were called, the picture

GRAECIAE ANTIQUAE SPECIMEN GEOGRAPHICUM. J.B.B. D'Anville, 1794. This dramatic map of ancient Greece covers the area from Macedonia to Peloponnese.

becomes extremely hazy. Even though Macedon became the dominant Greek power from the 330s B.C.E. onward and conquered virtually the whole known world, we know next to nothing about the daily life of the Macedonians and can say little about its distinguishing characteristics since they left no literary record. For the Hellenistic era (i.e., post-323 B.C.E.), we have abundant evidence about the Greeks living in Egypt in the form of letters and other personal documents written on papyri that have survived in the sand but not anywhere else in the Greek-speaking world (see p. 56).

There are other limitations to our study. The literary evidence that has survived from ancient Greece does not represent Greek society as a whole. Most of it is the product of well-to-do, leisured, adult male citizens. There are little data relating to those who were economically or socially disadvantaged, including the poor and the homeless, not to mention those who were enslaved, though it could be argued that the daily life of such persons, since it revolves primarily around keeping alive, is remarkably similar in all societies. An exception is Hesiod's *Works and Days,* which has much to tell us about the condition of subsistence farmers in Boiotia around 700 B.C.E. Virtually none of the literary evidence focuses on women, metics (resident aliens), slaves, the disabled, or those living in the countryside. Another way of putting this is that most of our sources focus upon a highly unrepresentative minority. A further drawback is the fact that often the only explanations for many of the rituals that the Greeks performed in the home, such as those pertaining to birth and death, are very late. Some of these explanations are likely to be imaginative retrojections.

Furthermore, the Greeks were almost wholly incapable of identifying a social trend, formulating a social theory, or implementing a social policy. What the modern world therefore identifies as "social evils"—such as vagrancy, criminality, homelessness, divorce, illegitimacy, and juvenile delinquency, for instance—could be observed and discussed only on the individual level as constituting so many separate and unrelated personal dilemmas or tragedies. They could not be perceived as phenomena that were embedded in society as a whole, nor could they be discussed within a conceptual framework. This was due in large measure to the self-evident fact that the Greeks did not keep statistics.

We are fortunate in possessing a rich storehouse of visual material relating to daily life primarily in the form of vase paintings, particularly those that date to the sixth and fifth centuries B.C.E. Although the focus of such paintings is the activities of the well-to-do, there are a few scenes of country life, depicting sowing and ploughing, viticulture, olive growing, and animal husbandry. We also occasionally see depictions of craft activities, such as woodworking, shoemaking, and scent-making, as well as of some industries, such as arms manufacturing. We should bear in mind, however, that scenes on vases are not photographs; like sculptures, they tell us rather more about how the Greeks wanted to be imagined than they do about how they actually looked. And while on the subject of art, we should note that a crudely made household utensil or terra-cotta figurine can often tell us as much—perhaps more—about daily life as can the most exalted and costly work in any medium.

It is important to emphasize that the tenor of Greek society was predominately shaped by the aristocrats, or *aristoi,* who, as this word implies, considered themselves to be "the best." Their social inferiors were known as "the bad" *(kakoi).* Athenian society remained elitist even after radical democratic reforms were carried out by Perikles and Ephialtes a decade or so before the middle of the fifth century B.C.E.; and even though Perikles claimed that poverty was no bar to advancement, aristocrats continued to exploit their economic, political, and social status and thus to dominate the political assembly for at least another half century. In fact, all Greek communities continued to privilege the nobly born and wealthy over the baseborn and poor, even after many had followed Athens' lead and established their own democratic institutions.

Investigations of daily life tend to assume relatively settled conditions, a regular daily routine, and an adequacy of resources. In antiquity, however, interruptions in the daily pattern of existence were very frequent, whether as a result of natural or manmade disasters. As a result, an individual's lifestyle was subject to upheaval and change much more frequently and more drastically than is usual in our society. In particular, relocation was extremely frequent, whether as a result of land hunger, warfare, or enslavement.

Some scholars regard the investigation of such questions as "What did the Greeks eat for breakfast?" ("not much" is the probable answer!) as an irrelevant distraction to the serious study of history, thereby adopting a Thukydidean rather than an Herodo-tean approach to historical inquiry by privileging political events over customs. They have a point. Viewed in a vacuum, many questions having to do with daily life do not help us understand what makes the Greeks so different from (and in some ways so similar to) ourselves. It is all too easy to depict the Greeks as nineteenth-century gentlemen of refined artistic taste who had a penchant for homosexuality, waxed philosophical all hours of the day, and seriously mistreated their wives. I have tried to do better than that. What I have attempted here under the general heading of daily life is to investigate what the French call the *mentalité* (or mental structures) of the Greeks, a branch of structuralist inquiry that is associated with the *Annales* school of historical inquiry founded by Marc Bloch and Lucien Febvre. Simply put, it is a school of inquiry that believes in a close relationship between mental processes on the one hand and climate, physical environment, biology, language, ties of kinship, and so on, on the other, and that these so-called structures condition and set limits upon human behavior. In the same way, albeit at a more mundane level, I believe we can

better comprehend the *mentalité* of the Greeks by grappling with the conditions of their daily lives. The fact that Perikles, like most Athenians, probably ate very little for breakfast tells us relatively little; the fact that, like so many Athenians, he lost two sons to the great plague before succumbing to it himself tells us a great deal, and both circumstances in the end are woven into the texture of daily life.

Some of the questions I consider to be especially important are the following: What did the Greeks do with their income? How did they treat their slaves? How did they treat their wives? How did wives treat their husbands? How stable was the family? How were old people treated? How did the young treat the elderly? Were the Greeks afraid of death? Did they share our notion of romantic love? What did they think of foreigners? Were they racist? Did they engage in premarital sex? How commonly did they perform abortions? Did they

A BLACK-FIGURE AMPHORA *depicts a group of men har-vesting olives, a scene common to country life. Antimenes painter, ca. 520 B.C.E.*

practice euthanasia? Were they all unquestioningly patriotic? Did they believe in progress—social, economic, or other? How did they relax? Were they in general more highly cultivated than we are? Questions like these are inherently worth asking, regardless of whether we consider the Greeks our spiritual, cultural, or intellectual ancestors, which, whether we like it or not, they are.

Investigating the daily life of the ancient Greeks can be as exciting and as path-breaking as any other branch of inquiry conducted in the social sciences. The study of ancient history is not frozen in time. On the contrary, few branches of learning have proved to be so receptive to new modes of critical thinking, including Marxism, feminism, structuralism, and deconstruction. To be an accomplished ancient historian today requires not only knowledge of the literary sources (and the languages in which they are written), the archaeology, the inscriptions, and the papyri, but also an understanding of anthropology, sociology, economics, and psychology.

Though our knowledge of the ancient world is always expanding, what we can know will only ever be a fraction of what we would like to know. This must not, however, stop us from asking impertinent questions. As Jacob Bronowski (*The Ascent of Man,* 153) once remarked about science, "Ask an impertinent question, and you are on the way to the pertinent answer." This is no less true of historical inquiry. I encourage everyone who picks up this book to ask impertinent questions.

The principal units of Athenian currency were the following:

6 obols = 1 drachma

100 drachmas = 1 mina

60 minas = 1 talent

One drachma was the equivalent of a day's pay for an unskilled workman in the second half of the fifth century B.C.E. The cost of living for a family of four is estimated at 3–6 obols per day. The most common unit was the tetradrachm or four-drachma piece.

ANTIQUE SILVER COIN *from Athens, ca. 566 B.C.E., depicting an owl. The Athenian tetradrachm was stamped with the head of Athena on one side and an image of an owl, the symbol of the Athenian polis, with an olive sprig on the other side.*

✵ 1 ✵
HISTORICAL OUTLINE

THE MYCENAENS

Most historians agree that the emergence of the people whom we call Greek was the result of a series of migratory waves into mainland Greece from the north. This belief is largely based on the Greek language, for which we have evidence perhaps as early as the fifteenth century B.C.E. and at the latest by the thirteenth century B.C.E. (see p. 53). This was the period of Mycenaean culture, so named after the hilltop fortress with its impressive encircling walls situated at Mycenae in the Argolid in northeast Peloponnese. Other important Mycenaean fortifications include Tiryns, which lies a few miles south of Mycenae, Pylos on the west coast of the Peloponnese, Thebes in central Greece, Iolkos in Thessaly, and the Acropolis at Athens. Several Aegean islands, the most important of which was Crete, also came under the influence of Mycenae. The Mycenaeans traded extensively in the Mediterranean, notably with the peoples of Egypt, Syria, Sicily, and southern Italy. On the basis of the profile of a Mycenaean-style sword engraved into one of the stones at Stonehenge, it has even been fancifully suggested that they traded with Britain.

Probably much later, the Greeks, who called themselves *Hellênes*—the name that they retain to this day—invented a legend tracing their descent from their eponymous founder Hellen. Hellen was the son of Deukalion and Pyrrha, the Greek equivalent of Adam and Eve. Deukalion and Pyrrha were the only survivors of the Great Flood, so they were also the equivalent of Noah. By claiming to be

A MODERN-DAY PHOTOGRAPH OF THE RUINS OF THE PARTHENON IN ATHENS. *The most significant extant building of Classical Greece, the temple is regarded as an enduring symbol of ancient Greece, Athenian democracy, and Western civilization.*

the oldest people on the face of the earth, the Greeks were able to feed their sense of national pride and to claim special status among the other peoples they encountered, although it is fair to state as well that educated Greeks, like the historian Herodotos, were open and forthright in acknowledging the debt of Greek culture to other, older cultures, notably that of Egypt.

The most striking evidence for the early phase of Mycenaean culture is the shaft graves at Mycenae. These graves, dated around 1650 to 1500 B.C.E., were cut into the living rock to a depth of several meters. They were excavated in 1876 by the German businessman-turned-archaeologist Heinrich Schliemann. The shaft graves, which have yielded some of the richest finds ever discovered on the Greek mainland, provide confirmation for Homer's description of

FOUND IN A ROYAL SHAFT GRAVE *in Mycenae, this 3,500-year-old artifact is known as the Mask of Agamemnon, named after the legendary Greek king of Homer's* Iliad.

Mycenae as "rich in gold." Around 1500 B.C.E., a different style of burial chamber was introduced in the form of beehive tombs, so named because of their domed appearance. The most impressive of these is the Treasury of Atreus, built perhaps as late as 1250 B.C.E., which was named for Agamemnon's father. About the same time, the fortification walls of Mycenae were rebuilt so that the walls had an ornamental gateway surmounted by a relief depicting two lions flanking a pillar.

The Mycenaeans were literate, though their script, which is known as Linear B, was used exclusively for inventories and other bureaucratic purposes. It was never put in the service of literature, which in turn says much about their priorities. Without literature, we cannot investigate thoughts and feelings. In short, we cannot know what kind of people the Mycenaeans were.

A MODERN-DAY IMAGE OF THE TREASURY OF ATREUS *in Mycenae. The domed appearance is indicative of a beehive tomb.*

The Trojan War

Later Greeks preserved the memory of a major expedition undertaken by the Mycenaeans against a town called Ilion or Troy. The Trojan War and its aftermath were commemorated in two epic poems ascribed to Homer, *The Iliad* and *The Odyssey,* both composed around 700 B.C.E., though whether they were the work of the same poet continues to be a subject of debate. Once again it was Schliemann who, in 1871, excavated the site claimed to be Troy, which he identified with a mound called Hissarlik, situated a few miles from the coast in northwest Turkey. Discovering a considerable horde of treasure, he overhastily identified it with Priam's city. In fact, doubts remain to this day as to whether the site that he excavated really is Troy. Although most scholars concede that Homer's legend contains at least a kernel of historical truth, as Bernard Knox (in Finley, *The World of Odysseus,* xii) has noted, "There is nothing to connect Agamemnon, Achilles, Priam, and Hektor with the fire-blackened layer of thirteenth-century ruins known as Troy VII A (the archaeologists' candidate for Homer's city) except a heroic poem which cannot have been fixed in its present form by writing until the late eighth century, at least four illiterate centuries after the destruction."

The Trojan War, which is perhaps dated around 1200 B.C.E., is said to have lasted ten years. It ended in the total destruction of Troy. Shortly afterward, the entire Mycenaean world collapsed. It seems that the war, assuming it was historical, represented the dying gasps of Bronze Age civilization.

The Dorian Invasion

In the period from about 1300 to 1100 B.C.E., almost every Mycenaean site was plundered and burned. Thebes was destroyed around 1300 B.C.E., Pylos around 1200, and Mycenae around 1150. Of the mainland sites, Athens alone provides evidence of cultural continuity. The cause of the collapse of the Mycenaean world is not fully understood. Later Greeks attributed it to an invasion by a people who swept in from the north. They called this people the Dorians. Those Greeks who traced themselves back to the Dorians were subsequently organized into three tribes known as Hylleis, Dymanes, and Pamphyloi. The original leaders of these tribes were said to be the sons of Herakles, the greatest of the Greek heroes.

The archaeological evidence for the invasion is, however, negligible. No distinctively Dorian pottery has come to light, and the only artifacts that *may* be attributed to an invader are an iron sword and a long bronze dress pin. It has been suggested by way of explanation that the Dorians were a pastoral people whose lifestyle did not encourage the production of pottery and other artifacts. In fact, the main evidence for the invasion is based on dialect. The Greeks spoke in a number of different dialects, Doric and Ionic being the main ones. The

Ionic dialect was spoken by the Ionians, a people who believed themselves to be autochthonous (i.e., inhabitants of Greece since time immemorial) and who traced their descent back to Hellen's grandson Ion. However, the distribution of Doric and Ionic falls far short of proving the racial theory, because Doric was also spoken in southwest Turkey and Crete. Another problem is that the earliest full account of the Dorian invasion occurs only very late—in the writings of Diodorus Siculus, Diodorus of Sicily, of the mid-first century B.C.E.

In light of such inconclusive data, some scholars doubt the existence of a Dorian invasion altogether. However, a majority favors an invasion or successive waves of invasions as the most likely explanation for the collapse of the Mycenaean world. At any rate, the most important points to grasp are that, first, the Greeks genuinely believed themselves to be descended from two main groupings, Ionians and Dorians and, second, they exploited the perceived ethnic divide for political purposes.

THE DARK AGE

The collapse of the Mycenaean world ushered in the so-called Dark Age, which lasted several hundred years. The art of writing was lost, poverty became widespread, communications ceased, and the arts declined. The period for which there are least archaeological data lasted from 1025 to 950 B.C.E. The pace of recovery varied from region to region. Until recently, it was believed that the Dark Age enveloped the whole of mainland Greece.

However, we now have evidence of an important tenth-century B.C.E. settlement at a site called Lefkandi (ancient name, Xeropolis) on the island of Euboia, just opposite Attica. A rescue excavation conducted by the British School at Athens in 1981 brought to light a long apsidal-ended building, the finest of its age to be found anywhere in Greece. No less sensational is the discovery of the burial of a wealthy warrior, who has been dubbed by archaeologists the "Hero of Lefkandi." Beside his bones, which were interred in a bronze amphora with an iron spear and sword, lay the skeleton of a young woman. In an adjacent pit were the bones of four horses. Both the woman and the horses had been ritually slaughtered, presumably so that they could accompany the hero to the underworld. Such is the importance of the site and the impressiveness of its remains that some scholars now question the appropriateness of speaking of a "Dark Age."

THE GREEK RENAISSANCE

The period from 900 to 725 B.C.E., conventionally known as the Geometric Period, is named for the profusion of geometric motifs (circles, zigzag lines, swastikas, triangles, and the like) that adorn the painted pottery of this era. Around 800 B.C.E. there occurred a resurgence in cultural activity of such intensity that it is appropriate to speak of a renaissance. One of the most important developments was the adaptation of the consonantal Phoenician alphabet to the Greek language. It is not known where this adaptation first took place, but a likely candidate is Al Mina, a mixed Phoenician and Greek community situated at the head of the Orontes River on the present-day border between Turkey and Syria. This invention conventionally marks the division between prehistory and history. In the century from about 750 to 650 B.C.E., writing became widespread throughout the Greek world. Written records indicate that the first occasion when the Olympic Games were celebrated was in 776 B.C.E., which is thus the earliest date in Greek history. From 683 B.C.E. onward, the Athenians began to keep a list of their magistrates inscribed on stone.

One of the principal reasons for the Greek renaissance may have been an increase in the size of the population. From an analysis of graves, some archaeologists have calculated that, in the first half of the eighth century B.C.E., the population of Attica (i.e., the territory surrounding Athens) quadrupled and that in the next half-century it almost doubled again. Others, however, interpret the increase in the number of graves as evidence of an unusually high mortality rate, perhaps occasioned by drought and disease. Whatever the truth, it is important to bear in mind for our investigation that epidemics were a perpetual hazard in the summer months throughout Greek history, even though we rarely hear about them in our sources. For all ancient and premodern peoples, as well as for those living in the developing world today, deadly disease was an almost daily occurrence.

Over time, the population of mainland Greece did undoubtedly experience considerable growth, and this would have had a profound impact on daily life. An agrarian economy now began to replace one previously based mainly on animal husbandry as much of the land was converted to the production of grain, because grain can sustain a large population more effectively. It was an economy and a society that was dominated by aristocrats with large estates.

The World of the Homeric Poems

The Iliad and *The Odyssey* are among the greatest achievements of the Greek renaissance. Although their origins as oral poems—poems handed down by word of mouth—probably lie in the Dark Age, they were brought to completion around 700 B.C.E. The world described by these poems is that of an

A WHITE MARBLE BUST *of the poet Homer.*

imaginary Mycenaean past as envisioned by an impoverished and vastly reduced society that is looking back nostalgically to an epoch of military power and material prosperity. Yet the poems also interestingly reveal the beginnings of an instinct for democracy that is a central feature of the Greek character and that significantly shaped its history, as in *The Odyssey* Book 2, when Telemachos calls an assembly of fellow citizens to complain about the behavior of his mother's suitors, who are eating him out of house and home.

Although *The Iliad* and *The Odyssey* are the earliest surviving examples of epic poetry relating to the Trojan War, they come at the end of a long tradition. Paradoxically, it was their success that killed off this flourishing genre. Other epic poems on the same subject, known generically as the Epic Cycle, have survived only in fragments. We know nothing about Homer, not even whether he (possibly even she) was blind. We do not know whether he was a single person or whether *Homer* was the name for the many singers who composed oral epics around 700 B.C.E.

The Odyssey provides us with our first glimpse of the daily life of the Greeks. From it we learn a great deal about a wide variety of subjects including seafaring, farming, entertainment, burial customs, judicial procedure, feasting, rules of hospitality, sexual mores, slavery, attitudes toward work, and much more. For that reason, it constitutes a major source for this study, and it shall be referred to frequently in this work. Homer's spotlight, however, is almost exclusively on the aristocracy. A central feature of Homeric society is the practice of gift exchange. The act of giving was a motivator for all manner of actions and transactions, incumbent upon the benefactor, not the beneficiary. When the goddess Athene, disguised as a Taphian chieftain, is taking her leave from Telemachos on Ithaka after receiving his hospitality, she says to him, "As for the gift which a friend's heart prompts you to give to me, give it to me on my way back so that I can take it home with me. And let it be a very nice one, so that you receive something equally nice in due course" (*The Odyssey* 1.316–18).

The common people, the *dêmos,* hardly appear at all in the poem. Even the slaves who are most prominently featured, including the swineherd Eumaios and the nurse Eurykleia, come from noble backgrounds, having been captured and then sold into slavery. We do, however, gain an interesting insight into the lives of beggars from the fact that Odysseus disguises himself as one and then competes with the resident beggar Iros for the right to beg in his own home. We also learn of the existence of specialized itinerants, who do not permanently belong to the household but serve it periodically, notably seers, architects, physicians, and—chiefly—singers. We need to bear in mind that *The Odyssey* is a literary construct, even though it possesses an inner coherence that suggests to some that the picture of life it supplies is based on a closely observed social reality. Moses Finley, author of one of the most engaging and most imaginative books on ancient history ever written (*The World of Odysseus,* 43), argues in favor of placing that social reality in the tenth and ninth centuries B.C.E. Other scholars regard it as a conglomerate that does not reflect any single historical epoch.

Social Unrest

Homer depicts a world in which monarchy prevails, although it is possible to glimpse a power struggle between kings and rebellious aristocrats. Probably about a century before Homer, aristocratic rule had replaced monarchic rule in most parts of Greece. The poems of Hesiod, a peasant farmer from Boiotia who was perhaps a younger contemporary of Homer, testify to a new power struggle, this time between the aristocrats and the common people, or *dêmos.* In *Works and Days,* Hesiod warns aristocrats who pervert justice that they will not escape the "all-seeing eye of Zeus."

The challenge to aristocratic authority at the beginning of the seventh century B.C.E. was caused by many factors. One of the most important of these was writing, which makes it possible to codify laws and establish a constitution. Writing also makes it easier to detect evasion and malpractice on the part of those in power. The first written laws date to the seventh century B.C.E. Literacy in the Greek world was not confined to a particular social group, as it was in Egypt, for instance, where only members of the priesthood were literate. This made for far greater openness, transparency, and accountability in all aspects of Greek life—civic, political, administrative, and religious. Writing had a profound effect upon the development of Greek history, for without it democracy could not have come to fruition.

THE RISE OF THE CITY STATE

From 750 B.C.E. onward, the most distinctive political unit in the Greek world was the polis or city-state, from which the word *politics* is derived. As Aristotle remarked, "Man is by nature a *zôon politikon* [a political animal]," meaning "Man is an animal that is designed to live in a polis," and, we might add, parsing the wording more fully, designed to achieve his maximum potential under this system of government and no other. Although no two *poleis* were identical in physical layout, all by definition, possessed an urbanized center and surrounding territory. Each polis formulated its own law code, kept its own army, developed its own system of government, and recognized its own set of gods. These gods were variations primarily on the twelve basic Olympian gods, but they were also particular to any given polis.

The polis system prevailed in the heartland of mainland Greece. Around its fringes lived peoples such as the Ambraciots, Thessalians, and Macedonians, who had no urban center and were organized much more loosely into tribes or *ethnê,* from which the word *ethnic* derives. Since, however, *ethnê* have left no literature and few artifacts, it is virtually impossible to investigate the lives of their peoples. So when investigating the daily life of the Greeks, as noted earlier, it is the lives of the *politai,* or citizens of the city-states, who will be the primary focus.

The polis system flourished throughout the Greek-speaking world. It has been estimated that there were as many as 1,500 separate political communities dotted around the islands and shores of the eastern Mediterranean, along the southern shore of the Black Sea, in eastern Sicily and southern Italy, and further west, on the southern coast of France and on the eastern coast of Spain. It proved to be a remarkably resilient and flexible entity. Even after the Greeks had lost their independence, first to Macedon and later to Rome, the Greek city-states continued to flourish. Their success over such a long period of time was due in part to the inherent particularism of the Greeks—their preference, that is, for living in politically independent communities.

It is for this reason that the notion of "Greekness" was largely confined to the linguistic, religious, and social spheres. As a political concept, it amounted to very little. Though the Greeks shared a common language, common social structures, and a common religion, in other respects they observed little sense of unity. Only when faced with an external threat, as at the time of the Persian invasion, did they temporarily succeed in forming an alliance and implementing a joint strategy. Most Greeks thought of themselves as Athenians, Spartans, Corinthians, and Thebans first, and Greeks a distant second. And that remained true as well when they fell under the sway of Rome. It is why they only coalesced into a military force at moments of crisis. Even so, the cohesiveness of that alliance was constantly being undermined by the competing interests of its different members. The strains upon such coalitions can be seen in the first book of *The Iliad,* where Achilles calls into question the military capability of Agamemnon, the commander in chief of the Greek expeditionary force to Troy, and threatens to return home.

COLONIZATION

The period from about 730 to 580 B.C.E. witnessed an enormous expansion of Greek civilization through the medium of colonization. This was made possible by a power vacuum in the Mediterranean, because the two most important states in the previous era, Egypt and Phoenicia, were both in decline and no other state presented a serious obstacle to Greek outreach. The influence of the Near East on Greek culture, which came about as a direct consequence of this movement, was so strong that historians have dubbed the century from about 725 to 625 B.C.E. as the Orientalizing Period. Visual evidence for Near Eastern influence is provided by the profusion of Oriental motifs that begin to replace the geometric designs of the preceding era. But Eastern influence also extended to astronomical and mathematical data, legal concepts, and medical ideas, all of which now colonized, so to speak, the minds of the Greeks.

The primary motivation behind colonization was to resolve the twin problems of land shortage and population expansion. The depth of the crisis is indicated by an anecdote told by the historian Herodotos concerning the plight of the citizens of the island of Thera (modern Santorini) in the Cyclades (4.156). The Therans were so badly afflicted by famine that they exiled some of their fellow citizens. When the exiles attempted to return after failing in their initial bid to find a suitable location for a colony, they were showered with arrows and forced to sail off again. Eventually they succeeded in establishing a colony at Cyrene in modern Libya.

Initial bands of colonists probably averaged no more than about two hundred and were drawn from all levels of society. Very likely women arrived only after a colony had been securely established. Given the fact that those who embarked on this kind of adventure were facing a common challenge and a common danger, some loosening of the divisions between social groups was inevitable. The colonization movement (the term is somewhat imprecise because, for the most part, states acted independently) thus further weakened the power of the aristocracy. The chief colonizing cities were Chalkis and Eretria on the island of Euboia, Corinth and Megara in central Greece, and Phokaia and Miletos on the coast of Turkey. Notably absent from the list is Athens, which had sufficient fertile land not to need to form colonies, and Sparta, which took the alternative course of expanding into its neighboring territory. When the colonizing movement ended, the number of Greek cities had probably doubled. Southern Italy was so densely colonized that it came to be called *Magna Graecia,* or "Great Greece." It was at the Greek colony of Kumai (Roman Cumae), just north of Naples, that the Etruscans and Romans first came into contact with Greek civilization. Here, too, the Greeks, who called themselves *Hellênes,* first acquired the name *Graeci* in the Latin language, which they have retained ever since. (*Graeci* was originally the name of an obscure Greek tribe.)

Although colonists brought with them sacred fire from the civic hearth of their founding city, the tie between a colony and its founding city was not a particularly close one. Corinth alone established something resembling a colonial empire by maintaining close ties with its colonies. Far from serving to forge links between various parts of the Greek world, therefore, colonization further contributed to its disunity and particularism. It is important to appreciate that the limits of Greek colonization did not define the limits of Greek influence. Greek artifacts have been found as far afield as northern France, Switzerland, Germany, and Sweden.

ARCHAIC GREECE

The period from about 650 to 480 B.C.E. is called the Archaic Period. This name, which derives from the Greek word *archaios,* meaning "ancient," was originally coined by the late eighteenth-century German archaeologist Johann Joachim Winckelmann to identify a period of Greek history whose artistic productions were regarded as crude compared with those of its successor. The term thus constitutes a value judgment on the achievements of an era to which many contemporary scholars, who now judge Archaic art much more favorably, would not subscribe.

Solon

We know little about Athenian history until the beginning of the sixth century B.C.E., when a lawgiver called Solon came to power. At the time, Athens was experiencing economic hardship and agrarian distress, probably aggravated by drought and famine. The crisis had become so severe that heavily indebted Athenians were becoming enslaved to their fellow citizens. Solon solved this problem by adopting the radical procedure of canceling all debts. In addition, he legislated that no Athenian was permitted to incur a debt on condition that if he failed to repay it he would become the slave of his creditor. Second, if a father omitted to teach his son a profession, the son was released from the obligation of having to support his father in old age. Third, Solon forbade the export of corn and other agricultural products, with the single exception of olive oil, of which Athens had a surplus. Finally, he introduced measures that set Athens on the road to democracy. An assembly of citizens now met on a regular basis, and a court of appeal was established to check the abuse of power by magistrates. His laws were written on wooden tablets and placed in revolving frames for easy consultation.

Solon boasted in his poetry that he had "thrown his stout shield over both parties" (meaning both the rich and the poor). In truth, it is likely that neither the rich nor the poor were satisfied by his reforms. His laws seem to have had a beneficial effect on both society and the economy in the long term, however, and Solon is justly remembered for his even-handedness.

The Tyrants

From the mid-seventh to the mid-sixth centuries B.C.E. (though rather later in the case of Athens), many Greek states were ruled by tyrants. Most tyrants were disaffected aristocrats who nursed a grudge against their peers. Their rise depended on the support of the common people, with whom they allied themselves against aristocratic power and privilege. This coalition of interests typically lasted for two or three generations, after which the ruling tyrant, having lost popular support, found himself isolated and beleaguered.

Although the Greeks vilified their tyrants in later times because of their detestation of unconstitutional power, tyrants played an important part in the progress toward democracy by serving as a catalyst at the point of transition from aristocratic to popular rule. This was particularly true in the case of the Athenian tyrant Peisistratos, who came to power in 546 B.C.E. and gave Athens a stable period of government that lasted until his death in 528 B.C.E. It was under his rule that Athens took the first steps to becoming a major military power. Although Peisistratos safeguarded his position by ensuring that prominent magistracies were filled by his own supporters, he left the constitution essentially intact. In the words of the historian Thukydides, "The Peisistratids observed the existing laws. They merely saw to it that the highest offices were always held by their friends" (6.54.6).

The Athenians took great pride in the fact that they overthrew Peisistratos' successor, Hippias, attributing this exploit to two courageous Athenians named Harmodios and Aristogeiton, whom they honored with a statue in the Agora. There was also a popular song celebrating their achievement sung at symposia (see p. 162). The story of the Tyrannicides, as they were called, became the charter myth of Athenian democracy, because it instanced the moment in their history when the Athenians comprehensively rejected tyranny and embraced self-rule. The true story, however, as Thukydides pointed out, was not quite so inspirational. The pair had been motivated not by patriotic pride but by pique: the tyrant's younger brother Hipparchos had made unwanted sexual advances to Harmodios. So it was the tyrant's brother, not the tyrant, whom they slew. And their action did not end the tyranny. That was the work of the Spartans four years later—a fact the Athenians conveniently chose to ignore. The episode reminds us that the construction of national identity is as often as not based upon a deliberate, if unacknowledged, act of collective self-deception.

The Father of Democracy

The ill-conceived title "father of democracy" is most appropriately applied to the politician Kleisthenes, who, in 507 B.C.E., responded to what was fast turning into a civil war by undermining the grip over the Athenian constitution that powerful aristocratic kin groups known as *genê* (singular, *genos)* exercised. Kleisthenes, who was himself a blue-blooded aristocrat, made every citizen's political identity dependent on the Attic deme or village to which he belonged. Henceforth, each citizen was required to identify himself as "X, son of Y, of the deme Z." Kleisthenes then assigned each of the 139 demes to one of ten new tribes. In this way, he broke the stranglehold previously held by the *genê*, since regions that had previously been dominated by a single *genos* were now divided among several tribes. Henceforth, aristocrats could no longer manipulate or intimidate ordinary citizens as they had done in the past. The new Kleisthenic system was complicated and artificial, but it was wholly successful in making the Athenian political system more representative.

Sparta

Sparta, which is situated in south central Peloponnese, was a highly distinctive city-state that never succumbed to tyranny. It flourished in the Mycenaean Period but experienced a decline, like most other Mycenaean centers, around 1200 B.C.E. We know very little about Sparta's history over the next two hundred years. In the ninth century, however, it began to expand into its surrounding territory, first northward and later to the south. In the second half of the eighth century B.C.E., it made further territorial gains to the west by conquering Messenia, one of the most fertile regions in mainland Greece. The consequence for the future course of Sparta's history was decisive, because overnight it was made prosperous and agriculturally self-sufficient. No less crucial was its treatment of the inhabitants of Messenia, whom it reduced to the level of helots or slaves. Sparta henceforth became extremely conservative, wary of both political change and foreign ventures, and incapable of making any decision without considering the consequences for its control over the helots.

Some time after the conquest of Messenia, Sparta acquired a new constitution, which it ascribed to a legendary lawgiver named Lykourgos. Even assuming that Lykourgos was a historical figure, this new constitution probably evolved over a period of many years. The bulk of it, nonetheless, was likely introduced around 700 B.C.E. Some of the enactments were enshrined in a document called the Great Rhetra (*rhêtra* means "the thing said"), which established a compromise between aristocrats and commoners (Plutarch, *Life of Lykourgos*, 6).

The Spartan constitution was greatly admired in antiquity because it was thought to exhibit a harmonious balance between three competing systems of government: monarchy, aristocracy, and democracy. At the head of the Spartan state was a dual kingship. The two kings, who had equal power, could campaign either together or separately. Aside from their military role, however, their powers were strictly curtailed. They were subject to constant scrutiny by five magistrates known as *ephors* (the word literally means "overseer"), who were elected annually. If found guilty of impropriety, they could be deposed or exiled. The aristocratic feature of the constitution was the *gerousia* or council of elders. This consisted of the kings plus twenty-eight citizens over the age of sixty chosen from the aristocracy. Finally, there was the *apella,* or assembly, which all citizens, known as *homoioi,* or "peers," attended, though its powers seem to have been extremely restricted.

In 669 B.C.E., following the introduction of the reforms ascribed to Lykourgos, the Spartan army was decisively defeated by the Argives at Hysiai in northeastern Peloponnese. The effect of this defeat on Spartan morale was considerable. Within a decade, and presumably as a direct consequence, the helots revolted. A protracted war ensued, which Sparta eventually won. It was during this war that Sparta developed its celebrated ethic of *eunomia,* or "obedience to the law," which was destined to become the hallmark of its culture for centuries to come.

In the second half of the seventh century B.C.E., Sparta continued to import luxuries from abroad, its potters and painters developed a lively and original style, and its poetry and music were second to none. Foreigners, too, were welcome. Around 600 B.C.E., however, a shadow fell over Spartan society, and its citizens became increasingly isolated from mainstream Greek culture. This is symbolized by Sparta's refusal to mint coins, placing it outside the nexus of trade in which most other Greek states participated. Its overriding purpose henceforth seems to have been to acquire military control over the Peloponnese. This it did very successfully at the head of the Peloponnesian League, to which most states in the Peloponnese belonged (Argos was an exception) and which pursued a single foreign policy under its leadership. By the end of the sixth century B.C.E., Sparta had become the dominant military power in the Greek world.

The Persian Wars

In the second half of the sixth century B.C.E., the Greek cities of Asia Minor on the western coast of Turkey fell under the control of the rapidly expanding Persian Empire. In 499 B.C.E., they revolted and appealed to the mainland Greeks for help in a war of liberation. Only Athens and Eretria responded. Such was the might of Persia that the revolt was doomed from the start. After it had been brutally quashed, the Persians launched a retaliatory expedition to punish those who had assisted their subjects in revolting. Having razed Eretria, they landed on the Attic coast close to the plain of Marathon in northeast Attica, intending to sack Athens. In view of their huge numerical superiority, the Persians confidently expected to achieve an easy victory. Instead the Athenians, aided only by a small contingent from a neighboring polis called Plataiai, achieved one of the most stunning military successes in history. The losses on the Persian side were reportedly 6,400; those on the Athenian side numbered only 192.

Ten years later, the Persian king, Xerxes, returned with a much larger expeditionary force intent on conquering the whole mainland. The Greeks declared a general truce and formed an alliance under the leadership of Sparta. Their resistance, however, proved to be poorly organized and *post eventum*. Such was their disorder that there was no force waiting to oppose the enemy when they invaded Thessaly in northern Greece in 480 B.C.E. Shortly afterward, a contingent of 300 Spartiates (i.e., full Spartan citizens), under the command of King Leonidas, took up a position guarding the narrow pass at Thermopylai, which provided entry into central Greece. Although all 300, including Leonidas, were slain, the prestige won by the Spartans on account of their bravery and self-sacrifice was enormous. On the same day, a naval battle took place off the coast at Artemision, close to Thermopylai. Both sides suffered heavy casualties, but the Greeks did not succeed in halting the Persian advance.

Shortly before the Persians invaded Attica, the Athenians consulted the Delphic Oracle and were told to "trust in the wooden wall" (Herodotos 7.141). The meaning of this puzzling phrase was hotly debated in the assembly. Eventually, a politician named Themistokles persuaded his fellow countrymen to interpret it as an allusion to Athens' newly built fleet. The majority of the population evacuated

LEONIDAS AT THERMOPYLAE. Jacques Louis David, 1814. Oil on canvas. The king of Sparta sits on a rock in the center of the painting, facing the viewer and contemplating his and his soldiers' fates.

Attica, but a few Athenians interpreted the words literally and took refuge behind a wooden palisade surrounding the Acropolis, the highest defensible spot in Athens. The Persians began devastating the Attic countryside, sparing neither sanctuaries nor grave monuments. They easily overwhelmed those who were trying to safeguard the Acropolis and destroyed its temples and statuary, including the Parthenon's unfinished predecessor. Because temples were roofed with wood, it was easy to start a conflagration, whether deliberately or by accident, and this is evidently what occurred. This was one of the most devastating acts in all of Athens' history, and it had a profound impact on how the Athenians viewed the Persians. The Greek alliance was in real danger of breaking up, but Themistokles managed to persuade his allies to engage the Persian navy in the straits of Salamis, a small island off the southern coast of Attica. As Themistokles had predicted, the Persians were unable to maneuver their tall ships in the straits and suffered a major defeat. A year later, their army was defeated at Plataiai, just north of Attica. The expedition was abandoned, and the Persians retreated in disarray. Though the defeat of the Persians was "heroic" in terms of the relative size of the two armies, it revealed the endemic disunity of the Greeks: only about thirty to forty states participated in the resistance, out of a total of more than 700 in the eastern half of the Mediterranean alone.

AN EARLY 20TH CENTURY ILLUSTRATION *by an anonymous artist depicts the death of a Persian admiral during the battle of Salamis.*

Classical Greece

The beginning of the Classical Period is conventionally put at 480 B.C.E. on the grounds that the defeat of the Persians ushered in a new era of self-confidence among the Greeks, particularly the Athenians. This self-confidence is allegedly demonstrated first by the artistic achievements of the age and second by the move to full democracy that followed soon afterward. It is worth bearing in mind, however, that some of the most remarkable features of Greek culture, including democratic representation, artistic innovativeness, scientific speculation, and the birth of drama, had taken root long before the Persian invasion.

Like *Archaic,* the term *Classical* is laden with artistic prejudice, because it implies that the era represents a peak of unequaled cultural achievement.

The Athenian Empire

Immediately after the defeat of the Persians, the Greeks went on the offensive by forming a voluntary maritime confederacy under the leadership of Athens known as the Delian League. It was so named because its administrative headquarters was on the tiny Cycladic island of Delos (close to Mykonos). This confederacy had the twofold objective of providing protection against the Persians and ravaging Persian territory. It is not altogether clear why Athens rather than Sparta took the lead, but the reason probably had as much to do with Spartan timidity and inertia as it did with Athenian enterprise. What the situation clearly called for was a maritime power to hold Persian expansion in check. Sparta was ill-equipped to take a leading role in such a venture both because its economy was wholly based on agriculture and it was reluctant to commit its forces abroad for fear of a revolt among the helots.

We do not know the names of all the signatories to the confederacy, but it is estimated that about 150 states initially joined. The principal requirement upon each member was to contribute ships to a common fleet; however, the smaller states were permitted to pay an annual tribute to a common fund instead. This annual tribute amounted to 460 talents in the first year of the confederacy's existence—a very considerable sum of money, equivalent to millions, if not billions, of dollars. Within a short space of time, however, larger cities also found it more convenient to pay tribute rather than provide ships. Eventually, only the islands of Lesbos, Chios, and Samos, situated off the Turkish coast, continued to provide ships. Although this development came about as the result of voluntary decisions on the part of member states, it had the inevitable consequence of converting Athens into an imperial naval power.

Although each state exercised only one vote in the council, it soon came to be dominated by Athens, because it could easily influence the votes of the smaller states. It did not take long for Athens to reveal its hand. When the Cycladic island of Naxos tried to secede in 470 B.C.E., Athens forced it back into membership. Four years later, a similar fate befell the island of Thasos, close to the coast of Thrace, after its inhabitants had appealed in vain to Sparta for help. By now it was evident that the confederacy had become an instrument of Athenian policy.

Radical Athenian Democracy

In the late 460s and early 450s B.C.E., Athens took the final steps along the road to a radical or participatory democracy. It was a political system without modern parallel. The Greek notion of *dêmokratia,* or "power in the hands of the people," was very different from our system of democracy. In the Greek world, there was no menacing equivalent of Big Government. Nor were policy decisions made by faceless bureaucrats accountable only to their immediate superiors. On the contrary, the Athenian citizenry or *dêmos,* which consisted of all adult males over the age of about twenty, was completely sovereign.

The *dêmos* wielded its formidable power through a voting assembly known as the *ekklêsia,* which met approximately four times a month, although extraordinary meetings could be called at times of emergency. Each citizen exercised one vote and had the right to speak on whatever issue was under debate. Magistrates and junior officials were in the strictest sense its servants, because they were subject to investigation both before taking up office and on laying it down. It was also the *dêmos,* sitting in court as the *hêliaia,* who constituted the supreme judicial authority.

THE AGE OF PERIKLES

In the late 450s B.C.E., Athens sent out an expedition to assist the Egyptians in their revolt against Persia. However, it suffered a major defeat, and the expedition ended in disaster. As a result, Athens transferred the league treasury on Delos to the Acropolis for safekeeping. Five years later, it concluded a peace with

Persia, which meant that there was now no compelling reason for the Delian Confederacy to continue to exist, though Athens made no move to disband it. Not surprisingly, there were signs of unrest among Athens' allies, initially in the form of nonpayments. Shortly afterward, several members tried to secede. Athens also suffered a defeat at the hands of the Peloponnesian League at Koroneia, which lies to the north of Athens. When Megara, Athens' nearest neighbor, also revolted, the Peloponnesians invaded Attica.

Largely due to diplomatic initiatives on the part of a rising political star named Perikles, however, a full-scale war was averted, and a peace was concluded that was intended to last for thirty years. The peace acknowledged Athenian supremacy in the Aegean and Spartan supremacy on the Greek mainland. The entire Greek world now became increasingly polarized. Less and less was it possible for any state, however small, backward, and insignificant, to remain unaffected by this central polarity. In fact, the Greek world was destined to become as divided as Europe had become on the eve of the outbreak of World War I.

It is against this background of growing tension that the so-called Age of Perikles must be set. It began in 447 B.C.E., when work commenced on the Parthenon, a temple erected in honor of Athens' patron deity Athene. The Parthenon is the symbol par excellence of the Periklean Age. Other important building projects on the Acropolis included an ornamental gateway known as the Propylaia, which provides the only access to the hilltop. Perikles held no executive position other than that of general, to which he was re-elected on an annual basis. The immense authority that he wielded over the assembly was mainly a result of his charismatic personality. The Periklean Age was one in which man's reliance upon his unaided intellectual capacity has rarely, if ever, been so paramount. "Man is the measure of all things. Of the being of things that are, of the non-being of things that are not," wrote Perikles' contemporary, Protagoras of Abdera (a town on the coast of Thrace).

Not all Athenians were prepared to tolerate this attack on conventional morality, however. Many, moreover, were deeply offended when Anaxagoras, a friend of Perikles, pronounced that the moon was not a god, as was popularly believed, but merely a lump of earth. Many who were not genuinely offended found it convenient to capitalize on the popular sense of outrage to make a veiled political attack on Perikles. Although the politician survived the attack, several of his closest friends were prosecuted. The Age of Periklean rationalism did not win universal approval.

Even so, the Age of Perikles was one of the most brilliant in human history. Any Athenian citizen could have been forgiven for believing that he was living in the foremost city in the world at the greatest moment in its history. If he was a sober-minded realist, he would also have understood it was too good to last. It was doubtful, however, whether even the most pessimistic could have imagined the horrors that lay ahead.

The Peloponnesian War

The Thirty Years' Peace with Sparta lasted no more than fifteen years. Hostilities broke out in 431 B.C.E., before work on the Propylaia had been completed. The reasons for the outbreak of the Peloponnesian War, described by its chronicler Thukydides as "the greatest disturbance in Greek history" (1.1.2), are highly complex. Both sides claimed that they were fighting in the name of freedom (*autonomia* or *eleutheria*)—a slogan that fast became meaningless in the context of interstate rivalry, as it has done in more recent times. The Spartan claim, however, had more credibility, because their objective was to free Greece from Athenian imperial domination (2.8.4). They also placed the blame for the outbreak of hostilities on Perikles, claiming that he had encouraged his countrymen to go to war in order to distract their attention from domestic affairs. However, it is difficult to see what advantage Perikles could hope to gain from war in view of the fact that Athens' power was steadily increasing. It is far easier to argue in support of the theory that it was the Spartans and their allies who engineered the war. As G.E.M. de Ste. Croix points out in his definitive study *The Origins of the Peloponnesian War* (1972), it was the Spartans who voted for war, they who committed the first warlike act, and they who launched the first major offensive.

The aims of the two protagonists were not identical: that of the Peloponnesians was to bring about the destruction of Athens; that of the Athenians was to convince the enemy that they were unbeatable. The Peloponnesians had the more powerful army, whereas the Athenians held undisputed mastery of the sea. On Perikles' recommendation, the Athenians abandoned their farms and took shelter within the walls that surrounded the city and the port of Piraeus. The hardship resulting from the move can hardly be exaggerated, because it meant that the population of Athens doubled overnight. As Thukydides tells us, the refugees took up residence not only in Athens and the Piraeus, but also in the space between the Long Walls, a narrow corridor some five miles in length joining the two cities. By turning their state into an island, the Athenians therefore nullified Peloponnesian superiority by land. Perikles was convinced that they could not be forced into submission if they adhered unwaveringly to this policy. What he failed to allow for, however, was the effect upon Athenian morale of having to watch the Attic countryside being devastated. In addition, and as a direct result of his strategy, there was a severe outbreak of plague, which is estimated to have carried off about one-third of the population. Among the plague's victims was Perikles himself.

The first part of the war ended in stalemate in 421 B.C.E. Then, in 415 B.C.E., Athens launched an expedition to conquer the island of Sicily. It was the failure of this expedition that led to the resumption of hostilities in 413 B.C.E. Athens' final defeat came about in 404 B.C.E. Its citizens expected that the city would be totally destroyed, as many of Sparta's allies urged. The historian Xenophon tells us that the Spartans did not adopt this course, however, because "they did not wish to destroy a city that had done so much for Greece when she was facing her greatest dangers" (*History of Greece* 2.2.20). The more cynical might argue that Sparta, thinking with foresight, wanted Athens to continue to exist as a counterweight to the growing power of its own allies.

The course and outcome of the Peloponnesian War inevitably fills the student of history with a sense of tragedy. When it breaks out, Athens, the city-state par excellence, is at the height of power. Its final defeat, which followed after a bitter period of civil war, provided the Greek world with no lasting peace but merely led to further attrition and fragmentation. And yet the war, though it solved nothing, had been inevitable, because Athens' empire had represented a challenge to the autonomy of the Greek city-states. It is scarcely possible to imagine what it must have been like to have lived through such extremes of success and misery.

THE RISE OF MACEDON

The early fourth century saw the rise of Thebes at the expense of Sparta, which quickly squandered its dominance by arousing resentment among its erstwhile allies. When Philip II came to the throne of Macedon in 359 B.C.E., the focus suddenly switched to northern Greece. Previously Macedon had played no significant part in Greek history. Situated north of Thessaly, its fortunes had been determined mainly by its neighbors. From this date onward, however, Macedon was destined to dominate Greek affairs until the Roman conquest.

Philip gained control of mainland Greece not by embarking on an all-out war of aggression but by exploiting the rivalries between the city-states. When a dispute broke out over the control of the sanctuary of Delphi, Philip marched south at the invitation of the Thessalians. Some years later, he made peace with Athens, his main rival, and then again marched south to take over control of Delphi, celebrating the Pythian Games under his presidency. The final showdown between Macedon and Athens took place in 338 B.C.E., when Athens, in alliance with Thebes, was overwhelmingly defeated at Chaironeia in central Greece. This year also marks the terminal point for the political freedom of the mainland Greek city-states, which henceforth were greatly reduced in political and military power.

Philip did not destroy Athens as the orator Demosthenes had often predicted. Instead he returned the prisoners whom he had captured without demanding any ransom. Several months later, he summoned representatives from all the Greek states to meet in a council known as the *synhedrion*. Each member had to swear to uphold the common peace. It was Philip's intention to create a federation rather than to impose direct rule. However, he also set up military garrisons in the hope of deterring any uprising. Despite the leniency of his settlement, the Greek cities continued to agitate for their freedom with all possible energy. It was at the second meeting of the newly formed council that Philip announced his intention to conduct an expedition against Persia. Each member state was required to contribute forces. Before the expedition departed, however, Philip was murdered at his court in Pella in 336 B.C.E. by an unknown assassin.

Hitherto a backward and insignificant region situated on the fringes of the Greek world, under Philip's leadership, Macedon came to dominate mainland Greece as no other state had previously done. A speech attributed to Philip's son Alexander by the second-century C.E. historian, Arrian, serves as a fitting obituary to his reign:

Philip found you helpless vagabonds, mostly clothed in sheepskins, pasturing a few sheep on the mountains and putting up a poor fight against the Illyrians, Triballians, and neighboring Thrakians. He gave you cloaks to wear instead of sheepskins and brought you down from the mountains to the plains. . . . He turned you into city-dwellers and civilized you by means of laws and customs. (*Anabasis of Alexander* 7.9)

The discovery, in 1977, of a number of magnificent tombs at Vergina in Macedonia by the Greek archaeologist Manolis Andronikos provides clear evidence of Macedon's technical and artistic accomplishment under Philip II. A reconstruction of the skull that was found in one of the tombs led Andronikos to claim that it belongs to Philip himself, on the grounds that it provides evidence of an injury that caused him the loss of his right eye. It contained a marble sarcophagus, gold larnax, and ivory bed.

THE EMPIRE OF ALEXANDER THE GREAT

When Philip died, his son Alexander by his wife Olympias became king. He was just twenty. With his accession, the Greek world underwent enormous changes. Few Greeks seriously believed that the Persian Empire could be destroyed, and yet this is precisely what Alexander accomplished. To finance the invasion of Persia, he relied heavily on plunder. His main striking force was the cavalry. This represented a new departure in Greek warfare, which until now had been waged primarily by infantry.

Alexander won three major victories against the Persians. After his second victory at the River Issos in 333 B.C.E., the Persian king Dareios offered to share his empire by ceding all his territory west of the River Halys. Alexander rejected the offer and pressed on south into Syria. He besieged Tyre for seven months before eventually taking it. Dareios now made a new offer, surrendering the whole of his empire west of the Euphrates and offering him the hand of his daughter in marriage. This offer was also rejected. Alexander continued south, capturing other cities and visiting Jerusalem. He then invaded Egypt, which fell to him without a struggle. Since the Egyptian pharaoh was regarded as the incarnation of Horus, the son of Ra and beloved of Ammon, Alexander now became a god in the eyes of the Egyptians, although there is no evidence of his deification elsewhere at this date.

It was in Egypt that he founded the first and most magnificent of his cities, Alexandria, at the mouth of the Nile, which he filled largely with his own veterans. By the first century C.E., its population would reach nearly 300,000.

BUST OF ALEXANDER THE GREAT, *Second-century Roman. The youthful face, the anastole (a wreath-like arrangement of hair, upswept from the brow), the long wavy locks, and a hole in the crown for the insertion of a star (a symbol of his deification) identify this work as a portrait of the celebrated ruler.*

Alexander's biographer Plutarch, writing four centuries later, credits him with founding some seventy cities and military outposts in the course of his travels, many of which he called Alexandria, but the number is greatly exaggerated. Even if Alexander founded only six, however, as a recent, highly conservative estimate has proposed, these six, given their geographical locations, would have spread Greek culture to parts of the world that had previously been entirely ignorant of it, including Baluchistan, Pakistan, Tajikistan, and Afghanistan.

During his stay in Egypt, Alexander was filled with a longing, as Arrian (*Anabasis* 3.3.1) tells us, to consult the oracle of Zeus Ammon in the Libyan desert. This episode is one of the most remarkable in his career, because it served no strategic purpose whatsoever. Dareios was raising a fresh army, and Alexander's first priority should logically have been to prepare for this decisive encounter. The purpose of his pilgrimage remains a complete mystery. On being questioned about his encounter with the god afterward, Alexander merely replied that he had heard "what was according to his wish."

In 331 B.C.E., he won the last of his great victories at Guagamela on the River Tigris. He followed it up by burning down Persepolis, the palace that had been built by King Xerxes, leader of the expedition against Greece in 480 B.C.E. Shortly afterward, Dareios was murdered and Alexander was able to proclaim himself king of Persia. Following the final defeat of Persia, he undertook two further expeditions, the first to Bactria and the second to India. On his return to Susa, the Persian capital, in 324 B.C.E., he held a great banquet at which he married Dareios's daughter, insisting at the same time that his Macedonian officers should marry Persian women. Not surprisingly, his policy caused bitter resentment, particularly among the Macedonians, who considered themselves racially superior to the Persians. He pressed on eastward as far as the River Ganges in India before his troops refused to go any further.

Alexander died of unknown causes at Babylon in the spring of 323 B.C.E. after a short illness following a prolonged banquet and drinking bout. He left behind him an empire that stretched from the Adriatic in the west to the Punjab in the east, from southern Russia in the north to Ethiopia in the south. He was thirty-two.

ALEXANDER THE GREAT FOUNDING ALEXANDRIA. Placido Costanzi, 1737. Oil on canvas. The Macedonian ruler founded cities—often named after himself—in strategic military and trading locations. The city of Alexandria in Egypt is the only one still thriving today.

It seems highly probable that the conquests of Alexander the Great were provoked partly by an increase in population. It is thought that mainland Greece was more heavily populated between the fifth and the third centuries B.C.E. than at any time in its history until the late nineteenth century, and that, on the eve of Alexander's departure for the East, it had reached a peak of about two million inhabitants.

THE HELLENISTIC WORLD

On Alexander's death, each of his generals tried to seize as much of his empire as he could. It took nearly half a century before three stable kingdoms finally emerged: Macedonia, ruled by the Antigonid dynasty, founded by Antigonos Monophthalmos, meaning "one-eyed"; southern Turkey, Babylonia, Syria, Iran, and central Asia, ruled by the Seleucids, founded by Seleukos I Nikator, meaning "conqueror"; and Egypt, ruled by the Ptolemies, founded by Alexander's bastard half-brother Ptolemy Soter, meaning "preserver." Historians refer to them collectively as the Successors, or the *Diadochoi,* of Alexander the Great.

In addition, in mainland Greece, there were two federated leagues, the Aetolian League in the north and the Achaean League in the south. The technical Greek term for each is *koinon,* which means literally "the common thing," perhaps "the commonwealth." Both leagues were evolved tribal organizations—that is, they were settled communities but without any acknowledged center. The era from the death of Alexander until the Roman conquest is called the Hellenistic Period, taking its name from the fact that Hellenic or Greek culture was now disseminated over a very wide geographical area and was influencing many other cultures. One culture that fell under Greek influence in this period was Jewish. In Alexandria, for instance, where there was a very large Jewish population, Ptolemy II is said to have authorized a Greek translation of the Torah (the first five books of the Hebrew Bible), principally no doubt for the benefit of Jews who could not speak Hebrew. The translation, the Septuagint, was so named because it was alleged to have been the work of seventy translators.

In numerous ways the spread of Greek culture affected the daily lives of peoples living within its orbit throughout the eastern Mediterranean. It did not, however, obliterate local traditions. On the contrary, for the most part Greek culture coexisted peacefully with them, though it did eventually clash with Jewish culture. We should not, however, assume that it infiltrated the entire land mass ruled by the Successors. Vibrant pockets of Hellenism existed in urban settings alongside local cultures, some of which—particularly those that thrived in rural areas—were hardly influenced by it at all.

The Roman Conquest

Rome first came into contact with Greece through Greek settlements founded in Italy and Sicily. As noted earlier, the concentration of Greek states was so dense in southern Italy that the entire region came to be called *Megalê Hellas,* meaning "Great Greece," and then later, when the Romans encountered the Greeks, *Magna Graecia.* The communities of *Magna Graecia* attained considerable material prosperity and achieved a very high level of cultural achievement. It was undoubtedly through contact with them that the Romans first fell under the spell of Hellenism, which was destined to have such a profound impact upon virtually all aspects of Roman life, including religion, art, architecture, education, literature, statecraft, mythology, language, philosophy, and science.

In the 280s B.C.E., the Romans answered an appeal from Thourii in the Tarentine Gulf in the instep of Italy, under siege from the neighboring city of Tarentum. In turn, the Tarentines appealed to Pyrrhos, king of Epiros in northwest Greece. After two costly victories, Pyrrhos was finally defeated at Beneventum in southern Italy in 275 B.C.E. Then, in 168 B.C.E., the Macedonian king Perseus was defeated by the Romans at Pydna in southern Macedonia. In 149 B.C.E., Macedonia was reduced to the status of a Roman province. Three years later, a doomed Macedonian revolt took place, which the Romans ruthlessly suppressed. The Seleucid dynasty in Syria surrendered to Rome in 69 B.C.E. The Ptolemies were Roman vassals until the death of Cleopatra in 31 B.C.E., when Egypt became a Roman province.

One of the most enduring legacies of Roman rule in mainland Greece was depopulation and economic decline. The population reached its peak in the fourth century B.C.E. and seriously declined in the second century B.C.E. A major reason for this was the enslavement of large numbers of Greeks, most of whom were transported to the capital. In fact, Rome's conquest of Greece constituted the single greatest interruption in the daily life of Greeks living on the mainland at any time in antiquity, and it is regrettable that we have very little evidence to help us form a picture of the consequences of this momentous event for those who remained.

> The following observation by a friend of the Roman orator Cicero is highly
> revealing of the condition of mainland Greece in 45 B.C.E. as a result of
> Roman intervention:
>
> At sea . . . on my way back from Asia I was looking at the shores
> round about. Astern lay Aigina, before me lay Megara, on my right the
> Piraeus, and on my left Corinth—all once teeming cities, which now lie
> ruined and wrecked before our eyes. (*Letters to Friends* 4.5.4)

Greece's economic and political decline notwithstanding, its people and culture
were to continue to exercise a profound influence upon the Romans, as they had
done from the fourth century B.C.E. onward, and indeed earlier. As the Roman poet
Horace memorably phrased it, *Graecia capta ferum victorem cepit,* or "Conquered
Greece conquered its fierce victor" (*Epistles* 2.1.156). From the middle of the first
century C.E., mainland Greece underwent a considerable revival in its fortunes.
Nero (reigned 54–68 C.E.) was extremely cultivated in all things Greek and did
much to foster an appreciation for Hellenic customs and culture, both among
the aristocracy and among the common people. In 66 C.E., he began a tour of
Greece, competing in dramatic, lyric, and chariot contests. He claimed to have won
1,808 first prizes. The fact that he did not compete in all the events for which he
was awarded first prize failed to deter the Greek judges from acknowledging that
he had no equal. In 67 C.E. the emperor announced that he was liberating Greece
and giving it immunity from taxes. Nero's policy toward mainland Greece was
informed by an awareness that the country was struggling economically and by a
desire to improve its condition, for which he deserves at least some credit, though
he plundered Greece's art treasures along the way. Vespasian, however, who came
to the throne in 79 C.E., lost no time in rescinding the decree granting the Greek
cities autonomy and immunity from taxation, justifying his action by declaring
that Greece had "unlearnt" the ways of freedom, a reference, it seems, to the fact
that there was some unrest in the province at the time.

Hadrian (reigned 117–38 C.E.) was arguably the greatest philhellene of all. As a child he was nicknamed *Graeculus*—"little Greek"—in acknowledgement that he was at least as fluent in Greek as he was in Latin. Hadrian made several visits to Athens and lavished the equivalent of millions, if not billions, of dollars on beautifying the city. The Athenians were so grateful to him that they erected an arch in his honor to mark the boundary between the old city of Athens and the extension that he built. Another great benefactor was a super-rich Athenian named Herodes Atticus, who, in 143–44 C.E., sponsored the building of a new Panathenaic stadium with seating capacity of 50,000—perhaps not accidentally the same number that could be accommodated in the Colosseum in Rome. The Greeks were nothing if not competitive.

✤ 2 ✤
SPACE and TIME

LANDSCAPE AND CLIMATE

Greek history, not to mention the Greek character, owes much to the imperatives of the landscape of mainland Greece. It is a landscape that is unfriendly to humans. The mountains are forbidding, the vegetation sparse, the trees few, the soil poor and stony, and the climate harsh. Only a few of the valleys—one-fifth of the total land surface—are capable of supporting agriculture and cattle rearing on a significant scale. Because of the thinness of the soil, cows and sheep are relatively rare, and the most common livestock are goats. None of the rivers are navigable, and only a few have estuaries wide enough to serve as ports. Although these rivers may be raging torrents in the winter, irrigating the lowlands, most dry up in the summer.

Despite the fact that Greece was probably more thickly wooded in Classical antiquity than it is today, it has always been a poor country agriculturally and incapable of supporting a large population. Most of the land is mountainous, and few of the fertile plains are large. From early times, many states found it necessary to import wheat from abroad, including Athens, whose soil is too thin to support wheat. Its only important agricultural product was olives. To compensate for this deficiency, however, its territory was rich in marble and silver. To this day, Attica, the territory surrounding Athens, continues to have extensive marble quarries, though its silver mines are no longer active. Sparta's agricultural land was so small that, by the seventh century B.C.E., it had conquered the rich plain of Messenia, which lies to the west.

A PHOTOGRAPH OF THE ENIPEAS VALLEY, *where Mt. Olympus—the home of the twelve Olympian gods of ancient Greece—is located.*

The prominence of the mountain ranges, combined with the difficulty of land travel, helped to generate the fierce individualism that is a hallmark of the Greek character. Another factor that played a vital part in shaping the Greek character was the sea. The perilousness and unpredictability of this element is a central motif in Homer's *The Odyssey;* it is due to the wrath of the sea god Poseidon that Odysseus loses all his companions and is prevented from returning home to Ithaca for nine years. It was precisely because they were compelled to trade owing to their lack of natural resources that the Greeks came to develop a flexible response to the challenges of the outside world, whereas landlocked states that had no contact with the sea were, by contrast, inherently conservative and backward. This principle is neatly demonstrated by the difference in character between Athens and Sparta, the two dominant powers in the Greek world in the Classical Period. Whereas Sparta, an inland state, remained conservative and unenterprising, Athens, whose power and wealth were based on the sea, became the cultural leader of the Greek world.

Only the region as far north as Thessaly was regarded as properly Greek by the Greeks themselves. Macedonia, which lies above Thessaly, was considered semibarbaric, notwithstanding the fact that its inhabitants spoke Greek or a reasonable approximation thereof. The Greek world was not, however, limited to the mainland. As a result of the colonization movement, which is conventionally dated 734–580 B.C.E., it also came to include the Ionian cities along the west coast of Asia Minor (modern Turkey); the islands of the Aegean, of which there

The climate of Greece has been likened to that of southern California. The summers are hot and dry, whereas in the fall westerly winds occur with frequent outbursts of rain. Twice as much rain falls in the west of Greece as in the east. The coastal region is mild, but snows lie in the mountains throughout the winter. The poet Hesiod, a born complainer, found little to recommend it. In *Works and Days* (line 639f.), he tells us that his father, who came from Asia Minor, "settled near Mount Helikon [in Boiotia] in a wretched village called Askra, bad in winter, oppressive in summer, good at no time." Objectionable though the climate was to Hesiod personally, it is nonetheless sufficiently mild to enable the population to live much of its life outdoors.

Only the region as far north as Thessaly was regarded as properly Greek by the Greeks themselves. Macedonia, which lies above Thessaly, was considered semibarbaric, notwithstanding the fact that its inhabitants spoke Greek or a reasonable approximation thereof. The Greek world was not, however, limited to the mainland. As a result of the colonization movement, which is conventionally dated 734–580 B.C.E., it also came to include the Ionian cities along the west coast of Asia Minor (modern Turkey); the islands of the Aegean, of which there

A TOPOGRAPHIC MAP *showing the mountainous landscape of Greece.*

are more than two thousand in all; the islands off the west coast of Greece; the cities along the east coast of Sicily; and coastal cities in southern Italy, Libya, and Egypt, as well as a handful in Spain and France. In the Hellenistic Period, the limits of the Greek world become almost impossible to define, because Alexander the Great established Greek colonies in a predominantly non-Greek world that stretched as far east as the Hindu Kush.

THE CITY OF ATHENS

Like any other Greek polis, the Athenian state was a combination of urban center, or *asty,* and countryside, or *chôra.* Ancient Athens is today best known for the magnificent buildings erected on the Acropolis. This is a small, artificially leveled hilltop no more than 300 meters long by 200 meters broad that was the home of Athens' patron goddess Athene and other major state gods. Here stands the monumental gateway known as the Propylaia, the Parthenon or temple of Athene Parthenos, and the Erechtheion or temple of Poseidon-Erechtheus, all justly renowned as the crowning achievements of Classical architecture. These monuments should not, however, so overwhelm us that we lose sight of the image of Athens as a city—a city, moreover, that possessed many of the same problems as any urban development in any period, as well as others that were peculiar to the ancient world.

A MODERN-DAY PHOTOGRAPH OF THE ACROPOLIS CITADEL IN ATHENS. *The Acropolis has been under restoration since 1975, hence the construction cranes that are visible.*

Civic Amenities

Despite the grandeur of its civic buildings, in many respects, Athens resembled a country town rather than a city. Most of the amenities that we take for granted today were virtually nonexistent. There was no street lighting, which meant that, after nightfall, pedestrians had to provide their own source, most commonly no doubt in the form of a lantern-bearing slave. There was no fire brigade. There were no hospitals. The police force, such as it was, consisted of publicly owned slaves, whose job primarily was to keep the peace, not to detect or prevent or investigate crime. Water was brought to the city from distant springs by means of terra-cotta pipelines that fed public fountains. With one or two notable exceptions, the majority of fountain houses were simple reservoirs cut into the living rock. Only a few major roads were paved. There were no public toilets. There was only a very rudimentary and highly inefficient method of waste disposal. Traces of a drain that began beside the Acropolis and descended into the Agora have been found dating from the seventh century B.C.E., and in the fifth century a more extensive drainage system was constructed. However, it was never remotely comparable in scale to the *Cloaca Maxima,* or Great Drain, that ran through Rome and there must have been many occasions when it overflowed. Individual households would therefore have been responsible for the disposal of their own waste. Perhaps there were designated dumps where garbage was deposited before being removed from the city.

It was the duty of municipal law enforcement officers known as *astynomoi* to determine that certain minimum standards of hygiene and safety were upheld. Their tasks included ensuring that dung collectors did not deposit dung within a radius of ten stades (approximately half a mile) of the circuit wall; that buildings did not encroach upon the streets; and that the bodies of those who expired upon the public highways were collected for burial. The checking of such abuses, particularly the proper disposal of dung, must have been an uphill battle. Disease was an ever-present hazard, especially during the summer months.

What was true of Athens would have been true of most Greek cities, though some of the great Hellenistic foundations, such as Alexandria in Egypt, Antioch (modern Antakya) on the banks of the Orontes River, and Apamea, also on the Orontes, which were laid out according to a grid, are likely to have had better municipal facilities. Incidentally, these were all cities with estimated populations of 200,000 or more.

City Limits

From 479 B.C.E. onward, and possibly earlier, the limits of Athens' growth were defined by a circuit wall built on top of a stone socle with mud brick in its upper courses. This wall, hurriedly constructed after the defeat of the Persians, was pierced by at least seventeen gates. Through these gates passed roads connecting the city with the outlying districts of Attica—Acharnai to the north, Eleusis to the west, Piraeus to the south. The most famous of these gates was the Dipylon, or Double Gate, on the western side of the city. It was so named because it consisted of an entrance at each end of a long corridor that was designed to entrap the invader. Outside the Dipylon lay the Kerameikos or Potters' Quarter, where the most impressive grave monuments have been discovered. Reconstructed according to its Classical plan, the Kerameikos is today a tranquil oasis of peace amid the bustle of modern Athens. In the Eridanos brook that ambles through it, tortoises wade and frogs frolic, just as they did in antiquity.

The Agora

The road from the Dipylon Gate joined the Panathenaic Way, which was one of the few paved roads in Athens. This was the route taken by the Panathenaia or All-Athenian Festival, held annually in honor of Athene and every four years with special pomp and circumstance. As it wound its way up to the Acropolis, the Panathenaic procession passed through the Agora, a flat, open space roughly rectangular in shape and lined on all four sides with administrative buildings.

The Agora, which has no equivalent in the modern world, occupied a central position in the life of the community until the destruction of Athens by a Germanic people from Scandinavia known as the Herulians in C.E. 267. It was the civic, commercial, administrative, social, legal, and political heart of the city. The Altar of the Twelve Gods in the northwest corner of the Agora marked the spot where all roads converged and from which measurements to other parts of Attica were taken. Temporary stalls selling agricultural produce and manufactured goods were also set up here. In addition, the Agora provided the setting for most trials. Its unique combination—or, more accurately, jumble—of functions is captured in a fragment from a lost play by the comic dramatist Euboulos, who lists the following assortment of items and persons on hand there (quoted in Athenaios, *Professors at Dinner* 14.640b): figs, issuers of summonses to attend the law courts, grapes, turnips, pears, apples, witnesses, roses, medlars, haggis, honeycombs, chickpeas, lawsuits, beestings, curds, myrtle berries, ballot boxes, bluebells, lamb, water clocks, laws, indictments.

RECONSTRUCTION OF THE STOA OF ATTALOS IN ATHENS, *created by the American School of Classical Studies created in 1956.*

The Agora was amply provided with colonnaded walkways or stoas, of which the Stoa of Attalos, reconstructed down to the last detail by the American School of Classical Studies, is the finest and most spectacular example. Originally financed by Attalos II of Pergamon in about 150 B.C.E., it is over 115 meters in length and dominates the east side of the Agora. Provided with shelter from the elements, Athenians gathered in the Agora to engage in their favorite pastime—lively and animated discussion. Here, at the end of the fifth century B.C.E., the philosopher Sokrates was invariably to be found. Here, too, a century later gathered the Stoics, philosophers who took their name from the Painted Stoa, so named because of paintings done on wooden panels that were displayed inside it, which came to light in 1981 in the northwest corner of the Agora. The Agora was also a place to pass the time of day, as suggested by the verb *agorazein,* which means to "loaf about." Groups of Athenians, as well as foreigners, had their favorite meeting places. As the speaker in a law court oration by Lysias states (24.20), "Each of you is in the habit of frequenting some place, a perfumer's shop, a barber's shop, a cobbler's and so forth." The Dekeleians, for instance, gathered at the barber's shop beside the Herms (stone pillars with the head of the god Hermes), whereas the Plataians could be found at the cheese market on the last day of the month.

One of the most frequented spots was the monument to the Eponymous Heroes, which stood in the southwest corner of the Agora close to the law courts. This monument honored the heroes who gave their names to the ten Athenian tribes that were created by Kleisthenes. Its base served as a public notice board that provided news about military conscription, forthcoming trials, agendas for public meetings, proposed legislation, and other public matters. Other important secular buildings located in the Agora include the public mint, the *bouleutêrion* or council house, the *metrôön* or public record office, and the *tholos*. This last was a circular building with thatched roof that served as the living quarters for the fifty members of the council who were permanently on duty day and night to deal with emergencies. Despite its importance, the Agora possessed only very rudimentary civic amenities. Storm water and sewage were disposed of by means of a stone channel that modern archaeologists have rather grandiosely named the Great Drain.

The Acropolis

The Acropolis, which means upper or higher city, dominates the countryside of Attica for miles around. In early times, it functioned as a palace, a sanctuary, and a fortress. Its massive surrounding wall dates to the late thirteenth century B.C.E. The Acropolis continued to be used for defensive purposes until the 460s B.C.E., when a new wall was built to encompass a larger area. All the temples that had been erected previously were destroyed by the Persians in 479 B.C.E., and little trace of them survives today apart from a few fragments of architectural sculpture. For forty years, the Acropolis remained in its ruined condition as testimony to Persian barbarity until 447 B.C.E., when an ambitious building program was instigated on the initiative of Perikles, financed by the surplus tribute paid by Athens' naval allies, which resulted in an architectural project of breathtaking beauty.

Entering the Acropolis through the Propylaia, one faces the diminutive Erechtheion on the left and the massive Parthenon on the right. The Parthenon stands starkly isolated at the highest point of the rock, surrounded by a wasteland of broken marble somewhat resembling a stonecutter's yard. Yet the Acropolis played host to many other temples, of which virtually no trace has survived. To appreciate the effect that it would have presented in antiquity, one must

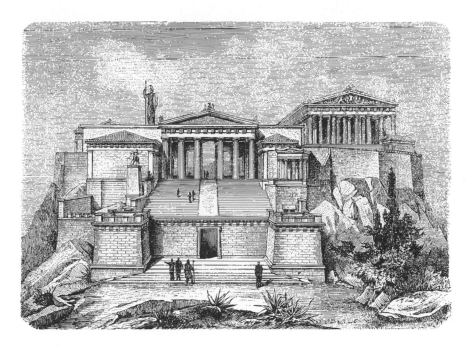

THE PROPYLAIA, OR GATEWAY TO THE ACROPOLIS. *Anonymous 1908 illustration from the Brockhaus Enzyklopädie.*

imagine several other temples, sanctuary walls, and altars, as well as a forest of dedicatory statues, all jockeying for attention like insistent petitioners. The Acropolis remained largely intact until the invasion of the Heruli in 267 C.E., when, in all probability, the Parthenon was severely damaged by fire, thereby reducing to a pile of carbonized rubble the chryselephantine (gold and ivory) statue of Athene by Pheidias, which it had housed.

Urban Growth

Before the beginning of the sixth century B.C.E., Athens possessed few public buildings. Nor, so far as we know, was any part of the city specifically laid aside for civic activity. Around the beginning of the sixth century B.C.E., however, the city began to expand dramatically, albeit in a haphazard fashion and without reference

THE ACROPOLIS FROM ABOVE, *as it would have looked in ancient Athens. The numerous buildings served a variety of functions and included palaces, temples, shrines, theatres, and stoas.*

to any master plan or guiding architectural principle. By the fifth century, the population had grown to such an extent that it could no longer gather in the Agora for public meetings. The *ekklêsia,* or assembly, was therefore moved to a hill overlooking the Agora called the Pnyx. The Theater of Dionysos, located on the south slope of the Acropolis, was also enlarged at this date. To the west, the Odeion of Perikles was built—a vast, roofed building capable of accommodating an audience of 5,000. Although Athens was damaged by Sulla in 86 B.C.E., it enjoyed a considerable architectural revival under the Emperor Hadrian (117–38 C.E.). Then, in 169 C.E. , the theater of Herodes Atticus was constructed, and the entire southern slope of the Acropolis became a vast cultural center, rather like the Kennedy Center in Washington, DC, or the South Bank Arts Complex in London.

Although fifth-century B.C.E. Athens was an urban entity, its growth and development did not bring about an exodus from the countryside. Even at the outbreak of the Peloponnesian War, most of the population still resided outside Athens, as Thukydides describes (2.16.1). It is difficult to gauge the extent to which those living in the countryside were incorporated into the life of the city. Although most Athenian citizens would have needed to travel to Athens at least once or twice a year for official business, few are likely to have done so on a regular basis, particularly those residing in the outermost demes such as Marathon and Acharnai, some twenty-five to thirty miles from Athens. It is therefore highly likely that there was a considerable gap in the lifestyle, as well as the political engagement, of city dwellers and country dwellers.

A City of Contrasts

Athens would have struck the modern eye as a curious amalgam of public magnificence and private squalor. It was a city to be admired for the breathtaking beauty of its public buildings, for which in the Classical Period there was no equivalent in the entire Greek world. In regard to its housing and public amenities, however, it may well have been inferior to many of its contemporaries. It may strike one as remarkable that the Athenians, who adorned their city with some of the most splendid buildings ever constructed, were prepared to tolerate such discomfort in private. It says everything about the difference in mentality between them and us that no one ever suggested that their priorities should be reversed.

TIME AND THE SEASONS

Dividing Up the Day

The Greek day was divided into twelve hours of daylight and twelve hours of darkness, a system which, according to Herodotos (2.109.3), the Greeks acquired from the Babylonians. As a result, the daylight hours were longer in the summer than in the winter. Hours were not subdivided into halves and quarters. In fact, the only way to tell the time accurately was by means of the sundial, which was first introduced into Greece in the sixth century B.C.E. and which they also borrowed from the Babylonians. Sundials were extremely rare, however, until the third century B.C.E. The natural divisions of the day—dawn, midday, and dusk—no doubt served most people for most purposes.

Only in the law courts was accurate timekeeping absolutely necessary, because, from the fifth century B.C.E. onward, speeches had to be timed down to the last second. This was done with the aid of a water clock known as a *klepsydra,* a clay vessel that could be filled to the level of an overflow hole just below the rim. When the speaker began his delivery, a plug was removed from a small hole at the base of one of the jugs. As soon as the water ceased to flow, the speaker would be required to sit down. This simple device guaranteed that both parties spoke for exactly the same amount of time.

KLEPSYDRA, OR WATER CLOCK. *This timekeeping device runs for six minutes, which was the time allotted for a speech in the law courts of ancient Greece.*

Marking the Passage of the Seasons

Hesiod's *Works and Days,* which was composed in the seventh century B.C.E., is a kind of farmer's almanac. It indicates that signs from the natural world, such as heliacal risings and settings, were used to mark the passage of the seasons and so served as a guide to the farming year. The time for plowing and harvesting, for instance, was indicated by the rise of a constellation called the Pleiades (also known as the Seven Sisters):

> When the daughters of Atlas [the giant who supports the earth on his shoulders] are rising [i.e., early in May], begin the harvest, and when they

are setting begin your plowing. These stars are hidden for forty nights and forty days, but they appear again as the year revolves again, which is when iron [i.e., for the blade of the plow] must first be sharpened. (lines 383–87)

Similarly, the moment to harvest grapes coincided with the appearance of particular stars:

When Orion and Sirius (also known as the Dog star) are in the middle of the sky, and rosy-fingered dawn sees Arktouros [i.e., in mid-September], then cut off all the grapes . . . and bring them home. (lines 609–11)

Hesiod also uses changes in animal behavior as an indicator of the changing seasons:

When the house-carrier [i.e., snail] leaves the ground and climbs up plants [i.e., in the middle of May], fleeing the Pleiades, then is not the time to dig vineyards, but to sharpen your sickles and rouse your slaves. (lines 571–73)

The blossoming of plants served as a further guide:

When the artichoke comes into flower [i.e., in June], and the chattering cicada sits in a tree and pours down his sweet song in full measure from under his wings and wearisome heat is at its height, then goats are fattest and wine is sweetest. Women are in heat, but men are at their weakest, because Sirius saps the head and the knees, and the flesh is dry because of the heat. (lines 582–88)

Hesiod scores top marks for the precision of his time-reckoning code and for his observation of the natural world. To quote the archaeo-astronomer Antony Aveni (*Empires of Time*, 48): "Hesiod's calendar codifies the association of celestial rhythms with the biorhythms present in all living things since their beginning.

His scheme is intricate and rich in detail in its predictive power . . . and his astronomic timings and crosschecks are . . . as accurate as any time-marking scheme, using these events, that can be written down."

Reckoning the Years

There was no universal method of reckoning the passage of years in the Greek world. Rather, each community adhered to its own idiosyncratic system. So when Thukydides wishes to indicate the year in which the Peloponnesian War broke out, he tells his readers that hostilities began "fourteen years after the capture of Euboia, forty-seven years after Chryses became priestess of Hera at Argos, in the year when Ainesias was ephor at Sparta, and in the year when Pythodoros was archon in Athens" (2.1.1).

The earliest preserved date in Greek history is 776 B.C.E., when the Olympic Games were first celebrated. However, Olympiads, which marked the four-year intervals between successive celebrations of the games, were not adopted as a basis for chronology until the third century B.C.E. Nor did all city-states seek to establish the year of their foundation. What they were primarily interested in proving was that their city had been founded earlier than their rivals, because this could lend legitimacy to territorial claims.

Athens' written records begin in 683 B.C.E., when it instituted a system by which a magistrate known as the eponymous archon gave his name to the year. There was nothing else significant about this date. It merely marked the adoption of a procedural convenience. Moreover, although the Athenians annually celebrated the birthday of their principal state deity, Athene Polias, on the tweny-eighth of the month of *Hekatombaion* (i.e., shortly after the summer solstice), they did not know the year in which the goddess had been born. They also held a festival called the *Synoikia* earlier in the month in commemoration of the *synoikismos* or unification of Attica, which they ascribed to their legendary king Theseus. However, because Theseus's reign could not be dated, this event did not provide a fixed date either. It was not until the Hellenistic Period that a determined attempt was made to establish a foundation date for Athens.

The Farmer's Year According to Hesiod

(after Claudia Carrington, *Omnibus* 17 [March, 1989]).
Reprinted with permission.

Hekatombaion

Now is the time to harvest figs. Be sure to have a sharp-toothed dog to keep away thieves

Anthesterion

When plowing time arrives, make haste to plow, both you and your slaves, on rainy days and dry ones

Pyanopsion

The sun's sharp fury and drenching heat subside and mighty Zeus sends autumn rain

Thargelion / Skirophorion

Thresh and winnow your grain. When all your work is done relax with good wine

Elaphebolion

Now is the time to tend your vines, pick off the caterpillars and pull out all the weeds

Maimakterion

When you hear the crane's voice, know that she means the time has come to plough

Munychion

When the one whose house is on his back climbs up the stems, sharpen your sickles and rouse your slaves

Metageitnion

Pluck the clustered grapes and bring your harvest home

Boedromion

Harvest your olives

Poseideon

Be on your guard! This is the hardest month, stormy, hard on livestock and hard on men

Gamelion

Wear a fleecy coat and tunic ... Do not be idle. Mend and repair old and broken tools

The author of an inscribed marble column known as the *Marmor Parium,* who claimed to have "written up the dates [of Athenian history] from the beginning," maintained that Kekrops, the first king of Athens, came to the throne 1,218 years prior to the setting up of the inscription in 264/3 B.C.E. In the same century, the geographer Eratosthenes devised a dating system that took as its departure the fall of Troy, which he assigned (not inaccurately, it may well be) to 1183 B.C.E.

Like other Greeks, Athenians did not celebrate the New Year, mainly because their calendar, which was based on the phases of the moon, was in a state of almost constant turmoil. A lunar calendar is extremely convenient in a subliterate society for arranging the dates of monthly festivals, payment of debts, public assemblies, and so forth. As a basis for marking the passage of the seasons, however, it is virtually useless, because the lunar year is eleven days shorter than the solar year. Because, however, the success of the harvest was thought to depend on ritual activity performed at precise moments of the year, the Greeks had to intercalate (i.e., insert) an extra month from time to time in order to keep their calendar in line with the annual circuit of the sun. In fact, over a nineteen-year cycle, they had to intercalate seven extra months.

The End of the World?

Although the Greeks were spared the anxiety that is associated with global warming, they did have an appreciation that the world's biological clock was running down. One indication of this was the perceived diminution in human stature and capability. In *The Iliad,* for instance, Homer claims that the heroes who fought at Troy were giants compared with the men of his day. A Greek warrior called Diomedes, for instance, effortlessly picked up a stone "which two men could not lift, of the kind that mortals are today" (5.302–4). Belief in the earth's biological decline was not confined to the hyperbolic medium of Greek epics. Herodotos tells us that, in Egypt, a sandal had been preserved two cubits in length, which had once belonged to the hero Perseus. Likewise, the image of a giant footstep made by Herakles was allegedly engraved on a rock in Scythia (2.91.3; 4.82).

A particularly bleak prophecy, which may well reflect deteriorating economic and social circumstances in the late eighth and early seventh centuries, appears in Hesiod's *Works and Days*. The poet informs his audience that they are presently living in the Age of Iron and that it is their lot "never to cease from labour and sorrowing by day, and dying by night" (lines 176–78). Yet if conditions seem bad now, they are destined to become much worse, for the time is fast approaching when infants will be born with the marks of old age upon them. Human life span, in other words, will have so contracted that infancy and old age will be virtually indistinguishable from one another.

> The father will have nothing in common with his sons, nor sons with their father, nor a guest with his host, nor friend with friend, nor will a brother be beloved as before. Men will dishonor their parents as they age rapidly. They will blame them, speaking harsh words. Stiff-necked, they will think nothing of the gods. Nor will they repay to their aged parents the gift of their own nurturing. (lines 182–88)

When that apocalyptic moment is reached, which reflects a decline in moral standards in line with the earth's biological decline, Zeus will annihilate the human race. Even so, the forlorn wish that prefaces the poet's description of the Age of Iron—"O that I was not among men of the fifth race, but had either died before it or been born after it" (line 174f.)—seems to hint at a cyclical repetition involving a return to the Golden Age. Hesiod does not appear to have regarded the invention of iron as marking an improvement in technology, nor does he seem to have been of the opinion that technological advance in itself represents a threat to the future of the planet, though the seeds of this modern belief lie embedded in the myth.

❊ 3 ❊
LANGUAGE, ALPHABET, AND LITERACY

THE ORIGINS OF THE GREEK LANGUAGE AND LINEAR B

By the thirteenth century B.C.E., at the very latest, the inhabitants of the Greek mainland and the island of Crete were speaking Greek. Indeed, some scholars, from the analysis of place names and archaeological data, believe that Greek speakers (or people speaking proto-Greek) had arrived by 2000 B.C.E. This makes Greek the oldest of all European languages with a continuous history lasting at least 3,300 years, possibly even 4,000 years. Although its origins are unclear, it belongs to the Indo-European family of languages, which extends from Iceland to Bangladesh. This includes Latin and all the Romance languages, the Germanic languages, Sanskrit, and many others.

Until the Hellenistic Period, Greek existed in a number of different dialects, the most important of which were Aeolic, Doric, Ionic, and Attic. These dialects do not, however, invariably correspond to ethnic divisions within the Greek "race." For instance, the inhabitants of Halikarnassos, modern Bodrùm on the Turkish coast, who were Dorians, spoke in an Ionic dialect. Following the conquests of Alexander the Great, a dialect called *koinê*, or "common," became the educated tongue of the entire Hellenistic world. *Koinê* is the dialect in which the New Testament is written.

LINEAR B INSCRIPTION, *found in Pylos, Greece, written on a terracotta tablet dating back to the second millennium B.C.E. The Mycenaeans used the Linear B script primarily for administrative records.*

The evidence for the existence of the Greek language in the Bronze Age derives from a prealphabetical Greek script called Linear B, which was deciphered by a thirty-year-old English architect named Michael Ventris in 1952. It is so named in order to distinguish it from an earlier, still undeciphered, script called Linear A, which may or may not have been Greek. (Linear A was used extensively throughout the Minoan world in the period from 1800 to 1450 B.C.E. Because it has not been deciphered, it is not known whether the Minoans were in fact Greek speakers.) Linear B was based on the principle that one sign represents one syllable. Objects are denoted by ideograms—that is, signs that were originally pictorial. Clay tablets engraved in Linear B by means of a sharp instrument have been found at Mycenai, Tiryns, Thebes, Pylos, and Knossos (Crete). Most of them date to the thirteenth century B.C.E. There is very little regional variation, which suggests a high degree of administrative centralization. It was used mainly for accounting records, as in the following tablet from Pylos: "Kokalos repaid the following quantity of olive oil to Eumedes: 648 liters; from Ipsewas 38 stirrup-jars" (Knox, in Finley, *The World of Odysseus,* viii). With the collapse of the Mycenaean world, the script died out and literacy disappeared.

Greece remained illiterate for over four hundred years. Then, in the early eighth century B.C.E., the Greeks came into contact with a seafaring people called the Phoenicians, who inhabited cities on the coast of Syria. They adapted the Phoenician alphabet to their own language by adding seven vowel sounds (i.e., *a,* short and long *e, i,* short and long *o,* and *u)* to the original sixteen consonants, making it a much more flexible script. Many of the Phoenician names for the letters entered the Greek alphabet virtually unchanged, including *aleph* (alpha) meaning "ox-head" and *beth* (beta) meaning "house." The same letters also functioned as a numerical system and were used for musical notation.

The earliest surviving examples of the Greek alphabet are dated around 740 B.C.E. Some scholars maintain that the Greeks first used the alphabet for trade and commerce, others for preserving epic poetry. The earliest examples of Greek writing are, in fact, lines written in epic verse. Before long, however, letters had come to serve a variety of purposes. Although some states had a few local variants, the alphabet became standardized by the early fourth century B.C.E.

The Greek alphabet was destined to become the basis for other European scripts, including Latin, modern Greek, and Cyrillic.

LITERACY

For many years after the alphabet was first introduced, only a small number of Greeks would have been literate. We do not know whether Homer was literate, though he certainly knew about writing because he makes reference to it in *The Iliad*. However, his poems were transmitted primarily through the oral tradition by *rhapsodes* (literally "song-stitchers"), professional reciters of poetry, who may or may not have been literate.

We do not know what percentage of the population could read and write at any period of Greek history. What is abundantly clear, however, is that mass literacy never existed on the scale that it exists today. William Harris, in *Ancient Literacy* (1989), has estimated that no more than 30 percent of the Greek population was literate at any one time. Levels of literacy varied from one place to another and from one social group to another. One of the highest levels was achieved by Classical Athens, whose democratic constitution was based on the principle that a substantial proportion of the (male) citizenry could read the often lengthy and extremely detailed documents that were recorded on stone, and that the majority at least achieved craft literacy, that is, they were able to read material related to their sphere of work. In Sparta, by contrast, where few written records were kept, most of the population was probably completely illiterate.

PAINTING *from an Attic red-figure cup depicting a teacher, Linos (on the right), holding a papyrus scroll, while his student, Mosaios (on the left), holds writing tablets.*

Literacy is likely to have been practically nonexistent among women, those who belonged to the lower social classes, and slaves. In each group, however, there were exceptions. Evidence from vase painting, including an Attic red-figure vase dated around 440 B.C.E. that depicts a seated woman sometimes identified as the poetess Sappho reading a roll, suggests, however, that some Athenian women were literate. Informal graffiti indicates that literacy was not exclusively limited to the elite. Lastly, the job of some slaves was to keep accounts of financial transactions or to read aloud to their masters and mistresses. It was slaves, too, who made multiple copies of literary works that went on sale.

Despite the importance of literacy in Greek society, much more information and learning was passed down by word of mouth than is the case in our society. At all periods and places, there was a ready audience for recitals of all sorts, not just musical but also literary. The historian Herodotos, for instance, first promulgated his work through oral recitation in Athens, and oral recitation remained a popular form of communication throughout antiquity.

PAPYRI

The commonest Greek writing material was *cyperus papyrus,* a plant that grows in the swamps of Lower Egypt, which had been used for writing in Egypt and Mesopotamia from 3000 B.C.E. onward. The Greeks called this plant *biblos,* from which the word *bible* derives. Stalks of papyrus were laid out in parallel horizontal strips, over which a second layer was placed vertically. The strips were then pressed flat and pounded with a flat stone so that they bonded together with their natural juices. A papyrus roll was read by unfolding with the right hand and rerolling with the left hand. To reread the roll, therefore, the reader (or more probably a slave) had to unroll the papyrus all the way back to the beginning.

The earliest surviving Greek papyrus, a commentary on the Orphic poems (see p. 201), dates from the fourth century B.C.E. It was found at Derveni, near Thessaloniki, in Macedonia. It is the only surviving papyrus to come from mainland Greece, and the reason it survived is because it was carbonized. The overwhelming majority of papyri came to light in Egypt, whose dry soil provides ideal conditions for their preservation, and postdate Alexander's conquest of that country. The largest cache has been retrieved from the rubbish dumps of a town called Oxyrhynchos (the name means "the city of the sharp-nosed fish"), situated about a hundred miles south of modern Cairo. Oxyrhynchos has so far yielded over 50,000 papyri.

To date, some 30,000 papyri have been edited. They include birth certificates, death certificates, lists of various kinds, receipts, marriage contracts, wet-nurse contracts, complaints to officials, tax returns, lawsuits, and last, but by no means least, private letters. They shed invaluable light on many aspects of the social, cultural, legal, and economic life of Greeks living in Egypt and of Egyptians who adapted to the Greek way of life (see Evans, *Daily Life in the Hellenistic Age,* 2008, in this series). One of the most interesting revelations the papyri provide is the degree to which Hellenistic Egypt was a truly multicultural society, as evidenced by the fact that a number of documents are bilingual.

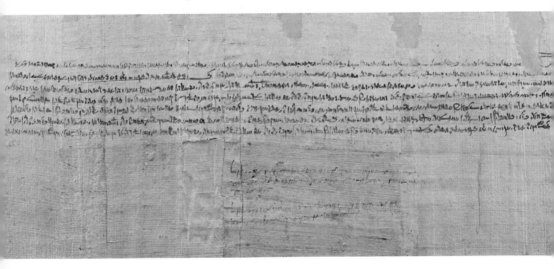

GREEK LEGAL DOCUMENT WRITTEN ON PAPYRUS, *documenting the sale and receipt of a plot of temple land on one side and listing the names of witnesses on the other side. This particular papyrus, found in Thebes, Egypt, dates to ca. 208 B.C.E.*

Many documentary papyri are written on scraps that contain fragments of Greek literature on the reverse. In fact, it is thanks to papyrology (i.e., the study of papyri) that several lost works of Greek literature have come to light. Among the most important finds are Sophokles' satyr play *Detectives,* Menander's comedy *The Ill-Tempered Man,* and Aristotle's *Constitution of Athens.* On the basis of the total number of literary papyri, the most popular author by far was Homer, with *The Iliad* outnumbering *The Odyssey* by three to one. This means that if a Greek owned any author's work at all, it was most likely to be that of Homer. Although the data pertain only to Egypt in the Hellenistic era, there is no reason to suppose that Homer would have been any less popular anywhere else in the Greek world.

Papyrology has been an important branch of historical inquiry since the final decades of the nineteenth century. Its discoveries provide us with a slice of Greek life that would otherwise be completely unknown to us. It is a life that sometimes comes across to us in heart-rending detail. We hear, for instance, of a slave called Epaphroditos, eight years old, who fell to his death out of a bedroom window when he was leaning out to watch castanet players down below in the street. On a more light-hearted note, we also hear of a schoolmaster named Lollianos who complained that he never received his salary "except sometimes in sour wine and worm-ridden corn."

OSTRAKA

Because sheets of papyri were relatively expensive to purchase, broken pieces of pottery, known as *ostraka,* frequently served for writing as well. Thousands of *ostraka* have been preserved in the soil of Greece because, unlike papyri, they are practically indestructible. Most are incised, though in Egypt the majority are written in ink. Although *ostraka* were mainly used for lists or official receipts, some were used for correspondence.

From *ostrakon* comes *ostrakismos,* which give us our word *ostracism.* An *ostrakismos* was a vote cast by the Athenian assembly to banish one of two leading politicians whose rivalry was judged to be harmful to the state. The ballot papers took the form of *ostraka* on which the citizens wrote the name of the candidate of their choice—or rather nonchoice. If more than 6,000 votes were cast, the leading candidate was exiled from Athens for ten years. The first ostracism occurred in 487 B.C.E. and the last in 417 B.C.E. We can well imagine that an ostracism was one of the most eagerly anticipated occasions in the political calendar. Many Athenians no doubt used their vote to express their displeasure with a policy that was closely associated with one of the candidates, whereas others acted purely out of personal spite. When a politician named Aristides, who was nicknamed the Just, was facing the threat of ostracism, an illiterate country bumpkin, failing to recognize him, asked him to inscribe his potsherd with Aristides' name upon it. When Aristides asked him whether the politician had done him any injury, the bumpkin replied "No. It's simply that I'm tired of hearing him called 'the Just.' " Aristides thus fell victim to what we would call today celebrity overexposure—a career hazard that overtook other prominent Athenian politicians.

In addition, the Greeks utilized wooden tablets coated with wax for messages, lists, and school exercises, as these could be used over and over again.

LIBRARIES

The first evidence for a trade in book rolls dates to the end of the fifth century B.C.E. A comic poet named Eupolis (*fl.* 420s–412 B.C.E.) alludes to a part of the Agora in Athens "where the rolls are on sale." Because rolls were copied by slaves, they were relatively inexpensive to purchase. At his trial in 399 B.C.E., Sokrates (Plato, *Apology* 26de) allegedly inquired of his accuser, "Do you think that the jury is so illiterate as to be unaware that the rolls of Anaxagoras of Klazomenai [a natural philosopher] . . . are on sale in the Orchestra [probably a part of the Agora where public performances took place, including singing, dancing, and drama] for a drachma at most?"

The earliest evidence for private libraries also dates to the end of the fifth century. The comic poet Aristophanes is thought to have possessed a substantial library because of the numerous allusions in his plays to the tragedians. (His surviving plays contain references to as many as 45 dramas of Euripides). Euripides, who is portrayed as an avid reader (e.g., Aristophanes, *Frogs* 943, 1409), almost certainly owned a library that contained the works of his fellow tragedians. Even so, very few individuals are likely to have purchased rolls. Probably the biggest library in private hands was that of Aristotle. The Greek geographer Strabo (*Geography* 13.1.54), who credits Aristotle with being the first serious bibliophile, describes in detail how successive private collectors kept it intact after his death, despite efforts by public libraries to acquire it. The anecdote reminds us that, even though rolls were relatively inexpensive, they were never plentiful, and once there had been an initial run of any work, copies were hard to come by.

Public libraries first came into being in the Hellenistic Period. They represented a claim to cultural status on the part of the dynasts who, for the most part, financed them. Strabo credits Aristotle with taking the initiative in "teaching the kings of Egypt how to organize a library." The largest library in the ancient world was, in fact, the Mouseion, or House of the Muses, in Alexandria, from which the word *museum* derives. Founded in the early third century B.C.E. by King Ptolemy I, it is said to have contained over half a million rolls, perhaps the equivalent of 100,000 books. (To give an indication of the sheer quantity of learning that existed in antiquity, we may note that when the first Bible rolled off Johannes Gutenberg's press in 1456, it is estimated that there were fewer than 30,000 books in all of Europe.) For several hundred years, the Mouseion remained the foremost repository of learning in the world. Among its famous librarians were Aristophanes of Byzantium, who annotated the earliest editions of Greek literature, and Aristarchos of Samos, who established the definitive text of both *The Iliad* and *The Odyssey*. Although the library was accidentally burned down, perhaps during Julius Caesar's siege of Alexandria in 48 B.C.E., it continued to function until 641 C.E., when it was closed on the orders of an Arab general.

Eventually, libraries became a feature of all Hellenistic cities and many medium-sized towns. The nearest rival to Alexandria, said to have possessed 200,000 rolls, was Pergamum, modern Bergama, about sixteen miles from the northern Turkish coast. (Pergamum, by the way, was celebrated for its parchment—the writing material that eventually replaced papyrus.) As they do today, libraries instituted rules governing the use of their rolls. A library in Athens, which was the gift to the city of a Romanized Greek named T. Flavius Pantainos around 100 C.E., contains an inscription that states: "No roll shall be taken out, since we have sworn an oath. It shall be opened from the first hour to the sixth."

In the absence of barcodes and an alarm system, it seems that the honor code prevailed. Somewhat paradoxically, what has survived of Classical literature owes nothing to the great libraries of antiquity and everything to the fact that manuscripts were copied and recopied, initially during the Roman Empire and later during the Middle Ages, first onto papyrus and subsequently onto parchment. Even so, merely a fraction of the total output of antiquity has survived. To give just one example of the scale of the loss, we have only seven of a total of 123 plays written by Sophokles—the ones that had been selected as set books for study probably around 200 C.E..

THE GREAT LIBRARY OF ALEXANDRIA. O. Von Corven (German), nineteenth century. This artistic rendering of the Library of Alexandria, or Mouseion, is partly based on archaeological evidence.

4

THE PEOPLE

SOCIAL ORGANIZATION

The Household

The basic social unit in the Greek world was the family, for which there is no exact linguistic equivalent. The nearest word is *oikos* (or *oikia*), which more accurately translates as "household." The head of the *oikos* was the oldest male, who was in charge of the religious practices that were conducted in the home. An *oikos* denoted all those living under the same roof: the master and mistress, their children and other dependents, and all their household slaves. It also included the landed estate, the movable property, the livestock, and any domesticated animals or pets. The commonest pet was probably the goose. Other favorite household pets included cranes, quails, small birds, and dogs. (When Odysseus returns home after twenty years, he is recognized by his dog Argos, who is so overcome with emotion that he promptly dies.) Cats, however, were regarded as oddities and were rarely kept as pets. Cocks were reared for fighting—a favorite pastime in Athens.

The Genos

The next largest unit after the oikos was the *genos* (pl. *genê*), meaning "noble kin group or clan." We don't know what proportion of the citizen body belonged to a genos but it may well have been less than 10 percent. Members of the same *genos* traced their descent from a common ancestor, who, in many cases, was

RELIEF SCULPTURE *showing a seated woman holding the hand of another woman, with a man in the background and a child to the left. A funerary stele such as this commemorates the deceased and their importance to the family unit.*

mythical or divine. We know of the existence of about sixty Athenian *genê* and they varied greatly in size; the most prominent was the Alkmaionidai, to which both Kleisthenes and Perikles belonged. All of Athens' most venerable cults were administered by *genê,* and the election to their priesthoods was hereditary. The priesthoods of both Athene Polias (Of the city) and Poseidon Erechtheus, the two principal state cults, were restricted to a small *genos* known as the Eteoboutadai. Precisely what *gennêtai* (i.e., members of the same *genos)* did in common apart from worship together is not known. We never hear of any social or other functions that brought them together, though they may have dined together periodically. Until the reforms of Kleisthenes at the end of the sixth century B.C.E., *genê,* because of their wealth and power, effectively controlled the political process. Even after the democratic reforms carried out around 462 B.C.E., they continued to wield very considerable influence at least for another half century.

The Phratry

Whereas only aristocrats belonged to a *genos,* all Athenians were members of a phratry. *Phratry,* from which the word *fraternal* is derived, means "brotherhood." Until Kleisthenes' reforms, membership in a phratry was the basis of Athenian citizenship. The blood ties between *phrateres* (i.e., members of the same phratry) are likely to have been much looser than those that bound together members of the same *genos. Phrateres* gathered together to perform religious ceremonies. They were also under an obligation to afford protection to one another. In particular, if one of their members was murdered, they were required to seek legal redress on the victim's behalf. The Athenian population was divided into at least thirty phratries, and they are attested in Athens from the seventh to the second century B.C.E. Phratries are, however, first mentioned in Homer and may be of Mycenaean origin. They also existed in Sparta, Argos, Delphi, Syracuse, and on the island of Chios.

A baby boy was admitted into his phratry usually in the first year of his life at a festival known as the Apatouria. Admission was contingent upon a vote of all the members of the phratry, who were required to substantiate the father's claim that his child "was indeed the offspring of an Athenian woman who was married." The boy was later reintroduced to his phratry at about the age of six-teen. The ceremony of induction, which included a sacrifice, was accompanied by a ritual cutting of the candidate's hair, an action that symbolically marked the end of his growing years. As before, all the members of the phratry voted to acknowledge his legitimacy. It is not known whether girls were also admitted to phratries, nor is it known what procedure was used to determine whether a girl was the legitimate offspring of Athenian parents.

The Deme

In the Classical Period, the whole of Attica, including the city of Athens, was divided into 139 local districts known as demes, many of which dated back to very early times. Some, in fact, may even have predated the foundation of Athens as a polis. It was Kleisthenes who converted the demes into political units, each with its own local assembly, cults, *dêmarchos* or local mayor, and treasury. Demes varied considerably in size and importance. Some were little more than hamlets, whereas others, such as Acharnai, situated on the northern borders of Attica, were very substantial settlements in their own right. A few even had their own theater. Each functioned as a kind of miniature polis. Every deme was required to keep a register, in which it recorded the names of all its demesmen who had reached the age of eighteen. This register served as an official record of the citizen body. For all public purposes, an Athenian citizen was required to identify himself by his *demotic*—that is, the adjective that designated the deme in which he was registered. He retained his demotic even if he went to live elsewhere in Attica. This meant that each Athenian family was identified in perpetuity by the demotic that it possessed at the time of Kleisthenes' reforms.

The Tribe

All Greeks believed themselves to be descended from one of two racial groups. Dorian communities, so named because they traced their descent to the Dorian invasion, divided themselves into three tribes, and Ionian communities, who took their name from their mythical founder Ion, son of Apollo, into four. The Athenians claimed to be Ionians, whereas the Spartans claimed to be Dorians.

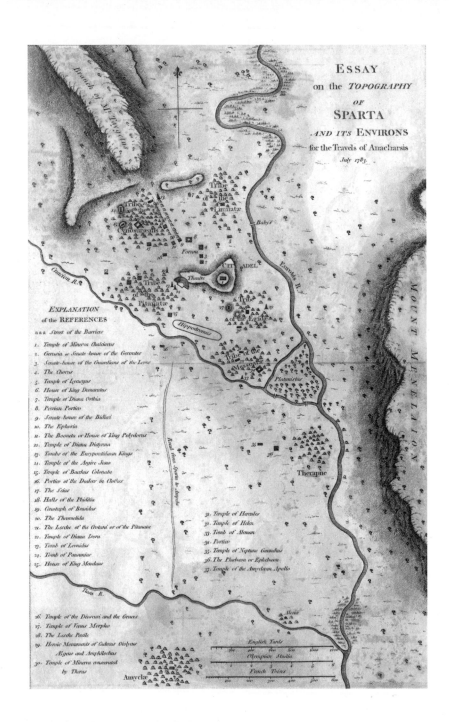

ESSAY
on the *TOPOGRAPHY*
OF
SPARTA
AND ITS ENVIRONS
for the Travels of Anacharsis
July 1783.

EXPLANATION
of the REFERENCES

a a a *Street of the Barriers*

1. *Temple of Minerva Chalcioecos*
2. *Gerusia or Senate-house of the Gerontes*
3. *Senate-house of the Guardians of the Laws*
4. *The Chorus*
5. *Temple of Lycurgus*
6. *House of King Demaratus*
7. *Temple of Diana Orthia*
8. *Persian Portico*
9. *Senate-house of the Bidiei*
10. *The Ephoria*
11. *The Booneta or House of King Polydorus*
12. *Temple of Diana Dictynna*
13. *Tombs of the Eurypontidaean Kings*
14. *Temple of the Argive Juno*
15. *Temple of Bacchus Colonata*
16. *Portico of the Dailers in Clothes*
17. *The Scias*
18. *Halls of the Phiditia*
19. *Cenotaph of Brasidas*
20. *The Theomelida*
21. *The Lesche of the Crotani or of the Pitanatae*
22. *Temple of Diana Isora*
23. *Tomb of Leonidas*
24. *Tomb of Pausanias*
25. *House of King Menelaus*

26. *Temple of the Dioscuri and the Graces*
27. *Temple of Venus Morpho*
28. *The Lesche Poecile*
29. *Heroic Monuments of Cadmus Oiolycus*
    Ægeus and Amphilochus
30. *Temple of Minerva consecrated*
    by Theras

31. *Temple of Hercules*
32. *Temple of Helen*
33. *Tomb of Alcman*
34. *Portico*
35. *Temple of Neptune Gaeaduus*
36. *The Phoebeum or Ephebeum*
37. *Temple of the Amyclaean Apollo*

English Yards

Olympian Stadia

French Toises

To what extent these tribal divisions corresponded to a genuine racial division is unknown, but it certainly helped to fuel tensions between the two rival groups.

Kleisthenes introduced a system based on ten tribes, which were named after ten eponymous Attic heroes. These tribes, into which the whole Athenian body was divided, became the basis of all civic administration. Although the Athenians continued to acknowledge the existence of the four Ionian tribes, these now ceased to play any significant part in the administrative process. The ten Kleisthenic tribes formed the basis for election to the council, or *boulê,* which consisted of five hundred citizens, fifty of whom were elected annually by lot from each of the ten tribes. No Athenian was permitted to serve in the council more than twice during his life time. Its principal function was to prepare the agenda for the assembly and advise the magistrates. For one-tenth of the year— that is, for thirty-five or thirty-six days, each of the fifty members of each of the ten tribes served on an executive committee known as a *prytany.* Each prytany was responsible for the welfare of the state throughout its period of office. Its members, who were on call twenty-four hours a day, slept and ate in a circular building known as the Tholos, the symbolic center of the polis, which housed the sacred hearth, situated on the west side of the Agora. Each day a new member was elected by lot to serve as the chairman of the prytany. This meant that every Athenian had an equal chance of assuming the highest executive office in the land for the duration of a single day, purely ceremonial though that office was, with responsibility for the state seal and the keys of the state treasury.

The Citizen Body

In most Greek communities, citizenship was limited to freeborn adult males over the age of either eighteen or twenty-one. Until 451/450 B.C.E. Athenians could claim citizenship as long as their fathers had been citizens. In that year,

MAP OF SPARTA *showing the five different tribes and their locations relative to one another. Since Sparta left very little in terms of archaeological ruins, it is assumed that much of this map is conjecture. It does, however, indicate landmarks such as the theater, hippodrome, and citadel. Drawn by M. Barbie de Bocage in 1783.*

however, and at Perikles' prompting, the Athenians passed a law debarring the offspring of a union between an Athenian citizen and a metic (i.e., resident alien) woman from claiming citizenship. Henceforth, Athenian citizens had to have Athenian mothers as well as fathers, though how they went about proving that their mothers were Athenian is anyone's guess. The motives behind the legislation are obscure, but one leading factor was probably the desire to restrict citizenship to a limited group at a time when its benefits were becoming more and more attractive. It is estimated that no more than between 6 and 10 percent of any Greek population were actually citizens (i.e., males over the age of about eighteen). The most detailed information about the size of a citizen body relates to Athens. Thukydides (2.13.6–8) tells us that at the outbreak of the Peloponnesian War there were 13,000 hoplites on full-time duty, 16,000 of "the oldest and the youngest" who manned the garrisons, 1,200 cavalry, and 1,600 archers excluding the *thêtes,* who may have accounted for between 40 percent or more. This gives us a citizen body of approximately 50,000–60,000. If we multiply that figure by four to include women and children, we arrive at a total of about 200,000 Athenians. There is no evidence to indicate in any Greek society whether men outnumbered women or vice versa except in the case of Athens at the time of the Peloponnesian War, when there was a drastic shortage of males as a result of military casualties. The evidence for the shortage of males lies in the fact that the offspring of common-law wives were now recognized as legitimate, which had not been the case previously. The population was reduced by perhaps as much as a third by the plague that ravaged Athens from 430 to 426 B.C.E., but it recovered and probably remained stable until the end of the fourth century, when it began to decline.

Evidence for the size of the population of other Greek states is extremely meager. Argos is thought to have had a citizen body roughly the same size as Athens, whereas that of Corinth was probably only half the size. Sparta, at its peak, had a very small citizen body. Herodotos (7.234.2) tells us that, even in 480 B.C.E., the year of the battle of Thermopylai, Sparta's fighting force numbered only 8,000. By 371 B.C.E., its citizen body had dwindled to a mere 1,500. The reason for this sharp decline is not fully understood, but it probably had as much to do with disenfranchisement as it did with depopulation. Many Spartans may have become impoverished and found themselves unable to contribute to the dining clubs that were a precondition of citizenship (see p. 128).

The most populous Greek states in the Classical Period were in southern Italy and Sicily. Judging by the extent of the archaeological remains, the largest was Syracuse. In the period of the Roman Empire, several Greek cities, including Alexandria, Apamea, Antioch (modern Antakya), Ephesos, and Pergamon, all had populations of at least 250,000.

Athenian citizens were divided into classes according to the economic productivity of their land. The highest property class was known as the *pentakosiomedimnoi,* so named because their land yielded five hundred bushels of corn annually. The next was the *hippeis* or cavalry, whose yearly yield was three hundred bushels. These were followed by the *zeugitai* or "yokemen," whose yield was two hundred bushels, so named because they served in close rank (i.e., yoked together) in the army. The lowest group of all was the *thêtes,* literally "hired laborers."

The right of citizenship went hand in hand with the requirement to serve in the army, although military service was regarded as a privilege rather than a duty throughout the Greek world. From the time of Solon onward, all Athenian citizens had the right to attend the assembly. The belief nonetheless persisted that the attainment of full citizen rights was dependent on wealth. The political importance of the *thêtes,* the most impoverished section of Athenian society, rose dramatically when Athens became a naval power, because it was they who constituted the bulk of the sailors. Even so, members of this group were not permitted to stand for political office, either as magistrates or as members of the council, until the second half of the fourth century B.C.E.

The Sense of Nationhood

Although the Greeks differentiated themselves from those who did not speak Greek by the pejorative term *barbaroi,* a word of uncertain etymology that may seek to reproduce the incoherent speech of non-Greeks, the idea of "Greekness" played little part in politics. The Greeks never had a shared capital, a single ruling family, or even a clearly defined boundary. As noted earlier, although they did occasionally form alliances against a common enemy, these were invariably fragile and short lived. On the cultural front, the idea of Greekness was promoted by common blood, a common language, a common set of gods, a common mythology, and a common set of institutions, such as the symposium and the gymnasium. There also were a number of panhellenic sanctuaries, including Olympia, Delphi, and Eleusis, home of the Eleusinian Mysteries. (Only Greek-speakers could be initiated into these mysteries.) On an everyday basis, however, being a Greek meant far less politically and culturally than being an Athenian or a Corinthian or a Macedonian.

WOMEN

In Book 1 of *The Odyssey*, Odysseus's son Telemachos delivers this stern rebuke to his mother Penelope, who, understandably pained by an allusion to her missing husband, has asked the bard Phemios to choose a theme other than that of the Greeks' homecoming from Troy:

> Go inside the house, and attend to your work, the loom and the distaff, and
> bid your handmaidens attend to their work also. Talking is men's business,
> all men's business, but my business most of all. (lines 356–59)

Telemachos's reprimand epitomizes the traditional view of Greek society, namely one that was both patrilineal and patriarchal. Women, the view goes, though necessary for propagation, served few other useful functions. They were to be subdued and secluded, controlled and confined. Greek society was sexist and chauvinistic, as a wealth of literary evidence suggests.

Recently, some scholars have begun to question this overly schematized view of Greek society, regarding it as based on a highly selective set of sources that present an "idealized" view of how Greek society *should* operate from a male perspective. In particular, they cite scenes of daily life on vases, which show women enjoying far more freedom in the company of other women than literary sources suggest. Even so, it cannot be denied that Greek society did practice a degree of sex segregation, even if women were not entirely secluded, and it was certainly the case that they had no political or legal persona.

Odysseus's Women

Already in *The Odyssey* there is some support for a somewhat complicated view of the dynamic between the sexes. Despite Telemachos's claim about the dominant role of men in Homeric society, his father Odysseus constantly finds himself in a position of weakness and dependency vis-à-vis women. As in the real world, so in the world of *The Odyssey,* female power takes many guises: beauty, intelligence, cunning, resourcefulness, wisdom, and charm. The women whom Odysseus encounters—Kalypso, Kirke, Nausikaä, Arete, and his wife Penelope—exercise power in ways that are always indirect, sometimes magical, and often dangerous. They possess access to privileged information. They control hidden forces that assist or impede him on his way. They counterfeit and deceive. And they kill. The source of all the mischief is Helen, the cause of the Trojan War, still exercising an iron grip over her cuckolded husband Menelaos in *The Odyssey* Book 4.

The power that wives wield is aptly symbolized by the different fates of Odysseus and his commander in chief. Whereas Odysseus was blessed in the possession of Penelope, who remained faithful to him for twenty years and had the skill to ward off no fewer than 108 suitors, Agamemnon was immediately murdered on his return from the Trojan War by his wife Klytaimnestra and her lover Aigisthos. The question, however, remains: To what extent does this picture of women's power in early Greece mirror reality, and to what extent does it constitute a fantasy on the part of the poet? There is no means of knowing. Furthermore, there is hardly a single Greek woman from any period of antiquity whose life is more than a hazy blur to us.

The Bride

Although we do not have any documentary evidence regarding age at marriage, literary sources suggest that girls in their early to mid-teens typically married men who were old enough to be their fathers. Hesiod, in *Works and Days,* recommended that a man should be "not much less than in his thirtieth year" and a girl "in her fifth year past puberty" (lines 695–99). Hesiod's view, though that of a peasant farmer, is by no means unique. Solon was of the opinion that the right time for a man to marry was between the ages of twenty-seven and thirty-four. Similarly, Plato claimed that a man was at his peak for marriage in his thirtieth year. Some brides would have been even younger than the age recommended by Hesiod, particularly those who came from wealthy families, as we know from a fifth-century B.C.E. law code from Gortyn on Crete, which decreed that heiresses should be married "in their twelfth year or older."

Arranged marriages were the norm in Greek society, though a mature suitor would negotiate on his own behalf with his future bride's parents. In the following passage, a fictional character called Ischomachos, invented by Xenophon, who is intended to be typical of many upper-crust Athenians, informs his wife how he came to choose her as his bride:

> Have you ever wondered why it was that I married you and why your
> parents gave you to me? It wasn't just because I wanted someone beside me
> in bed at night. You realize that, don't you? What happened was as follows.
> Your parents were looking for a suitable son-in-law and I was looking for a
> suitable wife. I chose you and they, from among a number of possibilities,
> chose me. (*Household Management* 7.10–11)

Evidently, his wife's wishes did not figure in the negotiations. Regrettably, Xenophon does not describe how she reacted on learning of her husband's passionless courtship of her parents. Although Ischomachos was able to exercise independence in the choice of his bride, younger men were required to follow their fathers' wishes.

Such evidence as we possess suggests that wealth and status, rather than emotional attachment, were the principal criteria for choosing a wife. Mercenary and cynical though this system may seem, we need to bear in mind that there were few opportunities for the creation of wealth in ancient Greece. A marriage alliance was therefore an opportunity both to produce offspring and to increase the family's finances. A girl would almost invariably have been provided with a dowry, because, without one, she risked ending her forlorn life "unwed and barren" (Sophokles, *Oedipus the King,* line 1502). The marriage was therefore preceded by a formal agreement (*enguê,* literally "pledge"), consequent upon both parties having negotiated the dowry. Dowries, which generally consisted of both money and valuables, varied greatly in size. The aristocratic politician Alkibiades received the huge sum of ten talents when he married the sister of Kallias, one of the wealthiest men of his day. Because the function of the dowry was to provide maintenance for the wife, legal restraints were imposed upon its use. In the event of divorce, for instance, the husband was required to return it intact either to his wife's father or to her legal guardian. If he was unable to repay the entire sum, he was required to pay interest on it. The wife's personal possessions were also returned to her family. The orator Isaios informs us that, when Menekles divorced his wife, he not only returned the dowry but also her jewelry and clothing. The clear purpose of this law was to provide some protection for women and to ensure that divorcees were not left financially destitute.

Athenian law also imposed strict regulations upon the marriage of a daughter whose father died leaving no male heir. (Athenians were required by law to bequeath the bulk of their estates to their sons.) Such a woman was known as an *epiklêros,* which literally means "attached to the *klêros* or estate." The estate in question did not actually belong to her but merely accompanied her when she married. Because it was the duty of the nearest male relative to claim an *epiklêros* as his wife, an *epiklêros* might, and occasionally did, marry her uncle. So strictly was the law upheld that, in some cases, existing marriages were dissolved in order to comply with it. Its purpose was to keep property within the family and thus prevent the amalgamation of several *oikoi.* For much the same reason, marriages were often contracted between relatives, especially among the wealthy.

The Wedding Ceremony

Marriage created a much more violent and abrupt disruption in the life of a woman than it did in the life of a man, because the bride went to live in her husband's house. Removed from her family at an age when she was scarcely past playing with dolls, she had to take on a number of onerous duties, chief of which was to produce an heir for her husband *toute suite*. One of the most moving Greek myths, that of the abduction of Demeter's daughter Persephone by Hades, the grim god of the underworld, explores the underlying tensions generated by this violent disruption. Persephone is innocently plucking flowers in a meadow when she is snatched away to become the bride of an aged and forbidding stranger whom she has never seen before. Although the myth in the version that has come down to us, an anonymous epic known as the *Homeric Hymn to Demeter,* focuses on the grief of Persephone's mother Demeter rather than on the trauma experienced by her daughter, it nonetheless reveals a profound insight into the institution of marriage from the female point of view.

The most popular time for marrying was in the winter month of Gamelion, which means "the time of wedding." The ceremony began with a sacrifice to the gods of marriage, Zeus and Hera, to whom the bride consecrated a lock of her hair. She also dedicated her childhood possessions to Artemis to appease the goddess's anger at her impending loss of virginity.

On the day of the wedding, an Athenian bride took a ritual bath in water. This was poured from a special vase known as a *loutrophoros,* which means, literally, "a carrier of *loutra* (sacred water)." This bath prepared her

PLUTO ABDUCTING PROSERPINE. *François Girardon, 1693–1710. Patinated bronze. This statue, commissioned by Louis XIV, depicts a mature Hades (Roman Pluto) attempting to kidnap the young Persephone (Roman Proserpine), while a maid struggles to assist her.*

for her new life. It was followed by a feast held at the house of the bride's father. Here, the bride, who was veiled, sat apart from all the men, including the bridegroom. Beside her sat an older woman called a *nympheutria,* who guided her through the ceremony. Instead of a tiered wedding cake with fruit filling covered in icing sugar, little cakes covered in sesame seeds were served to the guests. These were believed to make women fertile. Toward evening, the bridegroom led his bride, still veiled, from her father's house in

IN THIS TERRA-COTTA SCULPTURE, *a husband draws aside his new wife's veil in the bridal room. Created in the second half of the second century,* B.C.E.

a wagon drawn by mules or oxen. A chest containing her dowry probably accompanied her. The bride sat in the middle with the groom on one side and the best man, or *paranymphos,* on the other. A torchlight procession preceded the wedding party along the route, and wedding hymns were sung to the accompaniment of the flute and lyre.

On arrival at the bridegroom's house, the pair was showered with nuts and dried figs called *katakysmata,* symbolic of the prosperity that it was hoped would attend the marriage. Boys with both parents still alive offered the guests bread, which they served from a basket used for winnowing corn—another symbol of prosperity. Prayers were probably spoken or sung, but there was no state official or priest in attendance. In a play by Menander, the groom's father says to the bride, "I give you my daughter so that you can sow her in order to produce legitimate children." The groom replies: "I accept her." However, we know of no standard form of words corresponding to an exchange of vows. The pair then entered the bridal chamber, and the bride removed her veil. The bridegroom then presented his bride with gifts called *optêria* (from *opteuô,* meaning "to see"), celebrating the fact that this was the first time (officially at least) that he had seen her without the veil (see image on previous page). The door to the bridal chamber was closed, and a hymn called an *epithalamion* (from *thalamos,* meaning "inner chamber or bedroom") was sung outside. Its somewhat macabre purpose, according to a late source, was to cover the cries of the bride as she underwent the violence of penetration.

A Wife's First Duty

The overriding duty of a Greek wife was to provide her husband with offspring, preferably boys, to ensure that his household did not die out. In addition to the pressure to conceive that came from the husband and the husband's family, there would also have been pressure from society at large, because every Greek community expected its citizens to beget legitimate children in order to keep the population at parity. Because of the high level of infant mortality, it is estimated that each married couple would have had to produce four or five children to achieve this modest target.

> *The obligation to become pregnant was reinforced by medical theory, which taught that abstinence from sex was injurious to health. A text ascribed to Hippokrates, the legendary founder of Greek medicine, states:*
>
> Women who have intercourse are healthier than those who abstain. For the womb is moistened by intercourse and ceases to be dry, whereas when it is drier than it should be it contracts violently and this contraction causes pain to the body. (*Seed* 4)

Giving birth was hazardous, partly because the standards of hygiene were deplorably low and partly because women often became pregnant while still pubescent. Miscarriages were extremely common, as were the deaths of women in labor. Echoing, no doubt, the judgment of many Greek women, Medea in Euripides' play of that name sums up the perils of childbirth as follows: "I would rather stand in battle-line three times than give birth once" (line 250f.). Although we hear of a variety of contraceptives—including herbal potions, concoctions of vinegar and water, and pads of wool soaked in honey—there was no safe and reliable method of birth control. This meant that, for many women there would be little respite between pregnancies.

The failure to become pregnant was either regarded with grave suspicion or interpreted as a biological problem from which the woman was suffering. Not surprisingly, given their prejudices and the state of their medical knowledge, the Greeks had no concept of male infertility. However, once a woman had provided her husband with a male heir, her standing and respect within the household increased considerably. In a forensic speech, an Athenian husband who discovered his wife in bed with her lover and stabbed the man to death justifies his action by stating that, after the arrival of his firstborn, he had bestowed upon his wife complete control of his estate in the erroneous belief that "the two of us had now achieved a condition of complete intimacy" (Lysias 1.6).

Given the importance of producing offspring, it is hardly surprising that concern about fertility and pregnancy features prominently among the miraculous cures that are inscribed on stones in the healing sanctuary of Asklepios at Epidauros in the northeast Peloponnese. One inscription, for instance, states: "Agamede from Chios. She slept in the sanctuary in order to have children and saw a dream. A snake seemed to lie on her belly and as a result five children were born." Another tells of the curious case of a certain Ithmonike of Pellene, who dreamt that she petitioned Asklepios to make her pregnant with a girl. The god agreed to grant her request and asked Ithmonike if that was all that she wanted. Ithmonike said it was and in due course became pregnant. After remaining pregnant for three years, she returned to Epidauros to ask the god why she had not yet given birth. Asklepios mischievously replied that he had made her pregnant as requested, whereas what she had really wanted was to give birth. The story has a happy ending, however. Immediately after leaving the sanctuary, Ithmonike gave birth to a girl.

In later times, obstetrics aroused considerable interest in medical circles. The most famous work on the subject is the *Gynaecology*, which was written by a physician named Soranos in the early second century C.E. It provides a highly detailed account of the practices surrounding labor, childbirth, and nursing.

Household Chores

In the Funeral Speech delivered over the Athenian dead in the first year of the Peloponnesian War, Perikles states, "Women's greatest glory is not to be talked about by men, either for good or ill" (Thukydides 2.45.2). Likewise, in Euripides' *Trojan Women,* Andromache, the wife of Hektor, declares, "There is one prime source of scandal for a woman—when she won't stay at home" (line 648f.). As noted earlier, however, we should be wary of taking such statements entirely at face value. They may well reflect an idealized view of women that was somewhat at variance with everyday reality.

What such statements do unquestionably reveal, however, is an overriding concern, amounting to paranoia, on the part of Greek husbands concerning their wives' fidelity. Ischomachos, whom we met earlier, tells us that he gave his wife the following advice soon after they were married:

> You must stay indoors and send out the slaves whose work is outside. Those who remain and do chores inside the house are under your charge. You are to inspect everything that enters it and distribute what is needed, taking care not to be extravagant . . . . When the slaves bring in wool, you must see that it is used for those who need cloaks. You must take care of the grain-store and make sure that the grain is edible. One of your less pleasant tasks is to find out whenever one of the slaves becomes sick and see that they are properly looked after. (Xenophon, *Household Management* 7.35–37)

As this passage indicates, it was the mistress of the house who was in charge of the domestic arrangements and who was held accountable if anything went amiss.

In addition to running the home, a wife was expected to contribute to its economy by plying the distaff (i.e., spinning by hand) and working the loom. Spinning and weaving were regarded as essential accomplishments in a woman, not least because most garments were made in the home.

ATTIC BLACK-FIGURE LEKYTHOS *(oil flask) portraying women weaving cloth on a loom, a common task for women in ancient Greece. Terracotta, ca. 550–530 B.C.E.*

Garments were made as follows: The wool was first cleaned and scoured. Then the matted fibers were separated from one another with a comb by means of a semicircular instrument known as an *epinitron,* which fitted over the thigh and knee, providing a slightly roughened surface upon which the wool could be teased out. The wool was then dyed in a vat. Next it was spun by hand using a distaff, spindle, and spindle whorls in what is known as the drop-and-spin method. Finally, it was woven into fabric on a loom. The warp was suspended from a crossbar, and its strands, known as the weft, held taut at its ends by loom weights, were threaded together by means of a shuttle.

Escaping from the Daily Grind

The traditional view, as noted earlier, is that women spent most of their time at home. To what extent this was true is impossible to determine, but it is unlikely to have been universally the case. During the Peloponnesian War, say, when men were away for long stretches at a time, women must surely have enjoyed considerable freedom. There are even a few vase paintings depicting women holding a symposium. What is likely to have been true at all times, however, is that when a respectable woman went out of doors, she rarely did so unaccompanied, if only for her safety's sake.

There were also a number of socially approved outlets for women, primarily those connected with religion. Although most festivals were attended by both men and women, there were a few, such as the Thesmophoria, a festival held in the fall in honor of Demeter, from which men were rigorously excluded. Funerals provided another important occasion for women to associate with one another. Women played the major part in preparing the body for burial, as they do in most Mediterranean countries to this day. Some women may even have looked forward to the next death in the family as an opportunity to meet with their relatives and friends. The defendant in Lysias's *On the Murder of Eratosthenes* (1.8) claims that his adulterous wife first met her lover at a funeral. A frustrated Greek wife and her would-be lover had to seize whatever opportunity they could! Women were also permitted to leave the home to make visits to the cemetery to attend periodically to the needs of the dead.

The following extract from Idyll 15 by the Syracusan poet Theokritos provides a fascinating insight into the lives of two women who are planning to spend the day together at a festival in honor of Adonis, a handsome young man who was the beloved of Aphrodite. The poem, which was written in the first half of the third century B.C.E., is set in Alexandria, Egypt, but the dialogue could be imagined as taking place almost anywhere in the metropolitan Greek world.

GORGO: Is Praxinoa in?

PRAXINOA: Gorgo, my love, what a long time it's been since I saw you—yes, I'm in. I'm surprised you made it, though. (To her slave) Eunoa, go and get a chair and cushion for the lady.

GORGO: Oh, don't bother. I'm quite all right.

PRAXINOA: Sit down.

GORGO: What a silly thing I am! I was nearly crushed alive getting here. There are chariots, boots, and men in uniforms everywhere. And the road is endless. You are always moving farther and farther away.

PRAXINOA: It's that stupid husband of mine. He buys this house out in the wilds—it's not even a house—it's just a hovel—purely to stop us from seeing each other. He's spiteful, just like all men.

GORGO: You shouldn't talk about your husband like that when the baby's here. You see how he's looking at you. (To the baby) Don't worry, Sopyrion, sweetie, she isn't talking about Daddy.

PRAXINOA: Heavens above! The child does understand.

GORGO: Nice Daddy.

PRAXINOA: The other day I told that Daddy of hers to pop out and get some soap and red dye and the idiot came back with a cube of salt! (lines 1–17)

The Legal and Political Status of Wives

Athenian women had no political rights. Legally, too, their position was one of inferiority to men. A law quoted by the fourth century B.C.E. orator Isaios decreed that "No child or woman shall have the power to make any contract above the value of a *medimnos* of barley" (10.10). (A *medimnos* was a measure of corn sufficient to sustain a family in food for barely a week.) They were not permitted to buy or sell land, and, although they were entitled to acquire property through dowry, inheritance, or gift, it was managed for them by their legal guardian (i.e., their father, male next of kin, or husband). Women thus remained perpetually under the control, or, to use a more benign term, tutelage, of some man, whatever their age or status. A wife seeking a divorce would most commonly be represented in the courts by her next of kin. If she sought to represent herself, the law afforded her no protection from further abuse, as we learn from an anecdote told by Plutarch about Hipparete, Alkibiades' wife, who became so distressed by her husband's philandering that she went to live with her brother. When she lodged a complaint against him in the courts, Alkibiades "seized hold of her and dragged her back home through the Agora, with no one daring to stop him or rescue her" (Plutarch, *Life of Alkibiades* 8. 4). If a divorce was granted, no formalities were required other than the return of the dowry to the wife's *oikos*. The husband, too, was free to claim back whatever he had contributed, as the following deed of divorce from Hellenistic Egypt indicates. Although the document is dated to the beginning of the fourth century C.E., contracts of this kind may well have been drawn up in earlier times as well. It is interesting to note that the responsibility for the marital breakdown is ascribed to an evil spirit (*daimôn*)—the ancient equivalent of irreconcilable differences.

> Soulis, gravedigger, of the region of Kusis, to Senpais, daughter of Psais and Tees, grave digger, greetings. Because it has come about as the result of some evil spirit that we are estranged from one another in respect to our common life, I, the said Soulis, hereby admit before sending her away that I have received all the objects that I gave her . . . and that she is free to depart and marry whomever she wishes.

I, the said Senpais, acknowledge that I have received from the said Soulis all that I gave him by way of dowry. (*Select Papyri* 1 no. 8 in Loeb Classical Series)

Widows

Because of the large age difference between men and women at marriage, many wives became widows by the time they reached their late twenties or early thirties. Young widows were expected to remarry, whereas older widows probably enjoyed considerable freedom. In view of the fact that the dowry that a wife brought with her had to be returned to her natal household (i.e., to the head of the family into which she was born) in the event of her husband's death, widows, like divorcees, were guaranteed some degree of economic security.

Common-Law Wives

Athenians could also enter into a less formal and less binding arrangement than marriage with a *pallakê,* a term that approximates to a common-law wife. Such unions were made primarily with resident aliens, prostitutes, and women who had no dowries. The prostitute Aspasia, virtually the only woman in fifth-century B.C.E. Athens who is known to us other than by name, was the *pallakê* of Perikles. Most *pallakai,* however, were probably girls whose families were unable to provide them with a dowry. A *pallakê* was placed under the authority of the man with whom she lived in much the same way as a legitimate wife. There were, however, two important differences: first there was no transfer of dowry, and, second, the offspring of such unions were not regarded as citizens and had no claim on the man's *oikos.* In the last decade of the Peloponnesian War, however, this regulation was suspended due to the shortage of Athenian manpower. Citizens were therefore permitted to have a legitimate wife as well as a *pallakê.* (In 430 B.C.E. the Athenian *dêmos* had passed an extraordinary decree legitimizing Perikles' offspring from Aspasia, but this had been an exceptional privilege accorded to a leading public servant in recognition of the fact that his two legitimate sons had just died of the plague.)

The Working Woman

So far we have considered only the lives of well-to-do women. The wives and daughters of the poor, as well as many spinsters and widows, lacking slaves to fetch and carry, would have been frequently seen in the streets. The orator Demosthenes tells us that one of the effects of the poverty that afflicted Athens after its defeat in the Peloponnesian War was that many women had to go out to work, typically as wet nurses, weavers, and grape pickers (57.45). In Aristophanes' *Thesmophoriazousai,* or "Women at the Thesmophoria," a widow with five children describes how she earns a precarious living by weaving chaplets of the kind that might have been worn by symposiasts (lines 446–49).

Virtually the only career option available to freeborn women was that of prostitute. It is important to bear in mind, however, that the English word conjures up a very limited picture of the range of services that women performed under this general title. As the Greek word *hetaira,* which means "female companion," suggests, they charged for their companionship rather than their sexual favors. The ideal *hetaira* was gifted, charming, and intellectually accomplished. *Hetairai* were the only women permitted to attend symposia. The *hetaira* Aspasia, who, as noted, was the common-law wife of Perikles, was so respected that she was consulted on both political and philosophical matters. Such was her influence over Perikles that the latter's decision to lead an expedition against the island of Samos is said to have been taken on her advice (Plutarch, *Life of Perikles* 24.1–3). Aspasia was able to attain this status and influence in part because she was a foreigner who came from Miletus in Turkey and was therefore not subject to the same social constraints as her Athenian counterparts. It would have been inconceivable for a freeborn Athenian woman to hobnob with the leading intellectuals of her day, and the freedom she enjoyed, and perhaps flaunted, no doubt greatly offended the sensibilities of Athenian men and women alike.

In addition, many brothels existed in Athens, largely staffed by slaves. In fact, the state acted as pimp by farming out the right to collect taxes from prostitution to enterprising individuals in much same way, *mutatis mutandis,* that it farmed out the right to collect harbor dues.

Conclusions

To offer any final assessment regarding the condition and status of women in the Greek world is impossible. To begin with, almost all the evidence, such as it is, relates to Athens. (The principal exception to this claim is the Homeric poems, whose portrayal of women must be treated with obvious caution.) Because, moreover, we possess almost no testimonies by women themselves, all we have to go on are statements made by men about women. Furthermore, our ability to make an objective judgment is complicated by contemporary assumptions about the role and status of women in our own society—assumptions, moreover, that continue to be in a state of flux. Although some vase paintings depict a rather more rosy picture of women reading, playing musical instruments, and dancing that challenge the more conventional view of women as repressed and uneducated, we cannot know how typical such scenes are of daily life.

Certain unpalatable facts are not in dispute, however. For instance, a girl's chances of survival were poorer than those of a boy; her life expectancy was shorter than that of a boy; her opportunities for acquiring an education were virtually nonexistent; the law regarded her as a minor whatever her years; and, should she choose to abandon her traditional role as mother and housekeeper, virtually only one profession—the oldest of all—was available to her. Partly as a result of the imbalance in life expectancy—the reverse, of course, of what prevails today— men tended to marry women who were a decade or more younger than they were. And this had huge implications for relations between the sexes, because it meant that husbands tended to lord it over their wives.

At the same time, evidence suggests that men did not invariably have the upper hand. To give a humorous example, Sokrates' wife Xanthippe is said to have doused the philosopher in water on one occasion and to have stripped him of his cloak in public on another (Diogenes Laertios 2.36–37). Relationships between the sexes were no doubt complex, as they have been throughout history. As Hektor's wife Andromache observed, "I offered my husband a silent tongue and gentle looks. I knew when to have my way and when to let him have his" (Euripides, *Trojan Women* 655f.)—surely the recipe for a happy marriage in any age. Even so, we should not attach too much credence to a remark ascribed by Plutarch to the Athenian politician Themistokles, who claimed that his son was the most powerful person in Greece on the grounds that the Athenians commanded the Greeks; he, Themistokles, commanded the Athenians; his wife commanded him; and his son commanded his wife (Plutarch, *Life of Themistokles* 18.5).

MEN

For a citizen of any community, excepting Sparta, where duty to the state overrode every other consideration, the ideal status was that of a gentleman of leisure. There were two ways in which one became a gentleman of leisure: either by owning a large estate worked by slaves or by engaging in trade, again by using slaves. Released from the obligations of earning their living, such persons were free to fulfill their civic and political obligations, not only as a participant in the affairs of state, but also as an informed member of the community. It may seem strange to us that politics featured so centrally in the lives of the Greeks, but this was due primarily to the fact that Greek democracy was participatory, not representative, which meant that the ordinary citizen was central and indispensable to the democratic process. As indicated earlier, his duties included loafing about in the Agora (see p. 41)—talking about current affairs or forthcoming lawsuits, discussing the upcoming agenda of the assembly or council, and gossiping. If the spirit moved him, it also included joining in philosophical debate with one of the many thinkers, such as Sokrates or the Stoics, who also passed time in the Agora and who commonly chose subjects for discussion that had a political aspect. What percentage of the Greek population belonged to this privileged class is impossible to determine with accuracy, but it was probably somewhere between 12 and 20 percent.

The landed gentry had little in common with any other socioeconomic group. Certainly their lifestyle was in no way comparable to that of poor farmers, known as the *geôrgoi,* who either owned only a small plot of land or rented from the rich in return for receiving a percentage of the harvest. Thukydides tells us that, at the time of the outbreak of the Peloponnesian War, more than half the population of Attica was living in the countryside. This is another way of stating that more than half the population was engaged in agriculture, although some allowance should be made for fishermen and those who ran cottage industries. The rural poor were extremely vulnerable to natural disasters, such as drought or crop failure. A number of groups toiled on the land in various parts of mainland Greece, such as "the dusty feet" in Epidauros, "the wearers of sheep skins" in Sikyon, "the toilers" in Thessaly, and "the naked ones" in Argos. Their names alone indicate their wretchedness, though we cannot be sure whether they were indentured serfs or merely very poor citizens.

Another group comprised manual workers and artisans known collectively as *banausoi* (from the Greek *baunos,* meaning furnace or forge)—namely, blacksmiths, metalworkers, sculptors, jewelers, house painters, potters, vase painters, carpenters, shoemakers, and the like. Although there was considerable variety in the economic status of persons in this category, overall they would probably have been regarded with condescension by the landed gentry unlike the *gêôrgoi,* whose livelihood, like that of the landed gentry, was based on the land. Many artisans may well have been either foreigners or slaves, as evidenced by the fact that the names of several potters and vase painters are foreign. One Athenian vase is even signed by a certain "Lydos the slave." Some artisans at least were fairly well off. In Xenophon's *Memoirs of Sokrates,* Sokrates says, "Don't you know that by producing grain . . . Nausikydes not only supports himself and his family . . . but has so much to spare that he often performs liturgies (see p. 233); that Kyrebos feeds his whole household by baking bread, Demeas of Kollytos by making capes, and Mcnon by making cloaks?" (2.7.6).

PAINTED TERRA-COTTA FIGURINE *ca. 6th century B.C.E., of a man grating cheese into a bowl. Men of lower economic status didn't have the same freedom from chores as slave-owning gentlemen of leisure.*

At the top of the earning scale of the self-employed were the Sophists—that is, itinerant professors of rhetoric who moved from city to city and charged considerable sums of money for their services, as well as celebrity entertainers, including, in the Hellenistic period, professional actors.

One of the benefits of Athens' maritime empire in the fifth century B.C.E. was that it provided enough surplus in the economy not only to finance the ambitious Periklean building program, but also to pay poor Athenians to be rowers in the navy and elderly or infirm Athenians to be jurors. These groups are discussed later (see p. 243), but it is important to note here that the surplus wealth in Athens' coffers thus guaranteed many Athenians a living wage. The most despised group were those in the employ of other Greeks, whether on a permanent or on a temporary basis. When Achilles wishes to convey the worst social condition imaginable, he instances that of a man who works as a day laborer, rather than that of a slave, because the latter enjoyed security of sorts (*The Odyssey* 11.489–91). For this reason, when Sokrates recommends working as the bailiff of a large estate to a once wealthy individual who lost his fortune at the end of the Peloponnesian War, the latter comments, "I'd hardly like to be a slave" (Xenophon, *Memoirs of Sokrates* 2.8.4), on the grounds that he would not want to be bossed around.

Whatever his source of livelihood, every citizen was obligated to serve the state. This meant attending the assembly and the religious festivals that were funded at public cost, serving on the council, holding the office of magistrate when called upon to do so, or being a juror in the courts. In Athens, a magistrate's term of office lasted a year, whereas a council member served for about one-tenth of the year, and this was probably true of other Greek communities. It is estimated that, in any given year, at least 8,500 Athenians—about one-quarter of the entire citizen body—were engaged in public service if we include the 6,000 who served as jurors and the 1,500 who participated in dramatic performances (see pp. 244 and 285). In practice, however, the number was probably much higher if we include those who served in a junior or unofficial capacity. All citizens were also required to serve in either the army or the navy, and when called up to do so, could not recuse themselves. For those at the bottom of the economic scale, fulfilling their civic responsibilities would have entailed considerable financial hardship. Scenes on vases depict the world of men as primarily dominated by drinking parties, hunting, exercising in the gymnasium, and departing for war. Political scenes are nonexistent, and scenes of men engaged in work are rare. Although pictorial considerations are partly responsible for the selection, the images of daily life have much to tell us about the average man's view of the idealized man's world.

PARENTS AND CHILDREN

Birth

In the absence of hospitals, most births took place either in the home or out of doors. Male physicians were present only when there were fears for the mother's life. Medical texts indicate that the presence of male physicians would have caused embarrassment and shame to women in labor. One of the most important assistants was the *maia,* or midwife, who combined medical expertise with proficiency in ritual.

Birth and religion were inseparably bound together. Women in labor were placed under the protection of Eileithyia, or "She who comes." The goddess was so named because her arrival was believed to enable birth to take place. Artemis, herself a virgin who rigorously shunned sexual intercourse, was also prominent in the birthing ritual. It was necessary to appease the goddess's anger by invoking her in prayer before delivery and by dedicating clothing in her shrine afterward. An olive branch was hung on the front door when a boy was born and a tuft of wool in the case of a girl, perhaps as an indication that the house was polluted, as later sources claim. The walls were smeared with pitch, evidently to prevent the pollution from seeping into the community.

The Newborn Baby Officially Enters the Home

On the fifth day after birth, the newborn baby was ceremoniously introduced into the home and placed under the protection of the household deities. The ceremony, which was called the *Amphidromia,* or "Running around," was so named because the child's father would run around the domestic hearth holding his infant in his arms in order to consecrate it to Hestia, goddess of the hearth.

Relatives would bring gifts for the newborn called *optêria* (see p. 76), so named in this case because this was the first time they had set eyes upon the child, including charms for protection against bad luck or the evil eye. On the tenth day after birth, the child would be given his or her name. Most firstborn boys were named after their grandfather, as is still the custom in Greece to this day—evidence of the emphasis on the continuity of the family line.

Nursing

It was customary for the well-to-do to secure the services of a wet nurse to breast-feed their infants. The following contract between a mother and her wet nurse from Hellenistic Egypt dated to 13 B.C.E. lays down terms of hire. It is interesting to note that the infant in question is a foundling slave girl, which suggests that adopted infants were sometimes raised to be slaves and that well-to-do families sometimes expended considerable sums of money on such children:

Didyma agrees to nurse and suckle outside at her own home in the city with her own milk that is to be pure and unsullied for a period of sixteen months . . . the foundling slave girl . . . that Isidora has given to her. She is to receive from the said Isidora as pay for the milk and the nursing ten silver drachmas and half a liter of oil every month. (*Select Papyri* 1, no. 16 in Loeb Classical Library)

A SEATED WOMAN *hands her newborn child to a nurse in this funerary stele. Wet nurses were often utilized by the well-to-do in ancient Greece. Marble, c. 425–400 B.C.E.*

Nurses feature prominently in Greek tragedy, which suggests that they were important members of the household. The most sympathetically drawn is Orestes's now elderly nurse Kilissa, who makes a brief but memorable appearance in Aeschylus's Libation Bearers. *In the following passage, she is fondly reminiscing about the chores that she had to perform on behalf of her royal charge many years ago:*

How I devoted myself to that child from the moment that his mother gave him to me to nurse as a newborn babe! He kept me up every night, crying and screaming. He was a perfect nuisance and all for nothing. They're brainless things, you see, children. You have to nurse them as if they're animals and follow their moods. A babe in swaddling clothes can't tell you what the matter is—whether it's hungry or thirsty or wants to go to the potty—though of course babies can't control themselves. It just comes out and you can't do anything about it. You learn to tell the future in my profession, but, heavens above, I was wrong often enough and then I had to wash its clothing. I was a nurse and a washerwoman rolled into one. (lines 751–60)

Although most nurses were slaves, a few were impoverished freeborn women. Soranos in *Gynaecology* (2.19.1) recommended that the ideal nurse should be "self-controlled, sympathetic, well-tempered, Greek, and tidy." Servile or free, many won the confidence and gratitude of their masters and mistresses, as is indicated by the fact that they often retained a position of trust in the household even in old age. The following semihumorous sepulchral inscription in mock heroic verse testifies to the enduring bond that existed between a nurse and her former charge:

Mikkos looked after Phrygian Aischre [the name means something like "Commoner"] all her life, even in old age. When she died he set up this monument for future generations to see. Thus the old woman departed from this life, having received due recompense for her breasts.

Unwanted Babies

Despite the keen desire for children, inevitably some pregnancies were unwanted. One solution was abortion. Although the Hippocratic Oath contained a prohibition against giving a pessary to cause an abortion, it is unclear whether the ban was primarily due to ethical or medical considerations. Moreover, the oath did not ban abortion altogether, and there is a famous passage in a Hippocratic text entitled the *Nature of the Child,* in which a prostitute is encouraged to jump up and down, while kicking her buttocks with her heels, in order to expel the fetus (13.1). Abortion would have been extremely dangerous, particularly if surgery were employed, not least because of the risk of infection. Soranos recommended it only if a woman's life was in danger. The Greeks also had to contend with the fear of the polluting effect of an aborted fetus. A sacred law from the sanctuary of Artemis in Kyrene, for instance, decreed that "if a woman has a miscarriage or abortion when the fetus is fully formed the household is polluted as if by death [i.e., heavily], whereas if it is not fully formed, the household is polluted as if by childbirth [i.e., lightly]." Aristotle, who advocated performing an abortion only "before the fetus received life and feeling," seems to have been mainly concerned with the risk of increased pollution that a later abortion would cause (*The Politics* 1335b 24–26).

The only evidence to suggest that Athenians regarded abortion as a criminal act is provided by a fragment from a speech by Lysias, which prohibits it on the grounds that an unborn child could have survived to claim its father's estate in cases where the father died during pregnancy. Not until around 211 C.E., however, did the ancient world, in the reign of the emperors Septimius Severus and Caracalla, make abortion illegal—but only as a crime against the rights of the parents. Medical scruples, fear of pollution, and legal prohibitions notwithstanding, it is likely that many Greek women did resort to abortion, particularly victims of rape, unmarried girls, and *hetairai.*

The other solution to an unwanted pregnancy was exposure or abandonment (*ekthesis* or *apothesis).* Though the Greeks had certain reservations about terminating an unwanted pregnancy, they showed little concern for the rights, as we would phrase it, of the newborn child. They did not, however, go so far as to kill unwanted babies, for the simple reason that to do so would cause pollution and involve the murderer in blood guilt. Instead, the unwanted infant was carried outside the city and left to its fate. The legend of Oedipus tells of an infant who was abandoned because of a prophecy that he would kill his father and marry his mother. To reduce his chances of survival still further, his father took the added precaution of nailing his ankles together, from which in later time he received the name Oedipus, or "Swollen Foot."

In Sparta, the abandonment of handicapped and sickly infants was required by law. Plutarch informs us that the father of a newborn child had to present his offspring for inspection before the council of Spartan elders. If it was strong and lusty, the council ordered him to raise it, but if it was not, the father was ordered to expose it at the foot of Mount Taygetos "in the belief that the life which nature had not provided with health and strength was of no use either to itself or to the state" (*Life of Lykourgos* 16.1–2).

Girls were almost certainly abandoned more frequently than boys, partly because their usefulness in the home was more limited than that of boys and partly because they had to be provided with a substantial dowry to attract a suitable husband and therefore represented a drain on the family's finances. For this reason, families with more than two daughters were probably somewhat rare. In a lost drama, Poseidippos, a comic writer of the third century B.C.E., puts the following observation into the mouth of one of his characters: "If you have a son you bring him up, even if you're poor, but if you have a daughter, you abandon her, even if you're rich." The same preference for a son is poignantly revealed in a letter written on a papyrus from Hellenistic Egypt. The writer, a soldier who was billeted in Alexandria, informs his pregnant wife that if she gives birth to a boy she should raise him, but if to a girl she should expose her. Evidently the mother's feelings were regarded as irrelevant. The lower value placed on girls is also strikingly illustrated by Herodotos's comment about the Spartan king Kleomenes, who, he says, "died childless, leaving only one daughter, Gorgo, behind" (5.48). Other groups that were at risk of being exposed included the deformed and those who were the product of rape or incest.

Some estimates put the level of female exposure in Athens as high as 10 percent. However, almost everything that we know about the practice derives from literary sources. It is certain, too, that some exposed infants would have survived, as indicated in the contract with the wet nurse Didyma, quoted on page 108. Infertility was a serious problem in the Greek world, and many childless couples would have been only too happy to act as the foster parents of an unwanted child. This was the experience of the infant Oedipus, who, having aroused the pity of the servant entrusted with the task of exposing him, grew up believing that he was the offspring of the king and queen of Corinth, his adoptive parents. Evidently the fact that his feet were deformed as a result of his injury did not deter his parents from adopting him.

Orphans

Given the hazards of life coupled with the low life expectancy, a very large number of children must have grown up fatherless, the primary meaning of *orphanos,* which gives us the word *orphan.*

Hektor's wife Andromache paints a haunting image of the fate of their child Astyanax, who, she envisages, will become an outcast after his father's death (The Iliad *22.490–498):*

> The day a child becomes an orphan he . . . goes always with head bowed low and cheeks wet with tears. . . . Anyone who feels pity for him briefly offers him his cup and wets his lips but not his palate. But a child who has both parents living drives him from the feast, beating him and upbraiding him: "Clear off! Your father doesn't dine among us."

To safeguard fatherless children, and equally to encourage the fathers of young children to risk their lives in the service of the state, many Greek *poleis* made it their policy to support orphans at public expense until they reached their eighteenth year. Athens at the end of the fifth century B.C.E. set the maintenance that orphans received at one obol per day. Although their welfare was administered by the eponymous archon, we also hear of *orphanophylakes*, or "protectors of orphans," who may have been assigned to individual orphans to perform a role not dissimilar to that of social workers today.

A Child's First Years

In the fourth year of his life, an Athenian boy was brought to the *Anthesteria*, or Flower Festival, which took place in early spring. Here he was presented with a wreath to wear on his head, a small jug known as a *chous,* and a small cart. This was also the occasion when he experienced his first taste of wine. Since wine was the gift of the god Dionysos and the drinking of wine was, as we shall see later, invariably accompanied by religious ritual, the Anthesteria was thus a rite of passage, marking an important transitional moment in the child's life.

Athenians felt particular tenderness toward children who died before attending their first Anthesteria. A *chous* was placed beside them in the grave, evidently to compensate them for the fact that they had not received one in life. In the graves of even younger children, feeding bottles have been found. In some cases, the black glaze around the spout has worn away, indicating that the bottle had been used before the baby died. Infant mortality—deaths during the first year of life—was extremely high in Greece, accounting for at least a quarter of all live births. Diarrheal diseases resulting from a lack of clean drinking water and the absence of a satisfactory waste disposal system—the two main killers in the developing world today—were major causes.

Several Athenian funerary monuments commemorate the deaths of small children. One bears an inscription that informs us that the deceased, whose name was Philostratos and who bore the nickname Little Chatterbox, was "a source of joy" to his parents "before the spirit of death bore him away." Another monument shows a pudgy child of about three stretching out his hands in the direction of a bird that his adolescent sister is holding. The inscription on the gravestone states that it was erected in honor of Mnesagora and her little brother Nikochares "whom the doom of death snatched away," perhaps as the result of a joint accident or an illness to which they both succumbed.

Toys and Games

Most, if not all, toys were homemade. There is archaeological evidence for miniature horses on wheels, boats, spinning tops, and rattles. Dolls with movable limbs were also very popular, as, no doubt, were rag dolls and stuffed animals, though no examples have survived.

In the following passage from Aristophanes' Clouds, Strepsiades, a doting father, tells how his precocious son used to construct his own toys:

Oh he's clever all right. When he was only knee-high to a grass-hopper, he made houses out of clay and wooden boats and chariots from bits of leather, and he carved pomegranates into the shape of little frogs. You just can't imagine how bright he was! (lines 877–81)

A favorite game thought to have been especially popular among girls was knucklebones *(astragaloi)*. Each player tossed the knucklebones in the air and attempted to catch them on the back of her hand. If she dropped any, she attempted to pick them up without dislodging those already resting on her hand.

Another popular game, which resembled checkers, was played on a board with black and white squares. It is frequently represented on vases with Achilles and Ajax as players, as they enjoy an interval of repose from the battlefield. The best throw was three sixes, which incidentally was proverbial for good luck. Its invention was ascribed to Palamedes, a Greek warrior who fought in the Trojan War, which indicates that the game was believed to be very ancient.

Ball games were also extremely popular, despite the fact that it was impossible to produce a completely spherical ball. Children used to blow up a pig's bladder and then try to make it rounder by heating it in the ashes of a fire. Some ancient ball games are still popular today. In one, the player who was "it" threw the ball and the others had to drop out one by one as they were hit. Boys at puberty and girls at marriage customarily dedicated their toys to the gods.

TWO YOUNG CHILDREN WATCH A COCK FIGHT, *a popular form of entertainment for people of all ages in ancient Greece. This relief is a rare example of a multi-figured terracotta sculpture, ca. 330-100* B.C.E.

Growing Up

Both boys and girls spent a great deal of time in the company of their mothers and slaves. Fathers, being absent much of the time, played only a minor role in the rearing of their children, until the children reached puberty. In Sparta, where men spent most of their time communally with their peers, the matriarchal tendency of the home was especially pronounced. Spartan mothers had a reputation for reinforcing the Spartan value system. One is said to have remarked to her son as she handed him his shield before he departed for war that he should return, "Either this or on this" (Plutarch, *Moral Sayings* 241f). What she meant was that he should either be carried back dead on his shield or not disgrace himself by throwing away his shield in flight.

> The following comment, which Xenophon attributes to Sokrates, provides a
> moving and enduring tribute to motherhood:
>
> It is she who is impregnated, she who bears the load during
> pregnancy, she who risks her life for her child, and she who supplies
> it with the food with which she herself is nourished; and then, having
> brought it into the world with much labor, she nourishes it and cares for
> it, although she has received no good and the child does not recognize
> its benefactress and has no means of signaling its desires. But a mother
> guesses what it needs and likes and tries to satisfy it, and rears it for a
> long time, toiling day after day, night after night, not knowing what
> gratitude she will receive in return. (*Memoirs of Sokrates* 2.2.5)

Juvenile Delinquency

Although the mother was the primary figure in a child's growing years, authority, or *kratos,* was invested in the father or legal guardian. This authority was
formidable and entitled him to enslave his daughter if he caught her in an act of
illicit sexual intercourse.

Despite the fact that the Greek family was a much more cohesive unit than
is typical today, it was not immune to the ills that afflict contemporary society.
Although we never hear about children from broken homes, many must have
grown up separated from their mothers. Due perhaps to the unrepresentative
nature of our sources, we only hear of juvenile delinquency among the well-to-do.
A fascinating description of one such occurrence is preserved in a speech by
Demosthenes, which was written on behalf of a young man named Ariston
around the middle of the fourth century B.C.E. Ariston claims to have been the
victim of an unprovoked attack while walking home late one night through the
Agora. He subsequently indicted the father of his chief assailant, a man named
Konon, who played a leading part in the assault. In the speech that he delivered
while prosecuting Konon, he describes the assault as follows:

First they tore my cloak off me, and then, tripping me up and pushing me into the mud, they struck me so violently that they split my lip and caused my eye to close up. They left me in this sorry condition, so that I could neither get up nor utter a word. While I was lying there, I heard them making a number of abusive comments, many of which were so offensive that I would shrink from repeating them in your presence. One indication of Konon's insolence and proof of the fact that he was the instigator of the whole affair, I will tell you. He began to make a sound in imitation of the song made by fighting cocks when they have scored a victory, while his associates encouraged him to move his elbows around against his sides as if they were wings. After this I was picked up naked by some passers-by, for my assailants had carried off my cloak. (54.8–9)

Ariston warns the jury that the kind of defense that they are likely to hear from Konon is that there are many young men in Athens from good backgrounds who become infatuated with prostitutes and then come to blows over them with other young men. The father will argue, in other words, that such behavior should be treated with indulgence. Ariston, however, maintains that rivalry over prostitutes had nothing to do with the attack and that his assailants held a personal grievance against him. He claims that there was a history of bad blood between Konon's son Ktesias and himself. When they were serving as *ephebes* (or cadets, see p. 259) on the borders of Attica, Ktesias and his brother amused themselves by emptying the contents of their chamber pots over the heads of the slaves of their fellow soldiers! We do not have the speech for the defense, so it is impossible to determine what part Ariston himself might have played in stirring things up. What is likely, however, is that rivalry among gangs of privileged youths featured prominently in a society that encouraged a high degree of competitiveness among all social groups.

However, there is no evidence to suggest that Greek society produced a disaffected youth culture that set its face against the values of society as a whole. We hear of only one isolated instance of violence against property. This was perpetrated in Athens in 415 B.C.E. by the so-called *Hermokopidai,* or "herm mutilators."

Herms were stone pillars surmounted by a carved head. The rest of the pillar was in block form except for a carved phallus. They stood at street corners and served as boundary markers. The *Hermokopidai* disfigured their faces and struck off their phalluses. The crime, however, was not a mindless prank. On the contrary, it had a political objective, being intended to prevent the sailing of the Athenian expedition to Sicily. Because Hermes was the god of travelers, the destruction of his image was interpreted as an extremely bad omen, as the vandals no doubt intended. The identity of the perpetrators remains unknown, however, so we do not know for certain whether they were youths.

The Elderly

Life Expectancy

Although estimates vary considerably, it is generally claimed on the basis of comparative data that life expectancy was little more than half the length that is common in Western societies today. Explicit evidence is very hard to come by, however. Paleontology provides only a rough indication of age at death. Funerary monuments rarely record age at death except in the case of those who survived to extreme old age. Infant mortality was at least as high as 25 percent. Those who reached their tenth birthday, however, had a reasonable chance of surviving another twenty years or more. It is estimated that, in the Roman world, only about 21 percent of the population attained the age of fifty and 13 percent the age of sixty. Probably these averages were comparable in the Greek world. This meant that there was a preponderance of teenagers and a paucity of the elderly. The satirist Lucian wrote a book called *Longlivers*—"Geriatrics" might be an appropriate equivalent—in which he listed famous people who had achieved eighty or more. The oldest Athenian whose age is recorded was a man named Euphranor, whose gravestone records that he lived to the ripe old age of 105. Because birth certificates did not exist except in Egypt, such claims should be treated with caution, however, particularly in view of the widely reported tendency in preliterate societies to "round up" age at death into pentads and decades (i.e., 35, 40, 45, etc.).

Women's life expectancy seems to have been about ten years lower than that of men. There were many reasons for the disparity. First, other than in Sparta, girls were not as well fed as boys. This made them more susceptible to disease and, in some cases, permanently impaired their health. Second, the early age at which many girls became pregnant—shortly after puberty—imposed severe strains upon their bodies, as did the frequency with which they became pregnant. Third, women at the lower end of the social scale were required to do manual work, often of a highly demanding nature. Men, by contrast, tended to lead less strenuous lives than women, except when they went to war, the conduct of which in most parts of the Greek world was limited to the summer months.

Despite the brevity of human life, three score and ten years nonetheless constituted the proper quota of years, as is indicated in a fragmentary poem by the Athenian lawgiver Solon: "If a man finally reaches the full measure of his years [i.e., seventy], let him receive the apportionment of death, without dying prematurely."

Literary Portraits of the Elderly

One of the most memorable literary portraits of old age is that of Nestor, king of Pylos, who is a major character in *The Iliad*. Nestor claims to have "seen two generations pass away . . . and now be ruling over the third" (1.250–52). Although given to delivering over-lengthy diatribes about the superiority of the men of his generation to those of the present day, Nestor nonetheless commands respect from the Greek chiefs precisely because of his age. Indeed, Agamemnon goes so far as to declare that if he had ten men of his quality advising him on strategy, Troy would soon be captured. Nestor makes a second appearance in *The Odyssey* as Telemachos's host and is no less prone to speechifying than before. It is testimony to Telemachos's maturing social skills that he manages to extricate himself from his palace without giving offence.

In Attic comedy, the elderly are often caricatured as irascible and vituperative. A notable example is Philokleon, who appears in Aristophanes' *Wasps*. Philokleon is depicted as a superannuated delinquent who looks back wistfully on his youth with all the venom of a frustrated old age.

Retirement or Death in Harness?

We have no means of knowing what percentage of the Greek population was able to retire. Nor is there any way of estimating to what extent the Greeks regarded retirement as an attractive or even possible option. Probably most working Greeks soldiered on until they died. Although we occasionally hear of the head of the household handing over the management of his property to his son, as Odysseus's father Laertes appears to have done, we do not know whether this was a widespread phenomenon. Nor is there any hint as to the fate of elderly or infirm slaves. While domestics such as nurses and pedagogues would probably have been treated humanely in their declining years, the prospects for those who did not have a personal relationship with their masters must have been grim indeed.

Caring for the Elderly

The Greeks regarded the care of the elderly, which they called *gêroboskia,* as a sacred duty, the responsibility for which rested exclusively with the offspring. Greek law laid down severe penalties for those who omitted to discharge their obligations. In Delphi, for instance, anyone who failed to look after his parents was liable to be put in irons and thrown into prison. In Athens, those who neglected either their parents or their grandparents were fined and partially deprived of their citizen rights. There were no public facilities for the aged—the very idea of an old people's home would have been utterly abhorrent to most Greeks.

It was customary for a childless man to adopt a male heir of adult years to whom he would bequeath his whole estate. In return, the adopted son would look after him in old age, give him a proper burial, and pay regular visits to his tomb. The adopted son would lose all legal connection with the family into which he had been born, including the right to inherit. In this way, if he had an heir himself, he would prevent his adoptive father's household from dying out. To a limited degree, this arrangement may have served to redistribute wealth, because the majority of adopted sons are unlikely to have relinquished their entitlement to inherit from their natal homes unless they were guaranteed an improvement in their financial prospects. Adoption was, therefore, as much a practical as a sentimental arrangement, into which both parties entered with a firm calculation of their own advantage.

The majority of elderly Greeks probably remained physically fit and mentally alert until their final illness. Few households can have had the time, energy, or resources to attend to those who were either incapacitated or bedridden. Even the aged would have been expected to play some part, however small, in the family's economic well-being. Odysseus's father Laertes, who makes himself useful by working in the vineyard on his own farm, is, therefore, likely to have been typical of the majority (*The Odyssey* 24.205ff.).

Respect for the Elderly

Even in the aristocratic world evoked by the Homeric poems, the elderly seem to have been concerned about the degree of respect that they received from the younger generation. Harking back to a supposedly Golden Age when youths were inherently deferential to their elders, Nestor remarks at the beginning of one of his long speeches, "In former times I associated with better warriors than you and they never made light of me" (*The Iliad* 1.260f.). Although Athenians were required by law to look after their parents, mistreatment of the elderly seems to have been commonplace in the late fifth century B.C.E. or at least became a matter of public concern. This was in marked contrast to Sparta, where old people were held in high esteem. This difference in attitude is in part a reflection of the conservative temperament of the Spartan people. In Xenophon's *Memoirs of Sokrates,* Perikles despairingly demands, "When will the Athenians respect their elders in the same way that the Spartans respect theirs, instead of despising everyone older than themselves, beginning with their own fathers?" (3.5.15). According to Herodotos (2.80),

RED-FIGURE ATTIC VESSEL *from ca. 480–470 B.C.E. featuring the hero Hercules, and Geras, a personification of old age. Mistreatment of the elderly was relatively commonplace in Athens during the last part of the fifth century B.C.E.*

it was a characteristic of Spartan youths to stand aside for their elders when they passed them in the street and to rise when they entered the room. No such customs are recorded for Athens, a much more youth-oriented culture.

Medical Neglect of the Elderly

Greek physicians do not seem to have been much concerned with the welfare of the elderly. There is little discussion of the ailments of the elderly in medical treatises, still less about how to treat them. Given the absence of effective painkillers, many old people must have ended their days in extreme discomfort. A Hippocratic treatise entitled *Aphorisms* catalogues the ills to which old age is subject:

> Difficulty in breathing, catarrh accompanied by coughing, problems of the urinary tract, arthritis, nephritis, dizzy spells, apoplexy, cachexia, itching of the whole body, insomnia, watery discharge from the bowels, eyes and nostrils, dullness of vision, glaucoma, and deafness. (3.31)

It is unlikely, however, that many elderly persons would have sought to take their own lives in order to end their misery, in view of the fact that suicides were thought to constitute an unhappy category of the dead. Only among the Stoic philosophers was it regarded as a point of honor for the very aged to terminate their existence before entering upon their dotage.

THE DISABLED

The Prevalence of Disability

Most Greeks probably became at least partially disabled by the time they had reached middle, let alone old, age due to the demands and stresses of life in the ancient world. The price of survival to what we would identify as middle age for the average man or woman was an unpalatable assortment of rotting and rotten teeth, failing eyesight, increasing deafness, constant back pains, creaky joints, failing hips and knees, vicious stomach ulcers, and unpredictable bowel movements. Injuries to the foot and leg were very common, as we know from the fact that these generated the largest number of votive offerings in healing sanctuaries. Because there were only very limited means of alleviating any disability whether slight or severe, a relatively mild disability like, say, astigmatism or a badly set fracture, would often be as constricting as a major one. Among the poor, the onset of disability would have meant a further reduction in economic circumstances, thereby accelerating the pace of their decline. It goes without saying that those who were most at risk of becoming disabled as a result of both sickness and injury were slaves. Because no professional medical care was available for the bedridden, it would also have been the slaves who tended to the needs of the seriously disabled. Those who could afford round-the-clock medical attention probably received as good as anything on offer in the intensive care ward of a modern hospital. To use an example from the Roman world, we hear from Pliny the Younger of the deformed and crippled Domitius Tullus, who "could not even turn in bed without assistance." Domitius, an ungrateful old sod, was often heard to say that "every day he licked the fingers of his slaves," evidently because he required them to spoon-feed him (*Letters* 8.18.10). No doubt, Greek slaves also served as full-time caregivers.

In addition to those who became disabled in later life, many infants would have suffered permanent debility from contaminated drinking water, which encourages the spread of cholera and typhus. Viral diseases such as meningitis, measles, mumps, scarlet fever, and smallpox, which produce damaging side effects such as deafness and blindness, are also likely to have been common. As mentioned, malnutrition, which impedes the growth and composition of bones, is likely to have been especially prevalent among girls. Far fewer congenitally deformed infants would have survived to adulthood than is the case today, however, in part because the Greeks had little compunction about withholding the necessities of life from those deemed incapable of leading a full and independent existence. In Sparta, as we have seen, the abandonment of deformed infants was required by law. Likewise, Aristotle recommended that, in a well-ordered polity, there should be a law "to prevent the rearing of deformed children" (*The Politics* 7.1335b, 19–21).

Attitudes Toward the Disabled

Reports of persons exhibiting gross deformities were probably widely circulated in the Greek world, as the name of the one-eyed giant Polyphemos ("Much talked about") in *The Odyssey* suggests, even though Homer never specifically describes the giant's medical condition, known as synophthalmia. Hesiod hints that the birth of a congenitally deformed infant was an expression of divine ill will (*Works and Days* 235). Moreover, oaths frequently contained the proviso that, if they were broken, the oath breaker would give birth to children who were monsters (*terata*). Such a belief would surely have acted as an inducement to abandon a deformed child rather than let it live as a permanent reminder of its parents' shame.

There is no evidence to indicate that the Greeks took official notice of abnormal births, nor that they constituted a distinctive category of divination. This was in marked contrast to Rome, where the birth of a deformed child, such as a hermaphrodite, was regarded as portentous. The absence of physical blemish was, however, a requirement for holding a priesthood. Given the religious importance attached to physical wholeness, it is likely that the deformed were stigmatized as second-class citizens, such as the hunchbacked Thersites, whose humiliation at the hands of Odysseus is greeted with approval by the entire Greek army (*The Iliad* 2.211–77). No provision was made to facilitate the participation of the physically disadvantaged in ceremonies and rituals of a civic or religious nature. Not surprisingly, very few prominent individuals are known to have been congenitally deformed. A rare exception is the Spartan king Agesilaos, who was both diminutive and congenitally lame. Hunchbacks, cripples, dwarfs, and obese women were popular entertainers at drinking parties. The majority of the severely disabled and chronically deformed probably begged or claimed the indulgence of a well-to-do relative. The only state known to have made any provision for its disabled was Athens. The author of an Aristotelian treatise titled the *Constitution of Athens* provides the following details (49.4):

> The Council inspects the disabled. For there is a law that bids those who have
> less than three minai and who are disabled and incapable of work to be inspected
> by the Council, which provides them with two obols per day at public expense.

The primary candidates, no doubt, were those who had been injured or maimed while fighting for their country. Even so, there was a deep suspicion of malingerers, and those claiming disability pensions were required to undergo a physical examination by the council or *boulê*. There also existed an Athenian law that enabled high-minded (or meddlesome) citizens to bring charges against persons whom they suspected of claiming welfare under false pretenses.

Conclusion

"No one is responsible for the fact that I am deformed except my own parents," moans the crippled fire god Hephaistos in Book 8 of *The Odyssey,* "and I wish they had never given birth to me" (line 311f.). Nowhere else in Greek literature is there a similarly heartrending utterance from a disabled person. Although the disabled were numerous, they left little trace in the historical record. Evidently they saw no advantage in trailing their misery before the public eye. The defendant in Lysias's *Oration* 24, whose right to public support was challenged by a fellow citizen, provided the jury with no description of his affliction, even though appeals to pity were a conventional feature of Athenian law court speeches. Physical pain and discomfort were not the only burdens that the disabled had to endure. They were also routinely exposed to shame, stigma, disgrace, and ridicule. Overall, it seems likely that the disabled were expected to suffer in silence, make as few demands upon society as possible, and remain hidden behind closed doors, because their presence constituted a source of shame to both their families and themselves. Their plight is easily overlooked when we conjure up the image of godlike physical perfection bequeathed to us by Greek art.

SLAVES

The vast majority of Greeks from Homer to Aristotle and beyond regarded slavery as an indisputable fact of life. Its existence at the heart of the Classical world is thus a source of considerable disquiet to those who admire Greek culture for its supposedly enlightened humanism. It is important to appreciate, however, that every known ancient Mediterranean society practiced some form of slavery, though the percentage of slaves to free would have varied greatly even within the Greek world. And it goes without saying that there was no recognition of what we call today human rights anywhere in the ancient Mediterranean. We should also note that slavery was not an absolute condition but one that admitted many different statuses. It incorporated, in Moses Finley's phrase, "a continuum of unfreedom." At one end of the scale were the chattel slaves, those who, in Aristotle's telling phrase, had the same status as "an animate or ensouled piece of property" (*The Politics* 1253b 32); at the other end were those who lived independently and remitted a part of their income to their masters. There were three ways to become a slave: by being born a slave, by being sold into slavery (or selling oneself into slavery), or by being captured in war. At most times in Greek history, there were probably more people who were either born into slavery or who were sold into slavery than who became slaves as a result of war, though this situation began to be reversed from the third century B.C.E. onward, when the Romans enslaved Greeks whom they had captured in war. Although a small minority of slaves who had faithfully served their masters or mistresses earned their freedom, we know very little about their lives subsequently. It is highly unlikely, however, that they were integrated into Athenian society in the way that Roman freedmen were integrated into Roman society.

The Origins of Slavery

The origins of slavery are not precisely understood, but the institution was certainly in existence by the end of the eighth century B.C.E. In the world evoked by the Homeric poems, most slaves were obtained by piracy, kidnapping, or warfare. Odysseus's swineherd Eumaios, for instance, was captured and sold into slavery as a child. Enslavement is the fate that awaits the female members of the royal household when Troy is taken. It would also have been the common fate of women and children in historical times whenever a besieged city fell. In late eighth- or early seventh-century B.C.E. Greece, slavery appears to have been widespread even among the poorest section of society. Hesiod (*Works and Days* 405f.) is of the opinion that an ox and a "bought woman" are an essential part of a small farmer's holding. In the Archaic Period, many Greeks became enslaved as a result of debt bondage. Debt bondage was a temporary status, and at least some who entered it would have later bought back their freedom. In practice, however, it was a very difficult condition to escape from, and, more frequently than not, it became not only permanent but also hereditary. One of the great achievements of the lawgiver Solon was to free all Athenians who had become enslaved as a result of debt in about 594 B.C.E. In other parts of the Greek world, however, debt bondage remained common practice.

The Size of Athens' Slave Population

Slaves in Athens are thought to have greatly outnumbered those in any other Greek community, though we have no reliable figures to determine the size of the population. The only surviving slave census relates to the late fourth century B.C.E. The total, which is put at 400,000, exceeds all bounds of credibility. Modern estimates vary wildly, from 60,000 to 400,000. Paul Cartledge (*Oxford Classical Dictionary*, 1415), drawing on evidence from modern slave societies including Brazil, the Caribbean, and the antebellum South, estimates that "between 450 and 320 B.C.E. about 80,000 to 100,000 slaves of all kinds were active in Attica at any one time (out of a total population of perhaps a quarter of a million)."

In Classical times, the possession of at least one slave was regarded as not only a necessity but also a basic right. In a lawsuit written by Lysias, the speaker states, "I have a trade but I don't earn much. I find it difficult making ends meet and I can't save enough money to buy anyone to do the work for me" (*On the Refusal of a Pension to an Invalid* 6). It is a mark of his meanness that Theophrastos's *Tight-Fisted Man* refuses to buy his wife a slave girl and instead hires one from the women's market (*Characters* 22.10). Every Athenian, like virtually every other Greek, would have aspired to own at least one slave, though in reality only members of the middle and upper classes could afford to do so. Most well-to-do Athenians probably owned two or three slaves, whereas the wealthy possessed between ten and twenty. The super-rich, however, owned a great many more. Nikias, one of the richest men in Athens in the late fifth century B.C.E., owned a thousand slaves, whom he leased out to fellow citizens at the rate of one obol per slave per day (Xenophon, *Revenues* 4.14). In conclusion, it is probably accurate to state that the servile population of Athens did not exceed the freeborn population.

The Racial Diversity of Athens' Slaves

Athenian slaves were imported from a variety of regions, including Thrace, Skythia, Illyria, Kolchis, Syria, Karia, and Lydia. Most of them, in other words, came from the fringes of the Greek world or beyond. The Thrakians, who occupied the territory that approximately corresponds to modern Bulgaria, seem to have made it a custom to offer themselves and their children for sale as slaves. The names Thrax and Thratta, meaning Thrakian male and Thrakian female, were among the most common slave names in Athens. But, although slaves came from a variety of regions, what most of them had in common, from an Athenian perspective, was the fact that they were assimilable to the categorization "barbarian." It is unthinkable that Greeks from Corinth, Thebes, Sparta, or any other Greek polis would have served as slaves in Athens.

The purchase price of a slave varied according to such criteria as skills, age, looks, and place of origin. Obviously, an educated slave who could read and write fetched considerably more in the slave market than one who was only good for menial duties. Likewise, a pretty young girl cost much more than an ugly old hag. Slaves with management skills were extremely expensive. Nikias, mentioned above, paid a talent (6,000 drachmas) for a slave to manage his silver mines. A slave in good health probably cost the equivalent of half a year's salary. The inscription relating to the public sale of confiscated property that belonged to those who had been found guilty of either mutilating the Herms or profaning the Eleusinian Mysteries in 415/14 B.C.E. prices a Syrian male slave at 240 drachmas, a Thrakian female at 220 drachmas, and "a little Karian boy" at 72 drachmas.

Although most Athenian slaves were purchased from abroad, some were bred in captivity, as indicated by the following remark made by Ischomachos in Xenophon's *Household Management:* "As a general rule, if good slaves are permitted to breed, their loyalty increases, whereas when bad slaves live together as husband and wife they become more adept at causing trouble" (9.5). Sparta's slaves, known as helots, by contrast were racially homogeneous and spoke Greek (see p. 131). Racial homogeneity was generally rare among slaves, though in other Greek communities it was the rule, including Thessaly in northern Greece and Syracuse in Sicily.

Domestic Slaves

Domestic slaves, sometimes known as *oikêtai* (literally, members of an *oikos* or household) were the ancient Mediterranean's ultimate labor-saving device for the home. They served in practically every capacity, including that of washerwoman, cook, caregiver, reader, gardener, porter, cleaner, handyman, tutor, escort, messenger, nurse, and traveling companion. As traveling companions, they accompanied their masters when they were called up to serve in the army. No doubt in the larger households, there was some division of labor, as, for instance, among the female slaves in the palace of the Homeric king Alkinoös, "some of whom grind the yellow grain on the millstone, while others weave the web and turn the spindle" (*The Odyssey* 7.104f.). Whether slaves were also employed in large numbers as agricultural laborers is unclear. In other words, we do not know to what extent the Greek economy was based on slave labor—an ongoing debate in scholarly circles with huge implications for our appreciation and assessment of Greek culture and its contribution to Western civilization.

On becoming a member of an Athenian household, a slave underwent an initiation

WOMAN WITH HER SLAVE CHILD-ATTENDANT. *Gravestone from ca. 100 B.C.E. Slaves were commonplace in wealthier Greek households.*

ceremony similar to that which a bride underwent on first entering her new home by having dried figs and nuts showered over him or her. This was intended to place the slave under the protection of Hestia, the goddess of the hearth. The poems of Homer suggest that close ties sometimes arose between master and slave. When, for instance, Odysseus reveals himself to his faithful slaves Eumaios and Philoitios on his return to Ithaca after twenty years, they throw their arms around him and kiss him (*The Odyssey* 21.222–25). Depictions of mistress and maid figure prominently on Athenian grave monuments, testimony to the fact that the two spent much time together in the *gynaikôn* or women's quarters. In Classical Athens, slaves were occasionally buried in family plots beside their masters and mistresses. Slaves also occasionally received medical attention. Xenophon, in the *Memoirs of Sokrates,* implies that it not uncommon to summon a physician when a household slave fell sick (2.10.2), and some of the case studies in the Hippocratic work entitled *Epidemics* involve slaves.

Overall the treatment of slaves must have varied greatly from one household to the next, depending in large part on the temperament of the owner. A less complimentary term than *oikêtês* was *andrapodon,* which means "a thing with the feet of a man"—as dehumanizing a definition as could be devised. Although Athenian slaves were protected by law against violent abuse, in practice it was virtually impossible for them to lodge a complaint against their masters, because they could not represent themselves in court. Starvation and flogging were likely regular punishments for bad behavior. A runaway slave was branded with a hot iron upon capture. If a slave was required to be a witness in a lawsuit, his or her testimony was only accepted under torture. There are no actual descriptions of slaves being tortured, however, so we do not know what methods were applied.

Although we lack a single account written by a slave telling us what he or she felt about his or her condition, Aristophanes' *Frogs* provides some insight into the kind of gossip that slave owners *imagined* their slaves engaging in when out of earshot and, though humorous, it reveals the latent paranoia that probably characterized the attitude of many slave owners:

SLAVE A:	I'm absolutely thrilled when I can curse my master behind his back.
SLAVE B:	What about grumbling as you're going outside after being beaten?
SLAVE A:	That's great!
SLAVE B:	What about not minding your own business?
SLAVE A:	That's terrific!
SLAVE B:	You're a man after my own heart. What about eavesdropping when he's having a private conversation?
SLAVE A:	That's enough to drive me wild with delight!
SLAVE B:	What about gossiping to your friends about what you discover? Do you like that?
SLAVE A:	Do I like it? By Zeus, that's enough to make me wet my knickers! (lines 746–53)

Publicly Owned Slaves

Some of the most privileged Athenian slaves were those owned by the state. Known as *dêmosioi* ("the public ones"), they included the notaries, the jury clerks, the coin testers, and the executioner—a few hundred in all. Athens' force of Skythian archers, who kept the peace, was also the property of the state. In addition, a large number of publicly owned slaves toiled as road menders. As building accounts make clear, slaves sometimes worked on building projects alongside Athenian citizens.

Those "Living Separately"

Because Athenian citizens refused to satisfy the demand for wage labor in the second half of the fifth century B.C.E., the conditions and opportunities for a limited number of slaves improved dramatically. Such slaves, who paid a commission to their owners, were described as "living separately" (*chôris oikountes)*. They included the managers of shops and factories, bankers, captains of trading vessels, bailiffs, and artisans. Pasion, who, on earning his freedom, became one of the wealthiest men in Athens, previously worked as a banker and was eventually granted Athenian citizenship because he gave generously to the state at a time of crisis.

Industrial Slaves

The most dangerous and exhausting work performed by Athenian slaves was in the silver mines of Lavrion in southeast Attica. Inscriptions reveal that the vast majority of industrial slaves, of whom there were many thousands, were non-Greeks. Xenophon (*Memoirs of Sokrates* 2.5.2) informs us that the price of slaves who served in this capacity could be as low as fifty drachmas. Conditions in the mines were terrible, and work continued uninterruptedly for twenty-four hours a day. From the discovery of miners' lamps containing oil, it has been estimated that shifts were ten hours in length.

Only occasionally do sources shed light on the terrible living conditions that some slaves faced, as in the following passage.

Slaves who work in the mines produce unimaginable revenue for their masters, wearing their bodies out toiling day and night in the shafts underground. Many of them die due to the terrible conditions. They get no respite or interruption in their toil but are forced by their overseers, who beat them, to endure their terrible conditions. And so their lives are thrown away, though there are some who endure the hardship over a long period of time, due to their physical strength and psychological stamina. For them death is preferable to life because of the enormity of their sufferings. (Diodorus Siculus 5.38.1)

Greeks as Slaves

It has already been noted that Greeks were sometimes constrained to sell themselves into slavery as a result of debt, a practice that may well have persisted in parts of the Greek world throughout antiquity. From around 275 B.C.E. onward, Greeks as prisoners of war began to arrive in Rome, where they were sold into slavery. The first influx of Greek prisoners occurred after the battle of Pydna in 168 B.C.E., when the Romans defeated the Macedonian king Perseus.

VOTIVE CLAY TABLET DEPICTING SLAVES *laboring in a clay quarry. Mine work was extremely dangerous and exhausting, with terrible conditions, long hours, and low pay. Corinth, Archaic Greek, late 7th century B.C.E.*

A second wave occurred in the 80s B.C.E., following the conclusion of the wars fought against Mithradates VI of Pontos.

Most well-to-do Roman households would have aspired to own a Greek slave as a status symbol. It is therefore likely that Greeks would have been treated better than slaves of any other ethnicity. Since, moreover, Greek males tended to be literate, they were often placed in positions of trust and authority, notably as tutors. Because the Romans regularly freed their slaves, many Greeks would have eventually found themselves in competition with freeborn Romans, not least as clients of their former masters, who would have subsequently tended to their welfare. Ramsey MacMullen (*Changes in the Roman Empire,* 179) has suggested that, around the middle of the first century B.C.E., Rome may even have tied with Alexandria for first place as the city with the largest Greek-speaking population.

Conclusions

Although it had its critics, the institution of slavery was never seriously challenged in the ancient world. Even philosophers such as the Cynics and Stoics, who professed to believe in the brotherhood of mankind, were muted in their opposition. In *The Politics,* Aristotle goes so far as to justify slavery as part of the order of existence, though he makes a distinction between what he calls slaves by nature (i.e., those born in captivity) and slaves by law (i.e., those captured in war). Aristotle proposed this distinction in response to those who regarded the very existence of slavery as "contrary to nature" (1253b–1255b).

Our understanding of slavery in the Greek world is bedeviled by both Christianity and Marxism. Each imposes value judgments upon the institution, and these value judgments tend to distort our investigation of its place in ancient society. Christianity deplores slavery as barbaric and inhumane. Marxist historians identify slaves with the subjected European proletariat of the nineteenth century. Friedrich Engels went so far as to allege that the moral and political collapse of the ancient world was chiefly caused by slavery. Neither the Christian nor the Marxist viewpoint does full justice to the realities of life in the ancient world, however. Abhorrent and vicious though the institution of slavery was in so many respects, it nonetheless provided some measure of economic security in an otherwise dangerous and unpredictable world. It would, however, be quite wrong to give the impression that slavery was a benign institution. The fact that "more than 20,000 slaves deserted, most of them skilled laborers" (Thukydides 7.27.5) when the Peloponnesians established a permanent base at Dekeleia in Attica in 413 B.C.E. is testimony to widespread discontent, even if many of the refugees were mine workers. Nor does it seem to have occurred to anyone that the existence of such a large servile labor force depressed the wages of the poor—or, if it did, no one did anything about it.

With the exception of Spartan agriculture and Athenian silver mining, there is little evidence to suggest that the Greeks depended on slavery for what Marxists call their means of production. Overall, therefore, it remains questionable whether the achievements of Greek civilization were made possible by slavery.

Foreigners and Barbarians

The status of being a foreigner, as the Greeks understood the term, does not permit any easy definition. Primarily it signified such peoples as the Persians and Egyptians, whose languages were unintelligible to the Greeks, but it could also be used to describe Greeks who spoke in a different dialect and with a different accent. Notable among this latter category were the Macedonians, whom many Greeks regarded as semibarbaric though they probably spoke Greek, as the following judgment upon Philip II of Macedon by the Athenian politician Demosthenes indicates:

> He's so far from being a Greek or having the remotest connection with us Greeks that he doesn't even come from a country with a name that's respected. He's a rotten Macedonian and it wasn't long ago that you couldn't even buy a decent slave from Macedon. (*Third Philippic* 31)

Prejudice toward Greeks on the part of other Greeks was not limited to those who lived on the fringes of the Greek world. The Boiotians, inhabitants of central Greece, whose ethnic credentials were impeccable, were routinely mocked for their stupidity and gluttony. Ethnicity is a fluid concept even at the best of times. When it suited their purposes, the Greeks also divided themselves into Ionians and Dorians, as mentioned earlier (p. 4). The distinction was emphasized at the time of the Peloponnesian War, when the Ionian Athenians fought against the Dorian Spartans. The Spartan general Brasidas even taxed the Athenians with cowardice on account of their Ionian lineage. In other periods of history, the Ionian-Dorian divide carried rather less weight, though it no doubt helped to bolster Greek-on-Greek racism.

Metics

Metic, which comes from the Greek word *metoikos,* meaning "one who dwells among," denoted a foreigner with the right to live permanently in the host country of his or her choice. Classical Athens, because of its empire, wealth, and commercial importance, attracted a vast number of metics. In this respect, the city-state was rather unusual, as Perikles pointed out (Thukydides 2.39.1). It is estimated that approximately 60 percent of the metic population lived in demes located in or around Athens, 20 percent in the port of Piraeus, and the remaining 20 percent in rural and coastal demes. Sepulchral inscriptions reveal that at least sixty different Greek and non-Greek states are represented among their ranks. The numbers of metics perhaps reached a peak shortly before the outbreak of the Peloponnesian War in 431 B.C.E., and then fluctuated in line with Athens' changing fortunes and prosperity. However, it is difficult to arrive at even a rough estimate of the total. Athens was not the only Greek state that encouraged the immigration of foreigners, but it was undoubtedly the one that attracted them in greatest numbers, in part because of the opportunities it afforded for enrichment through mercantile enterprises. Athens' most celebrated metic, however, was the philosopher Aristotle, a native of Stageira in Chalkidike (the triple-forked peninsula to the east of Macedonia), who resided in Athens for much of his working life. The Spartans, by contrast, were notoriously xenophobic and actively discouraged foreigners from residing in their territory even on a short-term basis.

As noted earlier, in 451 B.C.E. Perikles introduced a law requiring those claiming citizenship to prove that their mothers as well as their fathers were citizens. The state also revised its citizen register at this time and struck off a number of suspected metics who were believed to be claiming citizenship under false pretenses. Although Athenians could marry metic women, metic men were subject to a fine of 1,000 drachmas—the equivalent of about three years' salary—for cohabiting with an Athenian woman. Each metic had to have an Athenian sponsor, called a *prostatês,* and be registered in a deme. He (or she in the case of *hetairai)* was required to pay an annual poll tax called a *metoikion.* Men were liable to service in the military but in the navy only in times of emergency. They were also required to undertake liturgies (see p. 233). Metics were not permitted to own land unless they had obtained a special grant called an *enktêsis.* This entitled them either to purchase a home or establish a sanctuary for the worship of a foreign deity.

It was partly through membership of private cultic associations that metics were able to consort together and retain their distinctive identity. Many such associations also functioned as dining clubs. One of these was devoted to the worship of the Phrygian god Sabazios, an exotic deity whose nocturnal rites included ecstatic dances accompanied by the flute and kettledrum. The cult of Sabazios aroused such animosity when it was first introduced into Athens that it was the butt of humor in no fewer than four comedies by Aristophanes. In one play, Sabazios, together with other foreign deities, is booted out of Athens. In the middle of the fourth century B.C.E., however, the Athenians received an oracle ordering them to desist from persecuting the followers of Sabazios. This had the desired effect, and in time the Athenians themselves became worshippers of Sabazios. An inscription dated to the very end of the second century B.C.E. records the names of fifty-one members of the cult, no fewer than thirty-six of whom were Athenian. Private cultic associations, in other words, sometimes provided a common meeting ground for metics and Athenians, and in so doing no doubt eased the tensions between the two.

Religion apart, to what extent were Athenians tolerant of foreign influences, let alone in the business of absorbing them? Very possibly the presence of Greeks from other communities in their midst did produce a more open-minded community than was the case elsewhere in the Greek world. Non-Athenian Greeks are sometimes ridiculed in Aristophanic comedy, but this circumstance hardly helps us ascertain the level of xenophobia. Certainly the Athenians would have encountered metics in a wide variety of cultural contexts. Metics participated in religious ceremonies organized by the state, including the procession that formed part of the Panatheniac festival, which suggests that they were to some extent integrated into the life of the community, as does the fact that they could attend dramatic performances. The Spartans in particular had their fans, even though it is unlikely that many Spartans would have been seen in the streets of Athens. Some Athenians, known as *Lakonizers,* even adopted the Spartan style of dress by wearing short cloaks and growing their hair long, out of admiration for Spartan practices. Only wealthy Athenians are likely to have had any personal dealings with Spartans, however, notably through ties of hospitality (see p. 8).

Barbarians

It is sometimes suggested that the Greeks more or less invented racism single-handedly by holding up their culture as a shining example of everything that was noble and praiseworthy, while at the same time rubbishing everybody else, particularly the Persians. The truth is more complex. Even if the Greeks considered their culture to be superior to others, we should not assume that they were all out-and-out bigots. Certainly some Greeks saw much to admire in Persian culture. The historian Herodotos was so enamored of the Persians that he was dubbed *philobarbaros,* or "barbarian lover." Overall, the Greek attitude toward the Persians was probably a complex mixture of fascination, envy, and contempt.

The notion of the barbarian was not inherent in Greek culture. There is no trace of racial prejudice against the Trojans in *The Iliad.* In fact, the word *barbarian* never appears in Homer, either as a noun or an adjective, even though there was ample opportunity for it. The word *barbarophônoi,* meaning "of barbarous diction," appears only once in *The Iliad,* in reference to a contingent of Karians, a half-Greek, half-Persian people who fought on the side of the Greeks. More than that, Homer suggests that the regard for civilized values on the part of the Trojans is equal, if not superior, to that of the Greeks, in part because we see the war as much through the eyes of the royal Trojan household, which is presented to us as a normative family (apart from a single, brief reference to polygamy), as we do through the eyes of the Greeks, who are presented to us as irrepressibly contumacious and bellicose.

Not until Aeschylus's *Persians,* which was produced at the City Dionysia in 472 B.C.E., are barbarians depicted as a stereotypical group with a homogeneous culture. This change came about as a result of the Persian invasion of Greece—an event that bred terror and loathing in the Greek population, similar in intensity to that felt toward the hated Hun by the Allies in World War I. The stereotype was also disseminated through art, notably in portrayals of the battle between the Lapiths and centaurs, which are found on the metopes of the Parthenon (see p. 306). The lascivious and aggressive centaurs stand for the Persians, the innocent and abused Lapiths for the Greeks. Depictions of this mythological

BLOCKS FROM THE SOUTH METOPE OF THE PARTHENON SHOW, *respectively, a centaur attempting to rape a Lapith woman and a Lapith fighting a centaur. The tension between the Lapiths and the centaurs serve as a metaphor for tensions between the Greeks and the Persians. Athens, ca. 447 B.C.E.*

encounter, in which right clearly triumphs over wrong, no doubt served to bolster Greek self-esteem in the aftermath of the Persian invasion.

Precisely what the category barbarian amounted to in practical terms is difficult to determine. The most plausible origin of the word is "the people who mutter ba-ba-ba." Barbarians, in other words, were people who could not speak Greek. Non-Greek speakers were excluded from participation in the Olympic Games and from other Panhellenic ceremonies, such as the Eleusinian Mysteries. In time, however, barbarian also came to acquire the pejorative meaning of ignorant, brutal, and savage.

"Typical" barbarian behavior included drinking neat wine, beer, and milk; wearing effeminate clothing; and practicing circumcision. Thukydides (1.6.1–3) was of the belief that contemporary barbarians behaved similarly to the earliest inhabitants of Greece, first by carrying weapons around with them and second by wearing loincloths when exercising. The most despised feature of barbarian society, however, was the degrading subjugation of its population to one man, as the following brief exchange from Aeschylus's *Persians* indicates. It takes place at the royal capital of Susa shortly after the Persian queen received news of her son's defeat at the battle of Salamis:

QUEEN:	Who is their leader? Who commands their army?
CHORUS:	They declare themselves to be the slaves of no one and to serve no one.
QUEEN:	How then can they withstand an enemy invasion?
CHORUS:	Well enough to destroy King Dareios' large and powerful army. (lines 241– 44)

Despite the highly negative view of barbarian culture that many Greeks held, there is no evidence to suggest that barbarians were unwelcome or subjected to mistreatment if they traveled to Greece. On the contrary, they figure prominently among Athens' metic population in the fourth century. The Sidonians, who were Phoenicians, a Semitic people, actually enjoyed a privileged status that was not extended to other metics: they were exempted from the metic tax and other financial burdens.

Ultimate Monstrosity

The outermost reaches of geographical knowledge were thought to be inhabited by monstrous races, descriptions of whom were brought back by travelers. They include the Astomoi or Mouthless Ones, who have holes in their faces instead of mouths; the Skiapods or Shadowfeet, a one-legged people who lie on their backs shading their heads from the sun with a single huge foot; and the Kynokephaloi or Dogheads, who communicate by barking.

No figure quite so succinctly epitomizes the horror of the Other, however, as the Cyclops Polyphemos, whom Odysseus encounters in Book 9 of *The Odyssey*. Solitary; monstrous in size; possessing a single eye in the center of his forehead;

stupid; contemptuous toward the gods; hostile toward strangers; ignorant of seafaring and agriculture; and a lacto-vegan to boot, except when human flesh comes his way, Polyphemos is everything that the Greeks despised. Who could fail to be repulsed by the description of the regurgitated pieces of flesh that surface at the corners of his giant maw, as he sleeps off a dinner that consisted of Odysseus's companions? And who could fail to applaud when Odysseus blinds his single eye with a stake, before escaping from the cave by grabbing onto the belly of Polyphemos's favorite ram?

This interpretation nonetheless ignores some important facts that are less than complimentary to our hero. In the first place, the encounter with the Cyclops could have been avoided altogether if Odysseus had listened to his companions instead of being guided by his own insatiable curiosity. It was his fatal curiosity that prompted him to wait for the Cyclops in his cave, and this, in turn, led to the deaths of several of his companions. Again, after he escaped, it was Odysseus's irrepressible ego that caused him to reveal his name to the Cyclops, enabling the Cyclops to curse him in the name of his father Poseidon and delay his homecoming by many years. In short, the encounter creates the distinct impression that a canny Greek is by no means intellectually light-years ahead of an ignorant and uneducated Cyclops. Already in Homer's day, the category *barbarian* was problematic.

THE SPARTAN ALTERNATIVE

Another community worth looking at in some detail is Sparta. Sparta had none of the civic amenities of Athens. Thucydides (1.10.2), in a characteristically perceptive exercise in time traveling, writes:

> If Sparta were deserted and only the shrines and foundations of buildings
> were preserved, hardly anyone would believe that its power matched its
> reputation . . . since the city is not unified and does not possess costly
> shrines and public buildings, but consists of villages in the old style Greek
> way, whereas if Athens were to suffer the same fate, people would believe it
> had double the power from its appearance alone.

HIGH-ANGLE *view of the ancient ruins of an acropolis in Sparta.*

It is even questionable whether Sparta was a polis in the strict sense of the term, both because it did not have an urban center that was comparable to Athens and because the five villages that it comprised retained a measure of autonomy.

All that we know about the Spartans suggests that their way of life was ideologically antithetical to that of most other Greek communities—so much so that Herodotos in his history treats them as something of an ethnographical oddity. The Spartans were antithetical to other Greeks foremost in the fact that the needs of the family were subordinated to the requirements of the state. The only categories of Spartans who were accorded the distinction of being honored with tombstones that recorded their names were soldiers who died in battle and (probably) women who died in labor, evidently because each had laid down their lives in the service of the state. Second, Spartan women enjoyed more privileges and exercised more freedom than their counterparts in other Greek communities, largely no doubt because their role as childbearers was valued so highly. Third, Sparta was extremely conservative, as we know from the fact that its constitution remained unchanged for hundreds of years. It was a constitution that originated in the seventh century B.C.E. and was attributed to a legendary lawmaker named Lykourgos, though it probably continued to evolve for some two hundred years. Sparta's conservatism was due partly to the fact that its servile population, known as helots, were ethnically homogeneous and thus more likely to revolt and partly to the fact that it only minimally engaged in trade. Fourth, Sparta was a militaristic society whose primary objective from the seventh century B.C.E. onward was to foster a high degree of conformity and discipline in its citizenry, largely at the expense of cultivating other values. It therefore differed radically from Athenian society, to which it is unflatteringly contrasted in Perikles' Funeral Speech, notably when he states, "We have procured many opportunities for the mind to refresh itself from toil, by holding games and annual sacrifices, and the elegance of our private dwellings is a source of pleasure to us, which helps to banish misery"— not like the Spartans, the argument runs, who never take time off from the daily grind (Thukydides 2.38.1).

Perikles' view notwithstanding, there were a good many Greeks who admired the Spartan system, which they celebrated for its good order or lawabidingness *(eunomia)*. Sparta's *eunomia* was reflected in the fact that it avoided tyranny and enjoyed political harmony for some four hundred years. Whether *eunomia* was also a judgment upon the conduct of its citizens is not clear, though in view of the fact that these were referred to as *homoioi* or "equals," Spartans may well have observed a greater uniformity of behavior than other Greeks did.

Sparta was also admired for its mixed constitution. That is, it had a dual monarchy, subject to scrutiny by an overseeing body known as the *ephorate;* a council of elders; and a popular assembly known as the *apella,* which exercised a limited right of veto. The mercenary leader Xenophon (*Constitution of the Spartans* 10.4), for instance, an Athenian who was born a generation later than Perikles, has this to say about it: "The state of Sparta with good reason outshines all other states in virtue, since she alone has made the attainment of a high standard of nobility a public duty."

It would be impossible to write a detailed account of Spartan daily life, because its people have left behind so few traces of themselves. Very little Spartan literature has survived, and nothing later than the seventh century B.C.E. Most of what we know about Spartan society comes from philosophers and historians, and they were not much concerned with the practicalities of daily life, although they do provide a detailed description of the educational system, so it is that which we will focus upon. Because these writers were foreigners, however, we see the Spartans from the outside, although our earliest source, Xenophon, who was writing around 400 B.C.E., did at least visit Sparta.

Upbringing

From birth onward, the obligation to the state overrode not only any duty to the family but also one's right to life, in that Spartans practiced the compulsory exposure of newborn males in the case of those deemed unfit for rearing. Plutarch (*Life of Lykourgos* 16.1), writing around the beginning of the second century C.E., tells us that the father was required to present his offspring to the elders of the tribes for inspection. Then, "If the child was strong and lusty, the elders ordered him to raise it; if it was not, he had to expose it at a chasm-like place called *Apothetai* (Place of Exposure)."

The Spartan home was hardly a home in our sense of the word, because children spent most of their time with their peers. Even the first years of a boy's life were not completely free of discipline, as Plutarch (*Life of Lykourgos* 16.3) goes on to tell us: "Spartan nurses taught Spartan babies to avoid any fussiness in their diet, not to be afraid of the dark, not to cry or scream, and not to throw any other kind of tantrum."

At the age of six, boys were removed from the care of their parents and subjected to a tough system of state education known as the *agôgê*, or training.

The aim of the *agôgê,* which had something of the character of a Victorian boarding school, was to instill obedience, discipline, and resourcefulness. It probably had the further consequence of turning the child first into a brat, then into a bully. Boys were divided into packs and placed under the general control of an educational director known as a *paidonomos.* At about the age of twelve, a Spartan boy became a *meirakion* or youth. He lived in barracks and was kept on a minimal diet, the expectation being that he would supplement it by stealing. Plutarch describes the educational process as follows:

> Learning how to read and write was not considered important. Mainly
> their education consisted in learning how to carry out orders, how to test
> themselves to the limits of their endurance, and how to succeed at wrestling.
> So their training got tougher and tougher as they got older. Their heads
> were close-shaved, and they learnt how to march barefoot and go naked
> when training. (*Life of Lykourgos* 16.6)

The courage that this kind of training was designed to instill is indicated by the well-known story of a boy who was apprehended with a stolen fox under his cloak. Rather than admit his crime to his captors and undergo the humiliation of punishment, the boy vehemently denied the charge. His courage cost him his life because the fox gnawed through his entrails while he was being interrogated. We also hear of a strange ritual that was enacted annually at the altar of Artemis Orthia. One group of youths would try to steal cheese from the altar while another group would use whips on them to keep them at bay. The ritual enjoyed considerable popularity in Roman times, attracting large numbers of what have been aptly described as "sado-tourists." Although physically weak babies were exposed at birth, there must have been a number of perfectly fit and healthy children who were bullied mercilessly and who found this brutal system quite intolerable.

When a youth reached the age of sixteen (or possibly eighteen), he became a member of the *krypteia.* This, as its name from the Greek verb *kryptô,* meaning "conceal," indicates, was a kind of secret police force. Its purpose was to

*THE LACEDONIAN WOMAN. Louis Lagrenee, eighteenth century.
In this painting, a Spartan mother giving her son a shield. Military
service was mandatory for all males in Sparta.*

intimidate the subjected helot population, sometimes by slaughtering them.
(The fact that the ephors declared war on the helots at the beginning of each
campaigning season meant that killing them was not deemed impious.) During
this period, the youth lived out in the wild and had to fend for himself.

Citizenship

At the age of about twenty, a Spartan youth's education came to an end and
he became an *eirên,* a word of uncertain etymology. He was now liable for
military service, though he did not yet possess full rights of citizenship. Even
now, however, he was still required to lead a communal life, eating with his peers
and sleeping in army barracks. Only occasionally would he be allowed to sleep

with his wife. Even on his wedding night, a Spartan bridegroom was permitted to spend only a short time with his bride and was required to return to his army barracks before dawn.

On reaching age thirty, a Spartan finally became a full citizen, the word for which is *homoios,* meaning one who is equal. He now enjoyed something resembling a regular home life, though he was still required to take a number of his meals away from home. Qualification for Spartan citizenship, in fact, depended on membership in a *syssition,* or dining club. Each *syssitos,* or member of a *syssition,* made a monthly contribution to his dining club. He would not only regularly dine and relax in the company of his fellow *syssitoi,* but also fight alongside them in time of war. The size of a *syssition* is not known. Plutarch (*Life of Lykourgos* 12.2) suggests that the number was as low as fifteen, but modern estimates put it much higher, perhaps as high as three hundred. He also belonged to one of three Spartan tribes and one of twenty-seven *phratrai,* or fraternities.

He was now a professional soldier, owning an exclusive obligation to the state. When not at war, he would be required to be training for war, with occasional breaks in the routine to celebrate festivals—a state of affairs that provoked Plutarch (*Life of Lykourgos* 22.2) to observe that the Spartans were the only people for whom war was a welcome respite from the business of preparing for war! Only when he reached age sixty was a Spartan man finally released from military obligations, though, like many other retired servicemen, he probably continued to feel as much at home in the army as he did at home.

Women

Although Spartan home life was extremely restricted, women enjoyed a number of privileges that were denied their counterparts in other parts of the Greek world. In particular, girls were allowed to mix freely with boys. They also underwent an intensive physical training program, which included running, discus and javelin throwing, and wrestling. The purpose of this training program was to ensure that they became fit and healthy breeders of Spartan babies. The extreme value that was put on childbearing in Spartan society is indicated by the fact that wives could be "loaned" to an interested third party with the agreement of the husband, presumably to exploit their fecundity in cases where the husband was elderly or infertile. Another unusual feature of Spartan society is that women were permitted to own property, which was not the case in Athens. In fact, given the dearth of Spartan citizens by the fourth century B.C.E., it may well have been the case that, over time, a great deal of landed property passed into the hands of women.

Spartan women were celebrated for their wisdom and outspokenness. One of Plutarch's minor works is entitled *Sayings of Spartan Women,* and it reveals a mordant sense of humor, though we should not necessarily assume that all the sayings are either authentic or even all attributable to women. Even so, Paul Cartledge (*Spartan Reflections,* 126) is surely right to warn us against concluding that the Spartans were proto-feminists, primarily because of the extreme emphasis that they placed on women's childbearing potential. In fact, they seem to have done much to reinforce the Spartan value system by undervaluing their own role as mothers (see p. 97).

Helots

When the Spartans conquered Lakonia and Messenia (the territory to the west), they reduced the entire population to servile status. The Lakonians, however, who were known as *perioikoi* or "those dwelling round about," enjoyed preferential treatment to the Messenians, though it is often difficult to distinguish between the two subject peoples in the historical record. The Messenians were known as *heilôtai,* or helots, a word that is probably connected with a verb meaning "to capture." Helots, who were state-owned, were required to till the land and pay half their produce to their masters. It was this arrangement that left Spartan citizens free to discharge their military duties, and it is no exaggeration to state that the Spartan way of life was more dependent on its slave force than any other Greek community of which we have detailed knowledge. We have no means of determining the size of the helot population, though some scholars estimate that there were seven times as many helots as citizens. Whatever the true figure, it is hardly surprising that the Spartans were reluctant to engage in lengthy campaigns for fear of a rebellion during their absence. Indeed, the Spartans may well have lived in greater fear of their slaves than did most other Greek communities.

Helots had no political or legal rights and could be executed without trial. They could be freed only by a decision of the Spartan assembly. Their condition was so wretched that the poet Tyrtaios describes them as "asses worn down with great burdens." They did, however, serve in the army as light-armed troops. In fact Herodotos (9.10) claims that no fewer than 35,000 helots served as such at the battle of Plataiai in 479 B.C.E. If that figure is even remotely accurate, it is no exaggeration to state that Greece's ultimate victory over the forces of barbarism was due in large part to the contribution of the downtrodden and degraded.

Helots were the property of the Spartan state, which assigned them to individual citizens, who did not have the right to dispose of them. They served as baggage carriers in war and in exceptional circumstances were recruited into the army. Because, unusually among slave populations, they were allowed to propagate without restriction, they were racially homogeneous. For this reason, the Spartans were constantly fearful of helot revolts and took extreme measures to safeguard against them, as this chilling incident reported by Thukydides indicates:

On one occasion [in 424 B.C.E.] the Spartans issued a proclamation to their helots offering freedom to those who judged themselves to have shown the most bravery in war. Their purpose was to make test of them, since they believed that those who came forward first to claim their freedom would also be the ones who were most likely to give them trouble. Two thousand were selected. They were crowned and did the rounds of the temples, thinking that they had been liberated. Not long afterwards, however, the Spartans eliminated them. To this day nobody knows exactly how any of them perished. (4.80.3–5)

The Economy

Sparta, above all Greek communities of which we have record, embodied the ideal of *autarkeia* or economic self-sufficiency (see p. 16). This had important consequences for daily life. It meant that the majority of Spartans had to be content to lead lives of the utmost frugality and simplicity. Most had virtually no means of acquiring wealth, because the Spartan economy was chiefly agrarian. Although some Spartan-made goods are found outside Sparta in the sixth century B.C.E., in the following century they become extremely rare. The limited importance of trade is further indicated by the decision that was taken soon after 600 B.C.E. not to mint silver coins. The alleged law banning Spartans from possessing coins is, however, almost certainly a later fabrication. Although we do not know whether every citizen possessed a *klêros* or holding assigned to him by the state at birth, most of the population must have been roughly at the same point on the economic scale. The only Spartans who had the opportunity to enrich themselves were the generals, who, once they were abroad and off the leash, turned out to be as grasping as anyone, though we may suspect that the charge of accepting bribes from the enemy that was regularly leveled against them in the field was, in many instances, politically motivated.

Conclusion

Sparta was not the only polis that put a high premium on military discipline, but it was the one that did so to an extreme degree. How the Spartans occupied themselves when they were not either exercising or fighting remains a mystery. Perhaps they were simply too exhausted to bother. From the sixth century B.C.E. onward, they seem to have had little interest in cultivating the arts, though the image of Sparta as a complete cultural backwater, as painted by Perikles in the Funeral Speech, is no doubt an exaggeration. Clearly, however, the pursuit of happiness was not a recognized Spartan ideal. It is, of course, the austerity of their lifestyle that gives us our adjective *spartan*. Faced with the choice of living either in Athens or in Sparta, few of us would have any hesitation in opting for Athens, given its vibrant cultural life, its openness to novelty, and its engagement with ideas. Hardly surprisingly, the Spartans also had a reputation for extreme economy in the use of language, and the adjective *laconic* derives from the Spartan aversion to long speeches. In the hands of the Spartans, however, brevity could be put to good effect. When Philip II of Macedon sent the Spartans a letter threatening to raze Sparta if he captured the city, the ephors are said to have sent him back just one word in reply: *If.*

There is one last point to note that has profound implications for our understanding of daily life. Although the population of mainland Greece reached its peak in the fourth century B.C.E., in that same period, Sparta was experiencing a sharp demographic decline. Herodotus (7.234.2) claims that, in 480 B.C.E., Sparta had 8,000 hoplites. By the time Aristotle was writing *The Politics* around the middle of the fourth century B.C.E., the number had dwindled to 1,000. Aristotle (1270a29–34) plausibly states that this decline was the reason for Sparta's military and political demise, which occurred after its defeat at the hands of the Thebans at Leuktra in 371 B.C.E. Although the causes for the demographic decline are unclear, it is safe to assume that it involved a serious social upheaval. Economic factors may have been chiefly responsible, but we should not rule out the possibility that infertility also played a part.

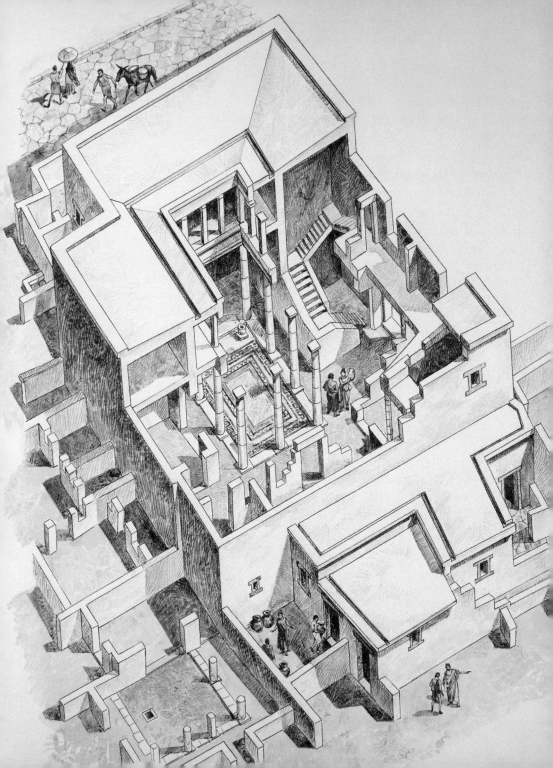

⚝ 5 ⚝

PRIVATE LIFE

HOUSING

The Greek household (*oikos* or *oikia*) typically comprised an extended rather than nuclear family, frequently with three generations living under one roof: the grandparents, the father and mother, their sons and unmarried daughters, their sons' wives and children, and the slaves. Quite commonly, therefore, there would have been about ten people living under one roof, often, one suspects, in rather cramped quarters. Only very trusted slaves would have lived in proximity to their masters or mistresses. Although we know next to nothing about slaves' living quarters, it is likely that most families domiciled them in a separate building, perhaps in some cases in a stall shared by livestock.

The residential area of Athens consisted of narrow, winding streets and small, poorly constructed houses. Most of it lay to the northeast of the Acropolis. Somewhat paradoxically, it was not until the fourth century B.C.E., when Athens' economy was declining, that houses began to be constructed in a more luxurious style. One ancient commentator named Herakleides was so contemptuous of Athens that in a fragmentary work he wrote, "Most of the houses are mean, the pleasant ones few. A stranger would doubt, on first acquaintance, that this was really the renowned city of the Athenians." Although Perikles, in the Funeral Speech, spoke proudly of the elegant private dwellings inhabited by Athenians, we would have found the majority of them to be sparsely furnished, simply decorated, and entirely lacking in the amenities of life.

BIRD'S-EYE-VIEW ILLUSTRATION OF THE HOUSE OF HERMES. *One of the more elaborate private structures on the island of Delos, the House of Hermes was probably a type of meeting space rather than a private residence.*

The cost of purchasing a house varied enormously. In Xenophon's treatise *Household Management,* Sokrates says to his wealthy friend Kritoboulos, "I expect that if I found a good buyer, everything including the house would fetch five minai, whereas your house, I bet, would sell for more than a hundred times that amount" (2.3).

One of the most serious defects in our knowledge of daily life is that there are so few remains of houses from anywhere in the Greek world dating to any period. Often all that survives of a house is discoloration in the earth with some accompanying debris. The one exception is the settlement of Akrotiri on the island of Santorini (ancient Thera) in the Cyclades, where in 1967 several well-preserved houses of Bronze Age date that were buried in a volcanic eruption came to light, complete with a stunning series of wall paintings. The best-preserved Athenian house was found in the Attic countryside near the modern town of Vari, a few miles to the southeast of Athens. Although it is a farmhouse, its plan is probably similar to that of many prosperous houses in Athens: a central courtyard with rooms leading off on all four sides. There was only one entrance to the house from the road. A south-facing verandah provided a place to work and relax, shaded from the summer heat or winter rain. Judging from the thinness of its walls, it is unlikely that the Vari house had a second story. In the southwest corner, however, the foundations are considerably thicker, suggesting that a tower of two or more stories once existed. It probably served as either a workroom or storeroom. Traces of other houses have been discovered in Athens, to the south of the Agora in the valley between the Pnyx and the Areopagos, including traces of semidetached houses. Like the Vari house, Athenian houses were built around a central courtyard and had an upper floor. Private houses are believed to have been very similar throughout the Greek world in terms of style and arrangements, whether they were built in the city or in the countryside, though very few have been uncovered. Towers, such as the one attached to the Vari house, also have been detected in connection with urban dwellings, though they were probably more common in the countryside. They could be used to store foodstuffs as well as to safeguard property and persons. Storerooms are already mentioned in *The Odyssey* as a feature of a well-appointed *oikos*. The one in Odysseus's palace was where "gold and bronze lay piled up, and clothes in chests, and an abundance of fragrant olive oil, and jars of aged wine, sweet to drink."

More impressive than the remains in Attica are those in Olynthos, a city in northeast Greece that was laid out in a grid pattern, as was common in the case of new foundations from the fifth century B.C.E. onward. Even the remains at Olynthos are, however, meager by comparison with the remains of Roman houses found in Herculaneum and Pompeii.

Building materials were extremely crude. Even the more sturdily constructed houses had lower courses of irregularly shaped stones simply piled on top of one another. Exterior walls were made of baked or unbaked mud brick, sometimes coated with lime. For the most part, walls were so thin and poorly constructed that, instead of breaking in by the front door, thieves sometimes knocked a hole through them. The word most commonly used for a burglar means literally a "wall digger." As the orator and politician Demosthenes once remarked, "Are you surprised, men of Athens, that burglary is so common when thieves are bold and walls are merely made of mud?"

Interior walls were generally covered with a coat of plaster, whitewashed or painted red, though a few wealthy Athenians may have decorated their rooms with frescoes. There was evidently a shortage of good interior decorators in fifth-century Athens, however, for the politician Alkibiades took the drastic step of locking his house painter inside his house for three months until he had finished the job. Floors consisted of beaten earth, clay, or paving stones occasionally covered in animal skins or reed matting. From the fourth century B.C.E. onward, they were commonly decorated with mosaics made out of small pebbles. Roofs were made of wood with terra-cotta tiling. Windows were very small and set close to the ceiling to afford maximum protection against the weather. In the winter, they were covered with boards or sacking to keep out the wind and rain, supplemented by shutters if the householder could afford them, because wood was both scarce and expensive. Doors were solidly made and supplied with locks and bars. When the Athenians residing in the countryside evacuated to the city at the outbreak of the Peloponnesian War, they took their doors and shutters with them.

> *Literary evidence suggests that men and women may, for some purposes,*
> *have had separate quarters. The speaker in an oration by Lysias describes his*
> *domestic arrangements as follows:*
>
> My small house has two stories. The layout was the same upstairs as
> downstairs, with the women's quarters upstairs and the men's quarters
> downstairs. Then our child was born, whom my wife decided to nurse
> herself. However, every time she wanted to bathe it, she had to come
> downstairs at the risk of falling down the staircase. So I decided to move
> upstairs and put the women downstairs. I soon adjusted to the new
> arrangement and my wife was frequently able to sleep with the baby, so
> that she could breast-feed it and stop it from crying. (1.9–10)

The Greek words for men's quarters and women's quarters are *andrôn* (or
andrônitis) and *gynaikôn* (or *gynaikônitis)*, respectively. Scholars used to believe
that women were largely confined to the *gynaikôn* on the grounds that Greek men
regarded it as a matter of honor that their wives and daughters not be exposed to
the public gaze. By contrast, the houses of the poor consisted of only one room,
divided into different living spaces by makeshift partitions. However, *gynaika*
cannot be securely identified in the archaeological record, and the only evidence
that can be cited for their existence is the discovery of finds such as loom weights
that are traditionally associated with women. More recently, some scholars have
argued that Greek houses were not primarily divided along gender lines and that
the principal spatial and architectural division was between household members
and outsiders.

The most favored location for the *andrôn* was on the north side of the courtyard,
which was warmed by the winter sun. The *andrôn* was the setting for the symposium
or drinking party and will be discussed later (see p. 157). No archaeological evidence
for the living quarters of slaves has come to light, though it is possible that male slaves
were separated from female slaves by a locked door or the like.

Lamps provided the main source of artificial lighting. Curiously, there are very few references to lamps in the Homeric poems, even though many of the scenes are set at night (e.g., *The Odyssey* 19.34). From the sixth century B.C.E. onward, however, small terra-cotta lamps become extremely common in the archaeological record. They were provided with a wick that floated in olive oil. Several would have been required to illuminate a single room, and often they were set on tall stands.

Because most furniture was made of wood, and because wood does not survive in the Greek soil, our knowledge of it mainly derives from illustrations found on vases and sculpted gravestones. Wood was so expensive that furniture was extremely sparse. Pieces were probably moved around the house as different needs arose. One of the most popular items was a chair with a curved back and curved legs known as a *klismos*. Three-legged tables also appear regularly, as do a variety of small stools. A basic necessity was the *klinê*, which did double duty as a couch by day and a bed by night. Furniture was rarely upholstered, though cushions and mattresses were common.

Cupboards were unknown, but wooden chests used for the storage of clothing and bed linen were popular. Musical instruments and other objects are sometimes shown hanging from walls. Small terra-cotta statuettes served as popular adornments. The only other display items were painted vases, such as the *lebês gamikos,* a bowl on a high stand that held the purifying water used in wedding ceremonies, which accompanied the bride to her new home.

We also hear of cramped and poorly constructed apartment blocks called *synoikiai*. These must have been death traps owing to the prevalence of earthquakes and the frequency of fires. *Synoikiai* were especially common in the port of Piraeus, where many poor people and foreigners resided.

Utilities

Most households had to fetch their water from outside, though some possessed a well in the courtyard that was cut into the bedrock to a depth of up to thirty feet. In later times, wells were lined with cylindrical drums made of terra-cotta to prevent their sides from crumbling into the water. From the middle of the fourth century B.C.E., however, and following a sizeable drop in the water table in Athens, bell-shaped cisterns became popular. These were designed to catch the rainwater that drained off the roof. The quality of the water obtained in this way must have varied greatly at different times of the year.

However, the majority of Athenians, and of Greeks in general, relied on the nearest public fountain for their drinking water. Collecting the daily supply of water was an arduous and time consuming task. For the most part, it was performed by slaves, though, in the case of the poor, this chore fell to the mistress of the house. (Daughters would not have been allowed out unaccompanied.) The public fountain was a popular place to gather and gossip, as scenes on vases indicate.

The earliest bathtub to be discovered, which is of Mycenaean date, was found in the Palace of Nestor at Pylos. Nearby it stood two large jars about four feet high, which probably contained water for the bath. In later times, small terra-cotta bathtubs became common in houses. Given the scarcity of water, however, only wealthy Greeks were able to immerse themselves in a full bath. Personal standards of hygiene thus varied considerably from one social class to another. Few houses possessed drains for the disposal of waste water. Although some cities had public bathhouses, these were never remotely comparable in size to their Roman counterparts.

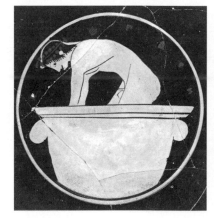

YOUTH WASHING IN A BATHTUB. *Detail from a terra-cotta* kylikes, *or drinking cup, ca. 510 B.C.E.*

Men relieved themselves in the home into a chamber pot called an *amis*. This was shaped like a salt container with an opening in the front. There were no public toilets, so men probably had no option but to relieve themselves in public. In the opening scene of Aristophanes' *Women in Assembly,* Blepyros defecates in the street as soon as he rises. Some houses, it seems, were not even provided with a cesspit (*koprôn*). Women used a boat-shaped vessel called a *skaphion*. Although babies could be dangled out of the window in an emergency (see Aristophanes' *Clouds,* line 1384), well-regulated houses possessed potties. One potty, which was found in the Agora, is provided with two holes for the baby's legs and a hole in the seat. Its detachable stand enabled its contents to be removed without disturbing the baby.

Urination was not without its dangers. Hesiod gives the following tips about how to avoid giving offense to the gods:

Do not urinate standing upright facing the sun but remember to do it either when the sun has set or when it is rising. Do not make water either on the road or beside the road as you go along and do not bare yourself. The nights belong to the blessed gods. A good man who has a wise heart sits or goes to the wall of an enclosed court. (*Works and Days* 727–32)

Facilities for the disposal of refuse were almost nonexistent. As a result, rubbish piled up in the streets in vast quantities, creating a terrible stench and constituting a serious health hazard, particularly in the summer months. Where houses were built close together, as in Athens and the Piraeus, the streets were ankle-deep in filth. Mosquitoes, rats, and flies were plentiful, carrying all manner of diseases and causing epidemics. One of the worst epidemics occurred in 430 B.C.E., when the entire population of Athens was cooped up inside the city walls. The Athenians claimed that the outbreak was caused by the Spartans poisoning their reservoirs. Although there appears to have been no substance to the charge, the Athenians were correct in their belief that the contamination of their water supply was the chief cause of the spread of the disease.

HOUSEHOLD RELIGION

The household, like every other community of Greeks, was a religious unit, and the head of the household was its priest. Many of the houses discovered in Olynthos were provided with an altar in the courtyard, and no doubt this was true generally in the Greek world. The role of priest would normally fall to the eldest son, who would have inherited it from his father. It was his duty to perform all the rituals pertaining to the welfare and prosperity of the household, in particular by making offerings, perhaps on a daily basis, to the three deities who were believed to safeguard its security and prosperity: Zeus Ktesios, or Zeus as protector of the household's wealth; Zeus Herkeios, or Zeus as protector of the boundary that surrounded it; and Apollo Agyieus, or Apollo as protector of the entrance to the house.

Each deity had its own sanctified spot. Zeus Ktesios, who took the form of a two-handled jar, was worshipped in the storeroom; Zeus Herkeios was worshipped in the courtyard, where he had an altar; and Apollo Agyieus was worshipped in the form of a statuette or a small pillar that stood beside the street door. In addition, each home possessed a hearth that was sacred to Hestia, the goddess of the hearth. Hestia had a particularly important role in the initiation of new members to the household, including brides, newborn children, and slaves, all of whom were formally introduced to her when they were showered with nuts and dried figs. We do not know of any religious rituals that were performed by the mistress of the house.

Because all the members of the household, as well as all its wealth, was placed under the protection of these gods, slaves sometimes participated in religious ceremonies, though the frequency of their attendance probably varied from household to household. Overall, however, the fact that the household was a religious unit may have helped to humanize relations between freeborn and slaves by reminding the former that the prosperity of the household depended in part on the well-being of its slaves.

The head of the household was also responsible for the proper conducting of funerals and for the rites that were performed at regular intervals on behalf of the dead, which are considered later in this chapter.

DRESS

Judged by current standards, Greek clothes were uniform and utilitarian in the extreme. It was virtually impossible to make a fashion statement by adopting an exotic or provocative style of dress. The blatant attention seeker Alkibiades was notorious both for the special shoes that were named for him and for his extravagantly purple robe (Athenaios, *Professors at Dinner* 12.534c). They hardly seem to us to constitute a serious aberration, yet the offense that they caused indicates how conservative the dress code must have been. Apart from shoes, we do not hear of any trade in readymade clothes. To the extent that fashions existed, they changed very slowly. The most popular fabric was wool, though, over time, linen became common. Cotton and silk were rare.

As noted earlier (see p. 80), most clothing was made on the loom in the home under the supervision of the mistress of the house. Almost every garment was rectangular in shape and required little stitching. Because very few items of clothing have been excavated, our knowledge derives mostly from vase paintings and sculpture. (A rare example of clothing from the second half of the fourth century B.C.E. is two pieces of tapestry-like cloth with gold and purple thread found in the tomb of Philip II at Vergina in Macedon.) Overall, this represents a huge loss, not only in terms of the garments themselves, but also in terms of what they would have had to tell us about women's handicraft, a field of expertise presided over by Zeus's daughter Athene. However, there can be no doubt that women produced work of the highest sophistication and refinement.

Women

In earlier times, Athenian women wore the *peplos,* a long, heavy woolen garment that revealed little of the figure beneath. The *peplos* hung from the body folded over at the top by about a quarter of its length. The turned-down material was attached to the shoulders by means of two long dress pins, and the garment was supported at the waist by a belt. Parts might be dyed purple or enlivened with woven geometric motifs. Embroidered decoration was, however, rare.

In the middle of the sixth century B.C.E., the *peplos* was replaced by a lighter and finer garment made of wool or linen called the *chitôn.* Because the *chitôn* hugged the figure more tightly than the *peplos,* it was more revealing of the figure, which may reflect a modest change in attitude toward women's sexuality at the time. The *chitôn,* being worn without any overfold, was held in place by a series of pins along the length of the arms. Whereas the *peplos* was sleeveless, the *chiton* had loose, elbow-length sleeves. It, too, was fastened around the waist by a belt.

The Athenians were of the opinion that the *peplos* was a Doric invention, whereas the *chitôn* was Ionic. More likely the change was a reflection of the increased wealth of the Athenians in the middle of the sixth century B.C.E., since linen, being more costly to produce than wool, had to be imported. As Herodotos reports, however, the Athenians gave a more sensational explanation. They claimed that, after a disastrous defeat at the hands of the Aiginetans, only one Athenian managed to escape. When he returned with news of the disaster, the wives of the men who had died in the battle were so outraged by the fact that he alone had escaped that they stabbed him to death with the pins of their dresses, demanding as they did so what had befallen their husbands. Herodotos concludes:

> So this man died but the Athenians thought that what the women had done was more terrible than the disaster itself. As they could find no way of punishing them, however, they made them change their dress to the Ionic style . . . as this did not require any brooches. (5.87.3)

FEMALE FIGURE, *perhaps a depiction of Persephone, wearing a* chitôn *and a* himation *as a shawl in this ca. 330 B.C.E. terra-cotta sculpture.*

Bronze dress pins eighteen inches in length have been found in excavations. They would have been more than adequate to the task of stabbing. The *peplos* remained popular in other parts of Greece, however—especially in the winter time, for which it was ideally suited.

Accessories

Earrings, hairpins, necklaces (fastened tight around the neck), pendants, brace-lets, diadems, and rings were frequently worn by well-to-do women. They were made from a variety of materials, but the commonest were gilt terra-cotta, cop-per, and lead. More expensive items were made of silver and gold, though it is noteworthy that few pieces of gold jewelry have survived from the Archaic

Period. In the Classical Period, however, goldsmiths produced highly intricate work, utilizing techniques such as filigree, granulation, and chasing. Infants were commonly given amulets to ward off evil.

The only item of jewelry commonly worn by men was the signet ring, which was used to put a seal on private documents and merchandise as a mark of ownership. Seal stones were made of both precious and semiprecious stones. The art of cutting stone goes back to the Minoan Period. In most cases, the artist cut the image into the stone, a technique known as intaglio; less commonly the image was in relief. Expensive seal stones were frequently buried with their owners because they were among the most personal items they possessed.

A simple cloth band called a *strophion* served as a brassiere for women. Other accessories used by women include the fan or *rhipis,* a flat object with a wooden handle. Another was an umbrella, or *skiadon,* used as a shield against the sun rather than as a protection against rain. Both men and women pulled up the fold of their *himation* to serve as a kind of hood. On their travels, men wore a flat, broad-brimmed hat made of felt or straw called a *petasos,* which they tied under the chin. When not in use, this often hung loose at the back of the neck. Workmen and slaves wore a conical cap called a *pilidion.* Women were less inclined to cover their heads than men, though in the Hellenistic Period they are often depicted wearing a sunhat with a broad brim and a pointed crown.

BRACELETS. *These are outstanding examples of Greek jewelry dating from the first century B.C.E. Using a variety of gemstones became popular after Alexander the Great conquered parts of the East, introducing the Greeks to Oriental styles and materials.*

The simplest form of footwear was the sandal. Fashionable women sometimes wore platform heels. In the home, both men and women usually went barefoot. All shoes and sandals were made of leather. On long journeys, men sometimes wore short lace-up boots, turned over at the top. But, while sandals and boots were fairly common, probably most Greek men went barefoot, even when performing military service.

Perfume was popular among both men and women. It was generally made by boiling the petals of flowers. Athletes applied perfume to their bodies after exercise, as is indicated by grave reliefs that show them carrying a small bottle attached to their wrists by means of a thong. Guests at a symposium also liberally sprinkled themselves with perfume. A highly prized perfume container was the *alabastron,* so named because it was carved of alabaster.

Makeup

It was a sign of beauty in a woman to have a pale complexion, which is why women on vases are frequently depicted with whitened faces. Their paleness was a natural consequence of spending most of their time indoors. However, some women sought to enhance their natural appearance by applying makeup. They also applied round spots to their cheeks and darkened their eyebrows with the soot produced by lamps. Eyes, eyelashes, and lips were painted a variety of colors. Not everyone approved, however. In Xenophon's treatise *Household Management,* crusty old Ischomachos makes the following acerbic observation:

> One day I noticed that my wife had put makeup on. She had rubbed white lead onto her face to make her complexion look paler than it really was and rouge onto her cheeks to make them look rosier than they really were, and she was wearing platform shoes to make her look taller than she really was. (9.19.2)

This drew the following stern lecture from him:

> You are to assume, my dear, that I do not prefer white paint and red dye to your real color, but just as the gods have made horses so as to give pleasure to horses, cows to cows, and sheep to sheep, so humans find the natural body most delightful. (9.19.7)

Ischomachos concludes his puritanical homily:

> Mix flour, knead dough, and shake and fold the cloaks and the bedclothes. This will increase your appetite, improve your health, and add redness to your cheeks. (9.19.11)

Men

The simplest male attire was a tunic a bit shorter than knee length. Known as an *exômis,* which means "off the shoulder," it was held in place by means of a brooch or knot tied at the shoulder. It was commonly worn by manual workers, including slaves, though, in the fifth century, the Spartans adopted it as a military tunic. On formal occasions, men wore a *chitôn,* similar to women. Another popular garment was the *himation,* which was considerably longer than the *chitôn* and worn either on top of it or without any undergarment. This was a rectangular piece of cloth that was generally wound over the

THE TWO MEN PAINTED *on this white terra-cotta vessel display typical men's attire from ca. 465 B.C.E. Greece. The younger figure on the right wears an* exômis *tunic and* petasos *hat, while the older figure on the left wears a* himation *and leans on a walking stick.*

left shoulder and under the right, with the surplus material hanging over the left forearm. There was practically no limit to the different ways of attaching it to the body, however. *Himatia* were often dyed and embroidered with a patterned border. In vase paintings and sculpture, those wearing a *himation* are often depicted leaning on a stick, which suggests that it was favored by older men. (Women also wore *himatia,* usually draping them over the right shoulder and under the left arm in the same way as men.) Another outer garment was the *chlamys,* which was also rectangular but shorter than a *himation* and commonly worn by travelers.

Men did not usually wear underwear. An article known as a *perizôma,* which roughly translates as "loincloth," seems to have served mainly as an apron that was used by athletes, priests, soldiers, cooks, and others.

There is some evidence to suggest that, in the Classical Period, the clothing worn by Athenian men became simpler and less ornate than it had been in the Archaic Period. According to Thukydides, "The Spartans were the first to adopt a moderate costume . . . and in other respects, too, the propertied class [of

Athens] changed their way of life to correspond as closely as possible to that of ordinary men" (1.6.4). As we have seen, some Athenians, known as Lakonizers, aped the Spartan dress code by wearing long hair and paying little attention to their personal hygiene.

Hairstyles

Women wore their hair long in a variety of styles. Some plaited it in tresses, others piled it up in a bun either at the nape of the neck or on top of the head. Head scarves were also commonplace, covering part or all of the hair. Athenian women only "let their hair down"—literally—on special occasions, notably at festivals and funerals. This gave them license to indulge in much freer behavior than was permitted them at other times. Some women either bleached their hair or dyed it. Female slaves wore their hair short and covered it in a hair net called a *kekryphalos*.

Freeborn men favored beards and moustaches, whereas slaves were often completely shaven. The Homeric heroes braided their hair and wore it long. This, too, is how men's hair is depicted in Archaic sculpture. In the Classical Period, the Athenians cut their hair much shorter.

The Spartans remained conservative in their preference for long hair. Plutarch writes,

> In wartime the Spartans relaxed the harshest aspects of their training and did not prevent young men from beautifying their hair and their armor and their clothing, happy to see them like horses prancing and neighing before competitions. For this reason men grew their hair long from adolescence onwards. Especially in times of danger they took care that it appeared glossy and well-combed, remembering a certain saying of Lykourgos concerning hair, that it made the handsome better-looking and the ugly more frightening. (*Life of Lykourgos* 22.1)

It was Alexander the Great who first made a clean-shaven chin fashionable and chic. Beardlessness was adopted by the Hellenistic kings who succeeded him, and no doubt by many ordinary people as well. Suddenly anyone with a razor could model himself upon the most powerful man in the world, though older Greek men probably continued to wear beards.

FOOD AND DRINK

The Greeks did not just eat to live; on the contrary, and from earliest times, dining had enormous social importance. In *The Iliad* Book 18, as long as Achilles grieves for his dead comrade Patroklos, he refuses all offers of food and drink. The hero's eventual acceptance of nourishment signals the abatement of that grief. Each day ends with a description of the warriors dining. Dining fills a bodily need and provides a necessary interruption to war. In historical times, the conditions of soldiers were less agreeable. On short campaigns, Athenian hoplites were required to bring their own provisions with them, whereas rowers were fed on a sparse diet of barley meal, onions, and cheese. At home, the whole family probably dined together. The most lavish dining parties were the symposia, which are discussed later in this chapter.

The basic diet was both frugal and, by our standards, monotonous. The Athenians ate two main meals a day—a light lunch, known as *ariston,* followed by dinner, known as *deipnon,* which was their main meal. The poor subsisted mainly on bread, soup, porridge, salt fish, eggs, and green vegetables. Well-to-do Greeks ate much more refined meals, though they were never as extravagant or as indulgent as the Romans. A sizeable percentage of the population would have experienced food shortage during their lifetime, whether as a result of war or crop failure. In Athens, corn buyers known as *sitônai* were appointed in times of crisis with the responsibility of purchasing and distributing corn, either free or heavily subsidized. Even so, catastrophic failure in cereal production over extensive areas of the eastern Mediterranean was exceptional, and we know of only once instance—in 338 B.C.E.—before the Common Era. The greatest threat to a city's food supply came about when it was under siege. Plutarch (*Life of Sulla* 13.3) tells us that, when the Roman general Sulla was besieging Athens in 87/6 B.C.E., the inhabitants subsisted in part on shoe leather and leather oil flasks.

In summer, meals were prepared in the open over a wood fire or charcoal grill, as is the case today in many rural parts of Greece. In winter, cooking was done inside the house on a portable brazier, which also provided the only source of heating. Boiling and roasting were the most common ways of cooking, but much food was served raw. Because chimneys were unknown, the

A FEMALE BAKER TAKES BREAD FROM AN OVEN. *Terra-cotta, early fifth century B.C.E.*

only way that the smoke could escape was through a hole in the roof. For this reason, charcoal was the preferred source of fuel, because it creates far less smoke than wood. Almost all cooking utensils were made of unglazed or partly glazed clay. The most common were kettles, saucepans on stands, shallow frying pans, casseroles, and grills. Although such mundane objects are rarely put on display in museums, they often have as much, if not more, to tell us about daily life in ancient Greece as the most beautiful painted pottery.

The well-to-do ate reclining on couches, leaning on an elbow and using their free hand to take food from a small table in front of them. This had important consequences for the preparation of food, which had to be served in small pieces. Although knives and possibly spoons were commonplace, forks were unknown. Most Greeks, however, probably made do with their fingers. A piece of flat bread would also have conveniently served as a kind of spoon. From the end of the fifth century B.C.E., the Greeks began to develop an interest in culinary art. The lead in this development was taken by Sicily, a region famed for its luxury, where a number of cookbooks were produced. *Professors at Dinner,* written by Athenaios, a Greek from Egypt, around 200 C.E., culls numerous extracts from these books and provides a vast storehouse of information on the subject of dining. As in the modern world, the most celebrated chefs tended to be men.

Cereals

Homer characterizes the human race as "bread-eating," and bread remained the basis of the Greek diet throughout antiquity. It has been estimated that cereals provided 70 percent of the needed daily caloric intake. The grain was separated from the chaff in a shallow mortar by pushing a flat stone back and forth across the millstone. The mortar was either made of baked clay or improvised from a hollowed-out tree trunk. There were two kinds of bread: *maza,* made from barley flour, and *artos,* a white bread made from wheat. Because barley was more plentiful than wheat, *artos* was something of a luxury, largely confined to the wealthy or served to the populace at festivals. The Greeks ate bread with honey, cheese, and olive oil. They also cooked it in a porridge or broth. The word *opson* described any type of food that was eaten with bread or other cereal.

Meat and Fish

Pigs, sheep, goats, and chickens provided most of the meat that was consumed by the Greeks. Large livestock, including cows and oxen, were in short supply, particularly in Attica. In general, however, meat was a rarity, particularly for those living in the city. Although most Greeks ate a simple casserole of game or poultry on a fairly regular basis, the only occasion when they would have tasted roasted meat was on feast days. The climax to every religious festival was the ritual slaughter of a large number of animals. This may be another reason why meat was rarely served in the home—because it was so closely associated with ritual. Although the ostensible purpose of a sacrifice was to honor the gods, the Greeks gave the least edible parts—the thigh pieces—to the gods. The rest they devoured themselves. All those who attended a sacrifice received a portion of meat, the choicest parts of which were reserved for the priests.

Fish, both fresh and dried and salted, seems to have been regarded as more of a delicacy than meat, judging by the fact that it is more frequently mentioned in cookery than meat. Some of the best fish, including mackerel, sturgeon, tuna, sea bream, and mullet, was imported from the Black Sea region. In Athens, a particularly common seafood was the anchovy or sardine, which was harvested close to the Attic coast. Archestratos of Gela, a mid-fourth-century B.C.E. poet who had a reputation for being a master cook, speaks of it as follows:

> Value all small fry as shit apart from the Athenian variety. I'm referring to
> sprats, which the Ionians call foam. Get hold of it fresh from the sacred
> arms of Phaleron's beautiful bay [off the south coast of Attica]. What you
> find in wave-girt Rhodes is also good, if it happens to be local. If you'd care
> to taste it, you should also buy leafy sea anemones. Mix this in and bake it
> all in a pan, grinding the fragrant flowers of the greens in olive oil. (quoted
> in Athenaios, *Professors at Dinner* 285b-c)

A favorite delicacy was eels from Lake Kopaïs in Boiotia. Aristophanes facetiously suggests that one of the greatest hardships that the Athenians had to face during the Peloponnesian War was the lack of Kopaïc eels, because the Boiotians had sided with the enemy. The Boiotians accorded them a quasi-religious status, as we learn from a Hellenistic historian named Agatharkides:

> The Boiotians sacrifice to the gods Kopaïc eels of extraordinary size,
> putting garlands on them, and praying over them, and casting barley seeds
> upon them, just as they do with other sacrificial victims. When a foreigner
> expressed amazement at the custom, a Boiotian replied that he had only
> one explanation for it, that one should observe ancestral customs. It wasn't
> his business to justify such things to other people. (quoted in Athenaios,
> *Professors at Dinner* 297d)

Vegetables, Fruit, and Other Foodstuffs

Popular vegetables included cabbages, asparagus, carrots, radishes, cucumbers, pumpkins, chicory, celery, and artichokes. Onions, garlic, and olives were also eaten in large quantities and provided the staple diet for those serving in the army and navy. Legumes, though high in protein, do not appear to have been regarded as an important foodstuff. Fruits included grapes, figs, apples, pears, and dates.

Nuts were generally harvested wild. Almonds, walnuts, hazelnuts, and chestnuts were widely distributed throughout Greece.

Olive oil, used in the preparation of many meals, was the principal source of fat. It also served in religious rituals and was applied to the body after exercise. The importance of olives for the Athenian economy is indicated by the fact that the goddess Athene caused an olive tree to spring up miraculously on the Acropolis when she was competing with Poseidon for the guardianship of the land. The use of butter was regarded as a mark of the barbarian. Cheese, which was mainly produced from the milk of sheep and goats, did not figure prominently in the Greek diet. Salt was used both as a preservative and as a condiment. Silphium, sage, and rosemary also were used as condiments. In place of sugar, which was unknown, the Greeks used honey and dried figs. The honey that came from Mount Hymettos in Attica was particularly prized in antiquity, just as it is today. (Beehive pots were discovered in the Vari house.) Notable absentees from the Greek diet included potatoes, rice, tomatoes, citrus fruits, and bananas.

Wine

The favorite Greek drink was wine, which was almost invariably served diluted and often artificially sweetened. The Greeks preferred to drink in quantity only after they had finished eating. The islands of Chios, Lesbos, Rhodes, and Samos had the reputation for producing the best wine. Wine was transported in clay storage jars called amphorae (see p. 230). The handles of these amphorae were stamped with seals bearing the name of the merchant and that of the city in which the wine was produced, rather like the label on a modern bottle of wine. Beer was associated exclusively with barbarians. Milk, though used in cooking, was not a common beverage. It is thus a sign of savagery in *The Odyssey* that the Cyclops Polyphemos drinks goat's milk and has never tasted wine.

DRINKING PARTIES

When the Greeks wanted to relax at the end of the day, the choices available to them were extremely limited. Institutions such as the cinema, theater, concert hall, jazz club, and dance hall had no ancient equivalent. As far as we know, no enterprising individual ever had the bright idea of charging admission to a place of public entertainment. There does not seem to have been anything comparable to the local pub or coffee bar. Confronted with such a barren landscape—as we at least would see it—the Greeks had no alternative but to entertain themselves. This they did foremost through the *symposium,* a word which means literally "drinking together." A symposium was not, however, the ancient equivalent to a few guys getting together to shoot the breeze and down a few drinks. On the contrary, it was a highly ritualized institution with its own precise and time-hallowed rules, even though some symposia, judging from illustrations found on vases, resulted in a drunken orgy.

Strictly speaking, symposium refers to the communal drinking of wine that took place at the conclusion of a dinner. Only after the tables containing food had been cleared away, garlands of flowers distributed, libations performed, and a hymn sung was it permitted to begin drinking. Symposiasts did not sit on chairs but reclined on couches, a custom that the Greeks probably learned from the Near East around the turn of the seventh century B.C.E. Although a symposium served a variety of purposes, for definition, we can hardly do better than quote Plutarch, a Greek writer living in the Roman era, who described it as "a passing of time over wine, which, guided by gracious behavior, ends in friendship" (*Moral Precepts* 621c).

Much of the evidence for symposia derives from images found on pots that were specifically designed for this purpose. In fact, scenes depicting the symposium outnumber any others relating to daily life—hardly surprisingly in view of the facts that a tastefully decorated set of drinking cups, *hydriai* (water jugs), *oinochoai* (wine pourers), and *kraters* (mixing bowls) was de rigueur in any well-appointed Greek house and that it was customary for scenes on vases to complement the function of the vase.

Agathon's Symposium

The most famous drinking party of all time was held at the house of a young tragic poet named Agathon in 416 B.C.E. The pretext for the party was a celebration in honor of Agathon, who had just won first prize in a dramatic festival held earlier in the day. Because some of the company were suffering from hangovers, they elected to consume only a modest amount of wine. They also decided to dispense with the services of a flute girl whom Agathon had hired for the evening. Instead, they entertained themselves by delivering encomia in praise of Eros, the offspring of Aphrodite, goddess of love. The last to speak was Sokrates. Just when he reached the end of his delivery, Alkibiades burst into the room. He was already somewhat the worse for drink and tried to make the other guests tipsy by forcing them to consume large quantities of wine. Eventually he settled down and agreed to follow the procedure adopted by the company by delivering a speech in praise of Sokrates. The party continued until dawn, by which time everyone had fallen

THE SYMPOSIUM OF PLATO. *Anselm Feuerbach, 1869. Oil on canvas. Feuerbach depicts the scene from Plato's* Symposium *in which a drunken Alkibiades, along with a crowd of revelers, enters the house of the poet Agathon. Note that the true focus of the painting is Socrates, on the far right, as he turns away from the loud scene. The two halves of the composition demonstrate the tension between fleshly pleasure and philosophical thought. The host, wearing a laurel wreath, stands in the center and uncertainly unites the two.*

asleep with the exception of Sokrates and Aristophanes, who were still conversing on the subject of poetry. Sokrates alone was completely unaffected by the alcohol that he had consumed, and around dawn, he rose, departed, took a bath, and went about his daily business.

Agathon's symposium is described by Plato in a work entitled *Symposium,* arguably his most charming dialogue. The image it conveys, however—one of learned gentlemen delivering carefully crafted speeches over a bowl of wine—can hardly be taken as typical of Athenian practice. Presented with the choice of either producing an impromptu encomium or listening to a flute girl, the majority of Athenians would have undoubtedly opted for the latter. Nor can there have been many drinkers who had the ability to conduct an elevated discourse when flushed with wine.

As we know from references in literature, any excuse could be used to party in ancient Greece: birth, marriage, or death, the departure or arrival of a loved one from abroad, a feast day, a birthday, or merely a change in the seasons. Probably in most cases, however, no pretext was required. Given the lack of alternative entertainment, we might suppose that drinking parties were an everyday occurrence. We do not know, however, whether they were exclusive to aristocratic society or whether poorer Athenians also held symposia.

Guests

It was customary for the host to inscribe the names of his guests on a wax tablet, together with the day and hour appointed for the symposium, and then hand the tablet to a slave who would make the rounds of the guests' houses. The usual hour for convening was the ninth. Generally, the ideal number of guests was nine, including the host. In Athens in the fourth century B.C.E., however, symposia grew so large that it became necessary to appoint a commission to ensure that the number of guests did not exceed the legal limit. Because wives and daughters were not permitted to attend symposia, the only women present were hired companions known as *hetairai,* who were discussed earlier (see p. 84).

Rooms Reserved for Drinking

The growing importance of the symposium as an institution from the fourth century B.C.E. onward was such that well-appointed houses frequently possessed a special room for drinking known as an *andrôn* (see p. 138). At Olynthos, such rooms were often located at the front of the house, next to the street. An *andrôn* can be identified in the archaeological record by its off-center doorway, which enabled the room to accommodate couches that were arranged alongside one another and set against the walls. The basic *andrôn* held four couches, though some were considerably larger. The couches were made of either wood or stone. In front of each couch was placed a three-legged table, on which food was laid out and the drinkers placed their cups. As private houses became more elegant, *andrônes* acquired floors adorned with mosaics and walls hung with tapestries.

Remembering the Gods

The taking of wine was a religious act, somewhat akin to the taking of communion by Christians. This religious aspect is prominent in descriptions of the origin of wine. In a late epic entitled the *Dionysiaka,* Nonnos (*fl.* 450–70 C.E.) tells us that a vine first shot up from the corpse of a youth named Ampelos (the name means vine), the favorite of Dionysos, as the god was lamenting the death of his beloved. While Dionysos drank the fruit of the vine, which was infused with all the beauty and grace of the dead youth, he gradually forgot his sorrow. The myth thus explains why wine has the power to enable humans to forget their cares.

Every stage of the symposium was marked by a traditional religious observance. Before being mixed with water, a few drops of wine were drunk in honor of the *agathos daimôn* or "good spirit." In a fragment from a lost work, Theophrastos states that the purpose of this toast was "to serve as a reminder, through a mere taste, of the strength of the god's generous gift." He continues, "Having bowed three times, they take it from the table, as though supplicating the god that they may do nothing indecent or have too strong a desire for the wine." This toast was followed by three libations, to Zeus Olympios and the other Olympian gods, to the heroes, and to Zeus Soter (Savior). While these libations were being performed, a hymn was sung to the gods. Before the party broke up, a triple paean or hymn was sung to Apollo. This was followed by a hymn to Hygieia, the personification of health, which began thus: "Hygieia, most revered of the blessed gods, with thee may I dwell for the rest of my life and may you be a gracious inmate of my house." A purificatory rite was performed both before the symposium began and at its close. So ingrained was the sense of religious occasion that Hesiod, as he sits alone under his shady rock in the heat of summer, his belly filled with good food, does not omit to perform a libation before drinking a cup of wine (*Works and Days* 592ff.).

The Master of Drinking

There were strict rules to which all symposiasts were required to adhere to ensure that the drinking did not get out of hand. Several Greek writers even compiled books of symposiastic laws, though none has survived. The philosopher Theophrastos (ca. 372–288 B.C.E.), however, provides us with a number of instances of bad form. It was, he tells us, the mark of an uneducated lout to drop his cup while the rest of the company was at prayer and burst out laughing, to tap or whistle in accompaniment to the flute girl, or to spit across the table at the wine pourer.

The enforcement of the rules was in the hands of the *symposiarch,* or master of drinking. The ideal symposiarch, according to Plutarch, had to be "the quintessence of conviviality," neither inclined to drunkenness nor averse to drinking. He had to be aware how each of his fellow symposiasts was affected by wine in order to determine what was conducive to the promotion of good cheer. He needed to be cordial and affable.

Election to this office was made on the throw of dice, which meant that it generally fell to one of the guests. The symposiarch had the authority to inflict a penalty on any drinker who infringed the rules. In exceptional circumstances, he could even order a guest to depart. Because the Greeks drank diluted wine, his inaugural duty was to determine the proportion of parts of wine to water—an important decision that would affect the tone of the whole evening. In addition, he decreed how many cups should be drunk, since only on rare occasions, as at Agathon's symposium, were symposiasts permitted to drink as much or as little as they wished. The purpose behind this rule was to ensure that everyone attained approximately the same degree of inebriation. Finally, the symposiarch proposed the entertainment and fixed penalties for those who failed to distinguish themselves in the games and competitions.

Despite these precautions, however, much no doubt happened that was not in accordance with the rules. A popular Greek saying, "I hate a drinker with a good memory," suggests that whatever was said or done by a symposiast when under the influence of alcohol was not to be held against him when he sobered up. What happened in Vegas, in other words, was expected to stay in Vegas.

Serving the Wine

For everyday use, the Greeks drank out of undecorated glazed mugs. The well-to-do, however, possessed a special set of drinking cups and wine containers, which they reserved for use at a symposium. Basic drinking equipment included a dozen or so *kylikes* or drinking mugs, a *kratêr* or mixing bowl, a *psychtêr* or wine cooler, an *oinochoê* or jug for pouring wine, and a *hydria* or jug for pouring water. The pottery was frequently decorated with figured scenes, often of very refined artisanship. As noted, these scenes provide a major source of information about conduct at these gatherings. Although the proportion of wine to water varied from symposium to symposium, there was usually a preponderance of water. Homer praises a much-diluted blend, and Hesiod went so far as to recommend three parts of water to one part of wine.

Games

One of the most popular symposiastic entertainments was the capping game. The rules were as follows: either the first player recited a well-known line from poetry and the second had to cap it by quoting the verse that followed, or, alternatively, the first player recited a whole passage of poetry and the next had to deliver a similar passage from a different poet on the same theme. Other variants are also known, such as having to quote a line of poetry that begins with the same letter as ended the line of the one previously quoted.

The Greek equivalent to darts was called *kottabos.* A piece of wood or bronze was fixed into a depression in the floor or attached to some other means of support and a crossbeam was placed on top with a vessel balanced at each end. Under each vessel stood a pan of water with an object fixed upright in the center. Players were required to flick a drop of wine from their cups into one of the vessels. The object was to cause the vessel to topple off and strike the object in the center of the pan. The winner was the one who spilled the least wine and made the most noise. Another game was to flick wine into nutshells that were floating in a *kratêr* or mixing bowl filled with water so as to make them sink.

YOUNG MAN PLAYING KOTTABOS. *Tondo from an Attic red-figure* kylikes *ca. 480–460 B.C.E.*

Dancing was also popular. One of the most famous symposiastic dances was the *kordax,* which, according to Theophrastos (*Characters* 6.3), a man would be out of senses to dance when sober. Unfortunately, we have no description of the *kordax,* though we do of other energetic dances that it probably resembled. At the end of Aristophanes' *Wasps,* the Chorus encourages the elderly Philokleon thus, "Whirl around, punch yourself in the belly, hurl your leg skyhigh, become a spinning top!" (line 1529f.).

Hired Entertainers

In Plato's *Protagoras,* Sokrates makes the following haughty pronouncement:

> Where the drinkers are men of breeding and culture, you won't see flute
> girls or dancing girls girls playing the harp. They are quite capable of being
> in one another's company without such frivolity and foolery, using their
> own voices and each taking his turn to speak or listen in sober fashion, even
> if they drink a lot. (347d)

It is questionable, however, whether Sokrates was quite such a killjoy as Plato suggests. Xenophon, who, like Plato, was a personal friend of Sokrates and also wrote a dialogue entitled *Symposium,* paints a strikingly different picture of the great philosopher in his cups. In it we encounter a Sokrates who delighted in the acrobatics of the hired entertainers and who even deigned to make a spectacle of himself by attempting to emulate their agile movements. Whatever the truth about Sokrates' liking for live entertainment, hired entertainers were in great demand among the drinking fraternity as a whole. They included flute girls, dancing girls (the ancient equivalent of lap dancers perhaps), jugglers, tumblers, and buffoons.

One of the earliest laws regulating hours of labor in the Greek world refers to the hire of flute girls according to three shifts: from dawn until noon, from noon until nightfall, and from nightfall until dawn. This law, passed in Kolophon (western Turkey), was intended to protect

A FLUTE GIRL PLAYS HER INSTRUMENT *for a banqueter in this detail from an Attic red-figure cup, ca. 490 B.C.E.*

professional entertainers against the excessively lengthy symposia to which the inhabitants of that city were addicted. Flute girls were also subject to price control. The Aristotelian *Constitution of Athens* informs us that, in fourth-century B.C.E. Athens, they were forbidden by law to charge more than two drachmas for their services (50.2).

The Political Dimension

The fact that a number of drinking songs were politically inspired suggests that many symposia were convened by those of the same political leanings. The most famous of these songs celebrated the murder of Hipparchos, the brother of the Athenian tyrant Hippias, in 514 B.C.E. The perpetrators of this deed were two young men named Harmodios and Aristogeiton (see p. 13), and a song in their honor by an anonymous author became a kind of Athenian national anthem.

> I shall carry my sword hidden in a branch of myrtle like Harmodios and Aristogeiton when they slew the tyrants and established Athenian democracy. Dearest Harmodios, you are not dead, but they say you live in the Isles of the Blest, where swift-footed Achilles lives and godlike Diomedes, the son of Tydeus.
>
> I shall carry my sword hidden in a branch of myrtle like Harmodios and Aristogeiton, when they slew the tyrant Hipparchos at the festival of Athene. Your fame shall live on the earth for ever, dearest Harmodios and Aristogeiton, since you slew the tyrant and established Athenian democracy.

Drunken and Rowdy Behavior

At the conclusion of a symposium, or when moving from one symposium to another, it was customary for drinkers to *kômazein,* or to roam about the streets in a gang. It was just such a gang of *kômastai,* headed by Alkibiades, that crashed Agathon's party. "No sooner had they sat down than the whole place was in an uproar," Plato writes in the *Symposium.* "Order went out of the window and they compelled everyone to drink huge quantities of wine." Assaults by drunken *kômastai* were not uncommon. The myth of the attempted

abduction of Lapith women by the centaurs, wild creatures half human and half horse whose bestial natures got the better of them under the influence of alcohol, is the archetypal drinking party gone wrong. It became a stock joke that the worst behaved guests at a symposium were the philosophers. In another work entitled the *Symposium,* written by the second-century C.E. satirist Lukian, a philosopher of the Cynic school called Alkidamas is the chief instigator of a bloody rumpus that leads to a broken head, smashed jaw, gouged-out eye, and several broken teeth. Comic writers, as was their wont, tended to see the more humorous side of drunkenness. Euboulos, in a fragment from a lost play, describes its effects as follows:

> The first cup is to health, the second to love and pleasure, the third to sleep, the fourth to violence, the fifth to uproar, the sixth to drunken revel, the seventh to black eyes, the eighth to the summoner, the ninth to bile, and the tenth to madness and throwing chairs around.

The symptoms of drunkenness were of scientific interest to Aristotle, who wrote a lost treatise on the subject containing the following observation:

> Under the influence of all other alcoholic beverages, people who become drunk fall in all directions, namely to the left, to the right, on their faces, and on their backs. But those who drink barley wine only fall on their backs and lie supine.

Conclusions

In Plato's *Laws,* an Athenian who claims to have made the symposium the subject of inquiry observes:

I have never yet seen or heard of one that was properly conducted from beginning to end. Here and there a few minor details may not have been amiss, but by and large I have found them badly conducted. (639e)

The *Laws* was Plato's last work, written a few years before his death, and this statement is no doubt a reflection of the bitterness of his old age. It has to be viewed in connection with his own disenchantment with the society around him. Apart from their social importance, symposia played a key role in the educational, cultural, and political life of the Greeks.

EDUCATION

Boys

Greek education was inevitably much more informal than its modern equivalent. Prior to the fifth century B.C.E., education was mainly in the hands of private tutors, which meant that only the wealthy could afford it. Most schools were extremely small, accommodating perhaps no more than about ten or fifteen pupils, although some were considerably larger. Herodotos (6.27) describes a school on the island of Chios that had 120 pupils. In 494 B.C.E., the roof caved in while the boys were learning their letters; tragically, only one boy survived. Even so, it is highly probable that most children were home-schooled. Not until the Hellenistic Period was a system of universal public education established in some communities for all boys, thanks to foundations that funded teachers' salaries. They include the city of Teos, which lies to the north of Ephesus, just off the Turkish coast, and the island of Rhodes. The exception to the rule was the Spartan state, which imposed a uniform system on both boys and girls that may well have been in effect long before the Classical era.

Athenian boys began their schooling around the age of seven. They continued as long as their parents could afford to pay their fees—or as long as the parents did not require their sons to be economically productive. We know very little about Athenian teachers, but they seem to have had little status. There is no record of the fees that were charged. and there is no knowing how widespread education was. Because democratic Athens required its citizens to be at least functionally literate, however, very few boys were completely unlettered. Aristophanes makes it clear in *Knights* (188f.) that even an ignorant lout such as a sausage seller knew how to read and write. As the Sophist Protagoras points out in Plato's dialogue of that name, it was a general rule that "the sons of the most wealthy went to school earliest and left latest" (326c).

Basic Athenian education consisted of reading and writing, physical training, and music. Reading and writing were taught by the *grammatistês,* which roughly translates as "teacher of letters." Pupils practiced their letters on waxed tablets using a pen called a *stylos.* Broken shards of pottery called *ostraka* served as scrap paper. The *grammatistês* also provided a grounding in literature by requiring pupils to learn passages from epic, lyric, and dramatic poetry. Memorization was a key element in the educational process. Nikeratos, who figures in Xenophon's *Symposium,* claims that his father made him learn by heart the whole of *The Iliad* and *The Odyssey*—some 27,000 lines in all (3.5). The poems of Homer were, in fact, the most widely read literature throughout Greek antiquity, as we know from the fact that more papyri have survived containing scraps of his poetry than of any other literary figure. Learning by rote sometimes paid off in later life. The Athenians who were taken prisoner by the Syracusans after the disaster of the Sicilian expedition were removed from the stone quarries and given domestic work if they were able to recite passages of Euripides.

The most popular musical instrument was the lyre or *kithara,* which was taught by a musician known as a *kitharistês.* This was regarded as such an important part of education that, in Aristophanes' *Wasps,* the hero Bdelykleon seeks to excuse a dog's thievery on the grounds that "he never learnt the lyre" (line 959). It was commonly played at symposia, much as a guitar might be played at a party today. Physical education, which took place under the instruction of a teacher known as a *paidotribês,* is discussed later. Only a few children learned how to draw. Little attention seems to have been given to mathematics.

Although the Athenian state did not require children to be educated and did not involve itself in the school curriculum, it sought to uphold certain values. In Athens, it was essentially the father's responsibility to ensure that his offspring

A *PAIDAGÔGOI with his young master. Terra-cotta, third-century B.C.E.*

received a proper upbringing. If he failed to do so, according to a law ascribed to Solon, the child was freed from the obligation of supporting his father in old age. The orator Aischines cites an Athenian law that forbade parents to send their children out of the home before daybreak and insisted that they be collected before sunset. With the exception of slaves called *paidagôgoi* (literally "child guides," from which the word *pedagogy* comes), who accompanied their young masters to school and sat behind them in the classroom, no adult was allowed to enter the school. If any did, it was a capital offense (*Against Timarchos* 9–12). Class size was prescribed by law. Publicly sponsored competitions sought to encourage high standards of accomplishment. At the festival known as the Apatouria, for instance, prizes were given to boys for recitation. Finally, no one seems to have raised any objections to corporal punishment, and it is very likely that it was commonly applied.

Girls

The education of Athenian girls was probably minimal. The majority received merely a basic training in how to run the household, generally from their mothers. Girls may even have been actively discouraged from becoming literate in order to keep them "unspoiled." A fragment from a lost play by Menander states axiomatically, "He who teaches his wife how to read and write does no good. He's giving additional poison to a horrible snake." Although some women were able to play a musical instrument, as we see from depictions in Greek art, few are likely to have been sufficiently well informed to express an opinion about the political issues of the day. Xenophon's fictional Ischomachos, therefore, probably speaks for a number of middle-class Athenians when he declares,

When I married my wife, she was not yet fifteen and had been so carefully
supervised that she had no experience of life whatsoever, seeing, hearing,
and saying very little. A man should be content, don't you think, if his
wife comes to him knowing only how to take wool and make clothes
and supervise the distribution of spinning among slaves. (*Household
Management* 7.5–6)

Even so, we should not discount the possibility that Ischomachos is being
portrayed as somewhat out of touch with reality. Athenian girls may not have
been quite so submissive as is sometimes assumed.

Elsewhere in the Greek world girls received little education, though there
may have been a few exceptions. The poetess Sappho, for instance, is thought to
have been associated with a school for young women that flourished on the island
of Lesbos in the second half of the seventh century B.C.E. The one society where
girls received some education at state expense was Sparta (see p. 128).

Higher Education

What we might describe as higher or tertiary education began for Athenian
youths around the age of sixteen. The principal subjects taught were rhetoric
and philosophy. The ability to speak in public was not only the hallmark of
a well-educated gentleman but also a vital attribute for anyone who wished
to make a mark for himself in a democratic society, whether in the political
assembly or in the law courts or in more informal contexts such as the
symposium. Rhetoric was first taught by the Sophists around the middle of the
fifth century B.C.E., although its importance is already evident in Homer, where
the ability to be persuasive in public is a prized asset among leading aristocrats.
The Sophists were roundly condemned by Sokrates, who regarded their
training as antithetical to the pursuit of philosophy. He did so in part because
they took a relativist stance on morality, whereas he and his pupil Plato were
idealist philosophers who believed that virtue was nonnegotiable, so to speak.
Similarly, the comic dramatist Aristophanes mocks Sophists in his play the
Clouds (first produced 423 B.C.E.), mischievously transforming Sokrates into

a quintessential Sophist who teaches his pupils to make the worse case appear the better without any regard for the truth. The hostility between practitioners of rhetoric and philosophy would endure almost throughout antiquity. Plato was particularly dismissive of Sophists in the *Gorgias,* which takes its name from one of its most famous and successful practitioners. Incidentally, Gorgias was one of the highest paid Sophists. He became so wealthy that he erected a gold statue of himself at Delphi—the first gold statue to be erected to a human in Greece—testimony to the high regard in which men of his profession were generally held, as well as to the enormous fees they commanded.

It is unlikely, therefore, that the criticisms of Sokrates and Plato had much impact on public sentiment, though it may well have been the case that many Athenians would have instinctively concurred with the characterization of Sophists as money-grubbing charlatans, especially those who could not afford their services. In the fourth century B.C.E., schools of rhetoric began to emerge in the Greek-speaking world, including one in Athens run by an orator named Isocrates, indicating that the discipline had achieved respectability. Aristotle also instructed his pupils in rhetoric as well as in philosophy, and he wrote a highly influential treatise on the subject. When the Greek states lost their independence, rhetoric ceased to have any political importance, but it still remained the centerpiece of higher education.

As well as hosting the Sophists, itinerant teachers who resided only temporarily in the city, Athens was also home to the four principal philosophical schools. The first two to establish themselves were Plato's Academy and Aristotle's Lyceum. Athens remained a leading center of philosophy into the Hellenistic Period and beyond and was the birthplace of both Epicureanism and Stoicism. Epicureanism was named after Epikouros, an Athenian who flourished around 300 B.C.E. Those who espoused his doctrine lived in seclusion in a complex called The Garden and maintained a simple style of living. They included women and slaves among their adherents. Very likely Epikouros also lectured to well-born Athenians, who, though they were interested in his philosophical theories, did not choose to dedicate themselves to a life of withdrawal.

Stoicism, which was founded by Zenon, a Phoenician merchant from Kition in Cyprus around 275 B.C.E., took its name from the Stoa Poikile or Painted Stoa, a colonnaded building in the northwest corner of the Agora in Athens, where the followers of this movement habitually assembled. (The building was discovered in 1981. It was called the Painted Stoa because of its spectacular wall paintings on wooden panels that were displayed inside). As in the case of Epicureanism, it is likely that well-born Athenians attended lectures on Stoicism, perhaps in a more formal venue, though we do not know of any designated space.

Only a very small percentage of Athenians would have had the means and the disposition to provide their sons with any form of higher education. One of the interlocutors in Plato's *Laches* (179a) states that most Athenian parents "allow their sons to do exactly what they like once they become lads," and this is likely to be a fairly accurate generalization.

Apprenticeship

Herodotos (6.60) informs us that, in Sparta, some trades and professions were exclusive to certain families, including those of herald, flute player, and cook. In Athens, too, many skills and professions were handed down from father to son, due partly to the law requiring an Athenian father to teach his son a skill if he expected to be supported by him in old age. For instance, the Athenian sculptor Praxiteles was the son of a sculptor, and both his sons and grandson were sculptors as well. Other professional skills, including the writing of dramatic poetry, were also handed down over several generations. Overall, however, it is likely that Athenian youths were freer in their career choices than their Spartan counterparts, given the less constricted tenor of Athenian society.

HEALTH AND SICKNESS

Ancient diseases are notoriously difficult to identify, even when paleopathologists have skeletal evidence to work with. Poor sanitation, the lack of a hygienic water supply, and malnutrition were probably the major sources of illness that caused death.

A particularly interesting source of information for the treatment of disease is a Hippocratic work called Epidemics. *It contains forty-two case studies of individuals, twenty-five of which resulted in the patient's death. In light of the very limited understanding of how epidemics spread, this is hardly surprising. The writer tells us, for instance, that on the island of Thasos one year (1.19):*

Most of those who fell sick and died were youths, young men, those in the prime of life, the smooth-skinned, those of fair complexion, persons with either straight hair or black hair, those with black eyes, persons who lived dissolutely and carelessly, those with either a thin voice or a rough voice, lispers, and those given to sensual indulgence. Very many women of this type (i.e., given to sensual indulgence?) also perished.

The passage also indicates how vulnerability to disease was ascribed to a wide variety of largely, if not wholly irrelevant factors, including gender, age, skin color, tone of voice, type of hair, and lifestyle.

Some of the most prevalent diseases in the ancient world are thought to have been gastroenteritis, dysentery, diarrhea, beriberi, rickets, scurvy, malaria, typhoid, pneumonia, and tuberculosis. There is evidence that, in some regions, arteriosclerosis affected as much as 80 percent of the population. We also hear of diphtheria, chickenpox, mumps, and whooping cough, but there is no evidence for either cholera or measles. Leprosy did not reach Greece until the Hellenistic Period. Cancer was known, with breast cancer, according to Galen, a physician of the second century C.E., being particularly common. Given the extremely high incidence of infant mortality, childhood diseases, including rickets and anemia, must have been widespread. Some sexually transmitted diseases were also known, though not syphilis or gonorrhea. Because most individual communities were fairly self-contained, epidemics did not often spread outside their borders.

Although diagnosis was of a high quality, there was very little understanding about how diseases were transmitted because there was no notion of germs. Drugs, surgery, purges, and bleeding were the most common forms of treatment. It is a chilling reflection that most people had to deal with physical pain on a level and with a frequency and intensity that is virtually inconceivable in the West today. It is also a fact that only when they were severely ill would most Greeks have had the luxury of taking to their beds; for the most part they would have had to grit their teeth and get on with it.

The Greeks attributed the rise of scientific medicine to the influence of Hippokrates of Kos, a shadowy figure about whom nothing is known for certain, although many early medical writings were ascribed to him. Among them is a book entitled *Aphorisms,* which begins with the statement, "Life is short. Art is long. Opportunity is brief. Experiment is dangerous. Judgement is difficult." It serves as a fitting comment about the risks attendant upon medical intervention throughout antiquity. Like other aspects of Greek life, however, medicine never wholly divorced itself from its religious roots. In fact, the growth of the cult of the healing god Asklepios at the beginning of the fifth century B.C.E. exactly parallels the birth of the tradition of scientific medical inquiry. Sickness and its cure were henceforth identified as areas of both professional and divine concern.

Temple Medicine

From the fifth century B.C.E. onward, sanctuaries of the healing god Asklepios, such as that of Epidauros in the northeast Peloponnese, functioned as both religious and medical centers. This is demonstrated by the fact that surgical instruments and votive offerings in the form of parts of the body are commonly found there, the latter in the hope of securing the god's intervention on behalf of the body part represented. Physicians, no less than their patients, would have regarded medical expertise as an art, which was, at root, a gift of the god. The fact that Hippocratic physicians took their oath in the name of Asklepios and other healing deities affords further proof of the complementarity of the two approaches. As late as the second century C.E., Galen claimed that he took up medicine because the god appeared to him in a dream and urged upon him a medical career when his father was sick.

The healing that was practiced at the sanctuaries of Asklepios is likely to have been a potent mixture of medicine, autosuggestion, faith healing, and perceived divine intervention. At night, the sick slept within the temple precincts waiting for a vision from the god to reveal the source of their cure (a process often referred to as incubation), while by day perhaps they entrusted their aches and pains to human physicians. Reports of miraculous cures (known as *iamata)* are preserved on tablets that were erected in the sanctuary, their purpose being to propagate the report of the god's miraculous powers to the Greek world at large and thus, too, *pour encourager les autres.* Forty-four cures are recorded at Epidauros, but the original number is thought to have been in the hundreds. A feature of some of the narratives is the emphasis upon the incredulity that preceded the cure, as we see in the following example from an inscription:

> A man came to the god as a suppliant who was so blind in one eye that all
> he had was an eyebrow with an empty eye socket. Some of the people in the
> temple laughed at him for his stupidity in thinking that he would be able to
> see when the eye socket was empty and contained nothing but a depression.
> When the man slept, however, a vision appeared to him. The god was seen
> to be preparing some medicine. He then opened the man's eyes and poured
> it over them. When day came, he could see with both eyes and departed.

The cures recorded include blindness, dumbness, paralysis, lameness, overextended pregnancies, infertility, headaches, and even baldness. Not surprisingly, we do not hear of Asklepios performing exorcisms or casting out devils, because these did not trouble the classical imagination. Nor did his expertise extend to the treatment of the mentally deranged. Incredible though many of the cures may seem to us, the part played by religious faith in the healing process should not be discounted. A 1995 study carried out at the Dartmouth-Hitchcock Medical Center determined that those with religious faith were more than three times as likely to survive heart surgery than those without faith.

Although relations between the advocates of faith healing and scientific medicine seem to have been essentially benign, some rivalry did nonetheless exist. The author of the celebrated Hippocratic treatise entitled *On the Sacred Disease* (2–5), for instance, vehemently opposed the prevailing orthodoxy that epilepsy was an affliction caused by the gods. Castigating "witch doctors, faith-healers, quacks, and charlatans" for seeking to alleviate the symptoms "by prescribing purifications and incantations along with abstinence from baths," he boldly asserted that epilepsy "is not more divine than any other disease." He concludes with the claim that any skilled practitioner could cure the disease "provided that he could distinguish the right moment for the application of the remedies." Similarly, the author of another Hippocratic work entitled *On the Diseases of Virgins* declared that menstrual irregularities in young girls could best be cured not by making sacrifices to the virgin goddess Artemis but by having intercourse—or rather (since it amounted to the same thing) by getting married.

Physicians

Basic first aid was practiced on the Greek battlefield from earliest times. Homer tells us that the Greek army at Troy relied on the services of two physician brothers named Machaon and Podaleirios, sons of Asklepios, who came from Thessaly, the original home of the healing god before he was elevated to godhead. Machaon extracted an arrow from Menelaos's midriff, sucked the blood from his wound, and then applied "healing medicines that Chiron [a centaur] had once generously given to his father" (*The Iliad* 4.218f.). Homeric physicians

THIS VOTIVE RELIEF *shows a physician treating the shoulder of a young man. In the background, the same young man lies on a bed while a snake licks his shoulder. Dates to the fourth century B.C.E.*

were not employed full-time but practiced medicine in a secondary capacity; Machaon had to be summoned from the battlefield to attend Menelaos. Not until the late sixth or early fifth century B.C.E. do we hear of professional physicians in the Greek world. One of the most famous was Demokedes of Krotona (a city in southwestern Italy), whose impressive career is reported at length by Herodotos (3.129–37). Demokedes had a truly international reputation. After curing Dareios, king of Persia, he was employed first by the Aiginetans, then by the Athenians, and finally by Polykrates, tyrant of Samos. His salary increased in line with his growing reputation. The Aiginetans offered him 60 *minai* for his services, the Athenians 100, and Polykrates 120 (1 *mina* was equivalent to 100 drachmas, and 1 drachma was probably the equivalent in the sixth century B.C.E. of at least two days' pay). Demokedes' career indicates that, as early as the beginning of the sixth century B.C.E., there were physicians who were prepared to move from place to place in response to local demand. The Hippocratic treatise entitled *Airs, Waters, and Places,* whose subject is the effect of climate, water supply, and location on the general health of a population, was probably written to assist physicians in their travels. We know of no Greek state that provided free public health service to its citizens, however. Public physicians, so designated, probably received a retainer in return for residing within the state's territory for a fixed period of time but were free to charge for their services. It is unlikely that they would have been able to administer to the needs of more than a small fraction of the total population.

The principal centers of medical learning and research were Krotona in southern Italy, Kyrene in Libya, the island of Kos (in the eastern Aegean), and Knidos on the west coast of Turkey. There were no medical institutions in the modern sense of the word, however. Physicians did not have to undergo any formal training. Nor did they possess anything resembling a medical license. Medical students attached themselves to established practitioners on a purely informal basis. Once they had acquired sufficient knowledge, they discharged themselves and were free to practice independently. The success of their careers would have depended on the size of their reputation, which means that the most successful of them must have been assiduous self-promoters. Given the absence of any objective criteria for determining commonly agreed-upon standards of medical competence, it is hardly surprising that allegations of charlatanism and quackery are commonplace in medical texts.

The Hippocratic Oath

Although anyone could claim to possess healing skills, some physicians organized themselves into guilds and agreed to abide by prescribed rules of medical conduct. The most important evidence for this is the famous Hippocratic Oath, which is attributed to Hippokrates himself and remained the cornerstone of medical ethics in the West until recently. Although we do not know what proportion of the medical profession observed it, those who took the oath seem to have constituted a "closed shop," since they swore to divulge their professional knowledge only to a select few. The Hippocratic Oath reads as follows:

> I swear by Apollo the healer and Asklepios and Hygieia [wife of Asklepios, the personification of health] and Panakeia [daughter of Asklepios, personification of recovery from sickness] and all the gods and goddesses, who are my witnesses, that I will keep this oath and this promise to the best of my ability and judgement.
>
> I will regard the person who taught me this art in equal honor to my parents and I will share my livelihood with him and make him a partner in my wealth when he is in financial need. I will esteem his family as I do my own brothers and I will teach them this art if they so desire to learn it, without accepting any fee or contract. I will pass on precepts, lectures, and all other instruction to my sons and to the sons of my teacher, as well as to apprenticed pupils who have taken the physician's oath, and to no others.
>
> I will employ treatments for the relief of suffering to the best of my ability and judgement, but I will abstain from using them for the purpose of causing injury or harm. I will not give lethal poison to anyone who requests it, nor will I suggest such a course. Similarly I will not give a pessary to a woman that would induce an abortion. I will keep my life and my art pure and holy. I will not use surgery even on those who suffer from stone but I will make way for those who are adept in that procedure. Whatever houses I

enter, I will do so in order to relieve sickness. I will refrain from all manner of intentional injury or harm. In particular I will not sexually abuse women or men, whether servile or free.

Whatsoever I see or hear in the course of my duties, or outside the course of my duties in my dealings with my fellow men, I will not divulge if it be matters that should not be gossiped abroad, but I will regard such matters as not to be spoken of. If I keep this oath and do not break it, may I prosper both in regard to my life and my art for all time. But if I violate it and break my oath, may the opposite fate befall me.

Epidemics

The most famous epidemic in Greek history was the plague that afflicted Athens from 430 to 426 B.C.E. The direct result of Perikles' controversial decision to crowd the entire population of Athens within the city walls, the plague carried off perhaps as much as one-third of the entire population. Although its identity continues to be disputed, typhus and smallpox are the most likely candidates. Thukydides, who was himself afflicted by the plague, has left us a description of its effects upon the body that is a masterpiece of succinct clinical analysis:

> People who were quite healthy for no particular reason suddenly began
> to experience violent fevers in the head together with redness and inflam-
> mation of the eyes. The throat and the tongue became bloody, and they
> emitted a breath that was foul and unnatural. After these symptoms came
> sneezing and hoarseness. Soon afterwards the disease descended to the
> chest with violent coughing fits. Once it reached the stomach that too
> became upset. Vomiting of every kind of bile that has been identified by
> the medical profession ensued, accompanied by great pain and distress.
> The majority were afflicted with ineffectual retching, which produced
> violent convulsions. In some cases the convulsions ceased at this point,
> but in others they continued afterwards. Externally the body did not feel
> very hot nor was it pale. Rather it was reddish, livid, and breaking out into
> blisters and ulcers. Internally, however, there was a burning sensation so

that sufferers could not endure to be covered by even fine linen but merely wanted to be naked. What they liked to do most of all was to plunge themselves into cold water. In fact many who received no attention threw themselves into cisterns, consumed by an unquenchable thirst. They were in the same state whether they drank a lot or a little. Restlessness and insomnia afflicted them throughout.

So long as the disease was at its height the body was not enfeebled but resisted the misery to a remarkable degree, so that the majority of people either perished on the seventh or eighth day as a result of internal burning while still having some strength left. Or, if they pulled through, once the sickness descended to the bowels and caused violent ulceration and watery diarrhea, most of them perished subsequently as a result of the ensuing weakness. For beginning at the top, in the head, the disease made its way down through the whole body and if anyone survived the worst of its effects, yet it still left traces by seizing onto the extremities. It made its way to the genitals, the fingers and the toes, and many who lost the use of these parts still survived, while there were others who lost the use of their eyes. (2.49.2–8)

Thukydides does not limit his analysis to a description of the progress of the disease within the body. He also focuses upon its social consequences in view of the high level of mortality, which undermined not only religious observances, particularly those relating to the burial of the dead, but also common standards of decency.

Chronic Illness

The majority of patients who received medical attention were wealthy individuals who suffered from curable illnesses and injuries. Probably the chronically sick, those suffering from degenerative diseases, and the aged would have had little reason to avail themselves of the services of the medical profession. None of the Hippocratic case histories describes patients with chronic illnesses. This is further corroborated by an observation made by Sokrates in Plato's *Republic* that Asklepios revealed the art of medicine only on behalf of those who "by nature and way of life are healthy but have some hidden illness in them" (407de). Sokrates continues:

> However, in the case of those whose bodies are inwardly diseased through and through, the god did not attempt . . . to prolong an already wretched existence for the individual concerned, who in all probability would foster other offspring like himself. If a man is incapable of living a normal existence he did not think it right to treat him, since such a person is of use neither to himself nor to the state.

Dissection

Despite the keen interest in medicine, knowledge of the internal workings of the human body was extremely rudimentary because dissection was not employed in the study of anatomy before the Hellenistic Period. Even then the practice was perhaps confined to Alexandria, Egypt. None of the works ascribed to Hippokrates is devoted to the study of either anatomy or physiology. Aristotle, writing at the close of the fourth century B.C.E., frankly states: "The internal parts of the body, especially those belonging to humans, are unknown. We must therefore examine the parts of other creatures that resemble humans" (*History of Animals* 494b 22–24). This refusal, or at least reluctance, to perform dissection was due largely to religious scruples, since the Greeks believed that the procedure could prevent the deceased from entering Hades.

Women's Bodies

Ignorance of dissection did not prevent physicians and scientists from inventing elaborate theories about the internal workings of the human body, particularly the female body. From Aristotle's perspective, women were failed males. It was their lack of heat that made them more "formless." Aristotle went so far as to propound the notion of a zoological hierarchy with men at the pinnacle and women one (giant) evolutionary step below. Women, in his telling phrase, represented "the first step" along the road to deformity (*Generation of Animals* 767b 8). Similarly, Galen, writing over half a millennium later, stated that, if it were not for the fact that the menses were needed to contain the hot male seed, we might suppose that "the creator had purposely made one half of the whole race imperfect, and, as it were, mutilated" (*On the Use of Parts* 14.6).

The fact that women needed to menstruate was proof in Aristotle's eyes that they could not burn up the residue that coagulated inside them. They were judged to be particularly susceptible to what we would call today hysteria, a word that is derived from the Greek for "womb" (*hystera*), meaning literally "the lower parts," though its symptoms were rather different from those of the condition we identify by this name today. The Hippocratic School believed that the womb took to wandering around the body if the menses were suppressed or if women did not engage in intercourse. So the theory supported the argument that women's sanity depended upon sexual intercourse.

Mental Disturbances

Although the Greeks lacked the scientific terminology to systematize and explain pathological states of consciousness, they were nonetheless capable of subjecting individuals to close psychological scrutiny. Greek tragedy manifests a keen fascination with mental abnormality, as the following outline of the plot of Sophokles' *Ajax* indicates.

After being defeated in his bid to win the prize for being the foremost soldier in the Greek army, Ajax goes completely berserk and slaughters cattle. He does this in the belief that he is murdering Agamemnon and Menelaos, the war leaders who awarded the prize to his rival. This delusional stage is followed by one of depression. When he returns to his senses, Ajax is overcome with intense shame—not because he tried to assassinate his superior officers but because he tried and so conspicuously failed. The hero now sees the world with unbearable clarity and realizes that he has no place in it. The nineteenth-century French sociologist Emile Durkheim identified three principal categories of suicide: egoistic, altruistic, and anomic. Sophokles' depiction of Ajax's suicide is so complex that it contains elements of all three.

It is not just in the realm of myth that we find incontrovertible evidence for major psychological disturbances. The madness of the Spartan king Kleomenes, as reported by Herodotos, has been cited as a classic instance of paranoid schizophrenia. The king's illness, which provoked him to strike anyone whom he met in the face with his staff, was variously explained either as a punishment brought on by the gods for having burned down a sacred grove or as a consequence of his fondness for unmixed wine, the consumption of which was believed to result in madness. Kleomenes ultimately became so violent that his relatives had him placed in the stocks. While in prison, he managed to intimidate his jailer into giving him a knife, whereupon, as Herodotos relates, "He began to mutilate himself, beginning with his shins. Cutting the flesh up into strips, he proceeded from his ankles to his thighs, and from his thighs to his hips and sides, until he reached his stomach, and while cutting that up he died" (6.75.3).

No one, it seems, tried to cure Kleomenes of his psychosis by medical means. Perhaps the Spartans were particularly unenlightened in such matters. Euripides at least was aware that those who have become temporarily deranged can be talked back to sanity, which may reflect the more advanced attitude toward the mentally sick that prevailed in Athens. At the end of the *Bacchai*, Kadmos gently coaxes his daughter into the realization that she has dismembered her son under the influence of religious ecstasy. Despite the horror of her act, he treats her state of mind as curable.

Plato's Madhouse

Paranoid schizophrenics and others who were judged to be a danger to the rest of society may have been kept in confinement for short periods of time. The local jail probably did double duty for criminals and the criminally insane. In a passage in *Laws* (11.908c–909d), which anticipates the use of asylums for the incarceration of political prisoners in the former Soviet Union, Plato refers darkly to a *sophronistêrion,* or "house of correction," where he proposes that those professing atheism should be imprisoned for five years at a stretch. While serving out their time, he goes on to state, they should be permitted to consort only with the members of the socalled nocturnal council, and then exclusively about matters connected with their moral welfare.

There is no external evidence for the kind of institution to which Plato alludes. It is, moreover, frankly inconceivable that the Greeks would have possessed the resources to provide long-term professional care for the mentally sick, any more than they had the resources to do so for the elderly or the chronically sick. If incarcerated briefly, the mentally sick were perhaps subjected to a type of treatment based on the principle of the short, sharp shock, as has been recommended in recent times for certain types of violent criminals.

SEXUAL MORES

The function of marital sex was procreation. So important was procreation that in Sparta it was acceptable for a husband to lend out his wife to another man for the purpose of impregnating her. Given the extreme emphasis that was placed both on virginity and on women's fidelity, it would have required much ingenuity and not a little luck to conduct a sexual liaison with a well-bred woman. Perhaps for this reason, the image of a Don Juan is alien to Greek culture, other than in the person of Zeus. In myth, even the Trojan prince Paris, the most notorious of all philanderers, remained faithful to the woman he seduced. The exception that proves the rule is Alkibiades, who was much admired by men and women, and who boasted that he had bedded (and impregnated) a Spartan queen.

At the same time, there was open acknowledgement of the fact that male sexuality could not be contained by marriage. Both married and unmarried men were, therefore, free to engage in sex with prostitutes or slaves. The famous myth of Pandora ("All-gifted"), told by Hesiod in *Theogony,* defines women as "a beautiful evil" which men cannot resist, evidently because of their sexual appetite and vulnerability to female charms. These characteristics are made comic sport of in Aristophanes' masterpiece *Lysistrata,* which presupposes that an international sex strike by women (or more accurately, by wives) will bring about peace by reducing all the combatants to another kind of impotence. The popular notion that men were slaves to their sexual appetites was balanced by the medical belief that women needed to have sexual intercourse for their physical and mental well-being (see section on Health and Sickness in this chapter).

Nakedness

The Greeks were remarkably unabashed about the depiction of male genitals in art. Statues of naked youths in the guise of Apollo served as funerary markers.

Herms, stone pillars with carved heads and phalluses, marked the boundaries of properties. Giant phalluses were borne aloft by Athenian virgins in Dionysiac processions. In the performance of comic plays, actors wore oversize phalluses made out of padding to draw attention to their sexual organs. It was also acceptable for a man to display himself naked before other men, particularly in a religious context. Male athletes practiced naked at the gymnasium—the word means "the place of nakedness"—and they also performed naked at the festival games. It was evidently for this reason that women were not allowed to approach the sanctuary of Olympian Zeus during the Olympic Games or indeed any other sanctuary where men were competing naked.

By contrast, the Greeks exhibited primness in regard to the naked female body, even when it was fully clothed. For this reason, it was virtually impossible to praise a woman for her beauty without at the same time impugning her chastity. Women in Homer are praised for their ankles, arms, and cheeks but never for their legs, breasts, or buttocks. For instance, when the Trojan elders catch sight of the drop-dead gorgeous Helen on the ramparts in *The Iliad,* they comment only very vaguely on her beauty. Even Aphrodite, the goddess of sex and sexual love, is described not as ample bosomed or possessed of juicy thighs but, very discreetly, as "laughter-loving" and "golden." In certain Spartan rituals, however, girls were encouraged to appear naked before Spartan youths in what appears to have been a kind of civic-sponsored incentive to marriage.

Homosexuality

The Greeks did not identify themselves as either homosexual or heterosexual. In other words, they did not perceive sexual orientation in terms of a life choice. Instead, they regarded homosexuality predominantly as an episodic phenomenon, a pattern of behavior that belonged to a particular period of one's life rather than as a permanent condition. A number of Greek communities, including those in Boiotia in central Greece, Elis and Sparta in the Peloponnese, and the island of Crete, even made pederasty a rite of passage to adulthood.

A homosexual union between males was acceptable only when asymmetrical, to use the modern jargon; that is to say, when it involved a younger and an older man and when it had a pedagogical as well as sexual dimension. Such associations provided the basis of aristocratic education in the Archaic Period and were institutionalized by the symposium. In later times, they seem to have been regarded less favorably. Whereas earlier, black-figure vases exhibit a preponderance of homosexual lovemaking, the red-figure vases that had become popular by the end of the sixth century onward more frequently depict heterosexual activity. Plato's *Symposion,* which elevates homosexual far above heterosexual love, provides a rather misleading picture of Athenian sexual mores at the turn of the fourth century B.C.E.

Although homosexual practice within certain limitations was regarded as normative by the Greeks, homosexual relations were not expected to replace heterosexual relations. Rather, they were intended to supplement them. In fact, those who committed themselves exclusively to homosexual acts were mocked and vilified, as we see from the abuse that was heaped upon such effeminates (as they were regarded) in the plays of Aristophanes. The most famous homoerotic relationship in Greek legend is that of Achilles and Patroklos, although Homer in *The Iliad,* for whatever reason, scrupulously avoids suggesting that it has a sexual basis. It is interesting to note that depictions of homosexual acts on vases are remarkably restrained. Anal and oral intercourse is practically never shown, although they both appear frequently on vases in a heterosexual context.

Male Prostitution

Male prostitution, though regarded with severe disfavor, was an ineradicable feature of Greek society. Athenians over the age of eighteen who became prostitutes were debarred from holding any executive or religious office and from addressing the assembly or council, although the law stopped short of depriving them of their citizenship. If a boy under the age of eighteen engaged in prostitution, his father or legal guardian was liable for prosecution. As further punishment for the father, the boy

A MAN SOLICITS A BOY *for sex in exchange for a purse containing coins in this tondo from an Athenian red-figure* kylikes *from the fifth century B.C.E. An inscription across the top reads "The Boy is Beautiful."*

in question was also released from the obligation to support him in old age, as the law otherwise enjoined on sons (Aischines, *Against Timarchos* 13–14).

Adultery and Rape

The penalty for adultery was much more severe than for rape. That is because rape was regarded as "merely" an act of violence, whereas adultery involved the transfer of a woman's affections and in so doing made it difficult to determine whether her offspring was legitimate. Whereas rapists were only required to pay recompense to the husband, convicted adulterers faced the death penalty. If an Athenian husband discovered his wife in bed with her lover, he was permitted to take the lover's life with impunity. The husband of an adulterous woman was required by law to divorce his wife. If he failed to do so, he could be deprived of his citizenship. Adulterous women were not permitted to attend religious rites conducted by the citizen body. If they disobeyed, the public was free to do to them any form of violence short of killing them.

Pornography

Pornography, a made-up word of Greek root that literally means "the writing about or the painting of whores, or *pornai*," was not regarded as having a corrupting influence, or if it was so regarded by some individuals, there is no surviving discussion devoted to the subject. Occasionally it even attained the status of high art. One of the most striking sculptural depictions of scantily clad women undergoing sexual abuse is the battle between the Lapiths and centaurs that is depicted on the west pediment of the temple of Zeus at Olympia (470–57 B.C.E.). To the right of the figure of Apollo, who stands in the center of the composition, we see the centaur Eurytion intent on raping the bride Deidameia (see p. 121). To the left of Apollo, another centaur is about to kick in the groin a Lapith woman who is scratching his cheek.

In vase painting, scenes of lovemaking were commonplace. Images of naked bathing women appear on the interior of red-figure cups as early as the late sixth century B.C.E.—far earlier incidentally than the first sculptural images of naked women. The bather was revealed as the (male) drinker drained the cup, thereby lending a certain air of comic prurience. Pornographic literature existed in the Hellenistic Period but seems to have been limited to sex manuals that enumerated the positions of heterosexual intercourse. There was no genre devoted to sexual fantasy, although fantasy is not absent from the Greek novel. A prime example is Longus's *Daphnis and Chloe,* which carries strong undertones of sexual violence.

Conclusions

Although there were no doubt many husbands who were faithful to their wives, the fact remains that it was not only socially acceptable but even expected that they would have sexual relations with a variety of partners, including prostitutes, slaves, and other males. What was not acceptable was having sexual relations with another man's wife. Society's tolerance of the male sexual drive came at a heavy price—one that was paid by the other half of the population, who did not enjoy such privileges themselves and who were evidently expected to turn the proverbial blind eye. One wonders how much Odysseus said about his sexual escapades to his wife Penelope when he returned home after his twenty-year absence, if indeed he felt obligated to say anything at all. It is a deep irony running through *The Odyssey* that Penelope is required to remain unwaveringly faithful to her husband when being persistently bullied into doing otherwise, whereas Odysseus's return is delayed some eight years by his cohabiting with the nymph Kalypso and the witch Kirke.

Death

The treatment of death and the dead divides us sharply from the mentality of the Greeks. In the modern industrialized world, most people die in hospitals. If they happen to have relatives beside them when they pass away, they may count themselves lucky. As soon as they have drawn their final breath, the nurse arrives to cover up the body and pull across the plastic curtains. Most relatives and friends forego visiting the corpse in the hospital if they have not been at the bedside earlier. Very few have any physical contact with the corpse. The hospital authorities then transfer the corpse into the hands of professional undertakers. In Britain, the deceased will never be seen again, because open caskets are extremely rare. In the United States, the deceased, thanks to the fashioning hands of the undertaker, will reappear in a completely transformed state when it goes on view in the funeral home.

In the Greek world, death was prevalent among persons of all age groups, whether as a result of warfare, accident, or illness, or, in the case of women, as a consequence of giving birth. It was incorporated into the life of the community to a degree that would strike many people today as morbid. In modern Greece, too, the business of the undertaker is not conducted behind heavily shrouded windows in subdued surroundings but under the full glare of arc lighting.

Physical Contact with the Dead

Different cultures permit different degrees of contact with their dead. Some accept the physical aspect of death as a natural and intimate fact of life. Others are deeply troubled by the idea of a dead body and regard it as an object to shun. Greek culture evinces both tendencies, permitting proximity to the corpse by family members but exercising vigilance in preventing pollution from escaping into the community.

Because there were no hospitals in ancient Greece, most people died either at home or on the battlefield. If death occurred at home, it was the duty of the relatives to prepare the body for burial. Fondling and kissing the corpse were acceptable and customary practices. And yet the Greeks were hardly more intimate with their deceased than their modern counterparts are. Significantly, *kêdeia,* the word for funeral, which literally means "a caring for," is still in regular use by the Greek Orthodox church.

Although we occasionally hear of undertakers, known as *klimakophoroi* ("ladder-bearers"), *nekrophoroi* ("corpse-bearers"), and *tapheis* ("buriers"), the duty of these hired hands consisted merely in transporting the corpse from the house to the grave and preparing the ground for burial. They were not, for the most part, specialists but merely odd-job men. Nor did they attend to the corpse's needs prior to its departure from the house, as modern undertakers do. Everything suggests that the Greeks would have regarded the idea of handing over the corpse of a dead relative to strangers as offensive and incomprehensible.

Helping the Dead to Reach Hades

This attitude had much to do with the belief that in the period between death and burial the deceased are in need of the solicitous attention of their relatives. Until inhumation or cremation has taken place, the dead were thought to be in what anthropologists describe as a liminal stage—a word that derives from the Latin word *limen* for "threshold." They were between two worlds, having not yet fully disengaged from this one while awaiting incorporation into the next. Entry to Hades, the world of the dead, did not occur automatically but was the consequence of strenuous activity on the part of the living. This betwixt and between status was regarded as extremely perilous, for which reason the unburied dead were believed to be at considerable risk. The primary obligation upon the living was thus to perform the burial as expeditiously and efficiently as possible. To fail in this sacred duty was to condemn the dead to wander up and down the banks of the River Styx, which surrounded Hades, for thousands of years. Thus, when Achilles delays burying Patroklos's corpse because of his overwhelming grief, his ghost appears to Achilles and urgently requests that he bury him "as soon as possible, so that I can enter the gates of Hades" (*The Iliad* 23.71f.).

Displays of Grief

Unlike many modern cultures, which encourage the presentation of a stiff upper lip in the face of loss, Greek culture not only tolerated but also expected highly demonstrative manifestations of grief. There are frequent references in literature to men and women tearing out their hair, rending their garments, beating and lacerating their breasts, rolling on the ground and wallowing in the dust, and going without food or drink for several days. This kind of behavior was prompted in part by a desire to honor the deceased, who were believed to take pleasure in witnessing the exaggerated displays of grief that their death occasioned. In *The Iliad* Book 23, Homer states that, when the Greeks were cremating the body of Patroklos, not everyone was grieving for the deceased. Some were using his death as a pretext to bewail their own private losses and griefs. To a Greek, there was nothing hypocritical or insincere in such transference. The loss of a loved one is common to all human experience, and Greek mourners brought to the funeral their own personal sense of life's pain.

Exeunt the Gods

Among persons of most faiths, the death of a loved one is an occasion to seek the consolation of religion, irrespective of the extent of their commitment to it at other times. The Greeks, by contrast, knew better than to approach their gods in the hope that they could either offer them some consolation or assist the deceased in their passage to the next world. At the graveside, as in the home, death was a domestic affair. Although the Olympian gods occasionally mourn the passing of their favorites, as Zeus mourns the death of his son Sarpedon on the battlefield outside Troy, this was the exception rather than the rule. For the most part, they give the impression of being indifferent to the experience of human loss.

We might seek to explain their indifference by arguing that their own immortality shielded them from a comprehensive understanding of the finite nature of human life. No less important, however, was the fact that proximity to the dead and dying put the gods severely at risk from the contamination caused by death. When, in Euripides' play *Hippolytos* (1437f.), Artemis's favorite Hippolytos is dying in agony after having been hurled from his chariot, the goddess swiftly takes her leave of him before he expires, since, as she explains to him, it is not permitted by divine law for a god or goddess "either to look at the dead or to sully their eyes with the expirations of the dying." For the same reason, no priest or priestess was permitted to enter the house of the deceased or attend a burial. Just as the gods needed to preserve their purity, so, too, did those who ministered to their needs.

The Funeral

No ritual was treated with more importance than that of burial. A popular view quoted by Plato (*Hippias Major* 291de) was that the best thing of all for everyone was "to be rich, healthy, honored by one's fellows, reach old age, and, after burying one's parents well, to be laid out well by one's own children and be buried in magnificent style." The Greek funeral, like our own, was a three-act drama. This

SCENE OF *PROTHESIS* *Notice how some of the family members surrounding the body tear their hair in grief. Pinakes were decorated plaques that were often dedicated as offerings. Holes at the top allowed them to be hung within sanctuaries on walls, trees, or even an image of the deity. Black-figure terra-cotta, sixth century* B.C.E.

comprised the laying out of the body in the home *(prothesis),* the funeral cortege from the home to the place of burial *(ekphora),* and the burial.

The *prothesis* was performed by the female relatives of the deceased. At the moment of death, the deceased's eyes and mouth were closed. A chin strap was commonly tied around the head and chin to prevent the unsightly sagging of the jaw. The body was washed, anointed in olive oil, clothed, and wrapped in a winding sheet. Finally, it was laid out on a couch with its head propped up on a pillow and its feet facing the door. This last practice, which seems to be nearly universal, has given rise to the expression about carrying someone out "feet first." From the fourth century B.C.E. onward, there developed a tendency to dress the dead more ornately, sometimes even to place a crown made of gold foil on the head, whereas in earlier times a simple wreath of ivy, laurel, or olive sufficed. When the body had been laid out, relatives were permitted to view the deceased and dirges were sung.

FOUND IN A TOMB *in northern Greece, these gold items, which include a mask, plaque, band, separate nosepiece, and ring, were likely buried with a warrior sometime in the sixth century B.C.E. The red discoloration of some of the gold indicates that the objects adorned a body that was cremated on a funeral pyre and they were then reassembled for burial.*

On the day of the funeral—which, in Athens, had to take place within three days of the death—the mourners accompanied the corpse to the place of burial. Some corpses were laid in a simple wooden coffin. However, because of the scarcity of wood, the poor had to make do with only a winding sheet, strewn with a few branches. The corpse was either borne by pallbearers or transported in a cart to the grave. Solon regulated that it had to be transported from the house before sunrise to avoid unseemly displays of grief that could cause a public nuisance and draw too much attention to the family.

The burial itself was performed by the relatives of the deceased. Little is known about the details. The service, such as it was, probably consisted mainly of ritualized laments. If a prayer was delivered at the moment of interment, we know nothing of it. Although both inhumation and cremation were practiced with differing degrees of popularity at different times, cremation was regarded as the more prestigious, since this is how the dead are disposed of in the Homeric poems. There is no clear evidence that the different methods of disposal reflected different beliefs, however. After cremation, the ashes were gathered and placed in an urn, which was then buried. Once the grave had been filled in, a grave marker was erected. The mourners then returned to the house of the deceased for a commemorative meal.

Keeping Pollution at Bay

Because a dead body constituted a strong source of pollution, relatives were required to take elaborate precautions to prevent its contagiousness from seeping out into the community. Such was the degree of public concern that many states passed detailed laws to ensure that the polluting effect of a corpse did not extend beyond the members of the immediate family. For this reason, too, Solon allowed only close family members and women over the age of sixty to enter the house of the deceased and take part in the funeral. Measures that seem to have been intended to combat the polluting effect of the dead include the following: placing a bowl of water brought from outside the house so that visitors could purify themselves upon entering and leaving; hanging a cypress branch on the door (a custom that may have served to warn passersby of the presence of a corpse within); placing oil flasks known as *lêkythoi* containing olive oil around the couch on which the dead was laid out; and, most important of all, bathing the corpse. Once the dead had been transported to the place of interment, the house was ritually cleaned. Inscriptions from different parts of the Greek world indicate that it was customary to debar relatives from participating in the life of the community for several weeks after the funeral.

Burial Grounds

The Greeks had no conception of a necropolis in the literal meaning of the word (though *necropolis* is, of course, a Greek word)—a city of the dead that is separate from the living. Those who dwelled in the country tended to bury their dead in a field on their estates, while city dwellers buried the dead beside a main road. The highways leading out of Athens were lined on either side with tombs, in much the same way that advertising billboards clutter the sides of our highways today. The most frequented roads provided the most favored burial spots for wealthy families, as indicated by the number of tombs located on the west side of the city in the area known as the Kerameikos or Potters' Quarter. The Kerameikos lay outside the Dipylon Gate and the Sacred Gate. The roads that passed through these gates led to the port of Piraeus and the deme of Eleusis, home of the Eleusinian Mysteries.

The practice of roadside burial may have arisen in response to a ban on burials within the city that that seems to have been imposed in the sixth century B.C.E. The ban may have been due partly to fear of the polluting effect of the dead and partly to the need to conserve as much space as possible for housing at a time of demographic growth, given the fact that Athens was surrounded by a wall. Roadside burial also provided the family of the deceased with an opportunity to advertise their wealth and prestige in a permanent manner, since the tombs so located would have attracted considerable attention. For this reason, gravestones invariably face the passerby, their sculptured adornments often looking down from an imposing height several meters above the ground.

> *Sepulchral epigrams frequently took the form of an address to the wayfarer, notably in the case of the celebrated epigram by Simonides, which was inscribed on the tomb of the three hundred Spartans who died at Thermopylai in 480 B.C.E.:*
>
> Tell them in Lakedaimon, passerby,
> That here obedient to their word we lie.

In Classical Athens, there seems to have been a belief that the family would be able to reunite in the hereafter if its members were buried in the same place. This may explain the popularity of the family plot, a large rectangular space walled on the front and at the sides, to which access could be gained only from the rear. Family plots, which had become popular by the end of the fifth century B.C.E., contained grave monuments commemorating all the family dead, including, in some cases, household slaves.

Expenditure on the dead came very high on the list of a rich citizen's financial priorities. We hear, for instance, of one family tomb erected in the final decade of the fifth century B.C.E. that cost at least 2,500 drachmas, although the defendant actually claims that the true figure was twice that amount (*Lysias, Against Diogeiton* 21). This was at a time when a rower in Athens' navy earned merely one drachma per day. Grave monuments increased in elaboration as the fourth century progressed and remained in vogue until 317 B.C.E., when

Demetrios of Phaleron introduced legislation severely limiting their costliness, evidently to curb unnecessary expenditure in a period of economic decline. Henceforth, the commonest form of grave marker was a simple marble column known as a *kioniskos,* some two to three feet in height above the ground and a foot or so in diameter. The great age of honoring the dead with sumptuous monuments was over.

Looking After the Dead

Bereaved relatives continued to maintain a close attachment to the deceased long after death had occurred, because their welfare in Hades was thought to depend on the attention they received from the living. Women were expected to pay regular visits to the grave, particularly on the anniversary of the day of death but also at other intervals throughout the year. We gain an insight into the importance of such rituals from the speaker of a forensic oration by Isaios (*On the Estate of Menekles* 46), who declares plaintively that, if his opponent prevails, "There will be no-one to perform the sacred ancestral rites on behalf of the deceased nor to offer the annual sacrifice to him either but he will be deprived of the honors due to him." Evidently, the speaker counted on the jury being outraged by such a prospect.

Because the dead were believed either to dwell in the proximity of their grave or at least to be capable of visiting it periodically, a variety of gifts judged necessary for their physical welfare were buried with the dead and deposited periodically afterward beside the tomb. The commonest grave gift in fifth-century Athens was the oil flask or *lēkythos,* which was decorated with images relating to the care of the dead set against a white background. Common objects that were deposited at the tomb include branches of myrtle, wreaths, cakes, and drink. It was also customary to anoint gravestones with olive oil and wind colored sashes around their shafts, almost as if gravestones in some sense embodied or ensouled the dead.

RELIEF FROM A WOMAN'S GRAVE *showing a man shaking the deceased's hand, a common trope on Athenian gravestones. Marble, ca. 375–350 B.C.E.*

Funerary Art

Images of death and the dead serve many different purposes, and understanding how these images function helps us to elucidate a society's attitude toward death. The Assyrians, for instance, adorned the walls of their palaces with skull pyramids to magnify their achievements and intimidate their enemies. The Greeks, however, were extremely reserved in their depictions of death. By and large, emotions such as sentimentality, fear, horror, disgust, and guilt played little part in the visual imagery they employed. In fact, Greek funerary art virtually excludes overt demonstrations of emotion altogether, preferring instead to situate grief in a timeless world where death becomes a subject for detached, philosophical contemplation.

A frequent image on Athenian gravestones is that of two persons, either seated or standing, shaking hands. In most cases, it is impossible to determine who is intended to represent the deceased and who the living. So we are left wondering whether the handshake signifies a farewell between the living and the dead or a reunion in the world to come. The motif of the handshake may have been deliberately chosen to blur the distinction between "here" and "there," as the Greeks prosaically termed the two worlds, in acknowledgment of the belief that those who part from one another in this world will soon be reunited in the next.

Whom the Gods Love . . .

Despite or perhaps because of its frequency, the Greeks were profoundly moved by the pathos of premature death. In the Archaic Period, this was evoked by the statue of a naked youth at the peak of his physical fitness, striding purposefully forward. Such statues, which historians have dubbed *kouroi* or "youths," frequently commemorated those who died on the battlefield. Their aesthetic beauty speaks keenly to the sacrifice made by the dead youth on behalf of the state. It is important to note, however, that *kouroi* depended on context and provenance for interpretation. Identical statues have also been found in sanctuaries of Apollo, the god who is eternally poised upon the threshold to adulthood. In other words, it is impossible to tell whether a *kouros* is intended to depict a dead youth or Apollo, other than by its provenance or inscription. This ambiguity tells us much about the way in which the Greeks sought to idealize death. By being assimilated to the youthful god, the deceased becomes ageless and physically perfect for all eternity.

Conclusions

Most of the evidence about the handling of death in ancient Greece relates to Athens. Yet attitudes toward the dead surely varied markedly from one Greek community to another. The Spartans, for instance, were far less circumspect in their dealings with the dead than the Athenians were. Legislation attributed to the lawgiver Lykourgos attempted to reduce the fears associated with death by permitting burial within the precincts of the city and even in proximity to sacred places (Plutarch, *Life of Lykourgos* 27.1). Let us take our leave of the recently deceased by considering a *lêkythos,* or olive oil container, on which is depicted a particularly charming woman moribund who is adjusting her coiffure in the presence of Hermes Psychopompos (literally "leader of *psychai* or souls"), the messenger and escort of the dead. Hermes is evidently waiting to escort the woman to Hades, while she dallies over the preparations for her final journey. We are struck by the unearthly patience of Hermes, which is reminiscent of the patience of a devoted, if long-suffering, husband. Is the scene intended to mock a woman's concern for her appearance at a time when she might be expected to have more pressing concerns?

Or is the artist conveying a message about how to confront our own exit from life—with equanimity, poise, and, above all, a sense of style?

Afterlife

It is extremely difficult to determine with any accuracy the kind of life that people expect to encounter in the world to come, because beliefs about the hereafter constitute a highly private and personal area of human reflection. They also tend to be self-contradictory, even where a strongly centralized religious authority like, say, the Roman Catholic Church provides certain guidelines. A fortiori in ancient Greece, where no centralized religious authority existed even within the same community, differences in belief are likely to have been extreme. It has been claimed, and with good reason, that no two Greeks shared exactly the same idea about the afterlife. If we knew more about Greek eschatology, the picture would doubtless be more baffling than it is.

Almost all our information derives from highly wrought literary descriptions supplemented by sepulchral inscriptions. These descriptions may or may not have been representative of popular belief, though they were almost certainly influential in giving it a basic outline. This is particularly true in the case of Homer, who, in addition to bequeathing to the Greeks their image of the gods, may well have bequeathed their prevailing image of Hades as well. After Homer, no detailed description of Hades has survived before the one provided by Aristophanes in his play *Frogs,* performed in 405 B.C.E. What modifications popular belief underwent in the intervening three hundred years is virtually impossible to determine.

The Topography of Hades

Hades could be approached by both land and sea. Homer places it "at the bounds of Okeanos (our word *ocean),*" the river that was believed to circle the inhabited earth, and "beneath the depths of the earth." In other words, it could be reached by sailing to the far west or by entering certain caves. In Book 10 of *The Odyssey,* the witch Kirke informs Odysseus, who is eager to consult the dead, that he must sail across Okeanos until he comes to the wild coast and groves of Persephone "where the tall poplars grow and willows that quickly shed their seeds" (508ff.). After beaching his ship, he is to seek the rock where the rivers Pyriphlegethon ("Blazing-like-fire") and Kokytos ("Wailing") flow into a river called Acheron (possibly "Sorrow"). Perhaps Odysseus is instructed to take this route because he is a seasoned seafarer, or perhaps it is simply less unpleasant than the land route.

In Book 24 of *The Odyssey,* Hermes, the escort of the dead, leads his charge by the land route. This traverses "the dark, mouldy ways"—a fitting path, we might say, for rotting cadavers. Hermes and his crew of gibbering dead then pass Okeanos, the White Rock, the gates of the sun god Helios, and the realm of dreams. Eventually they reach the asphodel meadow, so named for a type of wild flower that grows there. They are now officially in the realm of Hades, where "the spirits of the dead dwell, the phantoms of men who are worn out," as Homer puts it. And it is here, too, that Homer's description peters out. We learn nothing about the appearance of Hades, its size, its notable landmarks, or its divisions. All that we know is that it was dark and windy. Perhaps Homer's imagination failed him, or perhaps he thought it illomened to say more. It is possible, too, that the featurelessness of Hades may have something to do with its impenetrable darkness. The word *Hades,* which denotes both the god of the underworld and the underworld itself, means literally "that which is unseen." Not the least forbidding aspect of the kingdom is its essential unknowability.

It may strike us as something of a paradox that the Greeks had such an elaborate ritual for dealing with death and burial when their ideas about the afterlife were apparently so indistinct and colorless. Their pictorial imagination also seems to have stopped dead at the entrance to Hades. Vase paintings rarely provide more than a glimpse of what lies beyond.

The Miserable Homeric Dead

Everything that Homer tells us about the dead suggests that their condition was lamentable in the extreme. The quality of life in Hades is summed up well by Achilles' observation in Book 11 of *The Odyssey* that he would rather work as a day laborer for a man who had little property than be lord of all the spirits of the dead (lines 489–91). Because the dead have been worn out by their earthly existence, it is not surprising that they are described as "strengthless" and bereft of their physical powers.

Worse than that, the dead are condemned to experience for all eternity the mental anguish to which they were subjected when alive. The shade of Agamemnon, the leader of the Greek forces at Troy, can do nothing but eternally lament the untrustworthiness of women—a subject particularly dear to his heart in view of the fact that he was murdered by his wife Klytaimnestra on his return from the war. Similarly, the Greek hero Ajax is unable to forget the rancor that he feels toward Odysseus, who was judged more worthy than himself in the contest for Achilles' gold armor. Although we cannot know whether the Greeks would have drawn any edifying moral from such memorable images of unresolved mental torment, they serve as chilling reminders of the unending pain that awaits those in Hades who have left "unfinished business" up on earth. Equally pathetic is the preoccupation of the dead with the life that they have left behind. When summoned from below, they are eager, indeed greedy, for news of their relatives. Shorn of existence, however, they have nothing to report in return. All in all, it is as if the Homeric dead are caught in a time warp, unable to move beyond the recollection of their last moments on earth.

They remain, too, in the same physical condition as they were at the precise moment of their death. In *The Odyssey,* we hear that the shades include "marriageable virgins and much-enduring old men . . . and many who had been wounded with bronze spears and war-killed men holding their bloodied armor" (11.38–41). Similarly, in Sophokles' *Oedipus the King,* the king informs the citizens of Thebes that the reason why he blinded himself after discovering that he had killed his father and married his mother was so that he would not have to endure their gaze down in Hades (lines 1371–73).

The Perpetually Damned

Deep in the bowels of Hades was a windy region called Tartaros, to which were consigned all the most miserable sinners. This did not include serial killers and rapists—they would almost certainly have ended up among the general mass of mankind—but those who had outraged and insulted the dignity of the gods. Such was Tantalos, who served his son Pelops to the gods to test whether they had the capacity to distinguish human from animal flesh. Tantalos was condemned to stand in a pool of water with fruit trees dangling overhead. He is, to use the word that derives from his particular form of punishment, eternally tantalized, because whenever he bends to drink water it recedes and whenever he stretches for the fruit overhead the boughs sway out of reach. The overwhelming majority of the dead were spared the ordeal of having to go through any postmortem judgment. Although we hear of a judge named Minos in *The Odyssey,* his task appears to have been confined to settling disputes between the litigious dead. He did not have to determine their moral culpability, far less to distinguish between the saved and the damned.

The Privileged Few

In any system there often exists a privileged minority who do not endure the same miserable lot as the rest of humanity, and the Greek afterlife was no different in this respect. In *The Odyssey,* the old man of the sea, called Proteus, delivers the following prophecy:

> In your case, Zeus-born Menelaos, it is not fated that you should die and
> meet your doom in horse-rearing Argos [where Menelaos ruled as king].
> Instead the immortals will convey you to the Elysian plain and to the
> bounds of the earth, where fair-haired Rhadamanthys [presumably the king
> of this region] dwells, and where life is easiest for men. There is no snow,
> nor heavy storm, nor rain, but Okeanos always sends the breezes of soft-
> blowing Zephyros [the west wind] to refresh men. (4.561–68)

Menelaos is accorded this privileged status not because he has distinguished himself during his life time, but because he married one of Zeus's daughters. What kind of existence awaited those who dwelt in the Elysian fields is unclear. Apart from the extremely favorable climatic conditions, whose predictability would surely pall after a while, the environment appears to have been stultifying in the extreme.

Hadean Bureaucracy

Charon, the ferryman who transported the dead across the River Styx or the River Acheron, was elderly, unkempt, and disagreeable. It was certainly advisable to pay him for his services. A small coin called an *obol* was therefore placed in the deceased's mouth by caring relatives. Protecting the entrance to Hades was the two-, three-, or fifty-headed dog Kerberos. (Reports differ as to the exact number of his heads.) It was Kerberos's duty to fawn hypocritically on those who entered the region but menace them if they sought to leave. Hades, the lord of the dead and king of the entire region, who was the brother of Zeus and Poseidon, has few known physical traits, apart from dark hair. He is "monstrous" and "strong," "implacable" and "relentless"—no doubt because of the absolute finality of death itself.

ARRIVAL OF CHARON *upon entering Hades. Gustave Doré (French), 1857. Woodcut illustration for Dante's* Inferno, Canto III: *"And lo! toward us in a boat / Comes an old man, haory white with eld, / Crying, 'Woe to you, wicked spirits!'"*

For obvious reasons, he is also referred to as "all-receiving" and "ruling over many." We know little else about him, apart from the sinister fact that he abducted his wife Persephone when she was innocently plucking flowers in a meadow. His palace and its domestic arrangements are never described. But though the image of the god is not exactly attractive, he never assumes the role of tormentor of the dead. On the contrary, he seems to have been content to leave the denizens of his realm alone so that they could lead their miserable existences uninterruptedly.

PLUTO WITH CERBERUS. *Agostino Carracci (Italian), 1592. Oil on canvas.*

The realm of Hades also housed the three Furies—Alekto, Megaira, and Tisiphone—who sprang from the drops of blood from the severed genitals of Ouranos after his son Kronos had castrated him. The Furies were avengers of crimes, especially those committed within the family. They were, for instance, invoked by Klytaimnestra, after she had been murdered by her son Orestes. They pursued their victims with torches, snakes, or whips. They seem to have directed their enmity wholly against the living; we never hear of them taking vengeance against the dead.

By and large, those who ran Hades were inoffensive, if not wholly innocuous. It was the sheer boredom and dreariness of Hades that made it so awful. To be there for the duration must be hell indeed.

Toward the Hope of Something Better

Although the Homeric image of Hades probably continued to exert a powerful hold over the imagination throughout antiquity, as time passed, the Greeks became increasingly uncomfortable with the idea of equal misery for all. Accordingly, from the sixth century B.C.E. onward, they came to believe that those who had been exceptionally virtuous and/or had undergone initiation into certain rites pertaining to the afterlife could expect a more cheerful existence in the hereafter. Certain closed sects also held out the promise of a better afterlife than that available to the majority. Notable among them were the Pythagoreans and Orphics. Pythagoreanism was allegedly founded by the astronomer and mathematician Pythagoras of Samos, and Orphism by the mythic poet and musician Orpheus. Both sects advocated the belief that the soul (the Greek word is *psyche*) did not perish along with the body. Exactly what Pythagoreans and Orphics had in mind by the notion of soul is unclear, however. It was certainly a more distinctive and conscious entity than a disembodied Homeric shade, though it is anachronistic to equate it with the Christian soul. Both sects also maintained a belief in an underworld judgment involving rewards and punishments. Abstinence from eating meat and self-discipline were important requirements. Regrettably, we have no means of knowing how widespread such beliefs were, though they are likely to have been confined to a small minority.

Pythagoreanism also promoted belief in the transmigration of the soul at the moment of death. Securing a blessed lot in the hereafter could take several incarnations to achieve. Pythagoreans claimed that their founder was so enlightened that he could even remember his previous incarnations, a suggestion that exposed him to ridicule. In a lost work, the philosopher Xenophanes of Kolophon in Ionia tells the following facetious anecdote about the sage: "They say that Pythagoras was passing by one day when a puppy was being whipped. Taking pity on the animal, he said, 'Stop don't beat it. It's the soul of my friend. I recognize him by his bark.' "

Far more popular than Pythagoreanism or Orphism were the so-called mystery religions, which offered the condition of blessedness *(olbia)* in the hereafter to those who had undergone initiation into their secret rites. The most celebrated of these were the Eleusinian Mysteries, which took their name from Eleusis, an Attic deme situated about twelve miles west of Athens. Eleusis was visited by the goddess Demeter when she was searching for her daughter Persephone after she had been abducted by Hades (see p. 74). The Eleusinian Mysteries attracted initiates from all over the Greek-speaking world and were held for over a thousand years. They remained popular well into the late fourth century C.E. and numbered several Roman emperors among their initiates, including Hadrian and Marcus Aurelius.

Overall, the Greeks lacked a clear idea about the type of afterlife that was reserved for the fortunate minority. Even the Homeric *Hymn to Demeter,* which incorporates the founding charter of the Eleusinian Mysteries, merely states that those who have been initiated into the mysteries will become "blessed" (lines 480–82). A series of Classical reliefs, however, depict the dead savoring the delights of this world with no evidence of wasting or physical decay, as if taking their ease at the symposium. Although we do not know for certain whether this scene is situated in the hereafter, this cannot be ruled out, because the symposium was the nearest earthly equivalent to a sensual paradise that the Greeks ever devised. All this does not add up to much, however, and we are left with the impression that the Greeks found it as difficult to envisage paradise as most people have throughout history.

Conclusions

The afterlife is extremely resistant to clear and unambiguous conclusions. Ideas about it are inevitably a hodgepodge of contradictory and ill-thought-out hopes, fears, and fantasies. Our own beliefs and practices are no less conflictive than those of the Greeks. Few people are able to dispose of the belongings of a dead relative immediately after decease, and sometimes it takes years to do so, whether due to sentiment or to some vague notion that the dead are still present and needy. Even the passing of a cherished household pet provokes confused ideas.

At the beginning of the Republic, *Plato puts the following pronouncement into the mouth of the elderly Kephalos, which may serve as a fitting epitaph to the instability of beliefs concerning the afterlife within even the same individual at different periods of one's life:*

When a man gets to the end of his life he becomes subject to fear and anxiety about what lies ahead. The stories told about people in Hades, that if you commit crimes on earth you must pay for them down below, although they were ridiculed for a while, now begin to disturb a man's soul with the possibility that they might be true. (330de)

MAGIC

Magic is a difficult concept to identify in ancient Greece, because there was no category exactly equivalent to our modern notion. (The word *magos,* from which the word *magic* derives, referred to a Persian shaman.) It is likely that the use of what we might broadly describe as magical practices was widespread in all places and at all times, however. Although a number of Greek philosophers, including Plato and Aristotle, as well as members of the medical profession, tended to equate magic with fraud, there was never any systematic persecution of its practitioners, as there was, for instance, of witches in Medieval Europe and later.

This is all the more surprising in view of the negative image of witches in Greek mythology. A particularly chilling example is Medea, who, in Euripides' play of that name, uses her dark skills to fashion a deadly wedding dress for her ex-husband's bride and also murders her own children. As today, witchcraft seems to have been associated primarily with women, especially foreigners.

There are numerous references to magic in Greek literature. The earliest is in Book 10 of Homer's *The Odyssey,* where we encounter the witch Kirke, who uses a variety of magical devices, including salves, potions, and a magic wand, and who is capable of transforming Odysseus's companions into swine. Odysseus defends himself against her by means of a magical herb called *moly,* which the god Hermes provided for him. When Kirke has been subdued, she proceeds to instruct Odysseus in the art of summoning up the spirits of the dead, a magical practice commonly described in later Greek literature.

From the late fifth century B.C.E. onward, individuals who wished to evoke the dark powers beneath the earth commonly used the dead as their go-betweens. Favored messengers were those who died young and those who died violently, particularly suicides and murder victims. A popular custom was to inscribe a lead tablet with the names of the persons to be cursed and then to place the tablet in the grave alongside the gifts that were intended for use by the deceased in the world to come. In some cases, as many as fifteen names are mentioned on a single tablet. Many tablets allude to the parts of a person's body that are to be cursed—the tongue, the eyes, the soul, the mind, the mouth, the arms, the legs, and so forth. Various underworld powers are invoked, including Persephone and Hermes. To reach the other world, the lead tablet had to be "canceled" for use by the living. For this reason, tablets are often found with a nail driven through them. A variant on this device was a kind of antique voodoo doll—a miniature figure made of lead whose arms were bound behind its back. The doll was sometimes transfixed through the breast with a needle. One of the most common reasons for cursing in litigious Athens was a lawsuit, as we know from the discovery of tablets that curse individuals who have allegedly given false testimony. Magic also played an important part in religious rituals, notably in regard to birth. Midwives, who, in the absence of male physicians, presided unaided in the birthing room, also possessed a variety of skills of a magical, religious, and quasi-medical nature.

As a protection against curses, bad luck, and the evil eye, amulets were often worn around the body, particularly by young children. Many were made of cheap materials, though precious stones were believed to have special efficacy. Plutarch (*Life of Perikles* 38.2) tells us that, even Perikles, a confirmed rationalist, tied an amulet around his neck when he contracted the plague. It was taken as proof that the statesman really must be in a bad way "if he was prepared to put up with such nonsense." Herbs and plants were believed to possess magical healing properties. In addition, foreign and nonsense words were credited with magical powers.

FIGURINE DEPICTING ONE OF ODYSSEUS'S COMPANIONS *in the process of turning into a pig after the sorceress Kirke casts a spell on the men.*

✻ 6 ✻

THE PUBLIC SPHERE

RELIGION

Religion was at the center of daily life in ancient Greece, in both its domestic and public aspect. Just as the household comprised a religious community (see p. 141), so did the phratry, the *genos* (or noble kin group), the deme, the tribe, and the polis as a whole. And so, too, did temporary affiliations, including fellow drinkers at a symposium or soldiers preparing for battle or an audience at a dramatic production. Yet religion was something for which the Greeks, who had a word for most things, did not have a word. What we identify as religion was not regarded by them as something distinct and separate from other departments of life. On the contrary, the secular and the profane were constantly overlapping and intersecting with one another. The gods were everywhere and in all things. They were in the home, in the crops, in the city, on the battlefield, in the body, in the birthing room, in the weather, and in the mind. There was hardly any human activity or undertaking that was not susceptible to divine influence, and religion permeated every aspect of daily life, public as well as private. The Greek gods, however, were not mind readers. They were not, therefore, the least interested in whether their were, to use a Christian expression, "pure of heart." Much of what we know about the practice of Greek religion comes to us from highly unrepresentative authors, including the poets Homer, Hesiod, Aeschylus, Sophokles, and Euripides, the historian Herodotos, and the philosophers Plato and Aristotle.

STATUE OF ZEUS IN THE TEMPLE OF ZEUS *at Olympia. The statue, made by the Greek sculptor Phidias ca. 432 B.C.E., was one of the Seven Wonders of the Ancient World. Anonymous, 1879. Engraving.*

Because most Greeks took the existence of their gods for granted, they had no need for any creed or dogma, which is why they have not bequeathed to us any sacred literature comparable to the Bible or the Koran. The very Greek word *orthodoxy,* meaning "correct opinion," has no ancient equivalent, at least not of a religious nature. Ideas about the nature of the gods were as a result always fluid. As A. D. Nock (*Conversion,* 10) observed, "The place of faith was taken by myth and ritual (which) implied an attitude rather than a conviction." It follows that the focus of devotion was not upon belief but upon action. What mattered to the Greeks principally was securing the goodwill of their gods, and what mattered in turn to the gods were the respect and gifts that they received from mortals. Piety (*eusebeia*) thus consisted in the performing of traditional rites and in giving the gods what they wanted.

Although the Christian notion of sin had no Greek equivalent, certain forms of behavior did offend the gods and had fateful, even fatal, consequences, including *atasthaliê* and *hubris,* both of which translate approximately as overweening pride and presumptuousness. However, even though the gods preserved a healthy distance between themselves and mere mortals, the *nemesis,* or retribution, that presumptuousness engendered seems to have been regarded primarily as self-inflicted. At the very beginning of *The Odyssey,* Zeus complains that mortals blame the gods for their undoing when in fact it is their overweening pride that is the cause. Broadly speaking, however, Greek religion offered little guidance in conduct and no explanation for the ordering of the universe. For the answers to those and related questions, the Greeks turned to philosophy.

The main objective behind Greek religion was to secure advancement in this life. To come to terms with this priority, we have to step outside the assumptions of a monotheistic worldview and conceive of a universe not ruled by a single beneficent deity but by a host of warring deities whose interests frequently conflicted and who were only marginally concerned with the good of mankind. Greek religion was an inclusive and, by and large, essentially tolerant system, which operated from the following basic principles:

1. There are many gods.
2. Any community is necessarily eclectic in its choice of which gods to worship.
3. There will always be genuine gods who are left out of the community's pantheon.

Very few Greeks were what we would call atheists. A rare exception is Diagoras of Melos, a lyric poet who flourished in Athens in the final decades of the fifth century B.C.E. and who was accused of mocking the Eleusinian Mysteries. He was condemned to death but fled. A more common position was agnosticism, as manifested by the Sophist Protagoras of Abdera, who wrote: "Concerning the gods, whether they exist or whether they do not, I am unable to comment. The subject is inherently obscure and life is too fleeting." Incidentally, The tradition that Protagoras was condemned for impiety and fled from Athens is probably untrue.

Polytheism did not have to wage war against would-be intruders, unless the would-be intruder happened to come in the form of an exclusive monotheistic religion that challenged its fundamental belief in the plurality of the divine.

Getting the Gods' Attention

The gods presided over all aspects of daily life, including health and sickness, economic prosperity, the fertility of crops, livestock, and humans, childbirth, warfare, and seafaring (judged always to be a dangerous undertaking). However, they were only fitfully interested in human affairs. Their generally somewhat dismissive attitude toward the human race is indicated by the following words that Apollo addresses to Hephaistos when they are about to engage in battle outside Troy:

> Earthshaker, you would think I was out of my mind if I were to fight with you for the sake of wretched mortals, who are like leaves, now flourishing and growing warm with life . . . but then fading away and dying. So let us give up this quarrel at once and let mortals fight their own battles.
> (*The Iliad* 21.462–67)

The gods, in short, had better things to do than concern themselves with the plight of humans, and it follows from this that it was often something of an uphill battle to enlist their support. Their attention had to be attracted first by a prayer in which the petitioner reminded the deity of his or her relationship with the petitioner. Following the prayer, the petitioner made a sacrifice, poured a libation (drink offering), or offered a votive offering (an offering that was "vowed" or promised to the deity in recompense for his or her assistance), since the gods did not do anything for nothing. The sentiment is nicely epitomized in an inscription on a bronze statuette of a naked youth (or *kouros)* that is dated to the early seventh century B.C.E. The inscription, one of the earliest in Greek to survive, reads: "Mantiklos offers me as a tithe to silver-bowed Apollo. Give me something nice in return, Phoibos [Apollo]." It seems that Mantiklos was prepared to ascribe any windfall that came his way to Apollo. A sacrifice might consist merely of first fruits, grain, beans, cakes, wine, or milk. The most powerful sacrificial offering, however, involved the spilling of animal blood, preferably in large quantities, since the gods were thought to derive both pleasure and sustenance from the smoke of the victim that wafted up from the altar and entered their nostrils. Victims include chickens, goats, sheep, oxen, pigs, and bulls. Each deity had his or her favorite: Hermes favored goat, while Demeter liked pork. Before the battle of Marathon in 490 B.C.E., the Athenians, understandably apprehensive at taking on the vastly superior Persian army, vowed to sacrifice a she-goat to Artemis for every Persian they killed. Much to their surprise, they slew 6,400 Persians. Not having that number of she-goats available, they vowed instead to sacrifice five hundred per annum. As Xenophon (*Anabasis* 3.2.12) reports, they were still continuing the practice nearly a century later.

Votive offerings took many forms. They could be either as paltry as a crudely fashioned terra-cotta figurine or as costly and impressive as a temple. It was customary to offer a tenth of the spoils captured from the enemy after a victory in fulfillment of a vow made to the gods who had been invoked beforehand and who were believed to have contributed to it. The sacred way leading to the temple of Apollo at Delphi was lined with miniature temples, conventionally called "treasuries," that had been erected by victorious Greek states from the spoils filched from vanquished Greek states, because Apollo was invoked as a god of victory whenever states entered the fray.

Festivals

The most important festivals were those that were celebrated annually in honor of the deities who were worshipped and funded by the state. The high point of the festival was the sacrifice. At the Great Dionysia held in Athens in honor of Dionysos in 333 B.C.E., no fewer than 240 bulls were slaughtered. Just before the axe fell, barley grains were sprinkled on the victim's head to induce the animal to nod in pretended assent at its own killing. The animal was then flayed, chopped up, and roasted on top of the altar. Public sacrifices afforded one of the few occasions when the entire citizen body had an opportunity to eat meat, because everything except for the thigh pieces was later distributed among the priests and the celebrants. More importantly, from a religious perspective, public sacrifices helped to define the polis, since only citizens were permitted to partake of the meat. As such, it was an act of communion, in much the same way, *mutatis mutandis*, that the Eucharist is (in a double sense) an act of communion, in that only those who have been through the rite of initiation (termed confirmation) are permitted to partake of the host. (Only those who belonged to exclusive religious sects such as Orphism and Pythagoreanism, rejected sacrifice, which indicates that no vegetarian could participate fully in the civic, social, and religious life of the polis.)

TWO MEN SACRIFICE A PIG *in this tondo from a red-figure* kylikes, *created ca. 510–500 B.C.E.*

In addition to festivals that were financed by the state, each of Athens' demes funded festivals in which all the citizens of that deme participated. The religious calendar belonging to the deme of Erchia, which is preserved in an inscription dating to the fourth century B.C.E., records that sacrifices took place on twenty-five days of the year and that the total annual cost was about 547 drachmas (estimated to be equivalent to $54,700). Erchia was a medium-sized deme. Many were considerably larger and would have conducted more and larger sacrifices.

It was the civic responsibility of every citizen and demesman to participate in the festivals, because the goodwill of the gods was dependent in part on a good turnout. When Sokrates was brought to trial in 399 B.C.E., one of the charges against him was "not acknowledging the gods whom the state acknowledges." This was not a charge of atheism. It was a charge of nonparticipation in the major festivals.

The Olympians

The Greeks worshipped a pantheon comprising Zeus and eleven other deities who were thought to inhabit the peaks of Olympos, a mountain on the borders between Thessaly and Macedonia some three thousand meters high that is perpetually shrouded in cloud. The eleven were all siblings or offspring of Zeus. It may have been Homer who first constituted them into a family—it was certainly he who first gave them their vividly delineated personalities. The Olympian gods were not, however, identical everywhere in the Greek world; nor indeed were they held in equal honor. Later the hero Herakles was admitted into their ranks—a distinction never accorded Asklepios, the god of healing, notwithstanding his importance. Arrogant, fickle, cruel, and treacherous, the Olympians have been aptly described as superhuman in power and subhuman in morality. Neither good nor evil in themselves, they constituted a dangerous and unstable combination of both elements.

Because the gods were extremely jealous, the Greeks took extreme care not to succumb to hubris or overweening pride. Those who did so were punished with *nemesis* or vengeful destruction. Herodotos depicts a Persian noble giving this warning to Xerxes as he is contemplating invading Greece (7.10e): "It is always the biggest buildings and the tallest trees that are struck by lightning. The gods are accustomed to throw down whatever is too high." The difference between the Olympian deities and, in particular, the Christian God, who has been likened by comparison to an inoffensive celestial social worker of indeterminate gender, could hardly be more extreme. The Olympians cared little for the great mass of mankind, with whom their relations were, for the most part, distant and somewhat strained. As the author of the Aristotelian treatise

THE COUNCIL OF THE GODS. *Raphael (Italian), 1517–1518. Oil on canvas. In this painting, Olympian gods and mythological creatures look on as Zeus accepts Eros's wish to take the mortal Psyche as his wife (far right), while Mercury gives Psyche the drink of immortality (far left).*

entitled *Great Ethics* observes, it is impossible for gods and humans to be friends on the grounds that there can be no mutual exchange of feelings (1208b 27–31). Rare exceptions include the close bond between Odysseus and Athene in *The Odyssey* and between Hippolytos and Aphrodite in Euripides' play *Hippolytos*. Neither, however, can be held up as a model to emulate—not Odysseus, because he arouses the implacable enmity of Poseidon, and not Hippolytos, because he incurs the wrath of Aphrodite.

Although the gods were anthropomorphic—having the same physical shape as humans—in origin, they embodied aspects of the natural world and the human psyche. Apart from Hera, the first generation of Olympians— Zeus, Poseidon, Demeter, Hestia, and Hades—all personified natural forces, whereas the second generation—Hephaistos, Athene, Ares, Apollo, Artemis, Hermes, and Aphrodite—were representative of human accomplishments or attributes. Mercifully, there was no Prince of Darkness to prey on people's fears.

The Olympians did not create the world. They were not the first dynasty of gods to rule over it, nor was there any guarantee that they would go on ruling it forever. Kronos, who came to power by castrating his father Ouranos, sought to preserve his rule by swallowing his children alive. Likewise, his son Zeus, who acquired power by overthrowing his father in turn, took active steps to circumvent the prophecy that he would sire a son more powerful than himself. The following paragraphs describe the major deities and their spheres of influence.

ZEUS Although Zeus, "the father of gods and men," as Homer describes him, was supreme among the Olympians, his authority did not go unchallenged. Hera, his current wife, constantly sought to thwart his will. (Hesiod tells us that he had been married seven times previously.) Zeus alone of the gods concerned himself with justice, though he was far from consistent in his pursuit of that aim. Moreover, his own behavior fell lamentably short of setting a standard of morality for humans. His sexual appetite was insatiable, and later tradition credits him with having adulterous relations with at least 115 women, both mortal and immortal. In many cases, Zeus adopted a disguise, perhaps to evade, unsuccessfully for the most part, the watchful eyes of Hera. Among other incarnations, he turned into a bull to pursue Europa (Greek, Europê), a shower of rain to seduce Danaë, and a swan to entice Leda.

There were more aspects to Zeus than to any other deity. He was the god of rain, hospitality, justice, and persuasion. There was even a Zeus who was the averter of flies. Although, in theory, above Fate, Zeus tended to follow its dictates. A notable demonstration of this takes place in *The Iliad,* when, on the advice of Hera, he reluctantly decides not to save his son Sarpedon from his predestined death. Zeus's weapon was the thunderbolt, which he wielded with deadly effect against perjurers. The greatest temple built in his honor was located at Olympia, where the Olympic Games were celebrated every four years. The statue of the seated god in the temple, which was made by the Athenian sculptor Pheidias, was regarded as one of the seven wonders of the world (see p. 206). His biggest temple was erected in Athens. Begun around 520 B.C.E., it took about 650 years to complete—"a great victory of time," as one ancient writer aptly put it.

HERA Hera, Zeus's wife and eldest sister, was the guardian of marriage and queen of Olympos. Her symbol was the peacock, and the eyes of its tail feathers were believed to be the eyes of Argos, her hundred-eyed spy. In *The Iliad*, Homer depicts Hera as a nagging wife, ever suspicious that her husband is conniving behind her back but fully capable of paying him back. As indicated above, she had good reason to be suspicious of his philandering. Hera's temple at Olympia was older than that of Zeus, a fact that has suggested to some scholars that her worship on the Greek mainland predated that of Zeus. Another venerable shrine in her honor was erected at Argos. Oddly, there was no significant temple in Athens dedicated to her.

POSEIDON Poseidon, Zeus's brother, was god of the sea. His symbol was the trident, which he used to spear fish and stir up tempests. By taking the form of a colossal bull, he became the Earthshaker, capable of making the earth rumble and quake. It was Poseidon's animosity, aroused by the blinding of his son the Cyclops Polyphemos, that caused the detention of Odysseus on the island of Kalypso for seven years. Poseidon was defeated by Athene in the contest for the guardianship of Athens. His gift to Athens was a saltwater spring that he miraculously caused to spurt up out of the Acropolis, symbolizing Athens' mastery of the sea.

PORTRAIT OF ANDREA DORIA AS NEPTUNE. *Agnolo Bronzino (Italian), ca. 1540–1550. Oil on canvas.*

APHRODITE Aphrodite, the goddess of love and beauty, personified male sexual desire. The scene of her being awarded the golden apple by the Trojan prince Paris in the divine beauty contest is a popular mythological subject in Western art, one of the most notable examples being a painting by Reubens. Aphrodite defeated her rivals Hera and Athene by promising to bestow upon the judge the most beautiful woman in the world. The fulfillment of this promise led to the outbreak of the Trojan War, because Helen, the woman in question, was both married and a Greek. According to Hesiod, Aphrodite was born from the semen of Ouranos's castrated genitals, which his son Kronos had tossed into the sea. Homer, however, makes her the daughter of Zeus and Dione. According to some accounts, she was the mother of Eros, the winged boy who shoots arrows of desire into humans and gods.

APOLLO WEARING A LAUREL OR MYRTLE WREATH, *a white* peplos, *a red* himation, *and sandals. He's seated on a lion-pawed stool, holding a lyre in one hand and pouring a libation with the other. This tondo from an Attic white-ground* kylikes, *taken from a tomb in Delphi.*

PHOIBOS APOLLO Phoibos Apollo presided over a variety of activities including music, healing, plague, purification, and sunlight. In wartime, he carried a bow, in peace a lyre. It was he who sent a plague upon the Greek army encamped outside the walls of Troy in response to a prayer from his insulted priest at the beginning of Homer's *The Iliad*. He afflicted Thebes with plague when its people unknowingly harbored the parricide Oedipus. Apollo's two foremost sanctuaries were located on the tiny island of Delos, where he was born, and at Delphi, where he established his oracle. In art, he is depicted as a beautiful youth eternally poised on the threshold between adolescence and manhood. Despite his good looks, Apollo was consistently unlucky in love, often choosing partners who resisted his advances. One was Daphne, who prayed to Zeus to preserve her virginity and was transformed into a bay tree in consequence. Apollo is often regarded as the incarnation of the Hellenic spirit and embodiment of spiritual and intellectual enlightenment. This simplistic view ignores the darker side of his personality as the god of plague and unrequited love.

ARTEMIS Artemis, Apollo's twin sister, was both huntress and protectress of wild animals. She was also closely identified with the moon. Being a confirmed virgin, she was bitterly opposed to sexual intercourse. Women in childbirth were therefore advised to placate her fury by presenting her with offerings in advance of and after delivery. When the hunter Aktaion inadvertently observed her bathing, the goddess turned him into a stag and set his own dogs upon him. Artemis's temple at Ephesos on the coast of Asia Minor was one of the seven wonders of the world.

DIANA THE HUNTRESS. Anonymous, ca. 1550. Oil on canvas. The title of this French Renaissance painting refers to Artemis's Roman name, Diana.

ATHENE Athene, the daughter of Zeus and Metis (the personification of cunning), was born from her father's head when he was struck by Hephaistos's hammer during a quarrel. She emerged fully adult and dressed as a warrior. She was the goddess both of women's crafts and of defensive war. She became the patron deity of Athens by causing an olive tree to spring up on the Acropolis, symbolic of the fact that Athens' economic prosperity was based on the olive. The most sublime of all Greek temples, the Parthenon, which dominates the Acropolis, was dedicated to Athene in her capacity as a virgin or *parthenos*. It contained a statue sculpted by Pheidias that was over thirty-six feet high and covered in gold and ivory (see p. 300).

HADES Hades, the brother of Zeus, was the god of the underworld. Together with his wife Persephone, he ruled over the dead. The only myth associated with him is the abduction of Persephone.

DEMETER Demeter was the goddess of vegetation and the harvest. Her grief for her lost daughter Persephone after her abduction was believed to cause the "death" of the vegetative cycle in winter. Conversely, her yearly reunion with Persephone was thought to usher in the spring. In the outpouring of her grief for her daughter, we see her touched by emotion to a greater degree than any other Olympian deity. Almost uniquely, Demeter does not seem to have had a shadow side, although she played a prominent part in rituals pertaining to death and the afterlife, notably the Eleusinian Mysteries, which were open to all Greek speakers, male as well as female, slave as well as free.

BACCHUS. Michelangelo Merisi da Caravaggio (Italian), ca. 1595. Oil on canvas. Bacchus was the Roman name for Dionysos.

DIONYSOS Dionysos was the god of wine, fertility, nature in the raw, liberation, irrationality, and drama. His mother Semele was incinerated when Zeus manifested himself to her in his full glory as a thunderbolt. The god managed to rescue the embryo, which he sewed into his thigh. In due course, he gave birth to the infant Dionysos. According to another myth, Dionysos was killed and eaten by the Titans, who were subsequently destroyed by Zeus's thunderbolt. Out of their ashes arose the human race, part human and part divine. Dionysos was a latecomer to Olympos. His origins seem to lie in Thrace, although he is also connected with Asia Minor. His entry into Greece, and the opposition that he had to overcome, is the subject of Euripides' *Bacchai*.

HEPHAISTOS Hephaistos, the god of the forge, was the patron god of metalworkers. Being lame, he alone of the Olympians was not physically perfect. According to one version of his birth, his mother Hera bore him by parthenogenesis in order to spite Zeus. Somewhat paradoxically, Hephaistos's wife was the beautiful Aphrodite, who perhaps not unsurprisingly found the nimble-footed Ares a more agreeable partner. In *The Odyssey*, we learn that, when the pair began an adulterous affair, Hephaistos fashioned a miraculous net that locked them in an inextricable embrace. He then invited all the gods to come and witness the spectacle. An important temple to Hephaistos overlooked the Agora in Athens. In its vicinity, much evidence of bronze working has been found.

HERMES Hermes, the son of Zeus and Maia, was the god of trade, commerce, and thieves. He also served as messenger of the gods and guide of the dead to the underworld. For this reason, he is usually depicted wearing a traveling hat and winged sandals and carrying a herald's staff known as a *kêrykeion*. Statues of the god in the form of an upright pillar with sculptured head and erect phallus stood at street corners throughout Athens. These figures, known as herms, safeguarded gates and doorways.

ARES Ares, the god of war, was the son of Zeus and Hera. Despite his importance, he was little venerated by the Greeks, perhaps because of his bloodthirsty nature. Even in *The Iliad* he is treated with scant respect. When he is wounded and comes sniveling to Zeus, the latter describes him as a two-faced liar and sends him packing (5.889f.). Ares received little attention in Athens despite the fact that the most venerable council, known as the Areiopagos or Hill of Ares, bore his name.

THE HEAD OF ARES *from a Roman sculpture, copied from a Greek bronze original by Alkamenes dated 420 B.C.E.*

HESTIA Hestia, guardian of the Olympian hearth, was in some ways the most neglected of the Olympian deities. She features in no myths, and no temples were erected in her honor. Both the family hearth and the hearth that symbolized the city were, however, sacred to her.

Other important gods who did not reside on Olympos include Pan and Asklepios, both of whom gained entry into Athens in the fifth century B.C.E.

PAN Pan, who resembled a goat from the waist down, was in origin a rustic deity. He was worshipped in caves throughout Attica, the most prominent of which was situated on the north side of the Acropolis. The seven-reed *syrinx*, or panpipe, was his invention. He was capable of causing panic both in individuals and in armies. His cult was officially introduced to Athens after the battle of Marathon in 490 B.C.E., in recognition of the assistance he had rendered at the battle by instilling "panic" in the Persians.

ASKLEPIOS In his capacity as human physician, Asklepios, who was the son of Apollo and a nymph named Koronis, is first mentioned in Homer (*Iliad* 2.731f.). Legend had it that Zeus slew him with a thunderbolt because he had the presumptuousness to raise the dead to life. This detail is important because it speaks to a characteristic Greek caution—the need to respect human limitations no matter how great one's skill. Thanks to the priesthood of Apollo, however, Asklepios came in time to be awarded divine status and began to attract cult, so that eventually sanctuaries were established to him all over the eastern Mediterranean. His shrine at Epidauros in the northeast Peloponnese was the foremost healing sanctuary in the Greek world.

A number of minor deities were believed to reside in streams, rivers, and lakes (naiads), on mountains (oreads), and in trees (dryads). Although there was a multiplicity of deities to choose from, the forms of worship were remarkably similar. The main exception was the ecstatic cults, such as those belonging to Dionysos and the Great Mother, which provided a context for the abandonment of social constraints by encouraging the worshipper to "stand outside" of herself or himself (the literal meaning of the Greek word *ekstasis).*

Gods of the Earth

All the deities discussed so far dwelt in the sky, on the earth, or under water. There was, however, another powerful group of divine beings who were thought to reside underground. They are called chthonic deities, after the Greek word *chthôn,* meaning "earth." Chthonic religion was in many ways the exact antithesis to Olympian religion. Chthonic deities were worshipped in caves and subterranean passages. Whereas the Olympian deities, except for the lame, metalworking god Hephaistos, were physically perfect, chthonic deities tended to be loathsome and repulsive.

We know much less about them because they have left little trace in the archaeological record, but they may be older than the Olympian deities. Although few Greek writers make reference to them, there can be little doubt that they constituted an important and vibrant aspect of Greek religion, notwithstanding the fact that the state does not seem to have expended much money on them. Individuals, rather than groups, primarily conducted chthonic rituals to appease their anger or invoke their assistance. They were believed to exert a profound influence on human affairs, notably in regard to fertility and food production. They were also invoked to bring evil and destruction upon one's enemy. One form that this took was the so-called curse tablet, a lead tablet that was placed in a grave, a well, or a chthonic sanctuary (see p. 205). Among the dead the young were particularly favored, perhaps because they were deemed to be rancorous and willing to vent their anger indiscriminately. The tablet was inscribed with a text identifying the person being cursed and the parts of the body (e.g., tongue, hand, belly) to be affected by the curse. Sometimes the tablets were rolled up and pierced with a needle, and sometimes a small figure resembling a voodoo doll was included. Common targets were rivals in an athletic competition, a lawsuit, or a love triangle. Although we have no way of knowing what percentage of the population resorted to such measures, it is a fact that conditional curses (i.e., "If X does so-and-so, may such-and-such happen to him or her") were utilized by Greek communities to encourage conformity to their expectations and regulations. For instance, the oath that the Athenians took before the battle of Plataiai in 479 B.C.E. and later administered on an annual basis to ephebes is inscribed as follows: "If I remain faithful to the inscribed oath, may women give birth to children who resemble their parents. If I do not, may they give birth to monsters."

The most memorable appearance of chthonic deities in literature is that of the Furies at the opening of the *Eumenides,* the third play in Aeschylus's *Oresteia,* who are in pursuit of Orestes to Delphi for the crime of murdering his mother. They are described as follows: "They are women—no, not women but Gorgons rather. And yet they are not quite Gorgons either. . . . They are wingless, black, and they snore. Evil pus oozes from their eyes" (lines 48–54).

Later Apollo orders them from his sanctuary with the following menacing words: "Go to where heads are chopped off and eyes gouged out, to justice and slaughtering, to destruction of seed and of young men's pride, to mutilations and stoning, and to the lamentations of people being impaled" (lines 186–90).

Priests and Priestesses

The Greek word *hiereus,* which is roughly translated as priest, denotes an official who supervised the *hiera* (i.e., sacred objects) stored within a sanctuary and who conducted sacred rites connected with cult. The chief task was the supervision of sacrifices and the performing of other cult acts, particularly in connection with festivals. No Greek, as far as we know, ever regarded the priesthood as a vocation in the way that a Christian priest does. Eligibility to office was based on external qualifications rather than intellectual or moral attributes, though it is no surprise to learn that prostitutes, army deserters, and debtors were disqualified. The principal qualification seems to have been the absence of any physical blemish, because this was thought to constitute proof of divine disfavor. As far as we know, priests did not have to undergo any formal training. Nor do we know of any ordination that they underwent before assuming office. In most cases, a priesthood was only a part-time occupation. In democratic Athens, the newer priesthoods were annual appointments to which all members of the citizen body were eligible, whereas the older cults, such as that of Athene Polias ("Of the city"), were reserved for members of a particular noble kin group, or *genos,* and held for life. One such priestess, Lysimache, served for sixty-four years. It is suspected that Lysistrate, the heroine of Aristophanes' play of that name (produced 411 B.C.E.), is modeled upon her, as Aristophanes' pun on her name in the title of his play suggests. (Lysimache means "She who releases the battle," whereas Lysistrate means "She who releases the army"). In some parts of the Greek world, wealthy individuals paid considerable sums to become a priest, because of the prestige that the office carried.

In general, priests attended male deities, and priestesses attended female deities. They received only a modest fee for their services, though they were entitled to a choice piece of the sacrificial meat. Their duties were primarily of a liturgical and administrative nature. They were not expected to administer to the spiritual needs of , nor did they take any part in ceremonies that had to do with birth, marriage, and death. With the exception of those who officiated at the mysteries, they had no dealings with the afterlife. The Stranger in Plato's *Statesman* (290cD) aptly defines priests as those who "know how to offer our gifts to the gods in sacrifices so as to please them, and who know, too, the right way to pray to the gods so they bestow blessings on worshippers." Since there was no centralized religious authority either in Athens or anywhere else in the Greek world, priests were not able to exercise any influence over the political process, other than by virtue of their personalities.

Pollution

One of the most terrifying inventions of the Greek mind was the belief in *miasma,* or pollution. Miasma, whose workings were invisible, was analogous to a virus and capable of infecting a whole community if its course went unchecked. The belief in pollution may well owe its origins in part to the experience of contagious diseases such as plague or typhus, for which no medical explanation was available. However, miasma was not exclusively a physiological phenomenon. It had a religious dimension as well. In ascending order of magnitude, the principal causes of pollution were childbirth, death by natural causes, accidental homicide, and murder. The presence of an undetected murderer in a community could cause barrenness and blight among humans, livestock, and crops. Such at least is the premise underlying the plot of Sophokles' *Oedipus the King,* as we see from the following description of the city of Thebes at the beginning of the play:

> A blight is upon the fruitful plants of the earth, a blight is upon cattle among the pastures, and upon the barren labor pangs of women. A god who carries fire, a deadly pestilence, swoops down upon our city and ravages it, emptying the house of Kadmos [its founder]. Black Hades grows rich with groans and lamentations. (lines 25–30)

Whether Athenians of Sophokles' day actually believed that an undetected murderer could infect a whole community seems doubtful, though some of them may well have found it convenient to scapegoat a supposedly polluted individual for an otherwise inexplicable disaster. To prevent miasma from seeping into the community, elaborate rites of purification were conducted by priests in consultation with religious experts known as *exêgêtai,* or expounders. The most common purifying agents were saltwater, fire, sulfur, and blood, the most effective agent being the blood of a pig.

Foretelling the Future

An important reason for worshiping the gods was the fact that they had knowledge of the future, even though they did not control human destiny. Consultations mainly took place at oracular shrines, where the gods dispensed their knowledge through a medium who served as their mouthpiece. We know of ten oracular shrines in the Greek world. The most prestigious was at Delphi, where Pythian Apollo presided. No question was too important or too trivial to put to the oracle. Individuals might inquire, "Should I get married?," "Should I go on a sea voyage?," or "Should I adopt an heir?" States might ask, "Should we go to war?," Should we make peace?," or "Should we make a treaty?" Most answers came in the form of a simple affirmative or negative, but occasionally the petitioner received a more detailed and complicated response. In many cases, one suspects, he or she came to the oracle primarily to seek divine sanction for a decision that had already been reached.

An oracular response did not remove the responsibility of decision making from the petitioner, as the following anecdote told by Herodotos (1.53) clearly indicates. When Kroisos, king of Lydia, consulted Delphi about the advisability of declaring war on the neighboring kingdom of Persia, he was informed that, if he did so, he would destroy a large empire. Emboldened by this response, Kroisos duly declared war on Persia and fulfilled the prophecy—by destroying his own empire. What this cautionary tale reveals is that Delphi was not a place to get a quick fix on life's problems. On the contrary, the value of its utterances was nil if the petitioner did not inform them with a proper sense of his own limitations. Not for nothing was the injunction "Know yourself" engraved on the sanctuary wall.

Other means of foretelling the future included examining the entrails of sacrificial victims, observing the flights of birds, and interpreting the significance of dreams. Natural phenomena such as eclipses and earthquakes were also thought to presage the future. The reading of these signs was in the hands of itinerant seers, who hired out their services to individuals as well as states. Seers played a particularly important role on the battlefield, where they supervised the sacrifices that preceded any decision to join or delay battle. It was on the advice of a seer that the Athenian general Nikias took the fatal decision to delay withdrawing his forces from Sicily after an eclipse of the moon had taken place in 413 B.C.E., thereby bringing about the complete destruction of his army.

Breakaway Sects
Mainstream Greek religion offered a wide choice of deities from which individuals were free to choose on the basis of a variety of criteria. These included family

tradition, social status, personal preference, and last, but not least, ease of access to the deity's shrine. In addition to the worship of individual deities, there were cults that demanded unwavering and exclusive devotion by their adherents. Two such cults, as noted earlier, were Orphism and Pythagoreanism, both of which rejected state religion and sought to establish separate communities of worshippers. Neither Orphism nor Pythagoreanism appealed to anything but a tiny fraction of the population, however, and, as religious movements (if indeed they can be so called), they hardly feature at all in the Classical or Hellenistic Period.

Conclusions

Religion had a highly cohesive effect on Greek society. The major state festivals, such as the Panathenaia and the City Dionysia in Athens, were occasions when virtually the entire citizen body came together to honor the gods. It also drew together persons with similar backgrounds and of similar social status, because they would tend to worship the same gods. Similarly, each Athenian deme held festivals in which the entire deme population participated. A shared religion was, in fact, a hallmark of Greek identity. The historian Herodotus (8.144.2) tells us that, in 480 B.C.E., when a Spartan embassy arrived in Athens, fearful that the Athenians were going to side with the Persians at the time of the Persian invasion, the Athenians defined "Greekness" as, among other things, observing the same religious rituals.

The fortunes of individual deities ebbed and flowed according to necessity and need. Cults came and went, and, in extreme cases, sanctuaries were

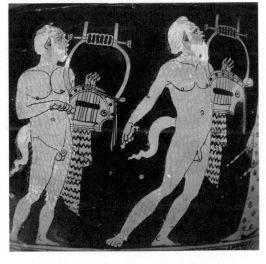

PAPPOSILENOI—SATYR-LIKE COMPANIONS OF DIONYSUS—*sing and play musical instruments during Panathenaia. Attic red-figure vase, ca. 420 B.C.E., depicts.*

leased out to new gods—or sold altogether. A new cult was accepted into the city's pantheon typically when the Greeks won a spectacular military victory; experienced a natural disaster such as drought, famine, or plague; or redefined their social and political identity. In other words, war, catastrophe, and social or political unrest were the main catalysts of change within a system of belief that was constantly in flux.

It is sometimes thought that Greek polytheism was no match for Christianity and that it went into terminal decline from the first century C.E. onward. In fact, polytheism endured long after the rise of Christianity. The Delphic Oracle was still issuing pronouncements in 267 C.E., when a barbarous people called the Heruli destroyed the sanctuary. In 395 C.E., Athens was saved from Alaric and the Visigoths by an epiphany of Athene and Achilles, who appeared, fully armed, astride the city walls. Not until 529 C.E. were the old gods officially laid to rest, when the Byzantine emperor Justinian forbade any pagan to teach philosophy in Athens. Even long after that, however, there are likely to have been pockets of resistance.

Economy and Trade

Although the word *economy* derives directly from *oikonomia*, which means literally "regulation of the household," the Greeks did not have a concept of economics comparable to our understanding of the word. Certainly there is no evidence to suggest that their behavior was determined by economic considerations of the kind that influence modern nation states. More fundamentally still, they did not regard the economy as an autonomous category over which the state might exercise control. There was no such thing as a budget prepared by officials in charge of the state treasury. Except in extreme circumstances, it is doubtful whether the Greeks had any way of determining what we would call today the health of their economy.

So far as there was anything resembling economic policy, this was generally limited to the supply of basic necessities, the most essential of which was corn. Prices fluctuated according to the law of supply and demand, and these fluctuations affected the standard of living. The Peloponnesian War had a profound effect upon wealthy and poor Athenians alike as a result of the devastation of the countryside by the enemy coupled with the heavy burden of taxation. Similarly, at the end of the Social War in 355 B.C.E., Athens was practically bankrupt. Its need to recoup its losses is evident in the subsequent reluctance of its citizens to engage in hostilities with the rising power of Macedon in the reign of Philip II. Because the Greeks, unlike ourselves, had no expectation that their standard of living would increase over the course of their lifetime, however, they were probably less unnerved by fluctuations than we are.

Coinage

Coinage first appeared in western Anatolia (modern Turkey) around 600 B.C.E. Legend also connects its origins with this region through Midas, the king of Phrygia, whose touch turned everything to gold. Prior to the invention of coinage, most transactions were conducted in kind. At the beginning of *The Odyssey,* Athene, in the guise of Mentes, declares that she has a cargo of iron that she is going to exchange for bronze (1.182–84). Elsewhere in the Homeric poems, bronze utensils and cattle are cited as standards of value. No doubt many exchanges throughout antiquity were conducted by bartering, even after the introduction of coinage.

The first kingdom to mint coins was Lydia, whose king's name, Croesus, has become a byword for wealth ("as rich as Croesus"). The earliest coins were made of electrum, an alloy of gold and silver found in the waters of the River Paktolos near the Lydian capital of Sardis. Later, the Lydians struck coins of pure gold and silver. Coinage was introduced to the Greek mainland in the first half of the sixth century B.C.E. The leader was the island of Aigina, which began

SOME OF THE EARLIEST COINAGE, *dating to ca. 600 B.C.E. Found at the Temple of Artemis at Ephesos.*

minting silver coins around 570 B.C.E. Aiginetan coins were stamped with a sea tortoise, the island's emblem, on the obverse (i.e., principal face of a coin). In time, all the cities that minted coins identified their own by stamping them with an emblem. For instance, Corinthian coins are identified by the figure of Pegasos, the winged horse, whereas Athenian coins bear an owl, the symbol of Athene. Because coin types were manufactured by artists of the highest caliber, many of them are outstanding works of art as well as being priceless historical documents. Arguably the most beautiful coins were minted by Syracuse and Akragas, two Sicilian cities. Their die cutters took such pride in their work that they even signed the dies.

In all, some 1,500 mints have been identified. A notable absentee is Sparta, which used iron spits known as obols as currency. These ranged from twelve to eighteen inches in length. This cumbersome system seems to have been intentionally designed to discourage the flow of trade across its borders. Not until the third century B.C.E. did Sparta begin to mint coins.

Athens first began minting its famous "owls" during the Peisistratid tyranny, so named because they bore the image of an owl, sacred to the goddess, on the reverse (see page xvii). On the obverse, they bore the helmeted head of the goddess Athene. Beside the head of Athene were written the letters "ΑΘΕ" (ATHE), an abbreviation for the name of the city.

To cope with the increasing complexity of financial transactions, money changers, known as *trapezitai,* set up tables in public places and operated a system based on letters of credit that anticipated the use of checks. In the Hellenistic Period, Egypt developed a centralized banking system with numerous local branches and a head bank in Alexandria. In the same period, coins bearing the heads of rulers became common. Particularly noteworthy are those issued by the Hellenistic dynasts, which depict Alexander the Great in the guise of Herakles wearing the skin of the Nemean lion. On the obverse, Zeus is seated on his throne. These coins performed an important propagandist function by illustrating the issuing dynast's claim to be the heir to Alexander the Great, who himself claimed descent from Herakles, the son of Zeus. They thereby helped to legitimize the dynast's shaky entitlement to kingship.

Imports and Exports

In *The Politics,* Aristotle claims that economic *autarkeia,* or self-sufficiency, was the goal to which each polis should aspire; an economy, in other words, that was not dependent on imports, but that supported itself by farming, fishing, hunting, trapping, and gathering plants, wild fruits, and nuts. It was an ideal that few, if any, *poleis* achieved. The extreme example to the contrary is Athens, whose economy by the middle of the fifth century B.C.E. was very largely dependent on imports. When the Athenians took the decision to abandon the Attic countryside at the outbreak of the Peloponnesian War and live off the revenue and trade from their empire, they were tacitly acknowledging the extent to which they had shifted from a land-based to a maritime economy. No doubt the abandonment of the countryside caused a great deal of economic hardship to many people; however, the fact that such a move was possible is a measure of the degree to which Athens was unable to support itself agriculturally.

Probably the main imports and exports throughout the Greek world were grain, wine, olive oil, and pottery. The most common form of commercial container was a two-handled jar with a narrow neck known as an *amphoreus,* meaning "carried on both sides," which gives us the word *amphora.* Amphorae varied greatly in size and shape, depending on what type of commodity they were intended to hold, though the average capacity in Classical and Hellenistic times was about five gallons. Plain on the outside, amphorae were often coated on the inside with resin or pitch to prevent seepage. They were generally stacked upright on ships and horizontally in shops and in the home. Some 40,000 amphora handles have been found in Athens, and 90,000 in Alexandria, making these cities the largest importers of wine—though, as indicated, not all would have contained wine. Few items are as ubiquitous as amphorae in the ancient world—or as expressive of the repetitive nature of daily life.

Athens' chief import was grain, its main supplier being the Black Sea region, particularly the Bosphoros. Other major sources included Egypt, Libya, Cyprus, Sicily, and Italy. Its dependency on imported corn was a leading factor in Athens' decision to develop the Piraeus, which in the second half of the fifth century B.C.E. became the foremost commercial port in the eastern Mediterranean. So vital was imported grain to Athens' survival that the *demos* made it a capital offense to ship it to ports other than the Piraeus. It was also illegal to extend a maritime loan other than to a merchant who agreed to convey grain to the Piraeus. In the high season, a minimum of six grain ships had to dock at the port each day to meet Athens' huge requirement.

Athens also had to import virtually all its shipbuilding supplies. These included timber, sailcloth, and ruddle, which was used for the painting of triremes. The chief supplier of timber was Macedon, supplemented by Thrace and southern Italy. Athens also imported slaves, particularly from Thrace, the Black Sea region, and Asia Minor. In the fourth century B.C.E., it probably needed to import approximately 6,000 slaves per annum in order to maintain its full complement. Other major imports included tin, iron, and copper.

Athens' essential imports were not its only ones. Perikles boasted with justification that "all the produce of every land comes to Athens" (Thukydides 2.38.2). An impressive list of the exotic commodities for sale in Athenian markets is provided by a comic writer called Hermippos in a play dated around 420 B.C.E. It includes silphium (a plant used in medicine and as a condiment) and ox hides from Cyrene in Libya; mackerel and salt fish from the Hellespont; pork and cheese from Syracuse; sailcloth, rigging, and papyrus from Egypt; cypress wood from Crete; ivory from Libya; raisins and dried figs from Rhodes; pears and apples from Euboia; slaves from Phrygia; mercenaries from Arkadia; tattooed and untattooed slaves from Pagasai; acorns and almonds from Paphlagonia; dates and wheat flour from Phoenicia; and, finally, rugs and cushions from Carthage. As a result of its imports, Athenians enjoyed a much more varied diet and lifestyle than any other Greeks until the Hellenistic Period.

The most valuable Athenian export was silver, which is discussed in the next section. Other exports included olives, olive oil, wine, marble, and honey. The only manufactured goods that were exported were pottery and armor.

Silver Mines

Athens was fortunate in possessing rich deposits of silver. Its mines were located at Lavrion in southeast Attica. Mining concessions were auctioned off annually by state officials to private individuals. They were purchased by both indigent and wealthy lessees, equally eager to make their fortunes. Each successful bidder was free to extract as much silver from his concession as he could for the duration of his lease. The monies accruing to the Athenian state from its silver mines were considerable. A strike made in 483 B.C.E. yielded a revenue of 100 talents. On the recommendation of the politician Themistokles, this sum was devoted to the building of a fleet of 100 *triremes*, or warships. When mining activity reached its peak in the middle of the fourth century B.C.E., production stood at around 1,000 talents per year. The industry was very much subject to external pressures, however, and, in time of war, it was sometimes suspended altogether.

The State Exchequer

Although the Athenians were incapable of planning an economic strategy, they did possess a public exchequer. In Thukydides' *History,* Perikles informs the Athenians on the eve of the outbreak of the Peloponnesian War that the state possessed 6,000 talents of coined silver, stored for safekeeping on the Acropolis (2.13.3–6). In addition, the gold that covered the statue of Athene Parthenos inside the Parthenon was worth forty talents. This, he suggested, could be melted down and used in the war effort, as long as it was replaced afterward. It became commonplace in the following century to plunder temple treasures for this purpose. Those that suffered the most included the sanctuaries at Delphi and Olympia.

The acquisition of its maritime empire greatly increased Athens' wealth. Although ostensibly the tribute exacted from the allies financed their fleet, the Athenians were in no doubt that they were the beneficiaries of an imperialist enterprise. This is evident from their custom of parading their tribute in the Theater of Dionysos at the City Dionysia, likely to loud applause. In Aristophanes' *Knights,* a character named Demos, who is an unflattering personification of the Athenian people, dotes idiotically on a diet of tribute, flattery, gifts, feasts, and festivals.

Taxation

Lower- and middle-income Athenians did not pay taxes. Only the wealthy were required to make a contribution to the state. The first instance of direct taxation occurred during the Peloponnesian War, when the state exacted a special levy called an *eisphora,* or "contribution," to meet the cost of soldiers' pay. In the fourth century B.C.E., the 300 wealthiest citizens were required to pay an annual *eisphora*. Wealthy Athenians and metics were also required to subsidize important and costly public programs called *liturgies*. Those selected to be *gymnasiarchs*, for instance, had to bear the cost of maintaining a public gymnasium, whereas *chorêgoi* had to pay all the expenses involved in training the chorus for a tragic or comic production. The largest group of all, the *trierarchs*, had the burden of equipping and maintaining a trireme. No fixed sum of money was laid down for any of these duties because it was confidently expected that gymnasiarchs, chorêgoi, and trierarchs would vie with one another for the reputation of financing the best gymnasium, the best production or the best fitted-out trireme. It is unclear how Athenians in this supertax bracket were identified. As a safeguard against abuse, however, any Athenian who was called upon to perform a liturgy and who believed that he had been wrongly identified had the right to issue a challenge to anyone whom he considered to be wealthier than himself. The person so challenged was then under an obligation to either undertake the liturgy himself or swap properties with the person who had challenged him.

Conclusions

With so much surplus wealth in the Athenian economy in the second half of the fifth century as a result of the empire, we might expect that the standard of living would have risen. Archaeological evidence, however, suggests no such thing. As we have seen, the residential quarters of Athens were extremely modest. Evidently the attainment of a luxurious standard of living was not seen as a necessary or even particularly desirable goal, though there was considerable interest in the antics of the super-rich Alkibiades, who devoted part of his large fortune to the training of expensive racehorses. If private luxury had been their goal, the Athenians would not have spent 2,000 talents on one of the most ambitious building programs ever conceived. Nor, for that matter, would they have used the revenue from their silver mines a generation earlier to build a fleet. In sum, though a few wealthy citizens became more wealthy, most of the poor tended to remain poor. There is little evidence for the existence of a middle class and nothing to indicate that it increased as a result of Athens' empire. What Athens' increased wealth did provide, however, was the means whereby a substantial proportion of its citizens could combine leisure with relative frugality.

LAW AND ORDER

Our knowledge of crime in ancient Greece is meager. We know much more about legal procedure than we do about criminals. Although we hear about burglary, theft, mugging, rape, and murder, we know only of isolated cases. We are unable to compare the prevalence of such crimes in antiquity with their occurrence today.

ANCIENT MUNICIPAL LAW *inscribed on a fifth-century B.C.E. building in Crete.*

Most of our evidence comes from law-court speeches that were written on behalf of well-to-do clients embroiled in cases of disputed adoption, inheritance, and the like. The following discussion, therefore, reflects the limitations of our sources.

No Greek community had a police force in the modern sense of the term. The Skythian archers whom Athens possessed had the primary task of keeping the peace. In the absence of any state-run means of law enforcement, it was up to the injured party to arrest any criminal caught in the act and to bring him or her before a magistrate. This must have been extremely difficult in the case of victims of violent crime, especially if they happened to be elderly or female. If the injured party was incapable of apprehending the criminal, he or she could summon the magistrate, who would then make an arrest on his or her behalf. Instances of this sort, however, are likely to have been rare. In the case of a wrongful arrest, a fine of 1,000 drachmas was imposed. Other than in cases involving theft, murder, rape, and adultery, the accused received a written summons naming the day that he or she was required to appear before a magistrate.

Bringing an Action

Athenian law was divided into public and private actions. Public actions involved the community as a whole, whereas private actions concerned individuals. There was no public prosecutor. Although in practice many cases would have been brought to the courts by magistrates or other officials, Solon legislated that "anyone who wishes" was free to initiate prosecution in a public action, or *graphê*. This privilege was regularly abused by individuals who had an aptitude for meddlesomeness and litigiousness and who used it to bring frivolous or unjustifiable actions, as we know from numerous complaints in literature as well as from remarks by prosecutors and plaintiffs, who preen themselves on the grounds that they have "never previously appeared before a jury of their peers." Indeed it seems to have been one of the major drawbacks in the Athenian judicial system. In the case of a private suit or *dikê*, it was the responsibility of the injured party to bring the action. In cases of homicide, the relatives of the victim were required to prosecute the killer.

A preliminary hearing called an *anakrisis* took place before a magistrate. Oaths were exchanged by the plaintiff and the defendant, the former swearing that his accusation was genuine, the latter either admitting guilt or swearing that he was innocent. The defendant was free at this time to enter a counterplea. The case was then assigned to a particular court on a particular date. All trials, irrespective of the severity of the charges, were confined in scope to the space of a single day. Only a limited amount of cross-examination took place. The testimony of slaves could be obtained only under torture.

Trial Procedure

Although magistrates presided over trials, they did not serve as judges in the modern sense of the term. They gave neither advice nor directions to the jury, nor did they sentence those who were found guilty. They merely supervised the proceedings. The *dikastêria,* or law courts, were served by panels of jurors, drawn from a pool of 6,000 citizens, annually selected from all those who applied. The only qualification was that a juror had to be over thirty years of age. Juries were often extremely large because it was believed that this reduced the likelihood of bribery. The more serious the charge, the larger was the number of jurors. One jury is said to have numbered 1,501. As we have seen, Perikles was the first to introduce pay for jurors. Although it was less than a day's wage for a laborer, it was no doubt much appreciated by the poor, the elderly, and the infirm. Given the advanced age of many jurors, scholars suspect that they tended to be rather conservative. Aristophanes' comic play *Wasps* (produced 422 B.C.E.), which takes its name from a chorus of elderly jurors dressed as wasps, lends support to this view, as the jurors are portrayed as taking malicious delight in delivering harsh judgments. Because leading politicians and indeed prominent individuals in general were in constant danger of being prosecuted, jurors who were assigned to important cases exercised considerable power and influence.

First the prosecution spoke and then the defense. The length of their speeches depended on the seriousness of the charge. Even a capital case, however, was over in a single day. Witnesses were not called, though their sworn testimonies were read out in court. A water-clock ensured that both the prosecution and the defense had exactly the same amount of time to present their cases. Once the defense had spoken, the jurors voted without deliberation. In the fifth century B.C.E., jurors cast their votes in secret. Each juror was provided with two tokens, one for conviction and the other for acquittal. The juror deposited one of these in a wooden urn whose tokens were disregarded, and the other in a bronze urn whose votes were counted. Judgment was passed on a majority verdict. In the fifth century B.C.E., a tie meant an acquittal. In the following century, odd-numbered juries were the norm. There was no procedure for an appeal.

Scholars often point out that Greek culture was intensely agonistic (meaning "competitive") in nature, a word derived from *agôn*, "contest," and trials are one of the ways in which this agonistic spirit would have manifested itself. We can well imagine that many Athenians regarded jury service as a type of spectator sport, particularly since it was common practice for prosecutors and defendants to resort to such underhand tactics as parading their children before the court, no doubt suitably prepped to win the jury's sympathy.

Sokrates on Trial

Athens' most celebrated trial took place in 399 B.C.E., just after the restoration of democracy at the end of the Peloponnesian War. The defendant was the seventy-year-old philosopher Sokrates, who was accused of corrupting the youth, introducing new gods (the technical term was "new daimonic beings," or divine beings who were not quite on the level of gods), and failing to acknowledge "the gods whom the city acknowledges."

The real, though unstated charge, however, was that Sokrates had consorted with highly undesirable aristocrats who had suspended the Athenian constitution in 404 B.C.E. and set up a very repressive government known as the Thirty Tyrants. In addition, many Athenians probably found Sokrates quite insufferable, because he never tired of pointing out their faults, often in a supercilious and patronizing manner. He also manifested a barely disguised contempt for democracy. In other words, it is fair to say that Sokrates' character, no less than his behavior, was on trial. Sokrates himself says as much in Plato's *Apology,* when he claims that his accusers include not only the three men who have brought charges against him but also all those who hold a negative opinion of him (18b).

Plato's *Apology* purports to be a record of what Sokrates said in his defense. (The Greek word *apologia* does not carry the same connotation of guilt as it does in English. On the contrary, it is the technical term for any speech delivered by the defense.) Plato, who idolized Sokrates, was equally contemptuous of democracy. For a variety of reasons, we therefore need to be wary of treating his *Apology* as anything remotely resembling a transcript of what Sokrates actually said.

Instead of trying to win over the hearts and minds of the jurors, Sokrates went out of his way to dare them to pronounce him guilty. He even had the temerity to summon the Delphic Oracle, which had declared him to be the most intelligent of all Athenians, as a defense witness. He likened himself to a gadfly that flutters around an indolent horse. The image was hardly calculated to make the jury feel well disposed toward the accused, not least because Athenians prided themselves on their energy and intelligence. Hardly surprisingly, a majority of sixty jurors found him guilty.

Sentencing

For certain crimes, statutory punishments were laid down by law. In private actions damages, dependent upon a conviction, were often agreed in advance. In the absence of any agreement, however, one-third of the trial day was put aside to determine the penalty. After a verdict of guilty had been pronounced, the prosecutor rose to propose a penalty, followed by the defendant, who would propose a more lenient penalty. The jury then voted again. Fines, exile, and partial or complete loss of citizen rights (atimia) were customary punishments. In civil cases, if the plaintiff failed to secure one-fifth of the votes or if he failed to put in an appearance at the court, the standard fine was one-sixth of the damages that he was claiming.

At Sokrates' trial, the prosecution actually demanded the death penalty. To show his contempt for this suggestion, for the charges themselves, and for the process, Sokrates recommended that he be given free meals in the Prytaneion or City Hall for the rest of his life—a privilege that was reserved for public benefactors, including athletic victors. This so infuriated the jury that they voted by a margin of eighty more votes in favor of his execution. In other words, eighty jurors voted to execute a man whom they had previously found innocent of all charges. Something was obviously wrong with a system that permitted rancor to prevail over reason, but we never hear of any attempts to reform it.

Imprisonment

Imprisonment was imposed only on a short-term basis, primarily for those awaiting trial or execution. Prisoners were supervised by a group of junior

THE DEATH OF SOCRATES. Jacques-Louis David (French), 1787. Oil on canvas.

magistrates known as the Eleven, who also had the task of supervising the execution of condemned criminals. Athens' most famous prisoner was Sokrates, who was detained for several days while awaiting his execution. (His execution was delayed because his trial and condemnation coincided with an important religious ritual that was taking place and to have executed him during this period would have aroused the anger of the gods.) It used to be believed that a building located in the southwest corner of the Agora consisting of twelve small rooms served as Athens' state prison, but recently doubts have been raised about the identification.

Execution

Although murder, larceny, theft, picking pockets, housebreaking, kidnapping, and temple robbing rarely resulted in execution, as Sokrates' trial indicates, any serious offense was punishable by death if the prosecution saw fit to demand it. In extreme cases such as treason and tomb robbery, the condemned was denied the rite of burial. Criminals of this sort were hurled off a rock and left to rot in the *barathron,* or pit, a rocky gully which probably lay a short distance west of the Acropolis. In Sparta, a similar practice took place at a site called the Kaiades. This practice ensured that the dead would never be granted access to Hades but wander disconsolately up and down the banks of the River Styx for all eternity. In Macedon, hanging was the preferred form of execution. There is little evidence to suggest that decapitation was ever practiced in the Greek world.

Conclusions

There were several weaknesses in the Athenian legal system, excellent though it was by the standards of the day. In the first place, a trial resembled a public spectacle, with skillful oratory playing a disproportionate part in the outcome. Second, the large size of many juries increased the possibility of a verdict being subject to crowd hysteria. We know of at least one instance in which the citizen body, sitting in assembly, made a decision in the heat of the moment and reversed it the next day; it is likely that comparable changes of heart among jurors occurred from time to time. Because no procedure existed for lodging an appeal, however, only exceptionally was a verdict overturned. Third, although some penalties were fixed, many were not. In the latter case, this meant that jurors often opted for one of the two choices before them on the basis of the impact that the accused and the defendant had made on them during the trial. Fourth, although the legal system was intended to uphold the rule of law, in practice it continued to countenance, if not actively encourage, the pursuit of a family vendetta. This was particularly true in cases of homicide, because it was the duty of the relatives of the murdered victim to take it upon themselves to prosecute the killer. Many actions of lesser import are also likely to have been motivated by revenge. In one trial, a prosecutor admitted as much, confident that his transparency would not count against him in the eyes of the jury.

WORK

Agriculture

Because of the importance attached to land ownership, the most respected occupation was farming. Even in the late fifth century B.C.E., at least half the population of Athens was still engaged in agriculture The overwhelming majority of farmers owned no more than two or three acres of land. Only a small minority were wealthy landowners, whose estates occupied several hundred acres. We learn most about farming from Hesiod, whose *Works and Days* provides a vivid account of the agricultural year. As the poet emphasizes, it was an extremely arduous occupation even at the best of times, owing to the poor quality of the soil. Although Hesiod is referring to Boiotia, this would have been true of many parts of the Greek mainland, including Attica. The fact that land had to be left fallow for a year after each season's cultivation in order not to exhaust its goodness made agriculture even more laborious.

From the fifth century B.C.E. onward, crops were rotated and manure was used. As a general rule, the cultivation of olives and grapes, along with animal husbandry, was more profitable than that of grain and vegetables. To economize on space, vines, planted in rows, were interspersed with vegetables and fruit trees. Plowing took place twice a year, in spring and in autumn. Wooden plows, sometimes tipped with iron, were pulled by teams of oxen. Behind them walked the farmer (or one of his slaves), breaking up the clods with a hoe and covering the seeds with earth. In the harvest season all available hands gathered in the ripe grain. The grain was threshed on a stone threshing floor by driving oxen around in a circle to separate the wheat from the chaff. Each agricultural procedure was accompanied by religious ceremonies to ensure the favor of the gods. Few small farms were entirely self-sufficient. Most farmers had to travel to market to exchange their produce. In the Hellenistic Period, Egypt became the most intensively cultivated region in the Greek world.

Commerce

Already in Homer's *The Odyssey* we can detect a marked disdain for those who made their livelihood by commerce. When the Phaiakians ask Odysseus whether he is a trader, the question comes across as an insult. Even in the Classical Period, much of Athens' trade was conducted by its metic population rather than by its citizenry, which reflects this same age-old prejudice. Yet despite their low status, traders played a vital role in the exchange of grain, wine, salted fish, and luxury goods.

Part of the odium that attached to those who made their living by commerce was due to the fact that there was no clear distinction between trading and piracy in early Greece, and pirates frequently pillaged coastal communities. It was because of the risk of seaborne raids that cities like Athens were founded several miles from the coast. When Athens took control of the Aegean in the fifth century B.C.E., piracy had virtually been eliminated. With the decline of Athenian naval power in the fourth century, however, it enjoyed a resurgence. So serious was the problem in the Hellenistic Period that several Greek islands passed laws requiring women to stay indoors, for fear that they might be snatched away by pirates.

Manufacture and Retailing

Most manufacturing enterprises were extremely small. The largest Athenian *ergastêrion,* or workshop, of which we have record belonged to Kephalos, a metic who employed 120 slaves in his shield factory in the Piraeus. The father of Demosthenes employed over fifty slaves in his knife factory. The majority of enterprises were probably much smaller. It is estimated that Athens' entire force of potters in the fifth century B.C.E. numbered no more than five hundred, most of whom worked in groups of about six. Athens and the Piraeus were major centers of manufacturing. Evidence of bronze working has been found in the vicinity of the temple of Hephaistos, god of metalworking, on the west side of the Agora, while potters and vase painters worked chiefly in a district just outside the city on the west known as the Kerameikos (from which the word *ceramic* derives).

Specific cities specialized in the production of specific products. Athens was noted for its painted pottery, Corinth for its metalwork, and Megara for its cloaks. Most citizens whose livelihood derived from manufactured goods were content to leave their businesses in the hands of trusted slaves rather than devote any time or energy to them themselves. Many more products were produced in the home than is the case today. Spinning, weaving, and baking were done almost exclusively by women.

The evidence for retailing is very meager. Most establishments took the form of temporary booths set up in the marketplace on specific days each month, since many retailers were both the producer and the manufacturer. Only a few permanent establishments have come to light. A notable example is a shoe shop in the Athenian Agora, which was identified by the discovery among its ruins of leather thongs for sandals and boots, bone eyelets, and hobnails. Although Athens and the Piraeus were the principal markets for the exchange of foodstuffs and wares, each deme possessed its own agora where local exchanges took place.

Employment

The Greeks regarded the condition of working for someone else to be worse than that of a slave, since slaves at least enjoyed some measure of security. Temporary employees, in addition to being laid off at a moment's notice, had to endure the indignity of taking orders from a fellow citizen. Contemptible though employment was, however, it was probably widespread. Athenians seeking to hire themselves out as wage laborers gathered on a hill overlooking the Agora.

The most acceptable type of employment was as an employee of the state, because this did not entail subjection to a fellow citizen. In the second half of the fifth century B.C.E., the livelihoods of an increasing number of Athenians were made possible by the tribute accruing to Athens' empire. Even when Athens had lost its empire, the state continued to be a major employer. Though Aristotle's claim that state pay supported "over twenty thousand men" in the fourth century B.C.E. is an exaggeration (*Constitution of Athens* 24.3), there can be little doubt that it provided the means by which the poor could participate in democracy.

Most of the revenue went to pay the rowers of Athens' fleet. Sailors' rate of pay reflected Athens' changing economic fortunes. When its naval expedition was dispatched to Sicily in 415 B.C.E., it stood at one drachma per day. At the end of the Peloponnesian War, when Athens' reserves were well-nigh exhausted, that figure was cut by half. Unlike hoplites, whose service was intermittent, rowers constituted a full-time professional body. Because Athens generally

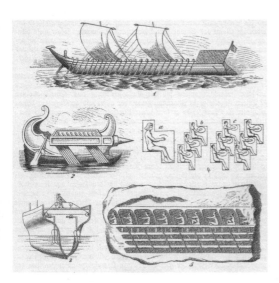

ILLUSTRATION REGARDING ANCIENT GREEK SEA VESSELS: *1. A Phoenician-style ship that carries fifty rowers; 2. A type of ancient ship called a hemiola; 3. Position of the rudder; 4. Arrangement of rowers; 5. A cross-section of a trireme shows the thwarts, or beams that run the length of the ship—note that the rowers use the beams as seats.*

maintained at least one hundred ships on active service during the fifth and fourth centuries B.C.E., its fleet must have provided employment for some twenty thousand men. Because its rowers were mostly drawn from the poorest class of citizens, the growth in Athenian naval power coincided with a growth in the political importance of the lowest social group, known as the *thêtes*. Maintaining the fleet in a seaworthy condition required the services of a large and highly specialized workforce of joiners, fitters, rope makers, painters, and sailcloth makers. Many of these were probably also rowers, who worked in these capacities when the fleet was laid up.

Because the size of its tribute exceeded the cost of maintaining its fleet, Athens was also able to support other programs that paid the wages of state employees. The most costly was the Periklean building program, instituted in 447 B.C.E. The building accounts for the Erechtheion indicate that citizens, slaves, and metics worked alongside one another on this project. Skilled workers, like rowers, were paid one drachma per day.

As we have already seen, the allied tribute also funded Athens' pool of 6,000 jurors, who served for a year at the rate of two obols per day, though this was increased after about 425 B.C.E. to three obols per day. Because most jurors were probably elderly or infirm, jury service therefore functioned as a kind of old-age pension-cum-disability allowance, if we assume, as seems likely, that most of the 6,000 were called upon to serve most days of the year.

Although being a state employee was preferable to being in the employ of another citizen, an Athenian who had to work for his living would have been regarded as socially inferior to one whose livelihood derived from the land.

Conclusions

Lacking any notion of job satisfaction, the Greeks were not much in favor of hard work. Why should they have been? Almost all the manual labor was done by slaves—cooking, cleaning, fetching and carrying, shopping, tending the garden, babysitting, nursing, sewing, taking down correspondence, and so on. Nor were they burdened with anything comparable to the Protestant work ethic. Most of them were probably fairly content with their economic status; or, at any rate, they did not make themselves miserable by entertaining grandiose dreams of one day becoming rich since they knew full well that movement up the economic scale was very hard to achieve. Besides, there wasn't a great deal to do with wealth anyway, other than to use it for conspicuous display—that is, to impress others. Just as the Greeks did not believe in the virtues of work for work's sake, so, too, they hardly had any notion of the concept of wasting time. Loafing about was an essential part of every citizen's life. It was by loafing about in the Agora each day that Athenians learned the latest gossip, exchanged ideas about the burning political issues of the day, and discussed the proposals that were tabled for the next meeting of the assembly. As already noted, they also used their time in the Agora to make their daily purchases, since respectable women were expected to stay at home.

TRAVEL AND TRANSPORTATION

Travel was widespread in all periods. From the eighth century B.C.E. onward, traders had regular contacts with non-Greeks such as Phoenicians and Egyptians. Already in *The Odyssey* we encounter itinerant experts, including bards, physicians, builders, and seers, who were known collectively as *dêmiourgoi* or "those who serve the community," and who, as Homer (17.386) tells us with a touch of hyperbole, were "invited from the ends of the earth." To this group in later times should be added Sophists, or teachers of rhetoric, who were much in demand in the fifth century B.C.E., and—a much larger group—mercenaries. In addition, many

Greeks made long journeys at some point in their lives to attend a Panhellenic festival, consult an oracle, or visit a healing sanctuary. We should also bear in mind that Greeks throughout the Mediterranean were frequently being uprooted as a result of warfare, famine, land hunger, and so on.

Land Travel

When Telemachos and his friend Peisistratos set off from Pylos to Sparta at the end of Book 3 of *The Odyssey,* they do so in a chariot with a single night's stop-over at Pherai (modern Kalamata). Homer's suggestion that chariots, which required both driver and passenger to stand alongside one another in a very restricted space, were used for long-distance travel is pure fantasy. The poet clearly thought it inconsistent with their status to have the royal pair traveling on mules, which in reality would have been the only way (other than on foot) to accomplish a long journey over land. There were, in fact, no roads for wheeled traffic over long distances anywhere in the Greek world, nor indeed was there any motivation to connect separate communities like Pylos and Sparta, which are separated by the Taygetos mountains. (It was only in the second half of the twentieth century that a highway was constructed through the Langadha Pass, linking Sparta to Kalamata.) Horses, too, were useless for long-distance travel, mainly because the custom of nailing metal shoes on their hooves was unknown. In addition, stirrups and saddles had not been invented, which made horseback riding over bumpy ground extremely painful and hazardous.

It follows that most Greeks would have been accustomed to walking considerable distances, often in the company of a slave who would carry their baggage. In Xenophon's *Memoirs of Sokrates* (3.13.5), Sokrates talks nonchalantly of the journey from Athens to Olympia, which is over one hundred miles, as a five- to six-day walk. Most of that journey would have been accomplished on well-trodden or not-so-well-trodden paths. The going was tough and quite dangerous at times, with brigands and footpads preying on the vulnerable. The story of the angry altercation that takes place between Oedipus and Laios on the way from Delphi, which leads to the death of Laios and some of his entourage, is clearly based on reality: travelers had every reason to be suspicious of those whom they

MODERN-DAY PHOTOGRAPH OF AN ANCIENT ROAD *that led to the acropolis in Stymphalos, Peloponnese.*

encountered along the way. That is why a favorite theme of Greek myth is the "culture hero," who cleared the roads of various unsavory individuals, as Theseus did for the stretch between Megara and Athens. The safest time to travel was when a large number of people were on the move, as when a Panhellenic festival like the Olympic Games was being celebrated. We do not know whether travel became substantially safer over the course of time.

None of Greece's rivers is navigable, and only a few have estuaries wide enough to serve as ports. The most common means of transporting goods over land was by a two-wheeled cart or a fourwheeled wagon, both of which had been invented by the third millennium B.C.E. Wagons and carts were mostly pulled by oxen, especially if the load was heavy. The top speed of an ox is about one and a half miles an hour, and the maximum distance that it can travel in a day is about eleven miles, so once on land goods traveled extremely slowly. Teams of mules and donkeys were somewhat faster but could only convey much lighter loads. Horses were rarely used partly because they were very costly and partly because the horse collar had not been invented.

Although roads only extended a few miles at most, road-building techniques were by no means unsophisticated. There is evidence of ramps, switchbacks, and pull-offs even in the Archaic Period. All roads, however, were local. There were none that joined one community to another. Mule and drovers' tracks provided the only link between communities. Many of the most important roads functioned as processional ways. In Athens, for instance, the principal paved road was the Panathenaic Way, which began at the Dipylon Gate on the west side of the city and ended up on the Acropolis. It served primarily as a processional way. Despite its importance, however, the surface along most of its length was simply packed with gravel. More functional was the paved road to Athens from the marble quarries on Mount Pentelikon. Goods were conveyed to Athens from the port of Piraeus—a distance of about five miles— along a cart road that also began on the west side of the city. (During the Peloponnesian War, when it was no longer safe to travel outside the city walls, a road running the entire length of the Long Walls that joined Athens to its port served in its place.) In many ways, the most impressive road-building project in Greece was the *diolkos,* or slipway, built by the Corinthians around 600 B.C.E. The *diolkos* enabled ships to be towed across the isthmus of Corinth rather than having to circumnavigate the Peloponnese. It remained in use until the ninth century C.E.

Sea Travel

The most common means of long-distance travel was by sea, though sea travel was hazardous due to weather conditions, piracy, and poor means of navigation. The sea god Poseidon's enmity to Odysseus, which delays the hero's homecoming and causes him the loss of all his ships, reflects a genuine paranoia about sea travel, notwithstanding its importance to Greek culture. Because there were no passenger ships, those seeking to travel by sea would have had to present themselves on the waterfront and bargain for a place on a ship heading toward their destination or at least toward a stop-off point along the way. They would have had to take their own bedding with them, along with food and cooking pots.

The busiest commercial port in the Greek world in the Classical Period was the Piraeus, which functioned not only as a center for the export of Athenian merchandise and the import of goods destined for Athens, but also as an *entrepôt*, or place of redistribution and transshipment for traders who found it more convenient to use its unrivaled facilities than deal directly with the source of supply. Given the unpredictability of the Aegean during the winter months, its commercial port, which was known as the *emporion,* must have hummed and buzzed with frenetic activity for half the year and been practically idle for the rest.

The volume of traffic that passed through the Piraeus required an extremely efficient system of loading and unloading to prevent a backlog of ships from clogging up the harbor with spoiled cargoes. After unloading their wares, merchants were under considerable pressure from the harbor authorities to sell their cargoes and depart as quickly as possible. The majority of dockers were slaves, hired out to ship owners on a contractual basis. Smaller merchant vessels unloaded from the stern, whereas larger vessels remained at anchor in the harbor basin while their merchandise was transferred onto barges. From the sixth century B.C.E. onward, cranes were used to unload the heaviest commodities such as marble and timber; pulleys were not in use until the fourth century. Loose merchandise was removed from the hold by means of a swing-beam with a weight attached to one end and a bucket to the other. Amphorae had to be removed singly with the assistance of a wooden pole supported at either end. Most cargoes were probably mixed. A duty was levied on all cargoes entering or leaving the Piraeus, which, in 399 B.C.E., amounted to more than 18,000 talents.

Hospitality and Hostelries

Because early Greece knew nothing of inns, an institution known as "guest-friendship" or *xenia* developed. This meant that aristocrats offered board and lodging to other aristocrats when they were on the road. Zeus Xenios protected the rights and responsibilities of guests and hosts alike. Being the guest of a host who was many years one's senior would have presented an exacting challenge for a young aristocrat poised on the threshold of adulthood. Homer's depiction of Telemachos in *The Odyssey* as the guest first of King Nestor in Pylos and then

WARRIOR HOLDING A SPEAR AND SHIELD *under a torrent of arrows. Detail from an Attic black-figure* lekythos, *or olive oil container, ca. 475–425 B.C.E.*

of King Menelaos in Sparta is clearly drawn from real life. The young man's ability to negotiate socially demanding situations without causing offence proves him to be the worthy son of his celebrated father.

By the end of the fifth century B.C.E. Panhellenic shrines like the one at Olympia were offering public accommodation for pilgrims, with separate quarters for foreign dignitaries. Outside the religious centers, facilities for travelers were much more limited. Even in a major commercial and tourist center like the Piraeus, the standard of accommodation was deplorably low. Aristophanes implies that its inns had a reputation for discomfort, prostitution, and bedbugs (*Frogs,* lines 112–15). By the middle of the fourth century B.C.E., the lack of decent facilities led Xenophon in *Revenues* (3.12) to recommend "the construction of more hotels for shipowners . . . around the harbors . . . as well as public hostels for visitors." Whether his advice was followed is not known. By the Roman Period, the situation had deteriorated even more. Cicero, in *Letters to Friends* (4.12.3), tells us that when a certain Servius Sulpicius journeyed to the Piraeus to collect the body of a friend who had died there, he found the latter stretched out under a tent. Evidently his friend had been unable to find any other accommodation in the port.

WARFARE

Warfare was an inevitable part of daily life in ancient Greece. As soon as the orange blossom came out in the Agora in April, the Greeks donned their armor and went off to war. Most Greeks were farmers and most Greek armies were citizen militias, so it was difficult to keep them in the field for long stretches of time. The exception was Sparta, whose citizens were fully enrolled in the army from age twenty to sixty. The Athenian orator and politician Demosthenes (*Third Philippic* 48) observed that it was customary practice for the Greeks to campaign only during the summer months (unlike Philip II of Macedon, who campaigned all year round). There were, however, many engagements that lasted considerably longer, notably during the Peloponnesian War. Every able-bodied Athenian citizen was required to serve either in the cavalry, the heavy or light infantry, or the navy. Which of the forces he joined depended on his economic status. Those who owned a horse generally served in the cavalry, those who could afford to purchase a suit of armor became hoplites, and those who were impoverished served as rowers in the navy. In practice, however, Athens had only a very small cavalry force until the late fifth century B.C.E., and this was true of most other states as well. (The exceptions to this rule were the Boiotian and Thessalian Leagues, which already had sizeable cavalry forces in the sixth century B.C.E.) Slaves were enlisted only in times of crisis, because, from the ideological standpoint of the polis, military service was regarded as a privilege rather than a duty.

Homeric Warfare

The very first glimpse that the Greeks offer of themselves is in the guise of warriors. It comes in *The Iliad,* which covers a period of ten days in the tenth year of the siege of Troy. Homeric warfare, which probably resembled the style of fighting that was actually current in Homer's day, was highly ritualistic. Although mass engagements occasionally take place, it is the individual encounters between heroes such as Achilles and Hektor that account for most of the action and that ultimately determine the outcome of the war. The plot of *The Iliad* rests upon the premise that the prowess of a single warrior like Achilles is such that his withdrawal from the battlefield causes a complete reversal in the fortunes of the two sides. Likewise, the death of Hektor at the end of the poem portends the destruction of Troy, because Hektor was Troy's most valiant defender.

ACHILLES DRAGGING THE BODY OF HECTOR AROUND THE WALLS OF TROY.
Pietro Testa (Italian), 1648–1650. Etching.

Heroes only did battle with warriors of comparable rank and fighting ability. They were seemingly oblivious to the possibility of being struck by a stray arrow or a rock hurled by one of the mob. Although usually conveyed to the battlefield in chariots, they fought almost exclusively on foot. Their chariots remained parked while the encounter was taking place, ready to provide a means of escape if their owners were forced to retreat or when they went in search of a new opponent. Having found a suitable opponent, heroes revealed their identity and issued a challenge. Ritual insults often preceded the exchange of blows. On rare occasions, combatants might decline to fight with one another should they discover that there existed a long-standing tie of friendship (*xenia*) between their two families, because these ties were thought to override ethic divisions. This happens in the case of the Greek Diomedes and the Trojan Glaukos in *The Iliad*

Book 6: after learning of each other's pedigree, the two men actually exchange armor with each other "so that everyone will realize that our families have provided hospitality for one another in days of yore" (230f.).

The armor described in the Homeric poems was made of bronze, as is consistent with the Bronze Age context of the Trojan War. It comprised *greaves* (leg guards), a corselet, and a helmet with a crest of horsehair. There was also a special kind of helmet worn by a few warriors made of ox hide, to which were attached plates made of boar's tusk. Shields were made of ox hide stretched over a wooden frame. The most common type of shield was small and round. Ajax, however, who was the tallest of the Greek warriors, had a rectangular shield with a rising curve on its top edge. Heroes fought mainly with a pair of throwing spears or a single thrusting spear, though, at close quarters, they also used the sword, frequently described as "silverstudded." The bow and arrow were chiefly limited to the common soldiery and to a handful of heroes, including Paris and Odysseus. The vanquished warrior, if not killed outright, typically offered the victor a ransom in order to spare his life. If the victor rejected his appeal, he might follow up the killing with an attempt to strip his victim's corpse of its armor. Where particular animosity existed, the victor might even despoil the corpse. Achilles engaged in this barbaric practice when he attached Hektor's corpse to his chariot and then dragged it around the walls of Troy under full view of his victim's parents. The death of a major hero on either side caused such disruption that it interrupted the whole war. Even on the battlefield, the aristocratic hero was provided with a full-scale funeral. Seventeen days were devoted to the obsequies for Achilles, nine for Hektor, and two for Patroklos. The extent of funeral rites conducted on behalf of any individual reflected his social standing and value to the army. Ordinary soldiers received only minimal rites of burial. The only method of disposing of the dead was cremation.

The primary objective of the Homeric hero was to win "imperishable glory" so that his deeds of prowess would be celebrated forever in epic verse of the kind written by Homer himself. His goal was "always to excel in battle and to outstrip others," as Peleus explained to his son Achilles (11.783). The value of the prize, or *geras,* that he received when the spoils of war were distributed to the army by his commander in chief reflected his individual worth and thus symbolized the honor in which he was held. Only marginally was the hero concerned with the collective good of the whole army. Warfare, in other words, primarily presented an opportunity for status enhancement and personal enrichment. At the beginning of *The Iliad,* Achilles, after being insulted by his commander in chief Agamemnon, withdraws to his tent, indifferent to the fact that this decision will cause the deaths of many of his comrades. What matters to him foremost is the public recognition of his own worth. Although he is criticized by his peers for his lack of judgment, none of them ever suggests that his behavior is selfish or immoral.

Even though Homeric warfare was highly ritualistic, the poet's description of what Achilles calls "blood and slaughter and the choking groans of men" (*The Iliad* 19.214) is virtually unsurpassed for its realistic evocation of the brutality of the battlefield. It provides an unforgettable picture of the warfare that depended primarily on a thrust of the spear. Homer describes the deaths of 240 warriors in *The Iliad,* of whom 188 are Trojan and 52 are Greek. A wide variety of wounds are described, not all of which are anatomically possible. We are told, for instance, that "the brain ran along the socket of the spear-head in blood-spurts" (17.297f.) and in another that "the point of the spear shattered the collarbone, tore through it, and stuck out by the base of the shoulder" (17.309–10).

Yet despite the poet's evident fascination with blood and guts, *The Iliad* is by no means a glorification of war. Brutality and cruelty are constantly exposed for what they are, while the achievements of the heroes are evocatively contrasted with the plight of the innocent, including women, children, and the elderly.

THE FAREWELL OF HEKTOR TO ANDROMACHE AND ASTYANAX. Carl Friedrich Deckler (German), ca. 1918. Oil on canvas.

The warrior arming as he is about to depart for battle is one of the most popular scenes on both red- and black-figure vases. All that changes over time is the style of the warrior's armor and weapons. It reminds us of a constant and unchanging event in the daily life of the Greeks, all the more charged with pathos in light of its repetitiveness.

Somewhat paradoxically, the most passionate denunciation of the futility of war is uttered by the bellicose Achilles:

A man suffers the same fate whether he holds back or if he goes into battle. The coward and the brave man are held in equal honor. I have achieved nothing with all the sufferings I have endured, forever risking my life in the line of battle. (9.318–22)

Hoplite Warfare

Around 700 B.C.E., a new style of warfare called hoplite was introduced, named for the *hoplon* or round bronze shield with which soldiers were equipped. The *hoplon,* which was made of wood or stiffened leather with a bronze covering, was about three feet in diameter and designed to cover half the body. It had a double grip and could be rested against the right shoulder, because it was concave on the inside. It was intended to protect not only its bearer but also in part the man standing to his left. For this reason, hoplite armies showed a tendency to drift to the right while they were advancing, as each hoplite sought protection on his exposed side from the shield of his companion standing on his right. Like Homeric heroes, hoplites wore helmets, corselets, and greaves made of bronze to a thickness of about half an inch. The principal weapon of attack was the thrusting spear, which was about eight feet in length and tipped with iron. As the unit advanced, the spears held by the hoplites standing in the first five ranks all projected beyond the front line. If a spear broke, it could be turned around, since the reverse end possessed an iron spike. Hoplites also carried a short sword, which they could use if they lost their spear or if they had no room to jab with their spear.

LEFT GREAVE FROM A HOPLITE SUIT, *sixth century B.C.E. A greave is a piece of armor protecting the kneecap and shin. This example has ornate decorations, including the face of a lion over the knee.*

Hoplite gear, though essentially uniform, is likely to have been highly individual in appearance. Because there was no government issue until the end of the Classical Period, hoplites were presumably at liberty to request from their armorer whatever minor modifications to the basic design they desired. Alcibiades, ever eager to court controversy, decorated his shield with the unwarlike device of Eros, the personification of love, shown wielding a thunderbolt. It was presumably intended as a witty and irreverent counterpart to the usual assortment of gorgons, lions, bulls, and boars favored by the majority. Hoplite armor was costly to purchase—approximately equivalent to a month's pay for an Athenian artisan—and, for this reason, it was often handed down from father to son (Plutarch, *Moral Precepts* 241f 17). It is estimated that between 30 and 40 percent of the citizen body could afford hoplite armor. Those who could afford to purchase a suit of hoplite armor could probably also afford to purchase and feed a slave, whom they would have taken on campaign to serve as their batman.

As noted earlier, service in a hoplite army was regarded as a privilege rather than an obligation, since, initially at least, only citizens were eligible. It is not accidental, therefore, that the introduction of hoplite warfare coincided with the rise of the city-state. Success in battle now depended not on individual deeds of prowess but on the collective discipline of the whole army, whose members were rewarded for their services by being given a role in the politics of the community they defended. Those who could not afford to purchase a suit of armor had to serve as light-armed troops known as peltasts, or, in Athens' case, especially from the 470s B.C.E. onward, as rowers in the navy. Certainly at the time of the Peloponnesian War, however, and possibly earlier, metics who could afford to purchase the requisite gear—presumably a sizeable proportion—were required to fight as hoplites alongside Athenian citizens.

Before a general gave orders for his army to engage in battle, a seer took the omens to determine whether they were favorable. Sacrificial victims were then slaughtered to the gods in the hope of securing their goodwill. The Spartans, for instance, drove whole herds of goats onto the battlefield for sacrifice. Armies advanced singing a *paean,* or hymn, in honor of Apollo. Because they often closed in on each other at a trot and because each hoplite was carrying approximately seventy pounds of bronze, the initial engagement must have resembled a head-on collision between two armored vehicles. When the Athenians advanced against the Persians at the battle of Marathon, they did so, Herodotos tells us, at a run. This tactic so unnerved the Persians that, although they heavily outnumbered the Athenians, they were instantly thrown into a panic.

The unit in which hoplites fought was known as a phalanx. This was a rectangular formation with a long battlefront usually eight ranks deep. Most hoplite battles took place on level terrain, since only thus could a phalanx maintain its cohesion. The objective was to break through the enemy ranks en masse. This meant that victory depended on each and every hoplite standing his ground. Most battles resembled a kind of tug-of-war, with both sides remaining evenly balanced for some time, while much pushing and shoving took place. Complicated maneuvers were rarely attempted, because these made it difficult for a phalanx to retain its formation. Because hoplite helmets had only small eye slots and no piercings for the ears, it was practically impossible for generals to give precise orders. Once battle had commenced, they could do little more than bark out words of encouragement.

The chief method of fighting was to jab repeatedly at the undefended parts of the enemy's body either above or below the shield. When one side finally began to yield, a swift outcome generally ensued, because it would have been practically impossible for a broken phalanx to regroup. It is estimated that most battles were over in under an hour. Casualties are put at around 15 percent. Because the victorious side put itself at risk if it broke rank and began pursuing a fleeing army, it was usually content merely to occupy the field. Thus, most hoplite battles ended in a tactical victory. The victors rarely sought to annihilate the enemy or render him incapable of waging further war. For this reason, often the only tangible consequence was the setting up of a trophy, or *tropaion,* at the spot where the victor had routed the enemy. A *tropaion,* which derives from the noun *tropê,* meaning "a turning around," generally took the form of the trunk of an oak tree decorated with the spoils of victory. It was believed to embody the *tropaios theos,* or trophy god, who was thought to have brought about the victory. None has survived, but from pictorial images we surmise that a trophy consisted mainly of weapons and armor that had been taken from the losing side. Most of the plunder, however, was either distributed among the army or auctioned off. It was also customary to dedicate one-tenth (*dekatê*) of the spoils to whichever god or gods had been invoked before the battle began.

Siegecraft

Legend reports that the Greeks besieged Troy for ten years and succeeded in taking it only by using the device of a wooden horse that they left outside the city, ostensibly as a peace offering. Although this story may well be pure fantasy, the supposition that Troy was able to resist for a whole decade the entire military capability of the Greek world is by no means inconsistent with what we know about the ineffectual nature of Greek siegecraft, which, even in the fifth century B.C.E., remained rudimentary. Virtually the only way to achieve success was by starving a city into submission, which was why Perikles was so confident that the Peloponnesians would never be able to defeat Athens if its population withdrew within the walls, because its navy could guarantee its supply routes. Sieges lasting months, if not years, were the rule rather than the exception. First a ditch was dug, and then a rampart was constructed to prevent food from being brought into the city, a procedure known as circumvallation. In the fourth century B.C.E., siegecraft became more sophisticated with the development of catapults and mobile towers. In response to these improved techniques, walls and towers became thicker and higher. Curtain walls, ditches, and postern gates were also introduced.

At the conclusion of a successful siege, the defeated population tended to be treated much more harshly than when hostilities were confined to the battlefield. As a result, they were commonly either killed or sold into slavery. Xenophon (*Education of Cyrus* 7.5.73) puts the following statement into the mouth of the young Persian prince Cyrus: "The custom is established for all time and among all peoples that when a city is taken in war, both the persons and their property belong to the captors." This was no doubt partly due to the protracted nature of siege warfare, and partly to the fact that besieging armies often suffered great hardship, notably from plague and other diseases.

Athenian Military Service

When Athenian youths reached the age of eighteen, they were required to serve for two years in the army as ephebes in the company of other members of their tribes (*ephêbos* means "poised at the moment of youth"). Though we do not know this for a fact, service in the ephebate was probably limited to those who had the resources to purchase a suit of hoplite armor. Their first year was devoted to training in hoplite and

A YOUNG MAN PREPARES TO LEAVE FOR WAR. *The warrior wears a hoplite breastplate and holds a spear. Red-figure vessel, ca. 470–460 B.C.E.*

light-armed warfare. Light-armed warfare included the use of the bow, the javelin, and the catapult. At the end of the year, a review was held, at which each ephebe was presented with a shield and spear. During their second year, ephebes served as patrolmen at forts situated along the borders of Attica.

> *Probably at the end of their second year of military training, ephebes were required to take the following oath of loyalty to the Athenian state:*
>
> I shall not disgrace my sacred weapons nor shall I desert my comrade at my side whenever I stand in the rank. I shall fight in defense of both sacred and secular things and I shall not hand down a fatherland that is reduced in size but one that is larger and stronger. . . . I shall be obedient to the laws that are established and to any that in the future may be wisely established. . . . I shall honor the sacred rites that are ancestral. (Inscription)

Having completed their two years of military training, ephebes became full citizens. They remained eligible for service until the age of fifty-nine, though it was between the ages of twenty and thirty that they were most likely to be called up. Athens first introduced pay in 462/1 B.C.E., and other city-states quickly followed suit. Although proficiency in warfare was an essential attribute of any state, Athens did not let it dominate its entire existence. As we see from the speech delivered by Perikles in honor of the dead who fell during the first year of the Peloponnesian War, Athenians took considerable pride in the fact that, whereas their enemies submitted themselves to a rigorous system of military training, they, by contrast, pass the time without such restrictions but are still just as ready to face the same dangers as the Spartans (Thukydides 2.39.4).

Trireme Warfare
In 483 B.C.E., Athens made the historic decision to build a fleet and become a naval power. Prior to that date, the state possessed only a skeletal navy of about

MODEL OF A TRIREME, *an ancient Greek sea vessel.*

fifty ships. It was with its navy that Athens helped the Greek alliance to defeat the Persian invasion two years later and subsequently acquired a maritime empire. Because rowers were not required to purchase their own armor, virtually all of them came from the poorest class, known as the *thêtes*. Athens achieved naval supremacy with the aid of a battleship known as a trireme. The word *trireme* is derived from the Greek *trierês,* meaning "three-fitted," a reference to its three banks of oars. Two banks of rowers sat in the hold of the ship and one on the crossbeams. The trireme was designed to achieve maximum speed and maneuverability with minimum weight. Its hull was about 170 feet in length and its width a mere fifteen feet, giving it a ratio of nine to one. It provided accommodation for 170 rowers, with ten hoplites, four archers, and sixteen crew members, making a complement of two hundred. Its objective was to ram the enemy by means of an iron ram mounted on its prow. It is estimated that a trireme could maintain an average speed of about eight knots and ram at twelve knots. In the Hellenistic Period, much larger warships, such as quadriremes (four-bankers) and quinqueremes (five-bankers), became common throughout the Greek world.

The headquarters of Athens' navy was in the Piraeus, which comprises three harbors. The navy occupied the southern shore of the Grand Harbor in the Piraeus and had exclusive use of the two other ports, Zea and Mounychia. The discovery of a circuit wall marking off the naval zone from the rest of the port suggests that entry was reserved for naval personnel. Naval inventories found in the Piraeus indicate that together the three harbors possessed some 370 shipsheds. Even if Athens was able to man only about two-hundred ships, however, which seems a more reasonable figure, it would still have needed some 40,000 rowers—approximately the size of the citizen body. Unsurprisingly, therefore, a sizeable proportion of these rowers would have been mercenaries.

Aristophanes evocatively tells us that, when a naval expedition was about to set sail, the Piraeus reverberated with the sound of "oars being planed, pegs hammered, and rowlocks banged into place, and all to the accompaniment of shouting, flutes and whistles of boatswains' orders" (*Acharnians,* lines 552–54).

At the outbreak of the Peloponnesian War, Athens possessed three hundred sea-worthy triremes. By the terms of its defeat in 404 B.C.E., it was required to surrender all but twelve. The size of its fleet increased during the fourth century, reaching an all-time peak of over four hundred in 322 B.C.E.—ironically, just before its sea power suffered a fatal reverse at the hands of the Macedonians.

Mercenaries

From the end of the fifth century B.C.E. onward, Greek states increasingly relied on mercenaries, particularly in specialist capacities as light-armed troops or as archers, though they were also hired as rowers. This development first came about during the Peloponnesian War, whose duration caused an acute manpower shortage on both sides. Many of those who enlisted as mercenaries came from such poverty-stricken regions as Arkadia, where farming was (often literally) an uphill struggle. Others came from outside the Greek world proper, like the Thrakians who were hired by the Athenians to assist their ill-fated expedition to Sicily. (We have already seen that the Thrakians were constrained to sell their children into slavery). Although it was economic hardship that primarily drove increasing numbers of men to seek mercenary service, new modes of fighting were now rendering hoplite warfare increasingly obsolete, since many engagements took place in rough terrain, where hoplite tactics were virtually useless. As a result, the previously indissoluble bond between service in the army and citizenship was undermined for all time.

In the fourth century B.C.E., Greek mercenaries enlisted in the armies of both Greeks and non-Greeks. Theoretically, therefore, Athenians could find themselves fighting in the same battle against other Athenians, though whether this actually ever happened is not known. Because they had an excellent reputation for discipline, Greek mercenaries were in considerable demand. In 397 B.C.E., a Persian prince named Cyrus hired 10,000 mercenaries from the Greek mainland in his bid to seize the throne from his brother. When Cyrus was killed in battle, the mercenaries succeeded in making their way from the Persian heartland back to friendly territory without suffering serious losses. The march, which is stirringly described by Xenophon in a work called *Anabasis,* or *The March Up-Country,* demonstrated the military superiority of Greeks over barbarians. This was to be proven even more dramatically when Alexander the Great invaded Persia in the 330s B.C.E. at the head of an army that consisted largely of mercenaries attracted by the promise of rich rewards.

Reliance on mercenaries from the end of the fifth century B.C.E. onward was not a completely new departure in the history of Greek warfare, however, as is illustrated by the following fragmentary poem written by the seventh-century B.C.E. poet Alkaios in celebration of his brother's homecoming from the wars:

> You have come from the ends of the earth, Antimenidas, my beloved brother, clasping your sword with its gold and ivory handle. You served alongside the Babylonians and you took on a mighty challenge when you rescued them by slaying a warrior who was all but a finger shy of eight foot in height.

Rules of Warfare

With the exception of siegecraft, which had its own specific rules, warfare tended to adhere to fairly civilized standards of behavior. Unlike their Homeric counterparts, hoplites did not make a habit of stripping their opponents' bodies or mutilating them in the way that Achilles mutilated Hektor's body. Nor was it their practice to despoil temples, sanctuaries, or tombs, which were regarded as sacrosanct. The destruction of property, whether public or private, was extremely rare, in part because warfare was confined largely to the battlefield. A notable exception was the Persians' destruction of the temples and statues that stood on the Athenian Acropolis in 480 B.C.E. The Athenians were so outraged by this act of vandalism that they left their temples in their ruined condition for thirty years as a vivid testimony to barbarian savagery.

Hostilities between Greek states were suspended for the duration of the Olympic Games and other Panhellenic festivals, including the Eleusinian Mysteries in accordance with a sacred truce (see p. TK). This guaranteed the safety of contestants and pilgrims on their way to and from the festival, as well as the state sponsoring the festival. Ambassadors were placed under the protection of the gods, and their persons were regarded as inviolate. Although local squabbles leading to bloodshed were endemic, wars tended to be short in duration. The campaign season began in the spring and ended in the fall. In Athens, its conclusion was marked by the mass burial of all those who had died in the preceding season.

Those who surrendered in battle were generally spared. A common fate for prisoners of war was to be sold into slavery or sent into exile. No doubt slave dealers, known as *andrapodistai,* meaning "people who deal in things with the feet of a man" (see p. 109), were as much a feature of the battlefield post combat as were carrion crows. Overall, however, we hear little about the fate of prisoners. A notable exception is the Athenian prisoners taken by the Syracusans in 413 B.C.E., who were put to work in their stone quarries. As noted earlier, those who could sing the lyrics of Euripides' tragedies eventually earned their freedom and returned to Athens.

Not until the Peloponnesian War did the Greek world experience anything akin to the modern notion of total war. Thukydides constantly emphasizes the decline in moral standards that this brought about. In 413 B.C.E., a contingent of Thrakian mercenaries, who had been hired by the Athenians, ran amok and

ANTIQUE MAP OF ANCIENT GREECE DURING THE PELOPONNESIAN WAR, *created ca. 1862.*

killed all the inhabitants of the town of Mykalessos in Boiotia, slaughtering "even the livestock and whatever other living creatures they saw," including all the pupils at a boys' school (7.29.4).

It was not only the barbarians whose standards declined, however, as Thukydides is at pains to emphasize. When the town of Mytilene on the island of Lesbos revolted from the Athenian confederacy and was forced to surrender in 427 B.C.E., the Athenians decided to execute all the men and enslave the women and children. The next day, however, they revoked their decision and opted instead to execute only the ringleaders, one thousand in number (3.50). Just over ten years later, the island of Melos (the most southwesterly of the

Cyclades), which was neutral, declined to join Athens' "alliance." After a short siege, the Athenians did not think twice about carrying out the punishment that they had originally intended for the Mytileneans. They slaughtered the men, enslaved the women, and repopulated the island with five hundred of their own citizens (5.116). Thukydides' point is that the decade-long war had brutalized the Athenians: acting initially with restraint when a trusted ally revolted, they later acted with none when a neutral state refused to toe the line. Thukydides sees this decline in moral standards extending to daily life, notably, as a we have seen, as a result of the plague that ravaged the city from 430 to 426 B.C.E.

Disposal of the Dead

Peter Krentz (quoted in Sekunda, *Greek Hoplite 480–323* B.C., 30) has estimated that, on average, 5 percent of victors and 14 percent of the defeated died on the battlefield in any single engagement, though sometimes the percentage of casualties was considerably higher. It was a universally upheld, albeit unwritten law to allow the defeated side to return to the battlefield to retrieve its dead. The law is already observed in *The Iliad*. In fact, the return of one's dead, which was made through a herald, was an acknowledgement of defeat. Only very rarely was this law violated, because sensibilities touching burial ran extremely high. One occasion was in 424/3 B.C.E. after the battle of Delion, when the Boiotians prohibited the Athenians from recovering their dead for seventeen days, which would have made identification of the bodies quite impossible (Thukydides 4.101.1). Euripides' *Suppliant Women,* whose plot is based around a mythical occasion when the Thebans refused to return the Argive dead, is likely to have been inspired by this event. During their retreat from Syracuse in 413 B.C.E., at the end of the Sicilian expedition, the demoralization of the Athenians was greatly increased by the fact that they were unable to care for their dead and wounded (Thukydides 7.75.3).

The dead were usually cremated on the field of battle. Their ashes were then placed in individual cinerary urns identified by name tags and brought home. The Athenians arranged their dead in ten piles according to their ten tribes and publicly interred their remains at the end of each campaigning season. Thukydides (2.34.1) describes this ceremony as "an ancestral custom," but it probably originated in the mid-460s—barely a generation before the outbreak of the Peloponnesian War. Only rarely, as in the case of the 192 Athenians who died fighting the Persians at Marathon, did they accord the war dead the honor of burial on the battlefield. Likewise, the Spartans buried the three hundred who died with their king Leonidas while guarding the pass of Thermopylai, where they fell. When the dead could not all be recovered, a *kenotaphion,* or "empty tomb" (from which the word *cenotaph* derives), was erected in the heart of the city.

Conclusions

Greek warfare was conducted on a miniscule scale in comparison with its modern counterpart. It has been estimated that at no time in history were the Greeks able to put more than 50,000 soldiers into the field. Another major difference is that it was not conducted under the full glare of publicity as it is today. Once an expedition had departed, only general reports of its fortunes reached home. Aeschylus in *Agamemnon* (line 437) memorably describes Ares, god of war, as the "gold-broker of corpses," who accepted soldiers in exchange for the ashes that were brought back from the battlefield in cinerary urns. Just as relatives waved good-bye on the quayside as the fleet set sail at the beginning of a campaign, so, too, the same relatives awaited the arrival of "urns in place of men" announcing the death of a husband, brother, or son.

In the course of his life time, an Athenian citizen would expect to be called up many times, because it is estimated that most Greek cities went to war three years in every four. It follows from this that he also had a fair chance of dying in battle, whether on land or at sea. Archaeology provides testimony to this fact in the form of casualty lists—inscribed monuments that were set up at public expense listing all the Athenian dead, tribe by tribe, on an annual basis. From them, scholars have calculated that 3 percent of the entire Athenian population died in battle annually. There is no reason to suppose that the average death toll would have been appreciably different in any other Greek community. Finally, we should spare a thought for those who returned from battle grievously wounded and who, in many cases, given the rudimentary state of medical knowledge, would have died a painful and protracted death.

⁂ 7 ⁂

PLEASURE
AND LEISURE

The importance of leisure is indicated from the fact that the nearest Greek equivalent to the word is *scholê* (which gives us the word *school*), whereas its antithesis, *ascholia,* means what we would describe as work. Leisure, in other words, was the normal condition of life, whereas work constituted an interruption. The enjoyment of leisure was justified on moral grounds. Aristotle, in Book 2 of *The Politics,* expressed the opinion that leisure was a precondition "both for the development of virtue and for the undertaking of affairs relating to the polis," and no doubt most well-to-do Greeks would have agreed. That is because scholê meant primarily having the time first to fulfill one's obligations as a citizen and second to devote oneself to self-improvement, by exercising in the gymnasium, congregating in the Agora, listening to philosophical exchanges, and participating in symposia at night. Those at the lower end of the social and economic scale, by contrast, enjoyed none of these diversions and had little recourse but to tumble into bed exhausted after a hard day's work. We may be confident, however, that the entire citizenry participated in the various festivals that were celebrated throughout the year, though one's level of participation would have depended on how much time one could take off work. Because there was no such thing as the weekend in antiquity, festivals would have provided the principal excuse to put down tools.

ATHLETICS AND THE CULT OF PHYSICAL FITNESS

Few peoples have attached so much significance to the cult of physical fitness as the Greeks. The notion of physical perfection was so central to their sense of

DISCUS THROWER. *Detail from a Panathenaic amphora dating to the fifth century B.C.E.*

selfhood that they seem to have been almost incapable of conceiving of themselves in any other terms. Greek art is saturated with images of perfectly formed men and women—so much so that it is tempting to conclude that the people who produced such impressive works were physically superior not only to their contemporaries but to every other race that has ever existed. Of course, this was far from being the case. To comprehend their deeply ingrained narcissism, it may be instructive to remember that theirs was a culture that made no distinction between what was *kalos* (beautiful) on the one hand and *agathos* (good) on the other.

The adoration of the human body found many outlets. Greek art, especially sculpture, gave it uninhibited expression. It was the Greeks who first identified the naked human body as the primary object of artistic attention. No less important, physical perfection was exemplified through competitive athletics, which occupied a central place at a number of major festivals. The assumption was that the gods, who themselves exemplified physical perfection on the divine plane, took delight in observing their human counterparts.

Every athlete aspired to win a simple crown of leaves that was awarded at the most prestigious games—the olive wreath at the Olympic Games, the laurel wreath at the Pythian Games, the celery wreath at the Nemean Games, and the pine wreath at the Isthmian. Nothing, however, quite equaled becoming an Olympic victor, or *Olympionikês*. In the Hellenistic Period, when the number of games that were held proliferated and cities vied with one another to attract the biggest sporting stars, cash prizes were offered as inducements, as well as gold and silver crowns.

Keeping Fit

Some form of athletic training was vital for boys from almost every social background, because one's ability to serve in the military was dependent on one's physical fitness. Many sports were, in fact, devised as a way of training for war, including javelin throwing and the *hoplitodromos,* a foot race in armor. As soon as they began school at about the age of seven, well-to-do Athenian boys were entrusted to a professional trainer known as a *paidotribês,* who worked in a *palaistra* or wrestling school. (*Paidotribês* means literally "boy-rubber," an allusion to the fact that he used oil to massage his charges.) Athens contained many *palaistrai,* but none has been fully excavated. Their general layout was similar to that of a Greek house. The training ground was probably enclosed by a wall with a verandah to provide shelter from the rain and sun. Most palaistrai possessed a changing room, a bathroom, and a place to store equipment.

Older athletes exercised naked in the gymnasium, a Greek word whose root is the adjective *gymnos* (meaning naked or lightly clad). Although many gymnasia were equipped with changing rooms and

THREE MEN PARTICIPATE IN THE HOPLITODROMOS. *Detail from an Attic black-figure Panathenaic amphora, ca. 323 B.C.E.*

other facilities, the basic requisite was a piece of level, open terrain where athletes could practice javelin and discus throwing as well as running. Gymnasia tended to be located near a river, enabling athletes to refresh themselves and bathe after exercising. Although only their foundations have survived, they were probably verdant oases with well-shaded walks. By the end of the sixth century B.C.E., Athens had acquired three principal gymnasia—the Academy, the Lyceum, and the Kynosarges—all situated outside the city. These were used by Athens' ephebes and hoplites as a fitness center, probably on a daily basis.

Socializing also went on in the gymnasium. Not only aspiring athletes but also older men would gather there to converse, gossip, and argue while sitting in the shade beside running water. Here, too, Sophists, would talk and give lectures. In the fourth century B.C.E., the gymnasia of Athens came to acquire a new identity as centers for philosophical discussion. Plato established his school in the vicinity of the Academy. The name, which derives from a local hero named Akademos, is the origin of our word *academic.* Half a century later, his pupil Aristotle established a rival philosophical school in the Lyceum. Aristotle's followers were dubbed peripatetics (from the verb *peripateô,* to walk up and down) because of their habit of pacing up and down as they pursued their philosophical inquiries. The topographical coincidence between intellectual and athletic excellence testifies to the Greek conviction that the two aspirations are complementary.

The Olympic Spirit

Competitive athletics was one of the principal means by which the Greeks promoted a sense of cultural unity. Although there were probably hundreds of local athletic festivals, four Panhellenic, or all-Greek, games attracted athletes from all over the Greek world. These were the Olympic and Nemean Games, both held in honor of Zeus; the Pythian Games, held in honor of Apollo; and the Isthmian Games, held in honor of Poseidon. The most prestigious of these were the Olympic Games, which were held every four years from 776 B.C.E. to 261 C.E. . It is a remarkable testimony to the Greek ability to rise above politics at least on a temporary basis that, in the course of this thousand-year period, never once, so far as we know, were they canceled. By contrast, our modern series, which was first held in 1896, has already been canceled three times, quite aside from being regularly exploited for propagandist or commercial advantage.

There were several reasons why the ancient Olympic Games were successful in promoting the spirit of Panhellenism. In the first place, Olympia, due to its location in a politically unimportant region of Greece, never fell prey to the ambitions of any neighboring power. For most of its history, the sanctuary was controlled by the neighboring city of Elis. Consequently, the games were never used for self-promotion by the host country in the way that the Nazis used the Munich games in 1936 to promote an image of racial superiority. The ancient Olympics did, however, occasionally serve the propagandist aims of individuals— notably in 69 C.E., when they were postponed for two years to enable the Roman emperor Nero to compete. To the credit of the Olympic authorities, his victories in the chariot race and musical contest were later expunged from the records.

Another reason why the Olympic Games genuinely embodied the Olympic ideal is that they formed part of a religious festival held in honor of Zeus Olympios. Olympia was the chief sanctuary of Zeus on the mainland. The religious component, which accounted for two-and-a-half of the five

WOODCUT RENDERING OF ANCIENT OLYMPIA. *In the distance on the left is the stadium where the original Olympic Games took place. Anonymous, ca. 1882.*

days devoted to the festival, was never overshadowed by the kind of hoopla that characterizes the modern series. A sacred truce, known as the *ekecheiria* ("restraining of hands"), which remained in effect for one month, was observed to allow spectators and competitors to travel to and from Olympia in safety. In later times, this was extended to two months, and finally to three months. Only once was the truce broken—by Sparta in 420 B.C.E. As a punishment, Spartan athletes were prohibited from participation in the games that year.

All Greek speakers were eligible to participate, and there was virtually no distinction between professionals and amateurs. Most cities subsidized the training of their athletes. Participants had to spend the entire month preceding the games training at Olympia under the supervision of the *Hellênodikai,* or "judges of the Greeks."

The Olympic Program

The first day of the Olympic Games was devoted to oath taking, checking the qualifications of the competitors, performing sacrifices, and praying. So important was winning that competitors prayed for either the wreath or death. All contestants participated naked and barefoot. The origin of this practice is attributed to a certain Orsippos, who was in the lead in a footrace when his loincloth fell off. Orsippos tripped and lost the race.

On the second day of the festival, the chariot race took place in the hippodrome. This was the most spectacular as well as the most dangerous event. It consisted of twelve laps up and down a straight track. The chariots had two wheels and were drawn by a team of four horses. Because there was no dividing barrier between the up and down track and because charioteers were required to perform 180-degree turns when they reached the end of each lap, head-on collisions were frequent. Increasing the likelihood of serious injury was the fact that charioteers tied their horses' reins around their bodies for stability, so if they fell they were dragged along the ground. Pindar, who wrote many odes commemorating victors in the games, claims that, in one race at Delphi, "forty drivers were laid low" (*Pythian Ode* 5.49). The chariot race was followed by a horseback race without stirrups or saddles over the same course. The victor in both events was not the charioteer or the jockey, but the owner of the horses. Because horses were extremely expensive, the victor was almost invariably a wealthy aristocrat or tyrant.

The remaining events took place in the Olympic stadium. The stadium was named for the stade, a unit of measurement approximately 210 yards in length. The stadium consisted of a level piece of ground covered with sand. Spectators watched from a raised bank

MAN IN A CHARIOT RACE. *Detail from a seventh-century B.C.E. clay hydria.*

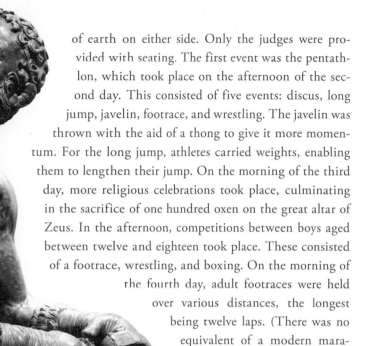

of earth on either side. Only the judges were provided with seating. The first event was the pentathlon, which took place on the afternoon of the second day. This consisted of five events: discus, long jump, javelin, footrace, and wrestling. The javelin was thrown with the aid of a thong to give it more momentum. For the long jump, athletes carried weights, enabling them to lengthen their jump. On the morning of the third day, more religious celebrations took place, culminating in the sacrifice of one hundred oxen on the great altar of Zeus. In the afternoon, competitions between boys aged between twelve and eighteen took place. These consisted of a footrace, wrestling, and boxing. On the morning of the fourth day, adult footraces were held over various distances, the longest being twelve laps. (There was no equivalent of a modern marathon.) The afternoon was given over to body-contact sports, including wrestling, boxing, and *pankration*. The *pankration*, which can be best translated as all-in combat, was a combination of wrestling and boxing. There were no rules, and serious injuries, even deaths, were not uncommon. On one occasion, the prize was awarded to a *pankratiast* named Arrachion, even though he had

THE THERMAE BOXER. *An athlete resting after a boxing match. Bronze, ca. third to second century B.C.E.*

been strangled to death. His opponent conceded the match just as Arrachion was expiring on account of the latter having broken his toe. The final event was a race over two laps by competitors dressed in full hoplite armor (*hoplito-dromos*). Proficiency in this event may have contributed to the Athenian victory at the battle of Marathon, in which the heavily armed hoplites unnerved the Persians by charging from a distance.

The only competition for unmarried girls was a footrace in honor of Hera. It is described by Pausanias as follows:

> The competitors are divided into three age groups, and they run in this way: their hair hangs down, a tunic reaches a little way above the knee, and they bare the right shoulder down to the bosom. They have the Olympic stadium reserved for the games, but the course is shortened to about one sixth of its length. The winning girls are presented with crowns of olive and a portion of the cow that is sacrificed to Hera. (5.16.2–3)

Winners and Losers

On the fifth and final day, prizes of olive wreaths were awarded to the victors. The victor first bound a band of wool around his head and the official then placed the wreath upon it. There were no prizes for those who finished second or third. Victors were permitted to erect statues in the sanctuary and were feted lavishly by their own cities when they returned home. Some were granted free meals at public expense for the rest of their lives. States whose athletes won prizes gained enormous prestige. Alkibiades, who placed first, second, and fourth in the chariot race, boasted that "the Greeks believed that Athens had even greater power than was the case because of my success in the Olympic Games, although earlier they had thought they had entirely worn us out in the war" (Thukydides 6.16.2). The most successful state was Elis, where Olympia was situated. Elis produced the first recorded Olympic victor, a baker named Koribos, in 776 B.C.E. Sparta was also prominent, whereas Athens, even at the height of its power in the mid-fifth century B.C.E., won far fewer victories. The most successful athlete was Milon of Kroton, who won the wrestling prize in five successive Olympiads between 536 and 520 B.C.E. Milon, a notorious show-off, used to challenge people to bend back his little finger—apparently no one could. He was also in the habit of tying a band around his head, taking a deep breath, and snapping the band with the aid of the veins of his head (Pausanias 6.14.7).

We should also spare a thought for the losers, whose plight is described as follows by Pindar:

> They, when their mothers meet them, have no sweet laughter around them,
> arousing delight. But in back streets they cower, out of their enemies' way,
> bitten by disaster. (*Pythian* 8.85—87)

Women were not permitted to enter the sanctuary of Zeus while the games were in progress. Pausanias (5.6.7) tells us that the ban was introduced after a woman called Kallipateira managed to disguise herself as an Olympic trainer in order to watch her son compete. She was exposed (literally) when she jumped over the trainers' enclosure. The judges decided not to punish her out of deference to her brothers, her father, and her son, all of whom had been Olympic victors. Although women could not watch the games in progress, handsome athletes had their fans and followers, who hung about the entrance to the site, eager to catch a glimpse of their favorites. Pindar writes of one such favorite as follows:

> On the many occasions that you won in the Panathenaia, Telesikrates,
> unmarried girls saw you and under their breath prayed that you might
> be their beloved husband or son, and they did the same at Olympia and
> Delphi, and at all the local festivals. (*Pythian* 9.97–103)

Although only a minute proportion of the Greek population actually participated in the games, young men were inspired to train in the palaistra in the hope that they might one day have the distinction of representing their city. The games thus functioned as a general incentive to physical excellence. Not everyone, however, approved of the adulation that victorious athletes received. A character in a lost play by Euripides inquires:

> Who has ever assisted his city by winning a prize for wrestling or running
> fast or throwing the discus or striking someone full on the chin? Will they

fight the enemy with a discus or kick them out of the country as if they were footballs? (*Autolykos* fr. 282)

The Bare Facts

The Greeks were not, of course, unique in their prejudice, as we might label it, for those who were physically perfect. The same prejudice was central to the Renaissance, as the numerous images of perfectly formed saints—the embodiments of physical and moral energy—by artists such as Michelangelo and Raphael demonstrate. So far as the common man figured at all in Renaissance art, he did so primarily as an adjunct to the central biblical and mythological scenes that were enacted by the Renaissance equivalents of the Holly wood idols of today. This remained the case until the seventeenth century, when commoners finally became objects of artistic interest in their own right.

In crafting an image of themselves that was at such variance with physiological reality, the Greeks were not wholly different from us, although they have bequeathed to us almost exclusively this image of themselves. If, by some quirk of history, all that survived of contemporary Western "art" were copies of *GQ, Vogue,* or *Woman,* posterity might be equally intrigued by the disjunction between representational image and physiological fact. It is a disjunction that hardly diminishes as we become wealthier, more leisured, and better fed. Results from the 1999–2002 National Health and Nutrition Examination Survey, using measured heights and weights, indicate that an estimated 16 percent of children and adolescents ages six to nineteen years were overweight. Physiological perfection was even less attainable in antiquity than it is in the modern world.

Festivals

Observances help to fill what Samuel Johnson, the great eighteenth-century man of letters, called "the great vacancies of life." Or, as a Greek proverb put it, "a life without festivals is like a road that has no inns." Festivals regulate the flow of life. Without them, the passage of life is in constant danger of becoming monotonous and undifferentiated.

Yet, today, festivals generally play only a minor part in the life of a community, notwithstanding the importance in the United States, for example, of the Fourth of July and Thanksgiving. This state of affairs is characteristic of societies that regard their holidays as peripheral and whose members do not closely identify with one another through the collective memory of shared experience. The Greeks would not have understood how society can function without a sense of shared experience that is reinforced at regular intervals throughout the year. Our lack of the celebratory would have struck them as uncongenial in the extreme. Moreover, because they did not divide the year into periods of seven days with an appointed period of rest at the end of each week, festivals constituted the primary pretext for recreation. They also afforded the Greeks an opportunity to express their common identity as citizens, tribesmen, and demesmen and to reinforce their sense of an inherited, if invented, tradition. In Athens, more than sixty days were devoted to state-sponsored festivals annually.

Greek festivals took many forms. At the lower end of the scale were the deme festivals. At the upper end were the civic festivals, in which the entire citizen body, including, in some cases, resident aliens, participated. The best attended of all, however, were the prestigious Panhellenic festivals, which attracted celebrants from all over the Greek world. In the Hellenistic Period, kings founded festivals at their capitals with the object of impressing their subjects as well as their rivals. One such was the Ptolemaia, which was instituted by Ptolemy II in the early third century B.C.E. at Alexandria, Egypt, in honor of his deified father. The procession he arranged under its auspices in 270 B.C.E. was one of the grandest events ever celebrated in antiquity.

Each festival was a unique expression of worship, tailor-made to the deity in whose honor it was held. A number of features, however, were common to many: a procession to a deity's shrine with ritual stops along the way; the singing of hymns; the decorating of a wooden object that embodied the deity's power; athletic, musical, and dramatic contests; and, finally, the most essential feature of all—a blood sacrifice performed on an altar in front of the deity's shrine, followed by the distribution of meat among the priests and worshippers.

Agricultural Festivals

Our knowledge of Greek festivals is not sufficiently detailed to permit us to fathom the precise significance that they held for the people who celebrated them. In general, the impulses that propelled the Greeks to congregate and perform elaborate and complicated rituals incorporated anxiety and fear on the one hand, relief and gratitude on the other. The majority of Greeks lived precariously between famine and surplus. Hardly surprisingly, therefore, many of their festivals were designed to secure a regular supply of foodstuffs, though we never gain a detailed insight into why precisely the celebrants did what they did. Indeed, much of what they did seems quite baffling to us.

One of the most puzzling was the *Thesmophoria,* a fall festival conducted exclusively by women. This was held all over the Greek world in honor of Demeter, goddess of the grain. The culminating ritual involved throwing the bodies of sacrificial pigs into snake-infested pits. Three days later, women were lowered into the pits to retrieve the pigs' putrefied remains, which were then placed on an altar and mixed with seed grain. This bizarre rite, which was perhaps seen as a kind of enactment of Persephone's descent to Hades, was evidently intended to facilitate the germination of the grain, but why it took this precise form is a complete mystery.

Other agricultural festivals included the *Oschophoria,* in which two youths carried branches known as *ôschoi* laden with grapes; the Haloa, held in honor of Demeter in mid-winter, when cakes in the form of phalluses were eaten; the Rural Dionysia, held in honor of Dionysos, during which a giant phallus was carried aloft; the *Anthesteria,* a flower festival held in early spring, when wine jars containing newly fermented wine were opened and blessed by Dionysos; the *Thargelia,* held in honor of Apollo, during which a pot of boiled vegetables called *thargela* was offered to the god, while a human scapegoat, who perhaps personified hunger, was beaten and driven out of the city; and finally, the *Pyanopsia,* in which branches laden with wool, fruits, cakes, wine, and oil flasks were borne by children in procession and later hung on the front door of every Athenian home.

Rites of Passage

Because the passage from one stage of life to another was thought to be fraught with danger, the Greeks paid very close attention to the junctures that marked these divisions. As we have seen, an Athenian infant went through his first rite of passage in his first year to gain entry into his father's phratry. His second rite of passage took place on the second day of the flower festival (*Anthesteria*), when boys aged between three and four were given their first taste of wine. It seems probable that this ritual signaled formal admission into the Athenian religious community, and hence into the polis itself, since wine, the gift of Dionysos, was a feature of almost every religious rite. Rites of passage were also conducted at later moments in his life—notably at adolescence and adulthood and, of course, at marriage and death. Overall, the various rites of passage signaled membership of the various affiliations to which each individual belonged—*oikos, genos,* phratry, tribe, deme, and polis, and, though our evidence is less than complete, we can be certain that entry to all these groupings was predicated upon elaborate ceremonial. Rites of passage have the effect of strengthening group solidarity, and virtually every freeborn Greek would have experienced a sense of multilayered communal belonging that is virtually unknown in the modern world. Women, by contrast, underwent far fewer rites of passage in the course of their life times—a reflection of their much more restricted social identity.

A CHUBBY EROS PLAYS WITH A TOY CART. *This small* chous, *or wine vessel, would have been gifted to a young child during Anthesteria, the festival in which Greek children first tasted wine. Red-figure chous, made ca. 410 B.C.E.*

Festivals in Honor of the Dead

Festivals in honor of the dead formed a major feature of the calendar. The most spectacular was the annual ceremony held in honor of the war dead. Known as the *taphai,* or burials, it took place at the end of the campaigning season in early winter. Thukydides describes it as follows:

Three days before the ceremony the bones of the fallen are brought and put in a tent which has been erected, and people make whatever offerings they wish to their own dead. Then there is a funeral procession in which coffins of cypress wood are carried on wagons. There is one coffin for each tribe, which contains the bones of members of that tribe. One empty bier is decorated and carried in the procession. This is for the missing, whose bodies could not be recovered. Everyone who wishes, both citizens and foreigners, can join the procession, and the women who are related to the dead make their laments at the tomb. When the bones have been laid in the earth a man chosen for his intellectual gifts and general reputation makes an appropriate speech in praise of the dead and after the speech everyone departs. (2.34)

Other festivals in honor of the dead include the third day of the Anthesteria, known as the *Chytroi,* or "Pots," which was so named because pots of porridge were offered on that day. *Chytroi,* in other words, was the Athenian equivalent to All Souls' Day, when the souls of the dead left their graves and wandered abroad. To counter their noxious presence, people would chew buckthorn and smear the doors of their houses with pitch. The dead were also celebrated at the *Genesia* and *Nemeseia.* The *Genesia* was in origin a private ritual celebrated on the birthday of the deceased, though under Solon it became a national festival. The *Nemeseia* (derived from *nemesis,* meaning vengeance) took place at night and was intended to placate those who had come to a violent end.

The Panathenaia

The most prestigious Athenian festival was the *Panathenaia* or "All-Athenian Festival," held annually on the birthday of Athene, the city's patron goddess. Once every four years, the festival was celebrated with special grandeur. This occasion is the subject of the great frieze that ran around the outer wall of the Parthenon. The procession assembled outside the city at the Dipylon Gate and proceeded through the Agora along the ceremonial Panathenaic Way in the direction of the Acropolis, its final destination.

Groups representing the entire population of Athens participated, the largest of which was a military contingent. On the Parthenon frieze, this takes the form of a cavalcade of naked horsemen. Young girls carried baskets containing barley meal to sprinkle on the heads of the sacrificial victims, as well as cushions for the gods to sit on. Youths carried water pitchers, old men brandished olive branches sacred to Athene, and metics bore offering trays. The central feature of the procession was a ship mounted on wheels with a woolen *peplos* rigged to its mast in place of a sail. The peplos, which was woven by Athenian maidens of noble birth who resided on the Acropolis, clothed an olive wood statue of Athene that was believed to have dropped onto the Acropolis out of the sky. The removal of the goddess's old peplos and its replacement by a new one evidently formed the climax to the entire Panathenaia, for this is the scene depicted on the portion of the frieze directly above the entrance to the Parthenon. A herd of cows was sacrificed to the goddess on the altar outside her temple, and the meat was then distributed to participants down at the Dipylon Gate, where the procession had begun.

The Panathenaia also featured competitions, including recitations of the works of Homer, contests on the flute and harp, athletic and equestrian events, dancing, and, in later times, a xnaval competition. Victors were awarded decorated amphorae containing olive oil in commemoration of the fact that the olive tree was the goddess's gift to the state.

BLOCK FROM THE EAST FRIEZE OF THE PARTHENON, *depicting an important scene from the Panathenaia festival—a bearded man, probably the* archon basileus, *or king magistrate, receives a folded cloth, likely the sacred peplos of Athena, from a child. Ca. 447–433 B.C.E.*

These bore the simple inscription, "One of the prizes from Athens," accompanied by an illustration of the event for which the vase was awarded.

THEATRICAL PERFORMANCES

When we talk about Greek drama, we almost exclusively mean Athenian drama, both tragedy and comedy. Only a few non-Athenian playwrights are known to us by name, and none of their plays has survived. Drama was both an invention and an integral aspect of Athenian democracy, so much so that it is quite impossible to talk about it other than as an expression of the distinctive political and civic realities of the Athenian state.

The origins of Greek drama are very imperfectly understood, but they probably derive from an opposition between the chorus and a single actor. From earliest times, the Greeks held choral performances in honor of the gods, in commemoration of military and athletic victories, and in mourning for the dead. *Tragoidia,* the Greek word for tragedy—which derives from *tragos,* or goat, and *oidê,* or song—probably owes its origins either to the fact that choruses were originally dressed in the loinskins of goats or to the fact that the prize for the song was a goat. The Athenians attributed the invention of tragedy to a shadowy figure named Thespis, who is credited with having won first prize in the first contest for tragedy held in about 534 B.C.E. Recently, however, scholars have argued that tragedy was only introduced after the establishment of democracy in 508/507 B.C.E. *Kômoidia,* which gives us the word *comedy,* means "*kômos* singing." A *kômos* was a band of tipsy revelers who wandered about the town, crashing drinking parties.

The promotion of drama to the level of Athenian national pastime par excellence owed much to the tyrant Peisistratos, who accorded it a central position in a new or revamped festival in honor of Dionysos, the patron god of drama—though why it was held in honor of this particular god was not entirely apparent even in antiquity. It was at this festival, known as the Great or City Dionysia, that plays were staged that rank today among the foremost achievements of Athenian culture—namely, the tragedies of Aeschylus, Sophokles, and Euripides and the comedies of Aristophanes. The City Dionysia was a four-day festival held in March. In the opening ceremony, a statue of the god was carried into the theater so that Dionysos could witness the performances. At the center of the playing area, known as the *orchêstra* (meaning dancing space), stood an altar. Both the statue and altar were reminders of the religious aspect of drama.

Because the City Dionysia coincided with the beginning of the sailing season, many foreigners and tourists would have been able to attend, including Athens' allies. The annual tribute that they brought with them was displayed in the theater (Isokrates, *On the Peace* 82)—a curious mingling of the secular with the divine that is so characteristic of Greek culture. On this occasion, too, orphans of the war dead paraded in battle gear and received the thanks and support of the citizenry. The Dionysia was initially devoted exclusively to tragedy, although, from 486 B.C.E., comedies were performed at it as well. This may well be the year when comedy first became part of the theatrical offering. Then in about 440 B.C.E., the Athenians established a festival devoted exclusively to comedy known as the *Lenaia* (derived from the word *lênê,* meaning a maenad or devotee of Dionysos), held around the end of January, which only citizens were permitted to attend.

Staging a Dramatic Performance

Every tragedian hoping to mount a production at one of the festivals had to submit three tragedies to a magistrate known as the eponymous archon (i.e., the Athenian magistrate who gave his name to the year). He also had to write a satyr play, so named because of its chorus of half-animal, half-human creatures, whose drunken and licentious antics provided an uproarious coda to the serious business of tragedy. Comic poets submitted only one drama. It was the archon's exclusive responsibility to choose which plays should be performed. Once he had made his choice of three tragic and three comic productions, he allocated to each a *chorêgos* (literally "chorus director"), who was a wealthy Athenian or metic. It was the obligation of the *chorêgos* to pay all the expenses of the production, chief of which, as his title implies, was the training and costuming of the chorus. Plutarch claims that the Athenians actually spent more money on dramatic productions than they did fighting the Persians and acquiring their empire (*Moral Precepts* 349a). It is estimated that the services of some 1,500 persons were needed to stage all the plays produced at the City Dionysia each year. This meant that a very sizeable percentage of the citizen body participated annually in the theatrical competitions and, if allotment was used, that a majority did so at least once in their lifetimes. To the best of our knowledge, all 1,500 participants would have been men, though it is conceivable that a few women assisted backstage, not least in preparing the costumes.

If a tragic trilogy or comedy failed to be selected by the archon, its chances of being performed in Athens or elsewhere were virtually nil. There was no equivalent to an off-Broadway theater devoted to experimental drama. Even so, as far as we know, no playwright ever questioned the conditions to which he was forced to submit in order to have his plays produced, nor did any ever complain that state funding inhibited the free expression of his ideas. In the first half of the fifth century B.C.E., playwrights were required to be composers, choreographers, designers, directors, and actors as well. Increasingly, however, these roles were taken over by specialists, though the playwrights still had to write the music for the chorus. Being a playwright hardly amounted to having a profession in the modern sense of the word, because they received payment only if they won first prize. Some, however, may have earned a modest income from the sale of copies of their plays.

The Theater

A Greek theater consisted of a *theatron,* or "seeing space", which was frequently cut into a hillside in the form of steeply raked tiers of seats, and a circular *orchêstra,* or "dancing space" about twenty meters in diameter, almost entirely surrounded by the *theatron.* Seats were arranged in the form of wedges and were divided from one another by vertical gangways. In the fifth century B.C.E., the seats were wooden, but in the next century stone became commonplace. The best-preserved theater is at Epidauros in the northeast Peloponnese, built in the fourth century B.C.E., whose acoustics are so refined that it is possible to hear a piece of paper being torn up in the center of the *orchêstra* from the back row of seats over fifty meters away. Recent research conducted by the Georgia Institute of Technology suggests that this is due in part to the limestone seating, which amplifies high-frequency sounds coming from the *orchêstra* while filtering out low-frequency sounds, such as the shuffling and murmuring of the audience.

The raised stage was an invention of the fifth century B.C.E., as, too, was scenery. The Greek *skênê,* meaning "hut" or "tent" and from which the word *scenery* derives, describes the actors' changing room, the outside of which could be painted to resemble the façade of a palace or temple and thus provide a sense of place. There was no other form of stage setting.

The Theater of Dionysos in Athens could probably accommodate about 20,000 spectators. (Plato mentions 30,000 in the *Symposium,* but this is almost certainly an exaggeration.) Even if only 10,000 attended, this probably amounted to a quarter of the citizen body. The front rows were reserved for priests, magistrates, and distinguished visitors. In the center of the front row was the throne of the priest of Dionysos Eleuthereus ("Liberator"). Special areas were reserved for ephebes, members of the council, and metics. Probably the rest of the audience sat in blocks allocated to each of the ten tribes. Even prisoners were let out on bail so that they could attend performances. The price of admission was two obols, though, from the fourth century B.C.E. onward and possibly earlier, citizens were admitted free. We do not know for certain whether women were permitted to attend. Although it may seem inherently unlikely that slaves were permitted to attend, we cannot rule out the possibility that some Athenians, particularly if they were elderly, were accompanied by slaves who assisted them to their seats and perhaps sat with them.

PRESENT-DAY RUINS OF THE THEATRE OF DIONYSUS *in Athens.*

Going to the theater was hardly a relaxing experience in the modern sense of the word, because the audience was expected to sit through four plays a day at least, or five if the tragic plays performed in the morning were followed by a comedy in the afternoon. That amounts to about ten hours of uninterrupted performance per day. There were no intervals, except between plays. Not surprisingly, audiences became extremely restless if they were bored or displeased. We hear of several instances when a hostile crowd pelted the performers with stones and fruit. In the fifth century B.C.E., plays received only a single performance when first produced. The only exception was Aristophanes' *Frogs,* first performed at the Lenaia in 405 B.C.E., whose political message was judged to be so relevant that the play was given a second performance, probably at the City Dionysia two months later. Deme theaters, however, regularly reprieved plays. In addition, some time before 425 B.C.E., the Athenians passed a decree permitting anyone who wished to revive Aeschylus's plays at the City Dionysia. (Aeschylus had died in 456 B.C.E.). In the fourth century, revivals of what were called "old tragedy" became commonplace even in the theater of Dionysos in Athens, as the plays of the three great tragedians became, in effect, canonized. Sometime between 340 and 336 B.C.E., a law was passed requiring that an official version of their plays be preserved in the state treasury.

Stage Equipment

Because theatrical performances took place in broad daylight, there was no opportunity to focus the audience's attention on a particular spot through lighting effects. Only two items of stage equipment were in regular use. One was the *ekkyklêma,* or "object that is rolled out." This was a low platform on wheels that was projected into the orchêstra from the central doors of the scene building to reveal the interior of a place or temple. The *ekkyklêma* was undoubtedly used by Aeschylus in *Agamemnon* in order to display the bodies of Klytaimnestra and her lover Aigisthos after they had been murdered by Orestes. The other device was the *mêchanê,* a word that simply means machine. The *mêchanê* was a kind of crane that enabled a character to be transported on or off stage by being swung through the air. The Latin phrase *deus ex machina,* (literally "a god from a machine"), which has entered our language, is a reference to the overworking of this device by dramatists who used it to extricate their characters from an otherwise insoluble plot.

The Chorus

The Greek word *chôros,* which to us suggests collective singing, literally means "dance" (as in the word *choreography).* Most choruses (in the Greek sense) were a combination of music, dance, and song. The central importance of the chorus in Greek drama is indicated by the fact that it was the orchêstra that formed the focus for a theatrical production. In earlier times, choruses numbered about fifty, but, around the middle of the fifth century B.C.E., they were reduced in size to fifteen or twelve. The training of a chorus was a lengthy and expensive undertaking. Costumes were often costly and elaborate. We are told that when the chorus of Furies entered in Aeschylus's *Eumenides,* their appearance was so frightful that pregnant women miscarried on the spot. However, since we are not even sure that women attended the theater, the anecdote may be apocryphal. In comedy, the costumes worn by the chorus were often extremely exotic, as suggested by the names of some of Aristophanes' comedies, such as *Birds, Wasps, Clouds,* and *Frogs.*

The chorus entered the orchêstra at the end of the first scene and remained there throughout the performance. During the choral passages, its members would sing and dance to the accompaniment of the *aulos,* a double pipe with reeds. The chorus leader might converse with the actors from time to time. One of the primary functions of the chorus was to comment on the action and urge caution. Its reactions also helped the audience to reach its own verdict about events, though the chorus was not the mouthpiece of the poet. At a more mundane level, it enabled the actors to change costumes between scenes. Its significance declined over time, and, in many of Euripides' late plays, it is little more than an adjunct. The exception to this rule is *Bacchai,* where the role of the chorus is central to the drama. Even the comic dramatist Menander, writing about a century later than Euripides, did not abolish the chorus altogether.

Choral performances were not confined to drama. They took place at all religious festivals, as well as at secular gatherings. They include a song of praise known as the encomium (*enkômion),* whose name derives from the fact that it was originally sung at a revel or *kômos;* the victory ode (*epinikion);* and the dirge (*thrênos).* The earliest surviving choral poetry was written by Alkman, who composed songs for choruses of Spartan girls in the seventh century B.C.E. Alkman's work provides us with a glimpse of a Sparta that is sensuous, delicate, and refined—very different from the militaristic state that it became in later times. Choral lyric reached its peak in the early fifth century B.C.E. Its chief exponent was Pindar, who wrote numerous odes celebrating victories in the Olympic, Pythian, and Nemean Games.

The Actors

All the speaking parts in both comedy and tragedy were performed by a maximum of three male actors. Because there could be as many as eight different dramatis personae in a play, however, actors frequently had to change parts. They did this by both switching masks and costumes and altering the pitch of their voices. Masks, which were probably made of stiffened linen, were fairly naturalistic in the case of tragedy but grotesque caricatures in the case of comedy. Because actors could not rely on facial expressions to convey their emotions, they had to be far more expressive in both voice and gesture than their modern counterparts.

In keeping with the idea of the heroic age that tragedy evoked, tragic actors wore brightly colored robes decorated with elaborate patterns. They also wore a calf-length boot known as the *kothornos,* which was loose enough to fit on either foot. In later times, the *kothornos* was provided with a high heel to make actors look more impressive. Comic actors were heavily padded to make them look completely ridiculous. Beneath their short tunics, they sported huge phalluses to depict the erect male organ, strapped around the waist by means of a belt. Actors were also provided with role markers, such as a scepter to indicate a king or a club to indicate Herakles.

A FIGURINE OF AN ACTOR *wearing the mask of a* rustic, *or peasant. Terra-cotta, second century B.C.E.*

Initially the main character in the drama, known as the protagonist, was played by the dramatist. By the end of the fifth century B.C.E., however, actors were professionals and allocated to each production by lot.

The Judges

Drama was a highly competitive activity. The prizes for first, second, and third place were decided by a panel of ten *kritai,* or judges. It is from *kritês* that the word *critic* is derived, although the English word is something of a misnomer, because Athenian *kritai* were elected by lot and in no sense constituted a panel of experts. Each wrote his choice for first prize on a tablet. The ten choices were then placed in an urn, from which the eponymous archon drew out only five. This system was intended to leave some part of the decision making to the gods. Regrettably, there is no way of telling to what extent the judges' verdict was based on dramatic content and structure and to what extent it was influenced by the quality of the production. Several of what today are regarded as the finest examples of Attic tragedy were not awarded first prize, including Euripides' *Medea,* which won third prize, and his *Trojan Women,* which won second prize.

The victorious dramatist received a wreath and a small cash prize, and the winning *chorêgos* was permitted to erect a column in his own honor. Of the three tragedians whose works survive, the most successful was Sophokles, who wrote 123 plays, won first prize eighteen times, and never dropped lower than second place. From 449 B.C.E., the judges also awarded a prize to the best protagonist.

Tragedy

Although we know the names of about 150 Greek tragedians, we have complete plays of only three, all of them Athenians. Of the works of Aeschylus (525–426 B.C.E.), the earliest of the three, we possess only seven out of about 73. Aeschylus introduced the second actor, which enabled a dialogue between two actors to take place on stage. He described his work as "slices from the great banquet of Homer," though his earliest surviving play is the *Persians,* a historical drama that deals with the Persian naval defeat at Salamis in 480 B.C.E. Aeschylus's masterpiece is the *Oresteia,* which was produced in 458 B.C.E., when he was sixty-seven years old. The *Oresteia,* the only complete trilogy that we possess (its accompanying satyr play has not survived), traces the fortunes of the house of Atreus from the murder of Agamemnon by his wife Klytaimnestra through to the acquittal of his son Orestes for avenging his father's death. Aeschylus, who fought at the battle of Marathon, allegedly met his death when an eagle dropped a tortoise on his bald head in the belief that it was a stone.

Aeschylus's successor Sophokles (495–406 B.C.E.) is also represented by only seven tragedies, out of about 123. His introduction of the third actor enabled more complicated dramatic interchanges to take place. This also had the incidental consequence of reducing the chorus to the role of spectator. His most celebrated drama, *Oedipus the King,* traces Oedipus's discovery of the fact that he has inadvertently killed his father and married his mother.

At the end of his life, Sophokles is said to have been taken to court by one of his sons, who tried to have him declared insane. The poet successfully refuted the charge by reading out one of the choruses from the play that he was currently working upon. He then turned to the jury and inquired, "Do you consider that to be the work of an idiot?"

Despite the fact that his plays illustrate the inscrutable will of the gods, Sophokles was a humanist. The following lines, which are delivered by the chorus in Antigone, *seem to echo the poet's own judgment on human achievement:*

Wonders are many, but none is more wonderful than man, who traverses the grey deep in wintery storms, making his way through waves that crash around him, wearing away the oldest of the gods, Earth, the indestructible, ploughing the soil year in and year out with his horses. . . . Only Death he has found no way to escape, though from irresistible sickness he has devised a way out. His ingeniousness and contriving are beyond everything. Now he makes his way to destruction, now to greatness. When he establishes laws and divine oaths and justice, his city rides high. (lines 322ff.)

Nineteen dramas of Sophokles' younger contemporary Euripides (480–406 B.C.E.) survive, out of about ninety-two. Euripides consistently depicts the gods as violent and inhumane. There is a tradition that he caused so much offense in Athens that he was prosecuted for atheism, though we do not know whether this is true. In the Bacchai, which was produced posthumously by his son in 405 B.C.E., the god Dionysos takes terrible revenge on the royal house of Thebes for having denied his divinity by causing a mother to tear her son limb from limb. The poet became so alienated and embittered at the end of his life that he abandoned Athens for Macedon, where the Bacchai was performed. It is said that he met his death by being torn apart by hunting dogs—another story of dubious authenticity.

All but one of the surviving tragedies are set in Greece's heroic past and depict the fortunes of its royal houses. Only a few are set in Athens. This does not mean that they were devoted to the exploration of outworn themes, however. Rather, the heroic past served as a backdrop for the lively investigation of contemporary political, moral, and social issues. Aeschylus's *Eumenides,* for instance, the third play in the *Oresteia,* contains what superficially at least appears to be an endorsement of the democratic revolution that took place in Athens four years earlier, though its true message seems to be rather more complex.

All tragedy, like comedy, is written in a variety of meters. The choral passages are punctuated by episodes that resemble the scenes of a modern play. A central feature of many plays is the *agôn,* which takes the form of a contest or dispute between two characters, each of whom seeks to defeat his opponent in argument. In Sophokles' *Antigone,* for instance, the *agôn* between Kreon and his son Haimon turns upon the justice of Kreon's decision to wall up Antigone alive in punishment for her having given burial rites to her brother, who has been condemned as a traitor.

Although most tragedies are concerned with violent and destructive actions, no actual violence is ever perpetrated on stage. Instead, it was common practice for a messenger to provide the audience with an extremely detailed description of a murder, suicide, self-mutilation, or other grisly occurrence that he has just witnessed off stage.

Most tragedies end with the chorus muttering a few platitudes along the lines of "What we expected to happen has not happened, and what we expected not to happen has happened." It has been suggested that the banality of such conclusions is probably due to the fact that the audience would have been heading for the exit by the time they were delivered. They should not be interpreted as the author's final judgment on the subject of the drama.

Comedy

Evidence for fifth-century comedy is even more meager than for tragedy. We possess only eleven plays by a single dramatist, Aristophanes (ca. 450–385 B.C.E.). Highly topical in subject matter, they contain plentiful references to events and personalities in contemporary Athens, many of which are lost on us. They are also extremely ribald and scatological. Frequently the plot turns upon a solution to a contemporary problem, such as how to end the Peloponnesian War. In *Acharnians,* for instance, the hero, who is a very average Athenian citizen named Dikaiopolis, achieves his goal by making a private peace with the Spartans. Similarly in *Lysistrata,* the women of Athens decide to jump-start the peace process by refusing to have sex with their husbands. Other plays are even more fantastic. *Birds,* for instance, is a fantasy about two Athenians who, fed up with all the pressures of modern life, attempt to set up a new city among the birds called Cloudcuckooland. In *Frogs,* Dionysos descends to Hades in order to bring back Euripides from the dead, though in the end he decides instead to

SCENE FROM ARISTOPHANES' *comedy,* Birds. *Note that the actors in this illustration wear masks.*

resurrect Aeschylus, on the grounds that Euripides' poetry is partly responsible for Athens' current troubles.

In the fourth century, a new style of comedy evolved that was almost entirely shorn of chorus and contained no contemporary allusions. Its greatest exponent was Menander (ca. 342–293 B.C.E.). Only one of his plays, *Ill-Tempered Man,* has survived in more or less complete form. Most of his plots explore the theme of romantic love through a complex intermingling of improbable devices including identical twins, broken families, and abandoned children. The genre, which is known as New Comedy, was taken over and adapted by the Romans. New Comedy was destined to provide the basis for comic inventiveness for centuries to come, an obvious example being Shakespeare's *Comedy of Errors.* Aristophanic Old Comedy, by contrast, was never revived and had no theatrical afterlife before the twentieth century.

Conclusions

Tragedy and comedy may be said to be two sides of the same coin. The principal difference is that, whereas tragedy explored the tragic consequences of conflict, comedy envisioned the possibility of some kind of reconciliation or resolution, however far-fetched. Between these extremes, there was little place for melodrama or sentimentality.

Publicly funded, profoundly civic in orientation, and fundamentally sacred in character, Attic drama might at first sight strike us as a covert means of reinforcing social conformity. The truth was far different. Although drama took place in a religious context, the playwrights did not see it as their objective to offer pious platitudes or promote supine obedience to the will of the gods. On the contrary, they were anything but shy of depicting the Olympians as degenerate and even morally repellent whenever it suited their purposes. Legend had it that, after witnessing Thespis's first tragedy, the Athenian audience was so mystified by its lack of religious content that they angrily demanded, "What's this got to do with Dionysos?" The question is still posed by scholars to this day.

What drama chiefly did was to provide a context in which issues of public and private concern could be literally aired in the open. Its purpose, in other words, was not to promote some kind of party line or function as a moral arbiter, but rather to give expression to the hard moral choices that define human existence, explore the problematic nature of man's relationship with the gods, and demonstrate the human (and divine) capacity for evil. As such, it frequently served subversive rather than conformist ends.

There is no more eloquent proof of the central importance of drama in the life of the Athenian community than the fact that the hard-line conservative Plato proposed expelling the playwrights, along with all poets, from his ideal city, being fearful of their influence on the morals of his contemporaries. And there is no stronger proof of the relevance of Attic drama to the contemporary world than the fact that the Colonels, who suspended democracy and ruled Greece from 1967 to 1974 as an oligarchy, found it necessary in the interests of public order to ban the performance of Euripides' works.

MUSIC

The Greek word *mousikê* identified a much broader range of cultural activity than our word *music*. It included all of the arts that came under the patronage of Apollo and the nine Muses—that is, singing and dancing as well as history and astronomy. The epithet *mousikos,* which means "muse-ish," was synonymous with good taste. Conversely, *amousikos* described a person who lacked refinement or education. In this section, however, we will consider the word music in its limited, modern sense.

Music was a central part of Greek daily life and, as such, was essential to an Athenian education. It was a feature of all social gatherings, including births, weddings, and funerals. Songs were sung by laborers to lighten the workload, especially at harvest and vintage, and by women in the home while they were grinding the grain, weaving, or kneading bread. Soldiers and athletes trained to the sound of pipes. Every religious event was marked by the singing of hymns. Nearly every genre of poetry, including epic, lyric, and dramatic, was written to be sung to music. Music was an essential accompaniment to the drinking party.

The various modes of music were believed to exercise a profound impact upon the mind. The so-called Dorian mode, being solemn and martial, was thought to induce courage, whereas the Phrygian mode, which was wild and perhaps atonal, was thought to encourage impetuosity. Philosophers were of the opinion that music contributed to

SAPPHO AND ALCAEUS. Lawrence Alma-Tadema, 1881. Oil on canvas. In this painting, set on the island of Lesbos in the late seventh century B.C.E., the poet Sappho and her companions listen intently as the poet Alcaeus plays a lyre.

a well-balanced and disciplined personality. Plato, however, was extremely skeptical of its influence and banished it from his ideal state. Greek vases depicting scenes at the tomb suggest that delight in music was not interrupted by death.

Music had the power to whip up a gathering to frenzy pitch, much as a rock concert does today. The poetry and music of Euripides in particular were well nigh irresistible. Plutarch tells us that when a singer from Phokis sang the opening chorus of the *Elektra* at a symposium at which Peloponnesian delegates were in attendance following the recent defeat of Athens at the battle of Aigospotamoi in 404 B.C.E., the delegates were so overcome by the rendition that they recommended not destroying Athens on the grounds that it would have been a crime to destroy "so great a city that had produced so great men" (*Lysander* 15.2–3).

Yet, although we have the words of numerous songs preserved as poetry, almost all the music has perished without trace. In total, some forty-six musical scores, mostly fragmentary, have survived. Sadly, not one of these fragments can be certainly identified as the work of any of the three great tragedians, all of whom were prolific composers, as they wrote the accompanying scores to the choruses. And despite all the research that has been done by scholars, it would be overbold to suggest that we actually know what Greek music sounded like.

Many people made their living as musicians in the Greek world. The earliest were the itinerant bards, who traveled from one aristocratic house to another reciting to the accompaniment of the lyre improvised tales about heroes and gods by relying heavily on the formulaic structure of epic verse. Demodokos, the blind bard whom we encounter at the court of the Phaiakians in *The Odyssey* Book 8 is often thought to be a self-portrait of Homer, who was himself in all probability a bard. Originally bards accompanied themselves on the lyre. Later they abandoned the lyre and carried a staff instead. Even after they ceased to accompany their recitations with the lyre, however, they probably continued to recite in a rather singsong style. It was at the instigation of the Athenian tyrant Peisistratos in the second half of the sixth century B.C.E. that Homer's poems were standardized and written down. Recitation contests now became part of the Panathenaic festival. Festivals also provided an opportunity for new works to be heard.

The most popular stringed instrument was the lyre, or *kithara,* which resembled a modern guitar. Even Achilles, the most violent of Greek heroes, is depicted playing the lyre in *The Iliad* Book 9 as a way of soothing his troubled feelings. In the simplest version of the instrument, the sound box is made of a tortoise shell with a hide stretched over the hollow underside. Music was produced by plucking the strings, usually seven in number, either with the fingers or with a plectrum. A variant on this instrument was the *barbiton,* which had longer strings. The barbiton was associated with scenes of revelry held in honor of Dionysos. Another stringed instrument was the harp, whose use seems to have been confined largely to professional musicians.

GIRL PLAYING THE AULOUS, *an ancient Greek double flute. Detail from an Attic red-figure* lekythos *made ca. 480 B.C.E.*

The most popular wind instrument was the *aulos.* This is often identified with the flute, although the sound it produced was considerably lower and closer to that of the oboe or bassoon. The aulos, which was played at the end, unlike its modern counterpart, consisted of a hollow pipe made of wood, bronze, bone, or reed. It was pierced with holes for the fingers and fitted with a reed mouthpiece. *Auloi* were usually played in pairs. The chorus of Greek drama sang and danced to the accompaniment of an aulos player, who also piped soldiers into battle and played an accompaniment to exercises in the palaistra. Another wind instrument was the *syrinx,* which consisted of a number of pipes of graduated length bound together. Variations in pitch were made by blocking the inside of the pipes with wax at different intervals. The syrinx was a somewhat crude instrument whose invention was attributed to the goat god Pan. No doubt it was especially popular among shepherds, for whom it would be the only source of distraction while minding their flocks.

The nearest approximation to a brass instrument was the *salpinx,* a long slender instrument terminating in a bell-shaped aperture. It was used primarily to herald the beginning and end of religious and other ceremonies. Several percussion instruments are known, including the *kymbala,* from which the word *cymbals* is derived; the *tympanon,* meaning a small drum; the *krotala,* or castanets; and the *sistra,* or rattles. They were all commonly used in ecstatic cults, notably those that had been imported into Greece from the East.

The Visual Arts

In modern culture, art carries a price tag and is often purchased either as an investment or as a status symbol. Most works of art are intended for private purchase. Art appreciation is a branch of connoisseurship that requires a highly trained, professional eye, not least in order to distinguish between an authentic work of art and a fake. By and large, the public plays a minor role in the changing fortunes of an artist's reputation, which is mainly determined by experts. Although the artist may ultimately become something of a public institution, he or she often remains a fashionable outsider. Finally, although some artists receive state sponsorship in the form of grants from the National Endowment for the Arts in the United States or from the Arts Council of Great Britain, not everyone agrees that this is an appropriate or valuable use of public funds.

Greek art shared nothing in common with the picture drawn above. It was never purchased as an investment. Other than perhaps in the minor arts, the connoisseur had no equivalent. The only "expert" was the community as a whole. The

Greeks did not regard costly works of art to be symbols of status and wealth. To our best knowledge, not a single marble or bronze statue ever graced a private home until the Roman era, which then witnessed a veritable craze for Greek statuary. Most major works of art were commissioned by the state and served a religious function, whether as temples, dedications to the gods, or monuments erected in commemoration of victorious athletes or the dead. Greek artists often found themselves in the pay of the state and had to work to a very strict set of specifications and guidelines. Greece never developed anything equivalent to the modern cult of the artist. We know the names of very few artists and virtually nothing about their private lives.

Sculpture

Greek sculpture originated around the middle of the seventh century B.C.E. Its initial inspiration owes much to Egypt. Marble, limestone, bronze, terracotta, wood, or a combination of gold and ivory known as chryselephantine were the chief materials. The 36-foot-high statue of Athene Parthenos, housed inside the Parthenon and designed by the sculptor Pheidias, was covered in ivory and gold to represent flesh and clothing. Stone statues were painted, which lent them a very vivid appearance. Accessories such as armor and jewelry and eyes were often reproduced in a different material. Statues were not cheap to purchase. It is reckoned that a bronze statue would have cost 3,000 drachmas, which is why very few have survived—most of them were melted down for reuse.

THIS ANONYMOUS, UNDATED ENGRAVING *shows what the statue of Athene Parthenos would have looked like in the Parthenon, where it was housed in the cella, or inner chamber.*

The Greeks did not make the same clear-cut distinction between reality and artistic illusion that we do, as the following anecdote makes plain. The statue of a famous athlete called Theagenes was erected in his honor on the island of Thasos. One of Theagenes' rivals was so incensed by this that he began to flog the statue at night. Eventually the statue toppled over and crushed him. The victim's sons proceeded to prosecute the statue in the courts. The statue was convicted and drowned at sea. This sequence of events only makes sense if we accept the fact that the image of a person or a deity was thought to embody—in the literal sense—his or her essence.

Greek sculptors did not see it as their goal to produce works of art that reflected the accidental and true-to-life deficiencies of authentic human anatomy. The chief artistic inspiration throughout antiquity was the physically perfect, primarily male, body, as exemplified by the god Apollo, who is invariably depicted as a youth in peak physical condition. A superb example of this is the Apollo who presides over a battle between the civilized Lapiths and the half human, half animal centaurs on the west pediment of the temple of Zeus at Olympia. Unperturbed and impassive, Apollo extends his right arm horizontally in a gesture that indicates his support for the Lapiths. Portraiture inspired relatively few works of Greek art. Many sculptures that purport to be portraits were produced long after the subject's death, so their resemblance to the sitter is questionable at best. Notable exceptions are the portraits of Sokrates, which probably do convey an authentic likeness. Even in the Hellenistic era, which saw the birth of a more realistic tendency, the depictions of careworn philosophers, aging athletes, and elderly women are more stereotypical than naturalistic. Among Hellenistic sculptures, only those depicting dynasts seem to have been truly individualized, especially the profiles on coins. One of the most memorable coin portraits is that of Euthydemos I of Baktria, dated about 200 B.C.E., which gazes at us across the millennia with disillusionment and disarming candor.

From the very beginning of full-size Greek sculpture in about 660 B.C.E., men were depicted naked. Statues known as *kouroi* (youths) stand frontally with one foot advanced, hands at side, fists clenched. The earliest examples are based on a sculptural formula that had been used by the Egyptians for two thousand years. Statues of women, called *korai* (girls), which have no antecedent in Egyptian art, are, by contrast, invariably clothed, albeit in diaphanous, clinging drapery that often leaves little to the imagination. They are depicted holding their skirt with one hand and holding out the other for an offering. Several dozen have been discovered on the Acropolis, where they were ritually buried in pits after being smashed during the Persian sack in 480 B.C.E. Some were in such mint condition when they were buried that the original paint survives. Because the proportions of many korai are not noticeably different from those of kouroi (with thick necks, broad shoulders, powerful thighs), they have been wittily described as "kouroi in drag." One of the reasons for their lack of naturalism is the fact that the naked female body was not, so to speak, available for anatomical study.

Only in the second half of the fourth century B.C.E. did the female nude become a socially acceptable subject in statuary. Even then, women are usually shown coyly covering the genital area with a hand or piece of drapery. A celebrated example is Praxiteles' sculpture of Aphrodite taking a bath, which was described by the Roman writer Pliny as "the finest statue in the whole world." Praxiteles actually carved two statues of Aphrodite, one clothed and the other naked. He then asked the inhabitants of the island of Kos which they preferred. They chose the clothed figure on the grounds that it was more chaste. The naked version of the goddess was subsequently purchased by the people of Knidos, a city that lies opposite Kos on the coast. Such, incidentally, was its erotic power that a man who was accidentally locked up with it overnight inside a temple is said to have indecently assaulted it.

Centuries later, when the Knidians were in dire financial straits, Nikomedes, king of Bithynia, offered to purchase the naked statue from them. Despite their hardship, the Knidians refused, claiming that it was the nude statue of Aphrodite for which their city was best known.

CNIDUS APHRODITE. *Restored Roman copy of a fourth-century B.C.E. original by the Greek sculptor, Praxiteles. Marble.*

Architecture

The Greek temple afforded the primary context for the expression of Greek architectural excellence. It was also the architectural medium on which was expended the greatest amount of energy. Built primarily to house a cult statue, it provided a showcase for the finest achievements of Greek architecture. The temple was by no means intrinsic to worship, since all cultic activity took place in the open air, around the altar. Its primary religious function was to secure the goodwill of the deity to whom it was erected.

The basic layout of the temple was established around the end of the seventh century B.C.E. A *pronaos*, or porch, leads to a central room, or *naos*. In some cases, there is a back porch, or *opisthodomos*, and a surrounding colonnade known as a *peristyle*. Temples were mostly aligned on an east-west axis, with the cult statue facing east so that it could witness the sacrifice being performed on the altar. At first, only the stepped platform on which the temple stood was made of stone, but later stone replaced wood for both the columns and the superstructure. The first temple to be made entirely of stone was that of Artemis on the island of Corcyra (Corfu). The best preserved temple is the Second Temple of Hera at Poseidonia, which was built of limestone around the middle of the fifth century B.C.E. The crowning achievement of Greek architecture is the Parthenon, which uses a numerical ratio of nine-to-four in all its proportions. Such are its stylistic refinements, which are intended to counteract the effects of optical illusion, that not a single line in the entire building is perfectly straight.

PRESENT-DAY PHOTOGRAPH OF THE SECOND TEMPLE OF HERA, *one of the best-preserved temples of ancient Greece.*

Greek temples are categorized according to three orders of architecture. The principal orders are the Doric and Ionic, which both evolved in the fifth century B.C.E. A third, known as the Corinthian, came into being somewhat later. (Corinthian is a misnomer. Paradoxically, it was the Doric Order that was invented in Corinth.) Doric columns, which are somewhat squat in appearance, rise from their platform without any base. They are decorated with twenty vertical grooves, known as flutes, in which shadows settle as the sky darkens, thereby lending a sense of drama and plasticity to the building. They are topped by capitals that resemble cushions. The Ionic column, which is considerably taller in proportion to its width, rises from a molded base and terminates in a capital that is surmounted by a pair of volutes. It has twenty-four flutes, separated from one another by a narrow band. The Corinthian capital also rises from a molded base but its capital resembles bands of acanthus leaves.

The differences in style extended up into the superstructure. A Doric frieze consists of rectangular blocks called metopes, interrupted by narrower rectangles with vertical grooves called triglyphs. By contrast, an Ionic frieze is continuous. The crowning member is a triangular gable known as a pediment, which is located at either end of the temple. A few temples, notably the Parthenon, combine elements of both the Doric and Ionic orders. Metopes, pediments, and friezes are frequently decorated with relief sculpture. Because these were painted, the overall effect would have been extremely colorful. Most large temples on the Greek mainland were built in the Doric style with a surrounding colonnade, whereas in Ionia (western Turkey) the fashion was for massive temples in the Ionic style with double colonnades.

Much of the sculpture that decorated a temple was narrative. A masterly example is found on the east pediment of the temple of Zeus Olympios at Olympia.

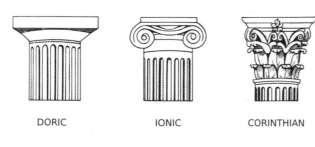

DORIC   IONIC   CORINTHIAN

THE THREE ORDERS *of ancient Greek architecture: Doric, Ionic, and Corinthian.*

ILLUSTRATION OF THE TEMPLE OF ARTEMIS AT EPHESOS, *one of the Seven Wonders of the Ancient World.*

Its subject is the chariot race between Pelops and Oinomaos. Pelops, who wished to wed Oinomaos's daughter, Hippodameia, had to defeat him in order to secure her hand. To assure his victory, he bribed Oinomaos's charioteer to tamper with the king's chariot wheels so that they would fall off during the race. Instead of portraying the drama of the collision, however, the sculptor has chosen to depict the tense moment before the race begins. The composition, which is dominated by the commanding presence of Zeus flanked on either side by the contestants, conveys an unearthly stillness. What shatters this mood is the reclining seer who raises his clenched fist to his cheek in a gesture of alarm. We comprehend that the seer is gazing into the future and envisions the catastrophe ahead.

It is testimony to the achievements of Greek architecture that no fewer than five of the Seven Wonders of the World listed in the second century B.C.E. by Antipater of Sidon for the benefit of tourists were Greek—though since Antipater was himself Greek, he may not have been entirely objective. They include the statue of Zeus at Olympia, the temple of Artemis at Ephesos, the Mausoleum at Halikarnassos, the Colossus of Rhodes, and the Pharos (or Lighthouse) of Alexandria.

Painting

Until fairly recently, our knowledge of the great paintings that decorated the interior walls of Greek temples and public buildings was mainly reliant upon literary descriptions, which failed to convey any real sense of the technical quality of the originals. Recently, however, thanks partly to the discovery of the Macedonian tombs at Vergina, we have direct evidence of these murals.

Even so, when we talk about Greek painting, we tend to think first of the relatively humble medium of vase painting, which happens to be far more durable. Vase painting is a major source of information about Greek life. Especially popular subjects are drinking parties and visits to the tomb, because most painted pottery was intended to be either used at a symposium or deposited in the grave. Other popular subjects include athletic activities and scenes taking place in the women's quarters. Earlier vases are decorated in the black-figure technique against a red background. Around 525 B.C.E., however, the process was reversed, and the background was painted in black, leaving the figure in red. Most scenes of daily life are rendered in red-figure pottery.

The Politics of Greek Art

Although art was predominantly religious in function and its subject matter was largely confined to the mythological, it was often used to make a political state-ment. When, for instance, in 447 B.C.E., the Athenians made the historic decision to rebuild the temples on the Acropolis destroyed by the Persians, they incorpo-rated a number of barely disguised references to Athens' heroic struggle for freedom into the sculptures. The Parthenon metopes, for instance, which depict the battle between the Lapiths and the centaurs, evoke the Persian Wars, since this involved a conflict between a higher order of civilization and a lower. It is possible, too, that the great frieze that ran around the outer wall of the naos, whose principal feature is a procession of Athenian cavalry, is intended to depict the 192 Athenians who died at the battle of Marathon, here shown as the heroized dead.

Conclusions

Greek artists were constantly learning new artistic techniques and addressing new problems. As a consequence, even in the absence of an archaeological context that would enable us to date a given artifact with chronological exactitude, we are often able to situate it to within a single decade. Coupled with this inherent innovativeness, however, was an inherent conservatism. For instance, although the different orders of architecture underwent refinement over the centuries, the temple remained the preferred medium of architectural expression. Similarly, the human body served throughout Greek antiquity as the focus for all sculptural and pictorial endeavor.

The Greek world did not foster artistic movements in the modern sense of the term. Nor did artists utilize their skills to make a personal statement. At all periods of history their level of achievement was remarkably uniform. They have bequeathed to us remarkably few bad or even indifferent works of art. Even in their poorest productions, it is generally the taste rather than the technical accomplishment that is deficient. Clearly artists were intimately familiar with one another's work and saw themselves as participants in a collective enterprise. Not the least distinctive feature about Greek art is its broad and undeviating acceptance of society's expectations of what constitutes art.

MYTHOLOGY

On the side panel of any cereal box, consumers might be enlightened about the differences between what the cereal maker calls myth, on the one hand and fact, on the other, in regard to the perennially fascinating subject of how to lose weight. Under the heading of myth might be claims that carbohydrates are fattening, that one does not need to exercise, and that one can eat as much diet food as one wants. *Myth*, in the sense that it is applied here, is synonymous with a fiction or falsehood that commands widespread assent but has no basis in fact. *Mythos*, from which the word *myth* is derived, however, carried no such negative connotation for the Greeks. Its basic meaning was word, speech, or story. Even in the sense of a story, mythos did not signify or imply a fiction. On the contrary, it denoted an exemplary tale that revealed what was perceived to be a fundamental truth (or possible truths), whether about the nature of the world, the deeds and activities of the gods and heroes, or the composition and evolution of Greek society. In the words of Walter Burkert (*Structure and History in Greek Mythology and Ritual*, 23), "A myth is a traditional tale with secondary, partial reference to something of collective importance," though with the important proviso that, despite being traditional, any myth can undergo limitless numbers of retelling and thus modification, even though the basic plot line remains stable.

The subject matter that the Greeks utilized for mythic treatment comprised all the events that had occurred from the creation of the universe to the aftermath of the Trojan War. This included the succession of divine dynasties that ultimately led to the current ruling dynasty of Olympian deities, the beginnings and evolution of human existence, the Trojan War itself, and the tales that took place in the Age of Heroes.

How Myths Were Transmitted

Although myths have reached us primarily through literature, this was not how they were transmitted in antiquity. Rather, they were the product of an oral culture that passed down its lore by word of mouth from one generation to the next. Although it is impossible to reach back in time to discover a myth's origins, surely many of them are rooted in Greece's preliterate past. It was a past that possessed no other means of preserving what needed to be preserved except by word of mouth. Precisely because they were transmitted orally, myths underwent considerable change in each retelling. Inevitably, some details were lost or modified while others were invented or recast. What has survived, in other words, is the result of a long evolutionary process that took place over several centuries and that remained in flux. It was a process that was organic in the true sense of the word. Indeed, it is hardly any exaggeration to state that once a myth acquired a canonical or fixed form, it ceased to retain its contemporary relevance for the teller and the audience.

The vitality of the mythic tradition can be aptly demonstrated by reference to the myth of Oedipus, the king of Thebes, who inadvertently fulfills the prophecy of the Delphic Oracle by killing his father and marrying his mother. It is a story that provides a stern warning about the terrifying power of coincidence. But in Sophokles' play, Oedipus the King it is much more than that. For when Oedipus discovers what he has done, he is so appalled by his crimes that he blinds himself. This act of self-mutilation, which is undertaken in response to his previous ignorance about his own identity, has a deeply symbolic meaning. Oedipus might have hanged himself, as he does in another version of the story. But it was central to Sophokles' interpretation that the king should go on living after learning the tragic facts about his identity. In other words, he lives on with his understanding enlarged but darkened, and in the full consciousness of his own unintended crimes. Sophokles thus infuses the myth with his own personal vision of the human condition, for which Oedipus is the quintessential symbol.

Myths were not, therefore, immutable artifacts written in stone. There was never any official version of a myth, though some versions inevitably became more popular than others. This did not prevent different versions from coexisting in different places and at different times—or even at the same time. Such a state of affairs was probably the rule rather than the exception. Although myths were the common property of all Greeks, they often bore a distinctly localized character. Each city-state disseminated its own versions and gave prominence to those myths that celebrated its own local heroes and local deities. That is why there can never be a "right" interpretation of what a myth "really means" in the way that some modern interpreters, such as Joseph Campbell, have fancifully suggested.

Our primary source for the study of Greek mythology is Greek literature. The oldest surviving myths are to be found in the poems of Hesiod and Homer. There is no evidence to suggest that Hesiod or Homer invented the myths they incorporate, however. Another important early source is an anonymous compilation of works called The Homeric Hymns, which contain charter myths that explain the establishment of cults in honor of the various Olympian deities. In addition, many of the best-known myths were dramatized by Athens' tragedians, who, as discussed earlier, for the most part set their

AN 1882 ENGRAVING *featuring the ancient Greek authors Herodotus, Aristophanes, Sophocles, Socrates, Euripides, Plato, and Aeschylus.*

plays in Greece's heroic past. The most comprehensive anthology is Apollodoros's Library, which was probably written in the late first or early second century C.E. It is the product of a period when myth had become foremost a subject of antiquarian interest. The visual arts, particularly vase painting and sculpture, also provide a useful source of information. In fact, mythology, along with scenes of daily life, are the two chief sources of inspiration for vase painting, though we should not think of them as necessarily separate from one another; scenes that depict myths may also shed light on daily life.

Most myths are preserved merely in part. The only one that receives exhaustive treatment in any surviving work is Jason's search for the golden fleece, as narrated in an epic poem entitled *Argonautika*, or *Voyage of the Argo*, by Apollonios of Rhodes in the third century B.C.E. Even the events of the Trojan War have come down to us only in a piecemeal condition. The lengthiest and most detailed treatment is provided by Homer's *The Iliad*; however, the action of this poem, which is limited to a period of ten days in the final year of the war, covers only a minor incident, namely Achilles' temporary withdrawal from the battlefield as the result of an insult from his commander in chief. The poem does not refer directly to either the cause of the war or its conclusion, nor does it contain a plot summary. So well known was its course, however, that Homer's audience could be relied upon to put the quarrel between Achilles and Agamemnon in its context and see within the events covered by the poem a foreshadowing and anticipation of the destruction of the city of Troy.

The following is a list of the most important literary sources for the study of Greek mythology:

Homer, *The Iliad*: The havoc that is caused among the Greeks and the Trojans as a result of Achilles' anger.

Homer, *The Odyssey*: Odysseus's return to Ithaka and his reunion with his wife Penelope.

Hesiod, *Theogony*: How the present Olympian dynasty came to power.

Hesiod, *Works and Days*: Zeus as the upholder of justice and champion of the common people against the kings, coupled with a breakdown of the agricultural year.

The Homeric Hymns: Stories about the early days of the gods and how they came to acquire their powers.

Aeschylus, *Agamemnon*: Agamemnon's murder at the hands of his wife Klytaimnestra and her lover Aegisthos.

Aeschylus, *Choêphoroi*, or *"Libation Bearers"*: Orestes' invocation of the shade of his father Agamemnon to aid him in a revenge killing of his mother and her lover.

Aeschylus, *Eumenides*, or *"Friendly Ones"*: Orestes' acquittal on the charge of matricide before an Athenian court.

Sophokles, *Oedipus the King*: Oedipus's discovery that he is guilty of murdering his father and marrying his mother.

Sophokles, *Antigone*: Antigone's defiant determination to give burial to her brother Polyneikes in violation of Kreon's edict.

Sophokles, *Oedipus at Colonus*: The elevation to heroic status of the blind and aged Oedipus.

Euripides, *Hippolytos*: Aphrodite's vengeance upon Hippolytos for his refusal to worship her.

Euripides, *Bacchai*: The dismemberment of Pentheus, king of Thebes, as a
result of his opposition to the cult of Dionysos.

Aristophanes, *Frogs*: Dionysos as anti-hero—cowardly, licentious, untrust-
worthy, and incontinent—and his descent to Hades in search of a poet
to save Athens.

Apollonios of Rhodes, *Argonautika*: Jason's search for the golden fleece in the
company of the Argonauts.

Ovid, *Metamorphoses*: A highly individualistic treatment of Greek and
Roman myth loosely bound together by the theme of shape shifting.

Apollodoros, *Library*: The most comprehensive collection of mythology to
survive from antiquity.

Myths of Origin

Where does the world come from? Why is there so much evil? Why do we give
the least edible parts of an animal to the gods when we sacrifice? Why is the year
divided into different seasons? Why are women so seductive? Why in the face
of all the terrible things that happen in the world do we still continue to hope
that things will improve? These and other perennial questions are just a few of
the issues that myths of origin (or charter myths, as anthropologist Bronislaw
Malinowski called them) seek to address.

The primary source for the mythic account of the origin of the universe
is Hesiod's *Theogony*. According to Hesiod, the primordial being was Chaos, a
word that roughly translates as gaping void. Next Gaia (Earth), Tartaros (the
lowest region of the underworld), and Eros (desire) came into existence. Chaos
then engendered Erebos (darkness) and Night, and Night, by coupling with
Erebos, gave birth to Aither (upper air) and Day. Whereas the book of Genesis
ascribes the creative act to a divine being who exists outside his own creation,
Hesiod proposed a model whereby the means of propagation emerged out of
nothingness. In other words, it was the instinct for mating rather than a series
of disconnected acts on the part of a divine will that caused the world to assume
its present form.

The Trojan War

The Trojan War represented the supreme military enterprise of all time. It was undertaken to avenge the honor of Agamemnon's brother Menelaos, king of Sparta. His wife Helen had been abducted by the Trojan prince Paris, who was the guest of Menelaos at the time. Contingents from all over the Greek world participated in the venture, which was placed under the command of Agamemnon, king of Mycenae. After a siege that lasted ten years, Troy was taken and destroyed.

The Trojan War, which elicited deeds of great courage on both sides, has all the makings of an epic in the modern sense of the word. It was, moreover, a just war, inasmuch as the Greeks were the injured party. Despite this, however, both in Homer's *The Iliad* and in the numerous dramas that treat incidents from the war, the emphasis is predominantly upon the sufferings of innocent victims, the intransigence of the victors, and the divided loyalties of the gods. Thus, far from being a nationalistic myth that jingoistically trumpeted the achievements of the Greeks, it served as a terrible reminder of the futility and horror of war. No image expresses the revulsion that this engendered in some Greeks more memorably than an Attic red-figure krater or mixing bowl dated 465 B.C.E., which depicts the Greek hero Neoptolemos using the body of Hektor's son Astyanax as a blunt instrument with which to batter to death the aged king Priam, who has taken refuge at an altar.

Deception, duplicity, and deceit all play a major part in the legends associated with the war. Book 10 of *The Iliad*, which is devoted to this theme, relates the capture of a Trojan scout, named Dolon, by Odysseus and Diomedes, who promise to spare Dolon's life if he will reveal the military disposition of the Trojan encampment. As soon as Dolon has fulfilled his side of the bargain, however, Diomedes decapitates him. He and Odysseus follow up this breach of faith by slaughtering the Thrakian prince Rhesos and his companions in their sleep. The famous incident involving the wooden horse, the example par excellence of Greek duplicity, leads directly to the fall of Troy. The giant hollow wooden horse contained a contingent of warriors who descended from it at night and opened the gates to admit the rest of the army. Although this incident lies outside the events of *The Iliad*, its central position within the tradition suggests that, in the eyes of the Greeks, their victory over the Trojans came primarily from cunning. Since, moreover, the wooden horse was ostensibly a ritual offering to the gods in appeasement for crimes committed by the Greeks, the gods, too, were implicated in the ruse.

Although the Homeric poems are among the greatest legacies of Greek culture, they demonstrate a strong influence of Near Eastern epic. A notable instance of borrowing involves the death of Achilles' dearest companion Patroklos in *The Iliad*. The description recalls the death of Gilgamesh's friend Enkidu in the so-called Epic of Gilgamesh, a Sumerian work the origins of which can be traced back to the third millennium B.C.E.—two thousand years before Homer. The source of many Greek myths ultimately lies in the Near East.

The Heroes

Greek mythology is full of tales about heroes such as Achilles, Orestes, Oedipus, Perseus, Herakles, Jason, Odysseus, and Theseus, all of whom are of divine parentage or ancestry. Achilles was the son of the sea goddess Thetis, Herakles and Perseus were the sons of Zeus, and Theseus was the son of Poseidon. Heroes are distinguished by their physical prowess, their appetite for adventure, and their willingness to take on challenges that would overwhelm the average mortal. The greatest challenge of all was the descent to the underworld, where the hero encountered what might be described as a negation of the self.

The range of heroic challenge is illustrated by the diversity of labors performed by Herakles, the greatest hero of all. Six of his labors take place in or around Olympia in the northwest Peloponnese, four send him to the cardinal points of the compass, and the last two—bringing Kerberos up from Hades and fetching the golden apples from the Hesperides—require him to journey beyond the confines of mortality. In meeting such challenges, Herakles stands as a symbol of the indomitability of the human, specifically Greek spirit.

The Greek hero was not merely an ancient version of the Lone Ranger, however. On the contrary, many of the myths emphasize the violent streak in human nature that is integral to man's lust for achievement. Many heroes, too, are less than heroic in their dealings with women. Herakles was repeatedly unfaithful to his wife Deianeira, whose death he inadvertently caused when she sought to revive his flagging affections. Theseus abandoned Ariadne on the island of Naxos after she had provided him with the means of killing the Minotaur, a creature half human and half bull that fed on a diet of Athenian youths and maidens. Jason rejected the sorceress Medea after she had assisted him in his theft of the golden fleece and had aided his escape by slaying her own brother Absyrtos.

Unlike his popular, much diluted, modern descendant, the Greek hero was a morally complex individual who frequently failed to conduct himself honorably, yet whose courage and prowess, in the eyes of the Greeks, did not release him from the obligation to live as a morally responsible human being.

HERAKLES AND THE HYDRA. Antonio Del Pollaiuolo, 1475. Tempera on panel. Here, the Greek hero kills the Hydra, a many-headed, serpent-like water beast. Notice that Herakles wears the pelt of the Nemean lion as he performs this labor.

The hero was, in other words, by no means a forerunner of the Christian saint. Nor was he primarily or predominantly a public benefactor. Although many heroic exploits did provide incidental beneficial consequences to mankind, this was by no means the only reason why they were undertaken. While Herakles' killing of the Nemean lion and the Stymphalian birds rendered the Greek world a safer place, his journey to the Hesperides in search of the golden apples was of no benefit to mankind whatsoever. In many cases, the principal motive for taking on the challenge seems to have been similar to that which inspires modern mountain climbers to risk their lives climbing K2: simply because it's there.

Despite or perhaps because of the questionability of their morals, heroes were a force to be reckoned with. Their powers did not cease upon their death, which is why hero worship (in the technical sense of the word), which took the form of blood sacrifice, was a central aspect of Greek religion. Heroes were only powerful, however, within the vicinity of their graves.

The Archetypal Dysfunctional Family

A number of myths explore the tensions, rivalries, and violence that lurk beneath the surface of family life as a result of Greek mythology's identification of the family as the major producer of neurosis and psychosis. The divine realm engendered more than its fair share of dysfunctionality. Kronos castrated his father Ouranos and attempted to kill all his children. Zeus's loveless marriage to Hera produced only one offspring, namely Ares, the god of war.

On the human level, the archetypal dysfunctional household was that of Atreus. The cycle of evil that characterizes its fortunes over the course of several generations began with the seduction of Atreus's wife by his brother Thyestes. Atreus then took revenge on Thyestes by inviting him to a banquet at which he served to him the cooked limbs of his children. Thyestes subsequently exacted his revenge on Atreus by inciting Atreus's son to murder his own father. Atreus's other son Agamemnon, who sacrificed his daughter Iphigeneia in order to obtain a favorable wind to carry the Greek fleet to Troy, met his death at the hands of his wife and her lover. The pair was murdered in turn by Agamemnon's son Orestes in revenge for his father's death.

Outlined simply thus, the myth of the house of Atreus strikes one as melodramatic and even absurd. In the hands of a great playwright like Aeschylus, however, it is transformed into a searching investigation of a very real human dilemma. That is because Aeschylus focuses almost exclusively upon the agonizing moral choice that Orestes faces by having to perpetrate the most abhorrent crime imaginable—matricide—in order to discharge the most sacred filial duty—that of avenging his father. Greek myths were not fashioned merely for the instruction of children.

Women in Myth

At first sight, Greek mythology seems to exhibit a strongly misogynistic strain. The chamber of female horrors includes Klytaimnestra, who murders her husband Agamemnon on his return from Troy; Medea, who kills her children in order to avenge the infidelity of her husband Jason; the fifty daughters of Danaos, who, with one exception, all murder their bridegrooms on their wedding nights; and Phaidra, who charges her stepson Hippolytos of raping her after he has scornfully rebuffed her sexual overtures. Only a handful of women are worthy of admiration, notably Penelope, who remains faithful to her absent husband Odysseus for twenty years, and Alkestis, who is so devoted to her husband Admetos that she volunteered to die in his place.

Simply enumerating myths about violent women merely reveals that the Greeks understood that women are capable of extreme violence. What is much more significant is that almost all these female acts of violence are perpetrated in response to extreme provocation on the part of husbands and lovers. Medea, for instance, who is one of the darkest figures in Greek mythology, betrayed everything that was dear to her—family, homeland, culture—to follow Jason back to Greece, only to be betrayed by him in turn when he found a more suitable wife to take her place. She is a woman who has lost all her identity. Even so, we can hardly ignore the fact that women in myth are anything but the shy, retiring, stay-at-homes that Thukydides spoke of (see p. 96), and there is something to be said for the view that they represent male paranoia about the hidden power of women—power, that is, that lies invested in the privacy of the home rather than in a public arena.

In addition to women whose acts of violence provide an outlet for their frustrations and disappointments, there is also a group of witchlike creatures who direct their destructiveness to all and sundry. These include the Gorgon Medusa, whose terrifying gaze turned men to stone; the half woman, half dog monster Skylla, who seized sailors and devoured them alive; a reptilian monster called Lamia, who stole children from their parents; the *Graiai*, or Grey Ones, women born old, who shared a single eye and a single tooth; the monstrous bird-women called the Harpies who kidnapped humans; and, finally, the Furies, who punished the guilty for crimes committed within the family.

MEDUSA. Michelangelo Merisi da Caravaggio (Italian), 1597. Oil on canvas mounted on wood.

Plato's Use of Myth

It is often stated that mythology lost its preeminence when Greek tragedy went into terminal decline at the end of the fifth century B.C.E., because, from this time onward, other ways of understanding human behavior came to the fore. In fact, however, myth continued to provide a vital means of interpreting the world even after the death of tragedy, not least in the philosophical works of Plato. In his Symposium, for instance, the comic poet Aristophanes claims that humans originally possessed four arms, four legs, and two heads. Being globular, they were able to propel themselves at high speed by using all eight limbs so that they moved "like tumblers performing cartwheels." They were so arrogant, however, that they attempted to scale Mount Olympos and attack the gods. By way of punishment, Zeus bisected them from head to toe, thereby creating the human body in its present form. Aristophanes ends with a stern warning that if human beings misbehave in the future, they run the risk of being bisected yet again and having to hop about on one leg! Fanciful though this myth is, it nonetheless makes some important points about human identity. Because these globular beings came in three forms before they were bisected— male-male, female-female, and male-female—the myth provides us with an explanation as to why some people are attracted to members of the opposite sex and others to members of the same sex: in Aristophanes' view, we are all seeking our missing half.

The primary importance that Plato attached to myth, coupled with the degree to which he regarded it as an indispensable tool for attempting to make sense of the world, is reflected in the following comment that he puts into the mouth of Sokrates at the end of *The Republic* (621bc). He tells the myth of Er, a man of Pamphylia who died and came back to life when he was about to be cremated and described what he had witnessed in the other world and concludes: "And so, Glaukos, the mythos was saved and did not perish, and, if we pay attention to it, it may save us."

Did the Greeks Believe Their Myths?

Giants with a single eye in the center of their foreheads, hideous hags with the capacity to petrify those who gazed upon them, monstrous snakes with numerous heads that doubled in number if they were lopped off—did the Greeks actually believe this crazy stuff? The question does not permit a simple answer. Even the ultrarationalistic historian Thukydides did not dismiss outright the monstrous Cyclopeans as purely imaginary. In his discussion of Sicily, where this fabulous race was thought to have once resided, he gives the following cautious pronouncement:

> The most ancient inhabitants are said to be the Cyclopes. . . . I cannot say
> who their relatives were nor where they came from or where they went. We
> have to content ourselves with what the poets said and with what anyone
> else knows. (6.2.1)

The Greek geographer Eratosthenes, however, who lived two centuries later than Thukydides, was openly dismissive. He is reported to have stated, "You will find the scene of Odysseus' wanderings when you find the cobbler who made the bag of winds in which Aiolos [king of the winds] deposited them" (in Strabo, *Geography* 1.2.15). On the other hand, it is probably fair to state that no Greek ever seriously doubted that the Trojan War was a historical event.

Although the Greeks in general did not question the veracity of their myths, from the fifth century B.C.E. onward, an effort was made to try to explain away some of their more fanciful elements. One that came in for rationalization concerned the god Dionysos, who was conceived when Zeus impregnated his mother Semele in the form of a thunderbolt. Having at the same time incinerated Semele, Zeus rescued the embryo by sewing it into his thigh. In Euripides' *Bacchai*, however, the seer Teiresias claims that this myth is based on a verbal confusion. What Zeus really did was to make a replica of the god, which he then "showed," rather than "sewed," to Hera. This laborious pun, which can be only approximately reproduced in English, demonstrates an attempt on the part of a rationalist to explain away an extravagant mythical claim without denying its essential veracity.

Conclusions

Myths express the patterns that underlie human existence; they do not determine the consequences of those patterns. Rather, they admit variants in line with the Greek belief in free will. Myths allowed the Greeks to live their lives freely while establishing certain parameters within which repetitive cycles occur.

Myth played a central role as a teaching tool. In Book 9 of *The Iliad*, when Phoinix, the tutor of Achilles, is trying to persuade his erstwhile pupil to return to the battle and accept the gifts that Agamemnon has offered him in reconciliation, he tells the story of Meleager, who refused to participate in battle and was ultimately compelled to return to the fray, forgoing the gifts that had previously been offered to him. This same fate, Phoinix suggests, awaits Achilles if he remains obdurate and does not accept Agamemnon's gifts. We can well imagine that conversations of this sort, in which a story from mythology was cited to teach one of life's important lessons, were taking place all the time.

In general, Greek mythology presents an exceedingly menacing and troubled landscape. Although it does not entirely banish what is generous and noble in human nature, few myths have happy endings, to the extent that they have endings at all. And such happiness as does occur is either fleeting or purchased at the cost of much misery. Through myth we encounter the dark side of human life, from which many of us would perhaps prefer to avert our gaze. Yet myth also provides us with an incomparably rich language for coming to terms with that dark side.

In the disunited and fractured world of Greece, mythology served as a powerful cultural unifier by providing people with both the sense of a shared past and the means of interpreting it. Nothing in the modern world performs a comparable function, and our society is much poorer for the lack of it. Yet, in Plato's words, if we pay attention to it, it may yet save us.

8

ANCIENT GREECE'S IMPACT ON MODERN CULTURE

> Greece has always been the favorite destination of those who seek to revive both body and soul. Because for centuries Greece's sun, waters, mountains and air have helped to refresh the body. While its culture, festivals, and warmth of its people have purified the soul. . . . Discover the part of Greece that lives in you. . . . And meditate upon the possibilities.
>
> —*Greek National Tourist Organization*

The school that I attended in the 1960s in north London produced a booklet in which all the pupils' names were arranged according to form. In pride of place on page one were those in Classical Sixth A. Although there were not many of us even in those days, in putting us at the top, the school was underscoring the point that nothing surpassed a classical education. My school was not alone in its prejudice for the Greeks and Romans, which it shared with many others of its kind throughout Europe. Its pupils today, however, are unlikely to be told that nothing equals a classical education or even that the literature of the Greeks and the Romans is superior to that of any other civilization. Contemporary teachers of classics, whether in schools or universities, are the guardians of a type of knowledge that has moved from the epicenter of the curriculum. Some of them even hold the Greeks and Romans responsible for many of the problems that society faces today.

PORTRAIT OF THE POET HOMER. In the style of Caravaggio (Italian), 1639. Oil on panel. This imagined portrait (no one knows what Homer looked like) shows the most famous poet of antiquity wearing a laurel wreath, a symbol of accomplishment and praise.

If this were all I could say about the current state of classical learning, there probably would be little point in reading this book. But while only a few—albeit a very dedicated few—submit themselves to the rigors of mastering the ancient languages, interest in the ancient world shows no signs of abating. Hollywood in particular has gone back to the Greeks repeatedly for inspiration over the last decade or so. Woody Allen's *Mighty Aphrodite* (1995) incorporates the device of a Greek chorus, which gives advice to the neurotic character played by Allen himself. The *Histories* of Herodotos became a bestseller, thanks to the retelling of a famous anecdote about woman's vengefulness in Anthony Minghella's award-winning film *The English Patient* (1996). Homer's *The Odyssey* sold like hotcakes at the newsstands in John F. Kennedy Airport and elsewhere in response to a blockbuster television miniseries directed by Andrei Konchalovsky (1997). An acclaimed Disney animated cartoon called *Hercules* was based on the exploits of the Greek hero Herakles (1997). The Coen brothers' *O Brother, Where Art Thou?* (2000) was loosely based on *The Odyssey*. Its central character is a fast-talking convict named Ulysses (the Latin name for Odysseus), who has escaped from prison in order to prevent another man from taking his wife and children from him. *Troy* (2004), directed by Wolfgang Petersen, which attempts to tell the whole story of the Trojan War from Helen's abduction to Troy's destruction (rather than just ten days in the war, as Homer does in *The Iliad*), cost $180 million and was one of the most expensive films ever made. Another hugely costly Hollywood venture was Oliver Stone's *Alexander* (2004), which was panned by the critics. However, *The 300* (2007), Zack Snyder's adaptation of Frank Miller's graphic novel loosely based on the Battle of Thermopylae, broke box office records when it was released in 2007. And Hollywood is just one of the ways whereby the ancient Greeks invade and continue to colonize modern culture.

Greek myths are also a major source of inspiration for modern literature. The structure of one of the greatest twentieth-century novels, James Joyce's *Ulysses*, is based on Homer's epic poem, while one of the most significant verse plays of recent years is Nobel prize winner Derek Walcott's *The Odyssey: A Stage Version* (1993). And while we are talking of the survival of Greek myth, we should reflect upon the fact that Greek tragedy, which is wholly inspired by myth, is now performed with extraordinary frequency in almost every country that has a theatrical tradition, not least because the plots are capable of almost endless adaptation to a multiplicity of political agendas. To cite just a handful of examples, Michael's Cacoyannis's film version of Euripides' *Trojan Women* (1971) was a condemnation of both the Greek junta and the Vietnam War; Seamus Heaney's adaptation of Sophocles' *Philoktetes*, entitled *The Cure at Troy* (1990), was critical of the culture of violence in Northern Ireland; and Ariane Mnouchkine's adaptation of Aeschylus's *Oresteia*, entitled *Les Atrides*, offered a feminist interpretation of the trilogy.

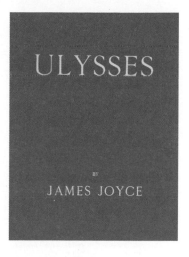

FIRST EDITION COVER OF *ULYSSES by James Joyce.*

THE CONTINUING CLASSICAL TRADITION

Whether we like it or not, it is virtually impossible to shake off the influence of our classical past. It is evident in our way of thinking, in our concept of government and political theory, in our aesthetic judgment, in our architecture, in our science and mathematics, in our medical tradition, and in our literature. In some branches of learning, its influence remains paramount. In philosophy its legacy is overwhelming. In the writing of history we remain dependent on our classical antecedents—notably Herodotos and Thukydides—who established the proper business of a historian. We could even claim that with Herodotos came the birth of anthropology, since the criteria for cultural differences that he established—style of dress, eating habits, burial customs, language, religion, and so on—remain at the center of any anthropological definition of the Other.

Over the past two hundred years, Greek words have been imported into the English language in vast quantities to describe new fields of inquiry and new scientific accomplishments. Modernity and the modern experience have been described and defined very largely by words of Greek origin. Examples include psychiatry, paranoia, schizophrenia, ophthalmology, euthanasia, pornography, cybernetics, cryogenics, eugenics, prosthetics, chemotherapy, orthodontics, pediatrics, pedagogy, and technology.

The Greek Revival in Architecture

What we call neoclassicism, so-named because it draws its inspiration from Greek architectural motifs and principles, was largely initiated by two Britons: the painter James Stuart and the architect Nicholas Revett. The pair visited Athens from 1751 to 1753 and produced detailed drawings of the buildings on the Acropolis, which they published in 1762 in Volume 1 of *Antiquities of Athens*. These drawings later served as the basis of design for many important buildings, including the British Museum. Stuart and Revett were among the first Europeans to associate Athenian democracy with Greece's struggle against Ottoman oppression, which later culminated in the War of Independence. Anticipating the publication of the second volume of Antiquities, they declared it was their intention "to treat of buildings erected while the Athenians were a free people."

AN ILLUSTRATION OF THE BRITISH MUSEUM *in London, ca. 1890–1900.*

In the same era, the German archaeologist Johannt Joachim Winckelmann produced a book entitled *Thoughts on the Imitation of Greek Works in Painting and Sculpture* (1755), in which he classified Greek art according to his own subjective notion of style. Winckelmann gave pride of place to what he called the "noble simplicity and calm grandeur" that he associated with the style of Pheidias, the chief sculptor of the Parthenon. Although contemporary art historians by no means unanimously concur with Winckelmann's judgment, and though the Archaic Period of Greek art is in some quarters more highly valued, Winckelmann's influence in shaping discussions of Greek aesthetics can hardly be overestimated.

The middle of the eighteenth century saw the birth of the great public museums, destined to become storehouses of the most prestigious works of art from Greco-Roman antiquity. They continue to serve as a palpable reminder to the public of the achievements of the classical world. A particularly controversial episode in the scramble to secure such treasures was the removal of the Parthenon's

RECLINING DIONYSOS, *created ca. 447–433 B.C.E, from the east pediment of the Parthenon. This was one of the sculptures removed from the Parthenon in 1801 by order of Lord Elgin, the British ambassador to the Ottoman Empire, and shipped to Britain for museum display.*

sculptures by Lord Elgin, the British ambassador to Ottoman Turkey, in 1801. Elgin not only took the sculptures that were lying on the ground, but he also removed pieces that were still in place on the buildings. His cache included twelve statues belonging to the pediments, fifty-six slabs belonging to the frieze, and fifteen metopes. After being initially rejected by the British Museum, the sculptures were eventually purchased and put on display in 1817. The legality of Lord Elgin's action, which was conducted with the consent of the Ottoman rulers of Greece, continues to be a matter of dispute between the British and Greek governments.

Philhellenism

The modern Greek nation-state owes much to the Romantic and Victorian image of classical Greece. When the Greeks rebelled against the Ottoman Turks in 1821, enthusiastic Britons like Lord Byron, who called themselves philhellenes and who cherished their classical roots, saw the struggle as a reenactment of the Persian Wars:

> The mountains look on Marathon
> And Marathon looks on the sea:
> And musing there an hour alone,
> I dreamt that Greece might still be free. (*Don Juan* 111.86)

As Richard Jenkyns (*The Victorians and Ancient Greece*, 14f.) has observed, the European philhellenic movement appealed all across the political and religious spectrum. The Romantic poet Shelley called the Greeks "glorious beings whom the imagination almost refuses to figure to itself as belonging to our kind." The Victorian poet Algernon Charles Swinburne called Greece "the mother tongue of thought and art and action." The English radical and revolutionary Thomas Paine saw "more to admire, less to condemn, in that great . . . people than in anything which history affords."

The Foundation of Modern Greece

The decision by the European powers to choose Athens as the capital of the newly created kingdom of Greece when the Greek War of Independence came to an end in 1832 is further evidence of the mesmerizing effect of Classical Greece on the European imagination in this period. At the time, Athens was merely a provincial town in what had been a backwater of the Ottoman Empire with a population of about four thousand. It had already sunk into obscurity by the period of late antiquity. The decision to choose it as the capital was therefore made in deference to its erstwhile role as cultural capital of ancient Greece. Hardly surprisingly, the favored style of architecture for the new capital was neoclassical. The revival of the Olympic Games, which the city hosted in 1896 in the refurbished Panathenaic Stadium, was further testimony to Athens' importance in the European intellectual tradition.

Contemporary with Greece's liberation from Ottoman rule, Greece acquired a new official language, known as *katharevousa*, meaning literally "the purified

PHOTOGRAPH OF THE OPENING CEREMONY AT THE 1896 OLYMPIC GAMES *in Athens.*

one," which had been devised by a classical scholar and revolutionary named Adamantios Korais. Katharevousa was based on the grammar of the ancient Attic dialect—the dialect that was spoken in Athens and its environs. It was introduced in opposition to *dêmotiki*, or demotic Greek, meaning popular Greek—the Greek that was currently spoken in Greece and that was thought to have been corrupted by borrowings from Turkish. As a result, many new words were coined based on ancient Greek roots. Examples include *leôphoreion*, literally "people-transporter," meaning bus, and *nosokomeion*, literally "sickness-tending-place," meaning hospital. Katharevousa remained the official language of Greece until 1976, when it was replaced by demotic, which had never died out. (The reason for the change at this date was that katharevousa had become associated with the junta that had ruled Greece from 1967 to 1976 and was thus discredited.)

Greece's past continues to haunt, even to shape, contemporary politics, not least through the medium of archaeology. As mentioned in chapter 1, a Greek archaeologist named Manolis Andronikos discovered a tomb at Vergina in Macedonia that is thought to have been that of Philip II. To the Greeks,

Andronikos's discovery proved that the region of Macedonia was exclusively Greek in character. This was contrary to the claim made by the predominantly Slavic Republic of Macedonia, whose appropriation of the name Macedonia caused deep offence to the Greeks when the state was established in 1977 on the breakup of Yugoslavia. "We have lost the shield of Macedonia," declared Prime Minister Konstantin Mitsotakis at Andronikos's funeral, indicating how centrally archaeology figures in matters of cultural heritage. The dispute about the name still awaits full resolution and is an ongoing irritant to the Greeks.

Postmodern Architecture

Postmodernism, the term often used to describe the prevailing cultural climate, signifies in effect a return to and reworking of classicism, following the rejection of the past, as exemplified by the preceding movement known as modernism. One of the most important skyscrapers to be erected in New York City in recent years is the AT&T Building, now owned by Sony, which was erected in 1984. Designed by U.S. architect Philip Johnson, it is topped by a broken pediment that is inspired by the designs of the eighteenth-century English furniture maker Thomas Chippendale, who was himself inspired by the design of a classical temple.

A more literal example of the influence of Greek architecture is the reconstructed Parthenon in Nashville, Tennessee. Built of concrete and gravel from the Potomac River, it is an exact copy of the Athenian original. In 1990, it acquired a forty-foot-high replica of the gold and ivory statue of Athene by Pheidias, made out of concrete and fiberglass. As Umberto Eco has said, "The post-modern reply to the modern consists of recognizing that the past, since it cannot fully be

RE-CREATION OF *the forty-two-foot statue Athene Parthenos from the Parthenon replica built in Nashville, Tennessee.*

destroyed, because its destruction leads to silence must be re-visited: but with irony, not innocently" (quoted in Taplin, *Greek Fire*, 25). In upstate New York, I reside between towns called Ithaca and Ilion and less than thirty miles from another town called Marathon—at the epicenter of the classical tradition, in other words.

Nor is the influence of Greek culture an exclusively Western phenomenon. Thanks to the conquests of Alexander the Great, Greek influence spread as far east as northern Afghanistan and the Indian subcontinent. Sculpture from Gandhara in northwest Pakistan, which laid the foundations for representations of the Buddha, was profoundly influenced by the canons of Greek sculpture.

THE CRADLE OF DEMOCRACY

And yet we should be careful not to go too far. It is too easy—and tendentious—to claim an unbroken tradition from antiquity to the modern day. Consider the following editorial that appeared in a center-left Greek newspaper called *Ethnos* in the summer of 1983:

> In this land of ours, throughout the centuries, the foundations of
> democracy were firmly laid by people determined to establish the right
> of the majority to manage freely their thought and activity. For the first
> time in the fifth century B.C., democracy shone and the basic principles
> governing society were established. Those principles were equality of rights,
> equality of political rights, equality of speech, and freedom of speech. . . .
> These four basic principles which have remained unchanged throughout the
> centuries should govern today all democratic regimes.

Although the sentiments expressed in this passage are not in dispute, we might question the accuracy of the claims. To begin with, the fifth-century democracy to which the editor alludes but does not mention by name is obviously that of Athens. Athens, however, was just one of some fifteen hundred city-states, the majority of which were ruled by oppressive oligarchies. It was not the case, therefore, that democracy "shone" throughout the Greek world. Far from it.

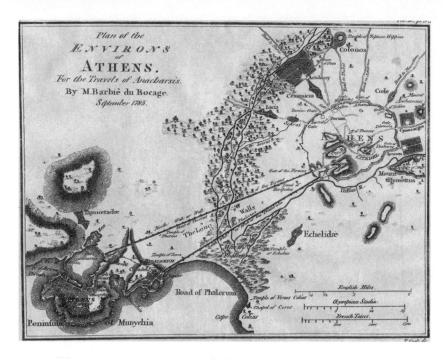

ATHENS WITH PIRAEUS. Jean-Denis Barbié du Bocage (French), 1785. This plan of Athens, based on excavations and ancient sources, provides impressive and accurate detail. The ancient city and its citizens originated Western democracy as we know it.

As for "the right of the majority to manage freely their affairs"— well, that is only true if one omits the slaves, metics, women, and children—well over half the population. We might even raise questions about the claim of freedom of speech, at least in the case of Sokrates, who was accused of corrupting the youth. Although we cannot know precisely what was meant by this obscure charge, it evidently referred primarily to his teachings.

There are other errors in the passage. The phrase "In this land of ours" refers, of course, to modern Greece. But modern Greece has been a nation-state only since 1833, and it is questionable, to say the least, whether the principles of democracy "remained unchanged throughout the centuries." For most of their history, the people whom we call Greeks have been denied democracy; that is, through the period of the Macedonian Empire (150 years), the Roman

Empire (500 years), the Byzantine Empire (1,100 years), the Ottoman Empire (400 years), the Greek monarchy (on and off about 100 years), the fascist dictatorship of General Metaxas (1936 to 1941), and the rule of the Colonels (1967 to 1974).

For more than a thousand years, in fact, democracy completely died out, not only in Greece but throughout the whole of Europe. The roots of modern democratic systems have much more to do with feudalism and the medieval republics that directly preceded them than they do with fifth-century B.C.E. Athens.

Problems of historical fact have not, however, deterred serious scholars from seeking to establish an unbroken democratic chain from antiquity to the present. In 1993, numerous celebrations were held in both the United States and Britain to mark the twenty-five-hundredth anniversary of the so-called birth of democracy—twenty-five-hundred years, that is, since Kleisthenes carried out his reforms. These celebrations begged another important question besides that of continuity: whether the origins of a process as complex as democracy can legitimately be pinned down to a single year and to a single historical personage. Situating the birth of democracy in 507 B.C.E. is ignoring the fact that a democratic tendency had been present in Athenian society long before Kleisthenes came to power.

OUR SO-CALLED CLASSICAL ROOTS: THE CONTROVERSY OVER *BLACK ATHENA*

The study of classical antiquity is also in the forefront of our current concerns about racism, cultural imperialism, and the like. In 1987, Martin Bernal, a professor of Chinese political history, wrote a highly controversial book called *Black Athena*, which investigated the origins of Greek culture. Bernal came to the conclusion that there had been a willful conspiracy of silence on the part of eighteenth- and nineteenth-century ancient historians, who ignored—or, at best, minimized—the decisive contribution made to Greek culture by the Afroasiatic (notably Egyptian) and Semitic (notably Phoenician) races. He then attempted to demonstrate the impact that their cultures had upon Greek culture by appealing to etymology and mythology. Bernal's hypothesis that earlier generations of classical scholars underplayed the contribution made by the African and Semitic races has some merit, and it is certainly appropriate, even laudable, to raise questions about the preconceptions of our predecessors, whose view of the human family was very different from ours. All historical inquiry is contingent and provisional, and our own prejudices will in due course come under scrutiny by our successors. This said, Bernal's claim to be able to detect an "Aryan model of Greek culture" propounded by nineteenth-century scholars carries little weight. Nor is it true that contemporary scholars are reluctant to ignore the contribution of Egyptian and Near Eastern cultures to Greek culture, though they do not, for the most part, consider their contribution to have been overriding.

More critically for Bernal's thesis, few classical scholars would concede that the Afroasiatic contribution to Greek culture was made by the black African races, and that is where the heart of the controversy lies. With the publication of Mary Lefkowitz's response to Bernal, entitled *Not Out of Africa: How Afrocentrism Became an Excuse to Teach Myth as History* (1996), the debate became so politicized that rational discourse between the two camps was almost impossible. Yet, if Bernal's work achieved nothing else, it has at least demonstrated the continuing importance of classical antiquity by reminding us that the enduring status of Greek culture in the West is such that cultural descent has come to be regarded almost as a precondition to cultural identity.

GLOSSARY
OF GREEK TERMS

Greek terms that commonly exist in English are Anglicized.

ACROPOLIS Citadel (literally "upper or higher city"), a defensible rock where many of a polis's most venerable cults were housed; when capitalized, the citadel of Athens.

AGÔGÊ Spartan public education system (literally "a leading forth"), intended to weaken pupils' ties to the family and strengthen their ties to the state.

AGÔN Contest of any kind; a scene involving a dispute between two characters in a drama.

AGORA A level space in the center of a polis that functioned as its commercial, civic, legal, and political heart. Every citizen was expected to spend time in the agora (verb, *agorazein*), both to learn about public affairs and to gossip.

ANDRÔN (OR ANDRÔNITIS) A room of the house primarily designed for holding a symposium. As the name (literally "men's quarters") implies, women, with the exception of *hetairai*, were not permitted inside when symposia were being held.

APELLA Spartan word for assembly; a political gathering of citizens.

ARCHON Senior magistrate (literally "leader"). In Classical Athens, there were nine archons chosen by lot, one of whom (the eponymous archon) gave his name to the year.

ASTY Urban center of a polis, in contrast to its surrounding agricultural territory.

ATTICA Territory of the Athenian state, comprising both *asty* and *chôra*.

AULOS Wind instrument similar to the oboe, which accompanied the chorus of a tragedy.

BARATHRON Pit in Athens into which condemned criminals were hurled to their death.

BARBARIAN Derived from *barbaros*, a word of uncertain etymology, this was the term used by Greeks to identify all non-Greeks. Although some *barbaroi*, such as the Egyptians, were admired for their culture, from the fifth century onward, and largely as a result of the Persian Wars, *barbaros* was increasingly used to stigmatize outsiders for lacking the moral, intellectual, and cultural qualities that defined the Greeks.

BOULÊ Council. Together with the assembly, the council was the chief organ of government because it set the agenda of the assembly. In Classical Athens, the council comprised five hundred citizens chosen by lot from each of the ten tribes.

CELLA Latin word used to describe the central room of a Greek temple. The cella of the Parthenon housed the gold and ivory statue of Athene by Pheidias. However, no rituals were performed inside it.

CENTAUR Mythological half human and half horse creature. Sometimes used to denote a barbarian in Greek art.

CHITÔN Ankle-length linen garment worn by women.

CHÔRA Territory owned by a polis.

CITY DIONYSIA Festival in honor of Dionysos at which tragedies were performed.

COLONY A somewhat misleading term used to describe an independent foundation sent out by a mother city. The so-called colonization movement lasted from about 734 to 580 B.C.E.

DÊMOS Citizen body of a polis, deme, or village.

DORIAN Term used by the Greeks to identify one of the two principal ethnic groups. Dorians, who occupied most of the Peloponnese and some of the islands of the Aegean, spoke a common dialect. See also **Ionian**.

DRACHMA Silver coin equivalent to a day's pay in the late fifth century B.C.E.

EKKLÊSIA Legislative assembly consisting of the citizen body. The Athenian *ekklêsia* met on the Pnyx, a hill overlooking the Acropolis, approximately forty times per year.

EKPHORA The act of transporting a corpse from the house of the deceased to the place of burial.

EPHEBE Athenian youth who, having reached his eighteenth year, was undergoing a two-year stint of military training (literally "one who is at the prime of youth").

EPHOR One of five Spartan magistrates elected annually by the citizen body, who was charged with extensive disciplinary powers, including the ability to prosecute the kings. Ephors (literal meaning probably "overseers") are found in other Greek states besides Sparta.

ETHNOS Large group of people who acknowledged their common ethnic identity and territory but who did not come together as a political unity. *Ethnê* (the plural form) probably existed at all times of Greek history but became especially important in the fourth century B.C.E. They left few material remains and no literature, so we know very little about their daily life.

EUNOMIA "Obedience to the law"; a term used primarily of Sparta to characterize the system of military discipline that was introduced in the first half of the seventh century B.C.E.

EXÔMIS Poor man's garment worn over the shoulder.

GENOS Kin group composed of aristocratic families claiming descent from a common ancestor. Members of Athenian *genê* (the plural form) remained politically important in Athens even after it became a radical democracy, the most notable example being Perikles, who belonged to the venerable Alkmaeonid genos.

GEROUSIA Council of elders (from *gerôn*, meaning old man). The Spartan *gerousia* consisted of twenty-eight elders and the two kings.

GYMNASIUM Training establishment or school (from *gymnos*, meaning "naked") where Greek males of all ages exercised and conversed together. Some gymnasia also accommodated philosophical schools.

GYNAIKÔN (OR GYNAIKÔNITIS) Women's quarters of a house.

HÊLIAIA Law court comprising Athenian jurors; also the building in which lawsuits were held.

HELOT A term of uncertain etymology used to describe the conquered peoples of Messenia, who worked as serfs for the Spartans. Although helots are most closely identified with Sparta, they are also known to have existed in other parts of the Greek world.

HERM Image of the god Hermes consisting of head and genitalia, which stood at street corners.

HETAIRA Term most commonly used for a courtesan, or female companion. *Hetairai* included some highly cultivated women as well as prostitutes.

HIMATION Woolen cloak worn by both men and women.

HIPPEIS Those eligible to serve in the cavalry; second-highest property class established by the Athenian reformer Solon.

HIPPODROME Horse track.

HOMOIOS Spartan peer or citizen.

HOPLITE Heavy-armed infantryman who carried a round bronze shield, or *hoplon*, from which the name derives. Hoplites fought in strict battle formation, a style of warfare that dominated land battles from the seventh century B.C.E. onward.

IONIAN Term used to identify one of the two principal ethnic groups. Ionians, who occupied Attica, Euboia, the Cyclades, and the central western coast of Asia Minor, spoke a common dialect. See also **Dorian**.

IONIC Term used to describe both one of the orders of Greek architecture and one of the dialects of ancient Greece.

KERAMEIKOS Cemetery outside Athens on the west side of the city where some of the most prestigious tombs have been discovered (literally "potters' quarter").

KITHARA Stringed instrument somewhat resembling a modern guitar.

KLÊROS Apportionment of land in Sparta sufficient to support a single family, passed down from one generation to the next.

KLINÊ Couch or bed.

KLISMOS Chair.

KOINÊ Greek dialect based primarily on Attic (the dialect spoken by Athenians). *Koinê* became universal in the Hellenistic Period as a result of the conquests of Alexander the Great.

KÔMOS Band of revelers.

KOUROS Term meaning "youth" that is used by art historians to describe marble Archaic statues of nude males that stood either in temples or beside graves.

KRYPTEIA Spartan organization resembling a secret police.

LITURGY The act of subsidizing important public programs by wealthy citizens or metics (from *leitourgia*, meaning "public service"). Liturgies included financing a chorus in a dramatic performance, maintaining a trireme, and paying for the upkeep of a gymnasium.

METIC Legal resident alien (from *metoikos*, meaning "living among"). Metics were obliged to serve in the army and pay metic tax, but they could not own property. Although metics probably existed throughout the Greek world, we only hear of them in Athens.

MIASMA Ritual pollution caused primarily by the shedding of blood.

MINA Unit of currency worth 100 drachmas.

OBOL Coin worth one-sixth of a drachma.

OIKIA, OIKOS Household or family. It comprised not only the family members but also the buildings, property, slaves, and animals.

ORCHÊSTRA Circular dancing floor.

OSTRACISM Athenian procedure by which a leading politician was sent into exile for ten years by vote of the assembly. See also **Ostrakon**.

OSTRAKON Broken piece of pottery used for writing; the votes cast in an ostracism were inscribed on *ostraka* (the plural form).

PAIDAGÔGOS Slave who accompanied a boy outside the home.

PAIDOTRIBÊS Athletic trainer (literally "boy-rubber," so named because it was his duty to anoint and rub youths with oil).

PALAISTRA Wrestling school.

PALLAKÊ Common-law wife.

PANATHENAIA The major Athenian festival in honor of Athene.

PANHELLENIC "All-Greek," a term that refers to events and institutions in which all Greek speakers were entitled to participate.

PANKRATION Combination of all-out boxing and wrestling.

PEDIMENT Triangular gable surmounting a temple.

PEPLOS Ankle-length woolen garment worn by women.

PERISTYLE Colonnade surrounding a building or inner court on all four sides.

PHALANX Hoplite formation, which, in the Archaic and Classical Periods, was usually eight men deep. Philip II of Macedon introduced a formation that was sixteen men deep.

PHRATRY Subdivision of the citizen body (literally "brotherhood"). Athenian citizenship depended on a child being registered in his father's phratry generally in the first year of his life.

PHYLÊ Division of the citizen body roughly translating as "tribe." Members of the same *phylê* traced their descent from a common ancestor. The Athenian politician Kleisthenes divided the Athenian citizenry artificially into 10 tribes.

POLIS Usually referred to as a city-state, the polis was an independent entity consisting of an urban center and surrounding territory. It was the most evolved political organization devised by the Greeks. Some fifteen hundred *poleis* (the plural form) are known to us.

POLITÊS A member of a polis who had full citizenship.

PROTHESIS The act of laying out the corpse in the house of the deceased and the ceremonies connected therewith.

PRYTANY Executive committee of the Athenian state consisting of fifty members of the council of five hundred. There were ten such bodies appointed annually, each holding office for one-tenth of the year.

SOPHIST Itinerant teacher of the fifth century B.C.E., who later offered instruction for a fee, notably in public speaking. Sokrates' (and Plato's) antipathy toward the Sophists has colored our modern perception of Sophists.

STADE A distance of about 210 yards (the length of a Greek running track), from which the word *stadium* derives.

SYMPOSIUM Drinking party (literally "drinking together") attended exclusively by men and *hetairai*.

SYNHEDRION Council of Greek city-states established by Philip II of Macedon.

SYRINX Wind instrument consisting of a number of pipes bound together.

SYSSITION Communal dining area where Spartans ate their evening meals.

THÊS Member of the lowest economic group instituted by Solon. *Thêtes* (the plural) gained considerable political influence in the fifth century, because they largely comprised the rowers in Athens' navy. The term was also used to identify hired workers.

TRIREME Three-banked warship that enabled the Athenians to dominate the Aegean Sea in the fifth century B.C.E.

TROPAION Trophy erected on the battlefield after a victory marking the spot where the enemy was routed (from *tropê*, "a turning around").

TYRANT Self-appointed ruler of a state, who was usually an aristocratic usurper. Tyrants, who first flourished in the seventh and sixth centuries B.C.E., often contributed significantly to the cultural development of their communities, though they were later vilified for their despotism.

XENIA Ritualized guest friendship between aristocrats belonging to different communities who were obligated to offer hospitality to one another when either of them was traveling. *Xenia* features prominently in Homeric society and existed in some form throughout Greek history.

FOR FURTHER READING

Translations of Selected Greek Texts (in Alphabetical Order of Greek Authors)

Aeschylus: The Oresteia. Translated by R. Fagles. Introduction and notes by R. Fagles and W. B. Stanford. New York: Penguin Books and Viking Press, 1979.

Archestratus: The Life of Luxury. Translated with introduction and commentary by J. Wilkins and S. Hill. Devon, U.K.: Prospect Books, 1994.

Aristophanes' Acharnians. Translation, introduction, and notes by J. Henderson. Bristol, U.K.: Bristol Classical Press and Focus Publishing, 1992.

Aristophanes' Clouds. Translation, introduction, and notes by J. Henderson. Bristol, U.K.: Bristol Classical Press and Focus Publishing, 1993.

Aristophanes' Lysistrata. Translation, introduction, and notes by J. Henderson. Bristol, U.K.: Bristol Classical Press and Focus Publishing, 1988.

Three Plays by Aristophanes: Staging Women. Translation, introduction, and notes by J. Henderson. New York: Routledge, 1996.

Aristotle, The Politics. Translation by T. A. Sinclair. Revised by T. J. Saunders. Harmondsworth, U.K.: Penguin Books, 1981.

Euripides' Bacchae. Translation, introduction, and notes by S. Esposito. Bristol, U.K.: Bristol Classical Press and Focus Publishing, 1997.

Euripides' Medea. Translation, introduction, and notes by A. Podlecki. Bristol, U.K.: Bristol Classical Press and Focus Publishing, 1991.

Herodotus: The Histories. Translated by A. de Sélincourt. Revised translation and notes by J. Marincola. New York: Penguin Books and Viking Press, 1996.

The Landmark Herodotus: The Histories. Translated by A. L. Purvis. Edited by R. B. Strassler. Introduction by R. Thomas. New York: Pantheon Books, 2007.

Hesiod: Works and Days and Theogony. Translated by S. Lombardo with introduction by R. Lamberton. Indianapolis, Ind.: Hackett Publishing, 1993.

Hesiod's Theogony. Translation, introduction, and notes by R. Caldwell. Bristol, U.K.: Bristol Classical Press and Focus Publishing, 1987.

Hippocratic Writings. Translated by J. Chadwick and W. N. Mann. Edited with introduction by G.E.R. Lloyd. New York: Penguin Books and Viking Press, 1978.

Homer: The Iliad. Translated by R. Fagles. Introduction and notes by B. Knox. New York: Penguin Books and Viking Press, 1990.

The Iliad of Homer. Translated by R. Lattimore. Chicago: University of Chicago Press, 1951.

Homer: The Odyssey. Translated by R. Fagles. Introduction and notes by B. Knox. New York: Penguin Books and Viking Press, 1996.

Homeric Hymns. Translation, introduction, and notes by A. Podlecki. Bristol, U.K.: Bristol Classical Press and Focus Publishing, 1991.

Homer's Odyssey: A Companion to the Translation of Richmond Lattimore. Introduction and notes by P. V. Jones. Carbondale: Southern Illinois University Press, 1988.

The Odyssey of Homer. Translated by R. Lattimore. New York: Harper and Row, 1967.

Plato: Complete Works. Edited by J. M. Cooper. Indianapolis, Ind.: Hackett Publishing, 1993.

Plato's Symposium. Translation and introduction by A. Sharon. Bristol, U.K.: Bristol Classical Press and Focus Publishing, 1991.

Select Papyri vols. 1–2. Translated by A. S. Hunt and C. C. Edgar. London and New York: Loeb Classical Library, 1932.

Sophocles' Oedipus at Colonus. Translation, introduction, and notes by M. Blundell. Bristol, U.K.: Bristol Classical Press and Focus Publishing, 1991.

Sophocles: The Three Theban Plays. Translated by R. Fagles. Introduction by B. Knox. New York: Penguin Books and Viking Press, 1986.

Soranus' Gynaecology. Translated by O. Temkin. Baltimore, Md.: Johns Hopkins University Press, 1991.

The Landmark Thucydides: A Comprehensive Guide to the Peloponnesian War. Translated by R. Crawley. Edited by R. B. Strassler. Introduction by V. D. Hanson. New York: Free Press, 1996.

Thucydides: The Peloponnesian War. Translated by R. Warner. Introduction and notes by M. I. Finley. New York: Penguin Books and Viking Press, 1972.

Anthologies of Translations of Greek Texts

Greek Lyric: An Anthology in Translation. Translated with introduction by A. M. Miller. Indianapolis, Ind.: Hackett Publishing, 1996.

Greek Lyric Poetry. Translated by W. Barnstone. New York: Schocken Books, 1972.

Greek Orations: 4th Century B.C. Translation with introduction by W. R. Connor. Prospect Heights, Ill.: Waveland Press, 1987.

The Murder of Herodes and Other Trials from the Athenian Law Courts. Translated with introduction by K. Freeman. Indianapolis, Ind.: Hackett Publishing, 1994.

Reference Works

Civilization of the Ancient Mediterranean. Edited by M. Grant and R. Kitzinger. 3 vols. New York: Charles Scribner's Sons, 1988.

The Oxford Classical Dictionary. Edited by S. Hornblower and A. J. Spawforth. 3d edition. Oxford: Oxford University Press, 1996.

The Penguin Dictionary of Ancient History. Edited by G. Speake. Harmondsworth, Middlesex, U.K.: Penguin Books, 1995.

General

Adcock, F. F. *The Greek and Macedonian Art of War.* Berkeley: University of California Press, 1967.

Amundsen, D. W. *Medicine, Society, and Faith in the Ancient and Medieval Worlds.* Baltimore, Md.: Johns Hopkins University Press, 1996.

Aveni, A. *Empires of Time: Calendars, Clocks and Cultures.* New York: Basic Books, 1989.

Baldry, H. C. *The Greek Tragic Theatre.* London: Chatto and Windus, 1978.

Baldock, M. *Greek Tragedy: An Introduction.* Bristol, U.K.: Bristol Classical Press and Focus Publishing, 1989.

Barrow, R. *Athenian Democracy: The Triumph and the Folly.* Surrey, U.K.: Thomas Nelson, 1992.

Barrow, R. *Greek and Roman Education.* Basingstoke, U.K.: Macmillan, 1976.

Beck, F. A. *Greek Education 450–350 B.C.* London: Methuen, 1962.

Becker, W. A. *Charicles or Illustrations of the Private Life of the Ancient Greeks.* Translated by F. Metcalfe. 6th edition. London: Longmans' Green and Co., 1882.

Bernal, M. *Black Athena: The Afroasiatic Roots of Classical Civilization.* New Brunswick, N.J.: Rutgers University Press, 1987.

Bickerman, E. *Chronology of the Ancient World.* Revised edition. London: Thames and Hudson, 1980.

Biers, W. R. *The Archaeology of Greece.* 2d edition. Ithaca, N.Y.: Cornell University Press, 1996.

Boardman, J. *Greek Art.* Revised edition. London: Thames and Hudson, 1973.

Boardman, J. *Greek Sculpture: The Classical Period.* London: Thames and Hudson, 1985.

Boardman, J., ed. *The Oxford History of Classical Art.* Oxford: Oxford University Press, 1997.

Boardman, J., J. Griffin, and O. Murray, eds. *The Oxford History of Greece and the Hellenistic World.* Oxford: Oxford University Press, 2002.

Bonnefoy, Y., ed. *Greek and Egyptian Mythologies.* Translated by W. Doniger et al. Chicago: University of Chicago Press, 1991.

Bremmer, J. *The Early Greek Concept of the Soul.* Princeton, N.J.: Princeton University Press, 1983.

Bronowski, J. *The Ascent of Man.* London: British Broadcasting Corporation, 1973.

Burford, A. *Land and Labor in the Greek World.* Baltimore, Md.: Johns Hopkins University Press, 1993.

Burkert, W. *Ancient Mystery Cults.* Cambridge, Mass.: Harvard University Press, 1987.

Burkert, W. *Greek Religion.* Oxford: Basil Blackwell, 1985.

Burkert, W. *Structure and History in Greek Mythology and Ritual.* Berkeley: University of California Press, 1979.

Buxton, R. *Imaginary Greece: The Contexts of Mythology.* Cambridge, U.K.: Cambridge University Press, 1994.

Cameron, A., and A. Kuhrt, eds. *Images of Women in Antiquity.* London: Croom Helm, 1983.

Camp, J. M. *The Athenian Agora: Excavations in the Heart of Classical Athens.* London: Thames and Hudson, 1986.

Cantarella, E. *Pandora's Daughters: The Role and Status of Women in Greek and Roman Antiquity*. Translated by M. Fant. Baltimore, Md.: Johns Hopkins University Press, 1987.

Carey, C. *Democracy in Classical Athens*. London: Bristol Classical Press, 2001.

Carpenter, T. H. *Art and Myth in Ancient Greece*. London: Thames and Hudson, 1991.

Cartledge, P. *Aristophanes and His Theatre of the Absurd*. Bristol, U.K.: Bristol Classical Press, 1990.

Cartledge, P. *The Greeks*. 2d edition. Oxford: Oxford University Press, 2002.

Cartledge, P. *Spartan Reflections*. Berkeley and Los Angeles: University of California Press, 2001.

Casson, L. *Ships and Seamanship in the Ancient World*. Princeton, N.J.: Princeton University Press, 1971.

Casson, L. *Travel in the Ancient World*. Baltimore, Md.: Johns Hopkins University Press, 1994.

Chadwick, J. *Linear B and Related Scripts*. London and Berkeley: British Museum Publications and University of California Press, 1987.

Clark, G. *Women in the Ancient World*. Oxford: Oxford University Press, 1989.

Clogg, R. *A Concise History of Greece*. Cambridge, U.K.: Cambridge University Press, 2002.

Dalby, A., and S. Grainger. *The Classical Cookbook*. Getty Trust Publications. Oxford: Oxford University Press, 1996.

Davies, J. K. *Democracy and Classical Greece*. London and Stanford, Calif.: Fontana and Stanford University Press, 1986.

de Ste. Croix, G. E. M. *The Class Struggle in the Ancient Greek World*. London and Ithaca, N.Y.: Gerald Duckworth and Cornell University Press, 1988.

de Ste. Croix, G. E. M. *The Origins of the Peloponnesian War*. London: Gerald Duckworth, 1972.

Dean-Jones, L. *Women's Bodies in Classical Greek Science*. Oxford: Oxford University Press, 1994.

Deighton, H. *A Day in the Life of Ancient Athens*. Bristol, U.K.: Bristol Classical Press, 1995.

Demand, N. *Birth, Death, and Motherhood in Classical Greece*. Baltimore, Md.: Johns Hopkins University Press, 1994.

Demand, N. *A History of Ancient Greece*. New York: McGraw-Hill, 1996.

Dodds, E. R. *The Greeks and the Irrational*. Berkeley: University of California Press, 1951.

Dover, K. J. *Greek Homosexuality*. London: Gerald Duckworth, 1978.

Dover, K. J. *Greek Popular Morality in the Time of Plato and Aristotle*. Oxford: Basil Blackwell Publishing, 1974.

Dover, K. J. *The Greeks*. Austin: University of Texas Press, 1961.

Drews, R. *The End of the Bronze Age: Changes in Warfare and the Catastrophe ca. 1200 B.C.* Princeton, N.J.: Princeton University Press, 1996.

Ducrey, P. *Warfare in Ancient Greece*. Translated by J. Lloyd. New York: Schocken Books, 1986.

Dunmore, C. W. *Studies in Etymology*. Bristol, U.K.: Bristol Classical Press and Focus Publishing, 1993.

Easterling, P. B., and J. V. Muir. Greek Religion and Society. Cambridge, U.K.: Cambridge University Press, 1985.

Etienne, R., and F. Etienne. *The Search for Ancient Greece*. New York and London: Harry N. Abrams and Thames and Hudson, 1990.

Evans, J. A. *Daily Life in the Hellenistic Age: From Alexander to Cleopatra*. Westport, Conn., and London: Greenwood Press, 2008.

Falkner, T. F., and J. de Luce, eds. *Old Age in Greek and Latin Literature*. Albany: State University of New York Press, 1989.

Fantham, B., H. P. Foley, N. B. Kampen, S. Pomeroy, and H. A. Shapiro. *Women in the Classical World: Image and Text*. Oxford: Oxford University Press, 1994.

Faraone, C. A., and D. Obbink, eds. Magika Hiera: *Ancient Greek Magic and Religion*. Oxford: Oxford University Press, 1991.

Ferguson, J. *Among the Gods: An Archaeological Exploration of Ancient Greek Religion*. London: Routledge, 1989.

Ferguson, J. *Morals and Values in Ancient Greece*. Bristol, U.K.: Bristol Classical Press, 1989.

Ferguson, J., and K. Chisholm. *Political and Social Life in the Great Age of Athens*. London: Ward Lock, 1978.

Finley, M. I. *The Ancient Economy*. London: Chatto and Windus, 1973.

Finley, M. I. *The Ancient Greeks*. New York: Penguin Books and Viking Press, 1963.

Finley, M. I. *Ancient Slavery and Modern Ideology*. London: Chatto and Windus, 1980.

Finley, M. I. *Early Greece: The Bronze and Archaic Ages*. London: Chatto and Windus, 1970.

Finley, M. I. *The Legacy of Greece: A New Appraisal*. Oxford: Oxford University Press, 1981.

Finley, M. I. *The Olympic Games: The First Thousand Years*. London: Chatto and Windus, 1976.

Finley, M. I. *The World of Odysseus*. Introduction by B. Knox. 2d revised edition. Harmondsworth, Middlesex, U.K.: Penguin Books, 1978.

Fisher, N. R. E. *Slavery in Classical Greece*. Bristol, U.K.: Bristol Classical Press and Focus Publishing, 1993.

Fisher, N. R. E. *Social Values in Classical Athens*. London: J. M. Dent and Sons, 1976.

Flacelière, R. *Daily Life in Greece at the Time of Pericles*. Translated by P. Green. New York: Macmillan, 1974.

Forrest, W. G. *A History of Sparta*. London: Gerald Duckworth, 1968.

Fox, R. L. *Alexander the Great*. London: Futura Publications, 1975.

Frost, F. J. *Greek Society*. 5th edition. Boston: Houghton Mifflin, 1997.

Gagarin, M. *Early Greek Law*. Berkeley: University of California Press, 1989.

Gantz, T. *Early Greek Myth: A Guide to Literary and Artistic Sources*. Baltimore, Md.: Johns Hopkins University Press, 1993.

Gardiner, E. N. *Athletics of the Ancient World*. Reprint of 1930 edition. Chicago: Ares Publishers, 1978.

Gardiner, E. N. *Greek Athletic Sports and Festivals*. London: Macmillan, 1970.

Garlan, Y. *Slavery in Ancient Greece*. Translated by J. Lloyd. Ithaca, N.Y.: Cornell University Press, 1982.

Garlan, Y. *War in the Ancient World: A Social History*. London: Chatto and Windus, 1975.

Garland, R. S. J. *Celebrity in Antiquity: From Media Tarts to Tabloid Queens*. London: Gerald Duckworth, 2004.

Garland, R. S. J. *The Eye of the Beholder: Deformity and Disability in the Graeco-Roman World*. London and Ithaca, N.Y.: Gerald Duckworth and Cornell University Press, 1995.

Garland, R. S. J. *The Greek Way of Death*. London and Ithaca, N.Y.: Gerald Duckworth and Cornell University Press, 1985.

Garland, R. S. J. *The Greek Way of Life: From Conception to Old Age*. London and Ithaca, N.Y.: Gerald Duckworth and Cornell University Press, 1990.

Garland, R. S. J. *The Piraeus: From the Fifth to the First Century B.C.* London and Ithaca, N.Y.: Gerald Duckworth and Cornell University Press, 1987.

Garland, R. S. J. *Religion and the Greeks*. Bristol, U.K.: Bristol Classical Press and Focus Publishing, 1994.

Garnsey, P. *Famine and Food Supply in the Graeco-Roman World*. Cambridge, U.K.: Cambridge University Press, 1988.

Garnsey, P., C. R. Whittaker, and K. Hopkins. *Trade in the Ancient Economy*. London: Chatto and Windus, 1983.

Glotz, G. *Ancient Greece at Work*. Translated by M. R. Dobie. New York: W. W. Norton, 1927.

Godwin, J. *Mystery Religions in the Ancient World*. London: Thames and Hudson, 1981.

Golden, M. *Children and Childhood in Classical Athens*. Baltimore, Md.: Johns Hopkins University Press, 1990.

Graf, F. *Greek Mythology: An Introduction*. Translated by T. Marier. Baltimore, Md.: Johns Hopkins University Press, 1993.

Green, J. R. *Theatre in Ancient Greek Society*. New York: Routledge, 1996.

Green, P. *The Greco-Persian Wars*. Berkeley: University of California Press, 1996.

Grimal, P. *Dictionary of Classical Mythology*. Translated by A. R. Maxwell-Hyslop. Harmondsworth, Middlesex, U.K.: Penguin Books, 1990.

Grmek, M. D. *Diseases in the Ancient World*. Translated by M. Muellner and L. Muellner. Baltimore, Md.: Johns Hopkins University Press, 1989.

Halperin, D. M., J. J. Winkler, and F. I. Zeitlin. *Before Sexuality: The Construction of Erotic Experience in the Greek World*. Princeton, N.J.: Princeton University Press, 1990.

Hanson, V. D., and J. Keegan. *The Western Way of War: Infantry Battle in Classical Greece*. Oxford: Oxford University Press, 1990.

Harris, H. A. *Sport in Greece and Rome*. London: Thames and Hudson, 1972.

Harris, S. L., and G. Platzner. *Classical Mythology: Images and Insights*. Mountain View, Calif.: Mayfield Publishing, 1995.

Harris, W. V. *Ancient Literacy*. Cambridge, Mass.: Harvard University Press, 1989.

Harrison, A. R. W. *The Law of Athens: Family and Property*. Oxford: Clarendon Press, 1968.

Hartong, F. *The Mirror of Herodotus*. Berkeley: University of California Press, 1988.

Hawley, R., and B. Levick. *Women in Antiquity*. London: Routledge, 1995.

Higgins, R. *Greek and Roman Jewellery*. London: Methuen, 1980.

Hope, T. *Costumes of the Greeks and Romans*. New York: Dover, 1962.

Hopper, R. J. *Trade and Industry in Ancient Greece*. London: Thames and Hudson, 1979.

Hornblower, S. *The Greek World 479—323 B.C.* London: Methuen, 1983.

Hughes, J. D. *Environmental Problems of the Ancient Greeks and Romans*. Baltimore, Md.: Johns Hopkins University Press, 1996.

Jenkins, G. K. *Ancient Greek Coins*. New York: Putnam, 1972.

Jenkins, I., and S. Bird. *An Athenian Childhood*. London: British Museum Publications, 1982.

Jenkins, I., and S. Bird. *Greek Dress*. Greek and Roman Daily Life Series no. 3. London: British Museum Education Service, n.d.

Jenkins, I., and S. Bird. *Greek Music*. Greek and Roman Daily Life Series no. 4. London: British Museum Education Service, n.d.

Jenkyns, R. *The Victorians and Ancient Greece*. Cambridge, Mass.: Harvard University Press, 1980.

Jeskins, P. *The Environment and the Classical World*. London: Bristol Classical Press, 1998.

Just, R. *Women in Athenian Law and Life*. London and New York: Routledge 1981.

Kagan, D. *The Outbreak of the Peloponnesian War*. Ithaca, N.Y.: Cornell University Press, 1969.

Kagan, D. *The Peace of Nicias and the Sicilian Expedition.* Ithaca, N.Y.: Cornell University Press, 1981.

Kebric, R. B. *Greek People.* 2d edition. Mountain View, Calif.: Mayfield Publishing, 1997.

Kirkwood, G. M. *A Short Guide to Classical Mythology.* Reprint of 1959 edition. Wauconda, Ill.: Bolchazy-Carducci Publishers, 1995.

Klein, A. *Child Life in Greek Art.* New York: Columbia University Press, 1932.

Knox, B. *Essays Ancient and Modern.* Baltimore, Md.: Johns Hopkins University Press, 1990.

Kraay, C. M. *Archaic and Classical Greek Coins.* Berkeley: University of California Press, 1976.

Kurtz, D. C., and J. Boardman. *Greek Burial Customs.* London: Thames and Hudson, 1971.

Lacey, W. K. *The Family in Ancient Greece.* London: Thames and Hudson, 1968.

Lawrence, A. W. *Greek Architecture.* 5th edition. Revised by R. A. Tomlinson. New Haven, Conn.: Yale University Press, 1996.

Lefkowitz, M. *Not Out of Africa: How Afrocentrism Became an Excuse to Teach Myth as History.* New York: HarperCollins, 1996.

Lefkowitz, M. *Women in Greek Myth.* London: Gerald Duckworth, 1986.

Lefkowitz, M. R., and M. B. Fant. *Women's Life in Greece and Rome: A Source Book in Translation.* London and Baltimore, Md.: Gerald Duckworth and Johns Hopkins University Press, 1992.

Lefkowitz, M., and G. M. Rogers. *Black Athena Revisited.* Chapel Hill: University of North Carolina Press, 1996.

Levi, P. *Atlas of the Greek World.* New York: Facts on File (Equinox Books), 1995.

Lissarrague, F. *The Aesthetics of the Greek Banquet.* Princeton, N.J.: Princeton University Press, 1991.

Luck, G. *Arcana Mundi: Magic and the Occult in the Greek and Roman Worlds.* Baltimore, Md.: Johns Hopkins University Press, 1985.

MacDowell, D. M. *The Law in Classical Athens.* London: Thames and Hudson, 1978.

MacDowell, D. M. *Spartan Law.* Scottish Classical Studies no. 1. Edinburgh: Edinburgh University Press, 1986.

MacMullen, R. *Changes in the Roman Empire: Essays in the Ordinary*. Princeton: Princeton University Press, 1990.

Marrou, H. I. *A History of Education in Antiquity*. London: Sheed and Ward, 1956.

Martin, T. R. *Ancient Greece: From Prehistoric to Hellenistic Times*. New Haven, Conn.: Yale University Press, 1996.

McAuslan, I., and P. Walcot. *Women in Antiquity*. Oxford: Oxford University Press, 1996.

McClees, H. *The Daily Life of the Greeks and Romans as Illustrated in the Classical Collections*. New York: Metropolitan Museum of Art, 1925.

Meiggs, R. *The Athenian Empire*. Oxford: Oxford University Press, 1979.

Meijer, F., and O. van Nijf. *Trade, Transport and Society in the Ancient World: A Sourcebook*. London: Routledge, 1992.

Melas, E. *Temples and Sanctuaries of Ancient Greece*. Translated by F. M. Brownjohn. London: Thames and Hudson, 1973.

Mikalson, J. *Athenian Greek Religion*. Oxford: Blackwell Publishing, 2005.

Mikalson, J. *Athenian Popular Religion*. Chapel Hill: University of North Carolina Press, 1983.

Moignard, E. *Greek Vases: An Introduction*. London: Bristol Classical Press, 2006.

Morris, I. *Death-Ritual and Social Structure in Classical Antiquity*. Cambridge, U.K.: Cambridge University Press, 1992.

Mossé, C. *The Ancient World at Work*. New York: W. W. Norton, 1969.

Murray, O. *Early Greece*. 2d edition. Cambridge, Mass.: Harvard University Press, 1993.

Murray, O., ed. *Sympotica: A Symposium on the Symposium*. Oxford: Oxford University Press, 1990.

Newby, Z. *Athletics in the Ancient World*. London: Bristol Classical Press 2006.

Neils, J., and J. H. Oakley, eds. *Coming of Age in Ancient Greece: Images of Childhood from the Classical Past*. New Haven, Conn., and London: Yale University Press, 2003.

Nutton, V. *Ancient Medicine*. London: Routledge, 2004.

Nock, A. D. *Conversion*. London: Oxford University Press, 1993.

Ober, J. *The Athenian Revolution: Essays on Ancient Greek Democracy and Political Theory*. Chicago: University of Chicago Press, 1997.

Olivová, V. *Sports and Games in the Ancient World*. London: Orbis, 1984.

Ormerod, H. A. *Piracy in the Ancient World*. Liverpool, U.K.: University of Liverpool Press, 1924.

Parke, H. W. *The Festivals of the Athenians*. London: Thames and Hudson, 1977.

Parke, H. W. *Greek Oracles*. London: Hutchinson University Library, 1967.

Parker, R. *Athenian Religion: A History*. Oxford: Clarendon Press, 1996.

Parker, R. *Miasma: Pollution and Purification in Early Greek Religion*. Oxford: Clarendon Press, 1983.

Peradotto, J., and M. Levine, eds. *Women in the Ancient World*. The Arethusa Papers 1984. Albany: State University of New York Press, 1984.

Pickard-Cambridge, A. *The Dramatic Festivals of Athens*. Revised by J. Gould and D. M. Lewis. Oxford: Oxford Clarendon Press, 1968.

Poliakoff, M. B. *Combat Sports in the Ancient World: Competition, Violence, and Culture*. New Haven, Conn.: Yale University Press, 1987.

Pollitt, J. J. *Art and Experience in Classical Greece*. Cambridge, U.K.: Cambridge University Press, 1972.

Pomeroy, S. *Families in Classical and Hellenistic Greece*. Oxford: Oxford University Press, 1997.

Pomeroy, S., S. M. Burstein, W. Donlan, and J. T. Roberts. *A Brief History of Ancient Greece: Politics, Society, and Culture*. Oxford: Oxford University Press, 2004.

Rhodes, P. J. *The Greek City States: A Sourcebook*. Norman: University of Oklahoma Press, 1986.

Rhodes, P. J. *A History of the Classical World: 478–323 B.C.* Malden, Mass.: Blackwell Publishing, 2006.

Richter, G. *The Furniture of the Greeks, Etruscans and Romans*. London: Phaidon Press, 1966.

Rider, B. C. *The Greek House: Its History and Development from the Neolithic to the Hellenistic Age*. Cambridge, U.K.: Cambridge University Press, 1965.

Robertson, D. S. *A Handbook of Greek and Roman Architecture*. 2d edition. Cambridge, U.K.: Cambridge University Press, 1945.

Robertson, M. *A Shorter History of Greek Art*. Cambridge, U.K.: Cambridge University Press, 1981.

Rohde, E. Psyche: *The Cult of Souls and Belief in Immortality among the Ancient Greeks*. Translated from 8th edition by W. B. Hillis. Chicago: Ares Publishers, 1987.

Sage, M. *Warfare in Ancient Greece: A Sourcebook*. New York: Routledge, 1996.

Sharwood Smith, J. *Greece and the Persians*. Bristol, U.K.: Bristol Classical Press and Focus Publishing, 1989.

Sekunda, N. *Greek Hoplite 480–323 B.C.* Oxford: Osprey Publishing, 2000.

Sekunda. N. *The Spartan Army*. Oxford: Osprey Publishing, 1998.

Simon, E. *Festivals of Attica*. Madison: University of Wisconsin Press, 1983.

Slater, W. J. *Dining in a Classical Context*. Ann Arbor: University of Michigan Press, 1992.

Smith, J. A. *Athens under the Tyrants*. Bristol, U.K.: Bristol Classical Press and Focus Publishing, 1989.

Smith, R.R.R. *Hellenistic Sculpture: A Handbook*. London: Thames and Hudson, 1991.

Snodgrass, A. *Archaic Greece: The Age of Experiment*. London: J. M. Dent and Sons, 1980.

Snodgrass, A. *Arms and Armour of the Greeks*. London and Ithaca, N.Y.: Thames and Hudson and Cornell University Press, 1967.

Sourvinou-Inwood, C. *"Reading" Greek Death: To the End of the Classical Period*. Oxford: Oxford University Press, 1995.

Soyer, A. *The Pantropheon: Or a History of Food and Its Preparation in Ancient Times*. Boston: Ticknor, Reed, and Fields, 1983.

Starr, C. G. *The Ancient Greeks*. Oxford: Oxford University Press, 1971.

Starr, C. G. *The Influence of Sea Power on Ancient History*. Oxford: Oxford University Press, 1988.

Stewart, A. *Greek Sculpture: An Exploration*. New Haven, Conn.: Yale University Press, 1990.

Stone, I. F. *The Trial of Socrates*. New York: Anchor Books, 1989.

Strauss, B. S. *Fathers and Sons in Athens*. Princeton, N.J.: Princeton University Press, 1993.

Swaddling, J. *The Ancient Olympic Games*. London: British Museum Publications, 1980.

Sweet, W. E. *Sport and Recreation in Ancient Greece: A Sourcebook with Translations*. Oxford: Oxford University Press, 1987.

Taplin, O. *Greek Fire*. London: Jonathan Cape, 1989.

Taplin, O. *Greek Tragedy in Action*. London: Methuen, 1978.

Todd, S. C. *Athens and Sparta*. Bristol, U.K.: Bristol Classical Press and Focus Publishing, 1996.

Todd, S. C. *The Shape of Athenian Law*. Oxford: Clarendon Press, 1995.

Tomlinson, R. A. *Greek Architecture*. Bristol, U.K.: Bristol Classical Press and Focus Publishing, 1989.

Travlos, J. N. *A Pictorial Dictionary of Athens*. London: Thames and Hudson, 1971.

Tsigakou, F.-M. *The Rediscovery of Greece*: Travellers and Painters of the Romantic Era. New York and London: Caratzas and Thames and Hudson, 1981.

Vermeule, E. *Aspects of Death in Early Greek Art and Poetry*. Berkeley: University of California Press, 1979.

Vermeule, E. *Greece in the Bronze Age*. Chicago: University of Chicago Press, 1972.

Vernant, J.-P., ed. *The Greeks*. Chicago: University of Chicago Press, 1995.

Walbank, F. W. *The Hellenistic World*. London and Stanford, Calif.: Fontana and Stanford University Press, 1981.

Wardle, K., and D. Wardle. *Mycenaean Greece*. Bristol and Newburyport, U.K.: Bristol Classical Press and Focus Publishing, 1997.

West, M. L. *Ancient Greek Music*. Oxford: Clarendon Press, 1993.

Whitehead, D, *The Demes of Attica: 508/7–ca. 250 B.C: A Political and Social Study*. Princeton, N.J.: Princeton University Press, 1986.

Wilkins, J., D. Harvey, and M. Dobson. *Food in Antiquity*. Exeter, U.K.: University of Exeter Press, 1995.

Wilkinson, L. P. *Classical Attitudes to Modern Issues*. London: William Kimber, 1978.

Williams, D., and J. Ogden. *Greek Gold: Jewellery of the Classical World*. New York: Abrams, 1994.

Wilson, P., ed. *The Greek Theatre and Festivals: Documentary Studies*. Oxford: Oxford University Press, 2007.

Woodford, S. *An Introduction to Greek Art*. London: Gerald Duckworth, 1986.

Woodford, S. *The Trojan War in Ancient Art*. London: Gerald Duckworth, 1993.

Woodhouse, C. M. *Modern Greece: A Short History*. London and Boston: Faber and Faber, 1991.

Wycherley, R. E. *How the Greeks Built Cities*. 2d edition. London: Macmillan, 1962.

Wycherley, R. E. *The Stones of Athens*. Princeton, N.J.: Princeton University Press, 1978.

Zaidman, L. S., and P. Schmitt Pantel. *Religion in the Ancient Greek City*. Translated by P. Cartledge. Cambridge, U.K.: Cambridge University Press, 1992.

NOVELS

Among the most celebrated novels about ancient Greece are those by M. Renault. They include *The Last of the Wine* (1956), *The Mask of Apollo* (1966), *The King Must Die* (1958), *The Bull from the Sea* (1962), *The Nature of Alexander* (1975), and *The Persian Boy* (1972). Nobel prize winner William Golding's final novel, *The Double Tongue* (1995), left in draft form at his death, tells the story of one of the last priestesses of Apollo at Delphi. Naomi Mitchison's *The Corn King and the Spring Queen* (1933), which has been described as "a triumph of empathy with vanished cultures," is set in Skythia and Sparta. Also highly recommended is Steven Pressfield's *Gates of Fire* (1984), which is about the Battle of Thermopylae. Nick Nicastro's *Isle of Stone* (2006) describes the plight of a group of Spartan hoplites during the Peloponnesian War. Margaret Doody has written several detective novels set in Athens, including *Aristotle Detective* (1978), *Poison in Athens* (2004), and *Mysteries in Eleusis* (2006).

MAGAZINES

A magazine called *Omnibus*, produced by the Joint Association of Classical Teachers (London), intended primarily for high schools, contains many very useful articles on classical themes. Somewhat more sophisticated, but intended for the general reader, is a magazine called *History Today* (London), which occasionally includes articles on the ancient world.

AUDIOVISUAL MATERIALS

There are numerous audiovisual materials about the Greek world. For a comprehensive list, see *Classical World*, Spring 2008, vol. 101 no. 3, pp. 335–419 (compiled by Janice Siegel and complete with prices).

CD-ROMs

Centaur Systems Ltd. (Wisconsin) distributes a number of CD-ROMs about classical Greece, including *Grammar: Drills for Greek Students*.

WEB SITES

historylink101.com/index.htm. *Ancient Greece*. Author Eric Rymer. Visited July 15, 2008.

www.perseus.tufts.edu/hopper/collections. Editor Gregory R. Cane. Tufts University. Updated daily.

www.fordham.edu/halsall/ancient/asbook07.html. *Internet Ancient History Sourcebook: Greece*. Editor Paul Halsall. Fordham University. Last modified December 10, 2006.

INDEX

IMAGE CREDITS

age fotostock
© Dea A Garozzo: 124; © Fine Art Images: 322

© akg-images
156

Alamy
© Ivy Close Images: 19; © Luc Novovitch: 330

Art Resource, NY
© The Trustees of the British Museum: I, XVI; © John Hammond/National Trust Photo Library: V; © DeA Picture Library: 44, 134; © Gianni Dagli Orti: 52; © Erich Lessing: 75, 173; © The Metropolitan Museum of Art: 79; © Hervé Lewandowski/RMN: 103; © Juergen Liepe/bpk, Berlin: 115; © National Trust Photo Library: 129; © Alinari: 200 bottom; © Stéphane Maréchalle/RMN: 211; © Scala: 268; © Album: 300

© Trustees of the British Museum
57, 228

Courtesy Dover Publications
217, 218, 315, 318

Dreamstime
© Szirtesi: 234

Getty Images
© Dmitri Kessel/Time Life Pictures: 46; © G. Dagli Orti/De Agostini: 87; 329

Courtesy Heritage Auction Gallery
325

iStockphoto
© ivanmateev: XVIII; © Snezana Negovanovic: 34; © Duncan Walker: 206, 265, 305; © ZU_09: 244; 273; © traveler1116: 310

Library of Congress
62, 326

© Mary Evans Picture Library
294

Courtesy National Gallery of Art
74, 252

Shutterstock
© Russell Shively: XVII; © Nick Pavlakis: 2, 41; © krechet: 3; © Kamira: 7; © Lefteris Papaulakis: 38; © Hein Nouwens: 43; © vlas2000: 297; © Jeff Grabert: 303

Walters Art Museum
27, 29, 97, 140, 145, 166, 189, 190, 205, 256, 259, 281, 297

Courtesy Wikimedia Foundation
II, 37, 61, 183, 200 top, 254, 216; Geographicus Rare Antique Maps: XII, 66, 332; Web Gallery of Art: 18, 213, 215, 239; Marie Lan Nguyen: 55; 90, 121, 144, 147, 150, 160, 161, 163, 194, 219, 226, 250, 271, 275, 290, 299, 302, 327; Wolfgang Sauber: 111, 274; Ulrich Tichy: 247; Deutsches Museum: 261; Yair Haklai: 283; Pearson Scott Foresman: 304

ABOUT THE AUTHOR

Robert Garland is Roy D. and Margaret B. Wooster Professor of the Classics at Colgate University. His research focuses on the social, religious, political, and cultural history of both Greece and Rome. He has written ten books and many articles in both academic and popular journals. His books include *Introducing New Gods* (2nd ed. 2008), *Celebrity in the Ancient World* (2006), *Surviving Greek Tragedy* (2004), *Julius Caesar* (2004), *The Greek Way of Death* (2nd ed. 2001), *The Piraeus* (2nd ed. 2001), *The Greek Way of Life* (1990), *Religion and the Greeks* (1994), and *The Eye of the Beholder: Deformity and Disability in the Graeco-Roman World* (1995). He has produced *Greece and Rome: An Integrated History of the Ancient Mediterranean* for The Teaching Company (2008), and has been a consultant and discussant for several television productions on the ancient world.